D1798714

B 5 499334 2

A History of Education for Citizenship

In this unique examination of education for citizenship the author covers two and a half millennia of history encompassing almost every continent. Education for citizenship is considered from its classical origins through to ideas of world citizenship and multiculturalism, which are relevant today. The book reveals the constants of motives, policies, recommendations and practices in this field and the variables determined by political, social and economic circumstances, which in turn illustrate the reasons behind education for citizenship today.

The subject-matter is analysed under the following headings:

- Classical origins
- The ages of rebellions and revolutions
- Education for liberal democracy
- Totalitarianism and transitions
- Multiple citizenship education.

A History of Education for Citizenship will be of interest to teachers and students of citizenship, particularly those concerned with citizenship education. It will also be of interest to those working in the field of politics of education and the history of education.

Derek Heater has taught at both secondary and higher education levels and was co-founder of the Politics Association. He has written widely in the field of education, more recently concentrating on the subject of citizenship education.

A History of Education for Citizenship

Derek Heater

RoutledgeFalmer
Taylor & Francis Group

LONDON AND NEW YORK

First published 2004
by RoutledgeFalmer
11 New Fetter Lane, London EC4P 4EE

Simultaneously published in the USA and Canada
by RoutledgeFalmer
29 West 35th Street, New York, NY 10001

RoutledgeFalmer is an imprint of the Taylor & Francis Group

Copyright © 2004 Derek Heater

Typeset in Times New Roman by
Keystroke, Jacaranda Lodge, Wolverhampton
Printed and bound in Great Britain by
Antony Rowe Ltd, Chippenham, Wiltshire

British Library Cataloguing in Publication Data
A catalogue record for this book is available from the British Library

Library of Congress Cataloging-in-Publication Data
A catalog record for this book has been requested

ISBN 0–415–30477–6

Contents

Preface

It is always good to start with an epigram from Aristotle. So, from the *Politics* let us take, 'The citizens of a state should always be educated to suit the constitution of a state' (Aristotle 1948: 1337aII). Remembering that his word *politeia*, which we tend to render as 'constitution', embraces way of life and social ethic as well as form of government, we almost have an epigraph for this book. Except for that little word 'should'. There can be no doubt that the practices of citizenship education in ancient Sparta and Athens, in the France of the Third Republic and the Germany of the Third Reich, for instance, revealed many differences, explicable by their different *politeia*. But the very choice of these examples raises the issue whether the variations were for the benefit of the state or for the citizen. Aristotle's 'should' derived from his concern for the stability of the state, and two moral questions arise from his proposition. Are the interests of the individual *qua* citizen always to be subordinated to the stability of the state howsoever that stability is secured? And are those who are learning to be citizens to be indoctrinated for the sake of that stability; and if so, what price the development of a civic conscience and political judgement, particularly when 'state' is considered to be synonymous with regime?

The history of citizenship education from ancient Greece to the contemporary world contains rich food for thinking about these and other, perhaps less fundamental questions. To be personal: the writing of this book has been an audacious undertaking and I believe that no one else has dared tackle this vast and complex subject, even in the relatively limited form presented here. For it requires an interest in history, political theory and education. Since I have spent half a century reading all three of these disciplines, in the twilight of my writing years I have decided it is time to pull them all together in this chosen theme.

The complexity of the subject has posed difficulties of organization. After much thought I have settled on a division into five chapters. The first two deal with chronological periods, namely the ancient world (though with a coda on its legacy) and the early modern age, which for our purposes also has a thematic unity of the political experiences of rebellions and revolutions. The other three chapters have themes, each treated chronologically through their particular time-spans: the liberal state, totalitarian regimes in their contexts and the diversification of citizenship into multiple forms. The amount of material to be covered varies greatly from chapter to chapter, so each is divided into sections for ease of comprehension.

I am very grateful for my wife's skill in helping me to cope with the computer and her faith that I could achieve a measure of success in bringing this project to a conclusion. The reader, the best judge of all, must assess whether I have been foolhardy in attempting the task.

Derek Heater
Rottingdean

1   Classical origins

Foundations and variations

Education for citizenship emerged in Greece during the Archaic Age (776–479 BC) and flourished in the following Classical Age, during which time it was the subject of some distinguished thinking. Both the pedagogical and literary activities were occasioned by the development of the status of citizenship: individuals needed to learn how to act in that capacity. By the eighth century the typical Greek socio-political entity was no longer the kingdom or tribe, it was the *polis*. The *polis* (we shall avoid the somewhat misleading translation 'city-state') – Sparta, Corinth, Thebes, for example – was a micro-state by today's standards. Even the demo-graphically bloated and democratically governed Athens at its apogee contained during its very brief maximum probably only about 50,000 members of citizen families, though to this number must be added resident foreigners and slaves. Population size and structure and geographical constriction indeed provide the basic clues to the origins of citizenship. The *polis* was a compact community dominated by a relatively small and ethnically cohesive group, for whom outsiders – the foreigners and slaves – undertook vital work. As a consequence, the dominant group enjoyed the privileges of relative wealth and leisure to participate in the government of the *polis*, to be, in short, citizens.

But behind this opportunity to be citizens lay two other determining factors. One was commitment to the well-being of the *polis*, including the willingness and desire to be involved in public affairs, which in themselves contained both a negative and a positive element. The negative was a hatred of an autocratic rule disrespectful of law. 'Arbitrary government,' it has been said, 'offended the Greek in his very soul' (Kitto 1951: 9). The positive element, the origins of which may be detected in the heroic era portrayed by Homer, was the habit of gathering to discuss the community's affairs, indicative of a deeply felt civic interest. The second determining factor was a product of the Greek capacity for abstract thought. The object of the citizen's political allegiance was no longer the chieftain, lord or king, but a conceptual entity, the state. The citizen was in fact, in the common phrase, an individual able 'to have a share in the polity' (see Hornblower and Spaworth 1998: 152); though the precise range of that share depended on the constitutional mode of the state, whether oligarchy or democracy, for example.

Whereas the Greek *poleis* (leaving aside the imperial expansion of Athens in the fifth century) remained small and their citizen-bodies tiny, the history of the Roman state is one of continual territorial expansion down to the first century AD and of episodic extensions of the rights of citizenship down to the third century AD. The difference is explained by a fundamental dissimilarity between the Greek and Roman notions of citizenship. The essence of Greek citizenship was participation; the essence of Roman citizenship was the ownership of legal rights. True, the principle of involvement in public affairs was by no means absent from the meaning of the Roman citizenship, but social and geographical realities placed very severe limitations on the practice. The division between patricians and plebeians, despite the winning of important rights by the latter, kept political and judicial powers in the hands of the former, privileged class. And the immense stretch of the Roman imperium inevitably meant that it was impossible for a citizen in, for example, Transalpine Gaul or Cappadocia to attend political meetings in Rome. Despite the myth that Rome remained a 'city', a *civitas*, only those resident in Rome itself or within easy travelling distance could live the full life of the citizen, *civis Romanus*.

Just as it would be misleading to make statements of too broad a generalization about citizenship in the Graeco-Roman world, so too there were variations in the forms of civic education that were devised in classical times. However, these differences were not related primarily to the dissimilarities in the ways citizenship was expressed in the Greek *poleis* and in Rome. The differences lay rather in a lack of complete agreement concerning the purposes and methods of the educational experiences which boys and adolescents should undergo.

It is possible to identify four areas in which different priorities or approaches were advocated and practised. First, and basically, was the issue of the objectives of civic education. Aristotle was quite clear about this. He explained that 'the polis . . . is an aggregate of many members; and education therefore is *the* means of making it a community and giving it unity' (Aristotle 1948:1263b). It is the responsibility of citizens to contribute to the cohesiveness and therefore the stability of the state, so they must learn how to make this contribution. The second objective was the specific and practical learning of the citizen's duties. Civic virtue was placed at the very heart of the classical concept of citizenship, and virtue meant performing one's duties. Learning these duties involved both understanding the range of activities expected of the citizen and training in the skills necessary for their efficient discharge. The third objective was to teach young citizens their rights, social, legal and political. Now, although these three objectives are distinguishable, they could and were identified simultaneously in programmes of education. Even in Sparta, where education for cohesion and duties was so paramount, the young citizens were also inducted into the rights of landownership.

However, balancing learning about duties and rights raises the question about the field of civic activity, which could be and was construed in both civil and military terms. This is the second of our four areas of differences. As one of the key functions of a Greek citizen was to fight for his *polis*, civic education, especially in the Archaic age, meant training primarily in the skills required of the hoplite (heavy infantry-man) and instilling the will to fight with valour, an essential feature of *aretē*. Pride in the state and its traditions was inevitably part of this element. However, induction into a civic inheritance had a civil as well as a military purpose and was a component of Roman as well as Greek citizenship education. As the generations wore on and the art and structures of politics were developed, it became prudent that citizens should be acquainted with the facts and processes of law and legislation, policy and policy-making. In Sparta alone, an unsparing military discipline persisted as the overwhelming characteristic of the citizen's educational programme.

It goes without saying that the military form of civic education was organized by the state. On the other hand, during the early centuries, citizenship education in the civil mode was provided, in both the Greek and Roman systems, by the family or by privately run initiatives; which brings us to our third area of variation – state or private arrangements. Private teachers – of whom the Sophists, Plato, Aristotle, Zeno of Citium and Quintilian are the most famous – offered education for a limited clientele: those youths with the intellect to benefit from and wealthy fathers to pay for these styles of schooling. For the majority, initiation into juridical and political matters was organized within the intimacy of the family or close friends: adult citizens, often fathers, taught novice citizens. Aristotle recognized both the distinction and the common practice in his own time: 'whether the education of children should be conducted on a private basis, as it still is, even today, in the great majority of cases.' Notice the 'even today'. He goes on to commend the provision of education by 'public action' (Aristotle 1948:1337a). We shall see that this did come about.

Visits to the lawcourts, assembly or forum gave youths, in pedagogical terms, a casual, unstructured introduction to citizenship. They were none the worse for that; but it is only one of the alternatives. This, then, is our fourth choice of approaches to citizenship education in the classical era – structured or unstructured teaching. Clearly, the military training form, as epitomized by Sparta, and the academic form as epitomized by Aristotle's Lyceum, were devised and prepared very carefully in the detailed ways apposite for teaching the required skills and understanding related to these kinds of curricula.

Our own structure for this chapter will be along the following lines. Partly because of their historical importance and partly because of the comparative wealth of our knowledge about them, we shall concentrate on the practices of citizenship education in Sparta, Athens and Rome, and the ideals as proposed by Plato, Aristotle and the Roman exponents of oratory. Through this investigation we shall see how the matters outlined above are illustrated in Greek and Roman history. Most dramatically Sparta provided a model, for ancient Greece and for some educationists down the ages, of the state provision of education and the control of education for stern citizenship training. Indeed, the Athenian Plato especially and Aristotle, who settled in Athens, regretted that their own *polis* lacked such an organized system. Sparta should therefore be our starting point.

Sparta and Athens

The training of Spartan youths for citizenship was the most extraordinarily determined undertaking by a state in the entire history of citizenship education to shape its citizenry to its perceived needs. Only Crete and Persia developed arrangements that approximated to this system (see e.g. Aristotle 1948: 1272a; Xenophon 1914: 4, 6; in Xenophon's work of 'faction', *Cyropaedia*, he paints a vivid picture of a deeply political society with even young children learning law and practising forensic oratory at school). In order to comprehend fully the experiences and indoctrinated behaviour of these trainee-citizens we must outline briefly the condition of the Spartan state and thus explain these needs.

During the final decades of the eighth century BC Sparta started on a campaign of expansion, overwhelming the Messenians to the west and subjecting them to a condition of slavery called 'helotry'. As Sparta extended her conquests throughout the southern Peloponnese (the region of Laconia or Lacedaemon) the numbers of the vanquished far exceeded the population of the metropolitan city. In order to hold the conquered people in thrall the Spartans evolved an elite military caste: these were the Spartiates, the citizens of the *polis*. And to exercise their task of imposing and maintaining the Spartan hegemony the Spartiates had to endure rigorous training. Accordingly, education of the Spartiate class, and so education for citizenship, became from the mid-sixth century a programme to develop physical fitness, military skills, utter adhesion and loyalty to one's fellow Spartiates, unquestioning obedience, and, above all, total dedication to the *polis*. True, Sparta had conducted the education of its youth, as all *poleis* had, as essentially military training; yet whereas – as other states emerged from the Archaic age – they partially demilitarized their teaching, with Athens leading the way, Sparta intensified hers. In Lacedaemonian tradition it was the statesman-lawgiver Lycurgus who consolidated the state's social, legal, political, military and educational institutions. Moreover, he is credited with confirming the aristocratic Spartiate system of citizens, who were relieved of the manual work, which was performed by the helots. Thus were the citizens freed for civil and military duties. According to Plutarch (whose *Lycurgus* and the work on *Spartan Society* attributed to Xenophon are our chief sources) Lycurgus 'accustomed citizens to have no desire for a private life, nor knowledge of one, but rather to be like bees, always attached to the community, swarming together around their leader' (Plutarch 1988: 37).

This regime, taken with the programme of upbringing and training (*agogē*) that was its essential preparation, set Sparta apart from all the other *poleis*. The really crucial facet of citizenship for Greeks and Romans alike, as we shall see throughout this chapter, was the quality of *aretē* (*virtus* in Latin, roughly translatable as 'goodness' or 'excellence' or 'civic virtue'). However, for Spartiates *aretē* meant virtually exclusively 'valour' or 'fortitude'. The famous elegiac poet Tyrtaeus, who wrote in the seventh century against the background of the Messenian wars, set the tone. He provided the uplifting messages which were learned and sung as marching songs by Spartan students. He praised the man who stands firm and steadfast in the forefront of the battle and whose heroic death is lamented yet glorified by the whole *polis* (see Edmonds 1961: 75).

In order to achieve this ideal, boys and young men of the Spartiate class were gathered into barracks of a homosexual and monastic life-style, where they underwent a strict and severe training programme which became increasingly vicious as the centuries wore on. For, in addition to the practising of military skills, the youths were forced to undertake feats of endurance, straining the limits of human physique and will-power. (Any Spartiate male baby judged to be potentially incapable of later withstanding these rigours was slung on the communal dung-heap.)

This *agogē* course lasted from the age of 7 to 20, arranged in three phases. Each boy was allocated to a pack or herd (the Spartan word *agela* means 'herd'), though the word 'troop' is sometimes favoured in the translation used here (see Plutarch 1988: 28, 168). (We need, in fact, to explain at this point that there are some detailed differences concerning the interpretation of the administration of the *agogē*. The view followed here is that presented in the edition of the Plutarch and Xenophon texts used in this chapter, but should be compared with Marrou (1956: 20, 364 n.23).) The overall command of the programme was in the hands of the *paidonomus*, the trainer-in-chief. As Xenophon explains, this man had 'authority to assemble the boys and to punish them severely whenever any misbehaved while in his charge. He also . . . [had] a squad of young adults equipped with whips to administer punishment when necessary' (Plutarch 1988: 168). Each *agela* was commanded by a senior student, *eiren*, aged 20. Xenophon provides us with an interesting insight concerning the recognition that in the second, adolescent stage, 'youths become very self-willed and are particularly liable to cockiness'; consequently at this age they were 'loaded with the greatest amount of work' and were 'occupied for the maximum time' (Plutarch 1988: 170).

The regime was stark, stern and brutal, both in the treatment of the students and in the behaviour expected of them. Clothing, particularly from the age of 12, was minimal, food was sparse; the only liberality was in the use of the whip, discipline being exerted by pain and shame, the flogging sometimes so unremitting as to cause the victim's death. Plutarch retails two famous examples of the kind of behaviour that was the outcome for the senior students of this fearsome training. One concerns a kind of Fagin-like induction. The boys were taught to steal as a means of developing initiative, cunning and practice in evasion. Theft was not crime; being caught was. The anecdote runs as follows: '[a boy] had stolen a fox cub and had it concealed inside his cloak: in order to escape detection he was prepared to have his insides clawed and bitten out by the animal, and even to die' (Plutarch 1988: 30). Apocryphal or true, Plutarch believed it to be a credible illustration of the Spartan mode of training. The other gruesome example concerns the *krypteia*, a kind of commando training. This is Plutarch's account:

> Periodically the overseers of the young men would dispatch into the country-side in different directions the ones who appeared to be particularly intelligent; they were equipped with daggers and basic rations, but nothing else. By the day they would disperse to obscure spots in order to hide and rest. At night they made their way to roads and murdered any helot whom they caught. Frequently,

too, they made their way through fields, killing the helots who stood out for their physique and strength.

(Plutarch 1988: 40–1)

The last sentence reveals the secondary purpose of these expeditions: to cull from the helot population any who might be dangerous rebels capable of threatening Spartiate control.

On the other hand, Plutarch does also give us a glimpse of what we might properly call education:

> As he reclined after his meal the Eiren would tell one boy to sing, while to another he would pose a question which called for a considered reply, like 'Who among the men is the best?', or 'What is your opinion of so-and-so's action?' Thereby boys grew accustomed to judging excellence and to making a critical appraisal of the citizens right from the start. When asked which citizen was good. . . . Answers had to be reasoned, supported by argument, and at the same time expressed with brevity and conciseness.

(Plutarch 1988: 3)

The transition from the status of student to that of full citizen was not, however, achieved suddenly. The young adult became first a quasi-citizen, performing military duties but denied civil rights or responsibilities. Then, when he was ready to be incorporated into the body of citizens, he had to be elected to a mess and be able to pay his 'mess dues'. Both election and payment of dues were crucial to becoming and remaining a citizen. Plutarch once more provides us with a vivid description of the election process:

> Each member would take a piece of soft bread in his hand and in silence would throw it, like a ballot, into the bowl which a servant carried on his head. Those in favour threw the bread as it was, while those against squeezed it hard with their hand. The effect of a squeezed piece is that of a hollow ballot. And should they find even one of these, they do not admit the would-be entrant because it is their wish that all should be happy in each other's company.

(Plutarch 1988: 21)

Thus, even enduring the trials of the *agogē* was no guarantee of being admitted into or remaining in the ranks of citizens.

Those who were adult citizens were known as *Homoioi* – 'peers' – because, within their privileged ranks, whatever their wealth, all were treated equally. In particular, all were required to eat frugally in the common messes (*phiditia*), partly as one means of ensuring their adult civic education. That the Spartans considered the continuation of education for citizenship crucial is attested by Plutarch in these sentences: 'Spartiates' training extended into adulthood, for no one was permitted to live as he pleased. . . . Unless assigned a particular job they would always be observing the boys and giving them some useful piece of instruction, or learning themselves from their elders' (Plutarch 1988: 36). The messes were particularly useful for cross-generational education, as, again, Plutarch reveals: 'The boys, too, used to frequent the messes: for them it was like being brought to a school for self-discipline, where they . . . heard political discussion' (Plutarch 1988: 21). Festivals, often dominated by the singing of martial songs, also contributed to bonding across the age-groups (see Plutarch 1988: 34).

The picture outlined above of Spartan education for citizenship bears virtually no resemblance to any interpretation of civic learning in the twenty-first century AD. Yet in both ancient and modern times it had its admirers. Xenophon is a prime example. Born in Athens *c*.430 BC, he later fought in the Spartan army against Persia, became a friend of the king of Sparta, and even sent his own two sons to that *polis* for their education. In the final section of this chapter we shall look at some examples in later periods of interest in Spartan educational practices. Here we record that, as a method of citizenship education, the Lacedaemonian system has provoked varying reactions for two and a half millennia. Some, notably Plato and even Aristotle, have admired the clarity of objectives and efficiency of administration of this state organization of the educational process; though even admirers, let alone detractors, have often regretted the obsessive narrowness of the 'curriculum', if such a word may be used of the *agogē*. The Spartiates have also been held in awe for their utterly unwavering patriotism and courage instilled by their upbringing. Yet its inhumanity, of course, has struck horror in the minds of those who have read Plutarch's account.

We must not, however, lose sight of the fact that reflections on the Spartiates have hitherto come from those interested in political theory and history, military history and, to some degree, pedagogical method; whereas our focus here is on citizenship. We need, therefore, to remember that the Spartiates were only a small elite – perhaps about 8,000 at their zenith *c*.500 BC. Not until the twentieth century was it possible, with the aid of modern techniques (as we shall see in Chapter 4), for totalitarian regimes to attempt a comparable shaping of a mass citizenry of millions. In the context of the history of citizenship, too, it is clear that the extraordinarily constricted education that the young Spartiates received during those thirteen years of *agogē* was devised precisely for an extraordinarily constricted form of citizenship. In the words of Aristotle, 'The whole system of legislation is directed to fostering only one part or element of goodness – goodness in war' (Aristotle 1948: 1271b). The story of Sparta is, indeed, a most graphic example of the interaction of a concept of citizenship and the related system of citizenship education.

In the Archaic age, as the Greek *poleis* were evolving, often in mutual suspicion, the need for citizens to have been trained in military skills can be readily understood. What is fascinating, however, as we have already observed, is that, just as the Spartans stiffened the training for their cadet-citizens in the mid-sixth century, almost simultaneously, the Athenians relaxed theirs. Moreover, as Athens became increasingly democratic socially, so demand for education broadened, and as she became increasingly democratic politically, so the broadening of educational facilities became increasingly needed. Consequently, whereas education had been confined hitherto to private tutoring of the offspring of aristocrats, the need for the education of large numbers led to the opening of schools. What is more, as the significance of education came increasingly to be accepted, so the state came to exert more control. Initially, as Plato reveals in the *Protagoras*, the sons of the wealthy were directed: 'When they have finished with teachers, the State compels them to learn the laws and use them as a pattern for their life' (Plato 1956: 326). Then, school attendance became universal among the citizenry and the state imposed regulations on the schools (see Gwynn 1964: 27). An indicator of the spread of at least basic literacy is provided by the introduction of ostracism. Cleisthenes, the author of key democratic reforms at the very end of the sixth century, devised this system of political censure; it assumed the ability of the members of the Assembly to write the accused's name on a potsherd. Indeed, Morrow has judged that, 'From the middle of the fifth century, at the latest, there must have been a highly literate public at Athens, and the other states of any size or wealth probably kept pace with her' (Morrow 1960: 320).

Even so, until the revolutionary changes in education which developed from the end of the fifth century, Athenians underwent very little in the way of explicit preparation for citizenship. The main medium for political awareness for young and adult alike was the range of oral arts – poetry, singing and drama. Solon, who was born *c*.640, was the great Athenian lawgiver; and his poems 'were cited not only in schools but in the public places of Athens as the "soul of Athenian citizenship"' (Castle 1961: 73–4). Plays offered the popular and powerful blend of entertainment and civic education. Sophocles' *Antigone* raised in sober tragedy the issue of the rule of law; in contrast, Aristophanes poked hilarious and bawdy fun at the jury system in *The Wasps*, at the idea of the political participation of women in *The Assemblywomen* and, with a bitter edge in the satire *The Knights*, at the whole Athenian political system and leadership.

Aristophanes also lampooned what he called the 'old education' (*archaia paideia*) in *The Clouds*, for, by this time (the play was first produced in 423), many new styles of education were coming into vogue. Socrates began his dialectical form of teaching, the Sophists delivered their lectures peripatetically, rhetoric was shaped carefully and skilfully as an oral art-form, the ephebic mode of military-civic training was established, and Plato and Aristotle contributed their thoughts to pedagogical theory. The work of the Sophists, rhetoric and the *ephēbeia* will occupy our interest for the rest of this section.

When, in the sixth century, the common Hellenic mode of government by dictator ('tyrant') began to wane and political power in many *poleis* became more widely distributed, the question naturally arose concerning the competence of the newly empowered to exercise that responsibility. To put the matter in moral terms, virtue (*aretē*), construed as the military valour of an elite citizenry, had to be supplemented by the *aretē* of political wisdom, even for the aristocracy, not to mention *hoi polloi* of Athens. How was that wisdom to be acquired?

The upper classes organized their own arrangements for adult members of the family to teach the older boys the city's laws, to take them on visits to the lawcourts and the theatre, and to encourage them to absorb the political ideas and gossip in the chatter of the public places. But this was haphazard. A more structured education was obviously necessary; and for those who could afford it, the Sophists satisfied that need. Their teaching, it is true, was not confined to Athens, though since much of what we know about them derives from Athenian sources, it is suitable to treat them in this section on Athens. The Sophists flourished during the second half of the fifth century; Plato, indeed, knew some of their number, including Protagoras and Gorgias, who appear eponymously in two of his dialogues. Their purpose was to teach all subjects, stretching their students' minds to demanding levels. However, their aim was also to teach for practical ends, to instil and promote in the students knowledge, understanding and intellectual skills that could be used. In pursuit of this prospectus they came into conflict with Socrates, who argued, on the contrary, the nature of *aretē* as personal morality rather than military and political commitment, and the fundamental purpose of education as the pursuit of truth rather than utility.

The prime concern of the Sophists was to teach their students the arts of politics, including the characteristics of good citizenship. Thus in the *Protagoras* Plato has Protagoras (who speaks first) explaining this to Socrates:

> 'from me [the student] will learn only what he has come to learn. What is that subject? The proper care of his personal affairs, so that he may best manage his own household, and also of the State's affairs, so as to become a real power in the city, both as speaker and man of action.'
>
> 'Do I follow you?' said I. 'I take you to be describing the art of politics, and promising to make men good citizens.'
>
> 'That,' said he, 'is exactly what I profess to do.'

Socrates, however, is sceptical: 'The fact is, I did not think this was something that can be taught' (Plato 1956: 318–19). For, by 'good', Protagoras meant 'skilful': his term was '*politikē technē*', the art of politics; and his particular contribution to political education was teaching his students the technique of winning an argument! Protagoras perfected his own pedagogical technique in the handling of any subject to such a degree that it has been described as both 'brazen in its cynical pragmatism' and 'astonishing in its practical effectiveness' (Marrou 1956: 51). So cynical, indeed, were some Sophists and their students in using this persuasive dialectical tool that the word 'sophistry' has entered the English language to describe this kind of verbal manipulation.

The effect of an argument may be enhanced by burnishing the skills of rhetoric through following the 'rules of the game'. Constructing the rules of effective oratory was accomplished first by another Sophist, Gorgias. But it was Isocrates who probably taught the skills most influentially. It is of interest to note that, just as in one generation, Socrates (b. 470) disagreed with Protagoras (b. *c*.490) on the subject of education, so too, though with deeper differences, did Plato (b. *c*.427) disagree with Isocrates (b. 436) in the next. Rhetoric, though by no means confined to political and forensic purposes, remained the stock in trade of civic education for a remarkably long time in the ancient world – from the expositions of Gorgias

(b. *c*.485 BC) to Quintilian (d. sometime in the 90s AD) – and schools of rhetoric persisted to the end of Roman Imperial times. Rhetoric even remained in the curriculum in Europe until the eighteenth century.

Much of the formal civic education we have outlined so far – the Spartan *agogē* and the teaching of the Sophists – was designed entirely or primarily for the elites of the city-state societies. Isocrates, a student of Gorgias, also aimed to educate an elite. He is important not only as an influential teacher of rhetoric, who drew students from great distances to his school in Athens, but as the originator of the prepared and published political speech also. For Isocrates' ambition was to improve civic consciousness and, ideally, panhellenic unity. For him the art of rhetoric had a moral political purpose. 'I do believe,' he wrote, 'that nothing helps as much towards the practice of virtue as the study of political wisdom and eloquence' (quoted Gwynne 1964: 47). A man of shy disposition and of remarkable longevity, he taught for over half a century, yet educated, in small seminars, only about a hundred students all told. His influence was none the less out of all proportion to these tiny numbers because of his published 'model' speeches and the dissemination of his ideal of moral political rhetoric by his dedicated and able former students.

Isocrates died in 338. Probably three years later, the system of *ephēbia* was regularized in Athens as part of the reforms of the Athenian administrator Lycurgus (not to be confused with his Spartan namesake). This was a style of training that became widespread throughout the Hellenic world at this time as a means of distinguishing citizens from non-citizens, though with variations in detailed application from *polis* to *polis* and over the many years of its institution. What follows is a description of the arrangements in Athens *c*.330 BC. The *ephēboi* (often translated as 'cadets') were young men aged 18 to 20, who pursued a course of education and training to prepare them for the duties and rights of citizenship. At first, probably entirely military in content, by the fourth century some moral and religious education with a civil purpose had been added to the course. It is likely that the reform of *c*.335 was introduced to restore the civic morale and military strength of Athens following the historic victory of Philip of Macedon over the Greeks at Chaeronea in 338.

The carefully structured Athenian ephebic system started with the registration of all 18-year-old youths who could prove the validity of their claim to be of Athenian citizen stock. There followed a two-year period of compulsory national service, though later this was reduced to a voluntary one-year period. The emphasis seems to have been placed heavily on military training and guard duties (see Aristotle 1984: 42.3–5). However, the oath, sworn at the end of their first year, reveals a political purpose to the training. The key sentences may be reconstructed as follows:

> I shall not dishonour these sacred arms, nor shall I abandon my comrades in battle; I shall fight for the gods and for hearth and home, and I shall not leave my country smaller, but rather [I shall leave it] greater and stronger than I found it, either by my own efforts or in the company of my comrades . . . and I shall submit to whosoever has authority [over me and exercises it] with wisdom, and I shall obey the existing laws and those that the wisdom of the rulers may

enact . . . and those that the people enact by common consent . . . and if anyone should attempt to subvert them I will not tolerate it, either by myself or in company with my comrades; and I shall venerate those whom my fathers venerated.

(quoted Marrou 1956: 106)

Notice, by the way, the democratic reference to the legislative power of 'the people'.

None of these approaches to citizenship education in Athens, it must be conceded, offered a full, balanced curriculum. In different ways, Plato and Aristotle put their minds to this matter, each reflecting his own judgement about the Hellenic civic education traditions.

Plato and Aristotle

Although theorizing about politics or education can rarely shake itself free of the social and intellectual environment in which the philosopher works, the theorist can produce ideas and proposals that are not confined tightly by practical considerations – indeed, that is the very function of the theorist. The contributions of Plato and Aristotle to thinking about citizenship education can therefore be appreciated only by taking into account both the influences of the time and place when they were working and the value of their ideas that may be judged to be perennial.

However, before examining their writings on our topic, we must try to clarify another issue, namely the loosely, perhaps too loosely, accepted range of what falls within the definition of citizenship education as assumed thus far in this chapter. This clarification is especially pertinent for an understanding of Plato's and Aristotle's ideas. We can best elucidate this problem of definition by recognizing that in both practice and theory different categories of individuals were the recipients of such education or were considered to be its proper beneficiaries. Let us picture these different categories as forming a spectrum drawn according to the numbers in each. Starting with the greatest numbers, we have the condition in democratic Athens where the citizen-body comprised a relatively large proportion of the total population and where compulsory ephebic training drew all novice citizens into its programme. In other states, notably Sparta, the numbers involved were relatively small simply because citizenship rights were not widely conferred. However, third and more importantly, many kinds of citizenship education were confined to only a small proportion of the total citizen-body because few had the leisure or money that private forms of civic education required. We may instance the instruction provided by the Sophists, by various schools, of which those of Isocrates, Plato and Aristotle were especially famous, and by families with the interest and leisure to undertake this form of initiation themselves. The fourth category – or a feature of the third, depending on how one views it – is defined by the purpose of much of this elite education. This was to provide a small number with the requisite understanding and skills for active political and juridical participation and leadership.

The question consequently arises as to whether, as we move from the first category to the fourth, the term 'citizenship education' may be properly applied to all. One could argue that what Isocrates was doing and what Plato was proposing in his *Republic*, for example, was not citizenship education but the education of young individuals to become professional politicians. The trouble is, one may also argue, in this Greek context, that those who became professional politicians, if educated morally as well as technically and intellectually, were in fact the best, or the elite, citizens.

This interpolation, though, has hindered the completion of our spectrum; because, as we proceed from mass to selected education, the final, fifth category can be an empty one: that is, that no education for citizenship should be attempted for anyone. This was a view propounded by Plato's master Socrates. In the *Protagoras* he draws the distinction between judging the skills of a tradesman or businessman and the 'virtue' of an individual acting as a citizen:

> But when it is something to do with the government of the country that is being debated, the man who gets up to advise them may be [of any trade or condition]. No one brings it up against any of these . . . that here is a man who without any technical qualifications, unable to point to anybody as his teacher, is yet trying to give advice. The reason must be that they do not think this is a subject that can be taught.
>
> And you must not suppose that this is true only of the community at large. Individually also the wisest and best of our countrymen are unable to hand on to others the virtue which they possess.
>
> (Plato 1956: 319 C–E)

We are now ready to analyse what Plato and Aristotle had to say on the subject, both of whom were drawn to it by the decay of social and political standards in fourth-century Athens: they felt that effective citizenship education was wanting and its lack went a considerable way to explain this parlous state of affairs. We start with Plato's two works in which he discusses citizenship education most fully: these are the *Republic* and the *Laws*. Plato completed the *Republic*, his plan for an ideal, utopian state, in *c*.375. He died in 347, leaving the *Laws*, a rather more pragmatic design, virtually completed. In addition, the *Republic* is more concerned with the advanced education of an elite, the *Laws* more with elementary courses for the generality of citizens. Both books reflect the educational practices of his day, especially of Athens, Sparta and Crete, the *Laws* being couched in the form of a dialogue engaged in by citizens from each of these *poleis*. Indeed, he had a qualified admiration for the Spartan system of education. In his own works he adopted the state provision of education and the institution of common messes, while yet regretting the over-emphasis of cultivating courage and military skills at the expense of fostering temperance and training the intellect (see *Plato* 1934: 630, 633–4).

Plato's educational philosophy is grounded in the belief that the proper purpose of *paideia* (education of the whole person) is to develop the mind and character of the individual, not to make the individual an athlete or a businessman, for example. Plato, in line with the pre-Cynic tradition, took it as axiomatic that human development could take place only within the political framework of a *polis*. Consequently, humane and citizenship education were, or rather should be, linked symbiotically by citizenship education. He makes this connection clear in the *Laws*, particularly in this passage: 'any training which has as its end wealth, or perhaps bodily strength, or some other accomplishment unattended by intelligence and righteousness, it [i.e. his argument] counts vulgar, illiberal, and wholly unworthy to be called education [i.e. *paideia*]' (Plato 1934: 644). In contrast, true education is 'that schooling from boyhood in goodness [i.e. *aretē*] which inspires the recipient with passionate and ardent desire to become a perfect citizen, knowing both how to wield and how to submit to righteous rule' (Plato 1934: 643). Faced with the twin perils of tyranny and anarchy, education to respect *eunomia* (balanced justice) was crucial: thus, 'education is, in fact, the drawing and leading of children to the rule which has been pronounced right by the voice of law' (Plato 1934: 659).

Accordingly, the citizen who rules must be educated to be wisely just and to rule lawfully, and the citizen who is ruled must be educated to accept that what he wants is what is lawful; that is, his behaviour must become virtuous. However, as Socrates declared, virtue cannot be taught. Plato's solution is to argue that goodness derives from an understanding of ultimate truth, and that truth can be discerned, *pace* the teachings of the Sophists, only by a very lengthy and carefully programmed student life devoted to the pursuit of knowledge and understanding and the cultivation of the faculty of reason. This prescription is expounded in its most thorough form in the *Republic*, where Plato requires a course, including a final fifteen years of on-the-job experience, which is completed by the age of 50. Then,

> They must lift up the eye of the soul to gaze on that which sheds light on all things; and when they have seen the Good itself, take it as a pattern for the right ordering of the state and of the individual, themselves included. For the rest of their lives, most of their time will be spent in study; but they will all take their turn at the troublesome duties of public life and act as Rulers for their country's sake, not regarding it as a distinction, but as an unavoidable task.
>
> (Plato 1941: VII, 540)

These are the 'Philosopher-Kings', the perfected citizens of Plato's course of civic education. Or, perhaps more properly, education of the political elite. His handling of education for citizenship in the *Laws* is more relevant for us. There, he makes it clear that, apart from the branches of mathematics, including astronomy, his curriculum is designed for all. It will be helpful, therefore, to examine this text in some detail, dealing with the organization of education in this hypothetical state, the roles of the various subjects and extra-curricular learning. (For a detailed analysis, the reader is referred to Morrow (1960).)

Plato was adamant that education must be administered by the state. His invention in the *Laws* of a position of 'minister of education', whom he calls by various terms, including 'educator', is especially revealing. Because human character and behaviour are the products of upbringing, this 'post is far the most important of the highest of offices of state' and must be occupied by one 'who is in all points best of all the citizens' (Plato 1934: 765, 766). He would be in charge of all forms of education, in school and extra-curricular. The Lacedaemonian influence is clear, though even Sparta had no overall magistrate. This influence is also evident in Plato's insistence that attendance at school should be mandatory as far as possible 'on the grounds that the child is even more the property of the State than of his parents' (Plato 1934: 804). Indeed, implicit in the *Laws* is that education has a primarily civic purpose. In a section on arts and crafts, Plato asserts that the citizen has no need of that kind of instruction because,

> A citizen has already a calling which will make him, in view of the constant practice and wide study it involves, in the preservation and enjoyment of the public social order – a task which permits no relegation to the second place.
>
> (Plato 1934: 846)

Although Plato was innovative in providing for a state educator in his hypothetical constitution, some of the content of his educational programme borrowed ideas from actual Greek practice, particularly Athens and Sparta. For instance, 'music' – the activities of the Muses in their various forms – was of capital importance in Greek education. The American musicologist Paul Lang has written:

> The Arcadians had state laws and regulations which called for compulsory musical education for every citizen up to his thirtieth year [for example]. . . . Not every sort of music was acceptable for educational purposes. The foremost place was assigned to melodies in the Dorian mode because their austerity was greatly valued as a character-building force.
>
> (Lang 1942: 15)

He goes on to explain that a different ethos was attached to different scales, or modes, and that these, in turn, were associated with the different Greek tribes. 'Thus there developed an ethical doctrine of the state-building properties of national music and the demoralizing effects of foreign music' (Lang 1942: 15). Plato was especially anxious that the greatest care be given in providing the exactly appropriate teaching in the musical disciplines, not just because of their positive qualities, but because he was apprehensive about the potential for social damage by using the wrong 'syllabus'. In the *Republic* he declares that 'rhythm and harmony sink deep into the recesses of the soul and take the strongest hold there' (Plato 1941: III, 401). Having established the beneficial modes of expression, these, as he insists in the *Laws* (Plato 1934: 798, 799), must at all costs be preserved in schools and festivals against any alteration; variation will endanger morality and undermine the stability of the state. In modern English terms, 'Land of Hope and Glory' good; rock'n'roll bad. (For the civically malign effects of the latter for producing 'rhythm-crazed' youngsters, see Bicât 1970: 324–5.) The study of literature (a form of 'music'), of poetry, drama and prose – for reading practice, recitation and memorization – was also restricted to the texts approved by the educator. Uninhibited by modesty, Plato puts into the mouth of the Athenian the judgement that 'of all the many compositions I have met with or listened to . . . I find [my own composition] the most satisfactory and the most suitable for the ears of the young' (Plato 1934: 811). In short, the *Laws* would be a 'set-book' – a somewhat bulkier document than the US Constitution studied by modern American high school students!

For the Greeks, patriotic citizenship meant training primarily for military service. Plato retains a two-year ephebic training in the *Laws*, though for young women as well as men. He also introduces gymnastics to complement 'music'. As we have seen, he scorned athletics as a competitive activity for its own sake: he believed that physical training should be designed to fit his citizenry both in stamina and skill to be called upon in the event of war to fight as hoplites. In passing, we note that the citizen's body would be developed and trained for agility in gymnastics as a necessary preparation for the peaceful activity of dance also, as inducing a civically beneficial sense of rhythm.

The skills and attitudes developed by the 'music' curriculum were to be put to good use in public festivals, many of which were planned in the *Laws*. By gathering together in these collective tributes to the gods, civic cohesion would be cemented and loyalty bonded. Anyone incapable of participating in such choral and Terpsichorean activities, says Plato, must be considered uneducated (Plato 1934: 654). The sense of civic union was to be reinforced diurnally by another form of lifelong education, that is, the institution of meals taken in common. Plato cites Sparta and Crete explicitly as his models for this intrusion of the state into what would normally be considered a part of private life, though in the *Laws* he includes women as well in this regulation (Plato 1934: 783): too much privacy weakens adherence to the law, he avers (Plato 1934: 780–1).

Aristotle shared his teacher's enthusiasm for 'common tables' (Aristotle 1948: 1330a), and, indeed, for many other of his recommendations, notably the state provision of education and the primacy of 'music'. However, before looking at the particulars of Aristotle's views on education for citizenship, we should recognize an important distinction that he draws between two possible kinds of political education, exemplified by the following extracts:

> A young man is not a proper student of [lectures on] politics; for he is inexperienced in *actions* concerned with human life, and discussions proceed from [premises concerning those *actions*] and deal with [those *actions*]. Moreover, being disposed to follow his passions, he will listen in vain and without benefit, since the end of such discussions is not knowledge but *action*.
>
> (Aristotle 1948: 1095a)

> The greatest . . . of all the means for ensuring the stability of constitutions – but one which is nowadays usually neglected – is the education of citizens in the spirit of their constitution. There is no profit in the best of laws, even when they are sanctioned by general civic consent, if the citizens themselves have not been attuned, by the force of habit and the influence of teaching, to the right constitutional temper – which will be the temper of democracy where the laws are democratic, and where they are oligarchical will be that of oligarchy.
>
> (Aristotle 1948: 1310a; see also 1337a11)

Do these two excerpts contradict each other, or are they reconcilable? They may be reconciled as long as we construe them in the following manner. We may translate 'lectures on politics' in the first passage as 'political science' (see Aristotle 1955: 28); and we should understand 'constitution' (*politeia*) in the second as including a system of social ethics as well as a form of government (see Aristotle (1948: lxvi), and 1289a where he adds to this definition 'the nature of the end to be pursued by the association and all its members is prescribed'). It then becomes clear that Aristotle believes young people should not be taught about constitutional structures and political policies, but should – indeed it is crucial that they should – be brought up to behave in harmony with the political culture of their particular *polis*.

This relative principle is, however, balanced by a second consideration, namely that education should make citizens as virtuous as possible. All wish to be virtuous because virtue is a pre-condition of happiness; but the individual's natural proclivity to virtue must be supplemented by the cultivation of good habits and reasoning power; that is, by education. Moreover, the felicity of the state and that of the individual are the same (Aristotle 1948: 1324a); the good state will therefore want all its citizens to be educated to goodness. Two consequences flow from this desideratum. One is that the state should provide schooling for the young. 'All would agree,' Aristotle asserts, 'that the legislator should make the education of the young his chief and foremost concern.' There are two reasons for this, namely the need to suit the style of education to the constitution, already mentioned, and that 'the constitution of a state will suffer if education is neglected' (Aristotle 1948: 1337aII). The second consequence of the desirability of educating citizens for virtue is that all who are capable of being educated (and he admits that some are not (1316a)) should have that capacity extended in accordance with what is possible for each individual.

What, then, are the implications of the co-existence of Aristotle's twin guiding principles for citizenship education, namely, to suit the constitution and to foster virtue? A modern authority explains:

> Education should form characters supportive of the regime yet should also prepare and encourage individuals to actualize their human potential. In calling for the actualization of potential, Aristotle is, one should remember, calling not only for excellence but for diversity, since a city's existence depends on the preservation of differences not inimical to virtue. . . . In short, education must make persons at once excellent citizens, excellent human beings, and excellent individuals.
>
> (Swanson 1992: 144–5)

We must now ask how Aristotle recommends that young people can best be educated to be good citizens. Basically, he argues, both non-rational habit and the reasoning faculty must be developed, the former in conformity with the understanding of what reason tells the individual is good. By 'good' is meant civic virtue; and civic virtue should comprise five qualities, namely moderation, trustworthiness, judgement, the spirit of protectiveness and goodwill. A combination of political exhortation to live virtuously, law to deter bad behaviour and education to teach and instil civic virtue is required.

A sound education, Aristotle understands, is a complex business, which no Greek *polis* has succeeded in translating into really good practice. What must be understood is that the soul is divided into a habituating sphere and a rational sphere. The former is related to action – undertaking necessary or useful acts and participating in war; the latter is related to leisure (or culture) – undertaking good acts and cultivating the arts of peace. The latter is superior (see Aristotle 1948: 1333b).

Education of the habits should be pursued through supervising children's moral behaviour and teaching them gymnastics and 'music'. The latter is vital for the cultivation and maintenance of good citizenship from puberty to mature adulthood; because performing or listening to the various rhythms and harmonic modes will evoke the various qualities of civic virtue (see Aristotle 1948: 1342b). Indeed, what Aristotle has to say about 'music' in the broad sense is no different from the views of the Greeks in general and Plato in particular, which we have outlined above. Since music affects the character of the soul, it is the prime fashioner of civic excellence (Aristotle 1948: 1340b).

However, music needs to be complemented by the less active kind of liberal education. The reason for this is that the good citizen must learn to be wise and prudent and to make good judgements – all requirements for proper engagement in public affairs. Yet this kind of contemplative, thinking education and the civic participation for which it is a preparation is scarcely possible if one's whole time is filled with being trained for and earning a living. Aristotle's programme of education, just as his definition of citizenship, therefore presupposes a society, like Athens, in which time-consuming and strenuous economic activities are undertaken by non-citizen slaves and foreign residents.

Without such free time, a thorough, extended, state-provided education for citizenship would not be possible. The alternative was the early Roman system of a basic civic instruction of boys by their fathers.

Rome

'Captured Greece took captive her brutish conqueror, and introduced the arts to uncivilized Latium.' Thus did the Roman poet Horace in his *Epistles* famously encapsulate the infiltration of Hellenic culture into Roman society increasingly from the second century BC. Although the effects were evident in education, yet distinctions between the two pedagogical systems in relation to citizenship education remained. Three differences of emphasis should – and partly to recapitulate – be especially taken into account. First, Greek citizenship, especially Athenian, was an essentially political concept and status, defining the citizen's political function; the Roman was primarily legal, defining who was a citizen and his rights in law, though, in truth, both peoples expected of their citizens the quality of virtue – *aretē* and *virtus* in their respective languages. Second, Greek education, conceived in its civic purpose distinct from military training, focused on leading the soul or personality to virtue by the affective moods of the musical disciplines. The Roman citizen of any culture rated music beneath his dignity and dancing as positively degrading, undermining his prized *gravitas*, and Roman civic education was pragmatically concerned mainly with learning about, living within and interpreting the law. Third, the Greeks – apart from the special cases of Sparta and Crete – came to accept the necessity of the institutionalization of education in schools; Rome retained more firmly, though not entirely, the conviction that education was essentially a familial responsibility.

The family was, in fact, the essence of Roman life. Throughout republican times and even, probably, as early as Rome's monarchical era, parents of citizenly status undertook the education of their children. The mother or another female member of the family moulded the characters of the youngest, as Tacitus, for example, revealed, explaining that,

> Whilst the child's character was still fresh and open and unspoiled by wrong, he should be taught to embrace the practice of virtue with all his heart; and that whether destined to be soldier, jurist or orator, his whole energies should be solely devoted to duty.
>
> (quoted Gwynne 1964: 14)

The father continued the education and training of his sons from the age of 7 to about 16 in every facet of living. Indeed, in his capacity as *paterfamilias* he had the right to wield dictatorial power over his family throughout the whole of his life. Underlying these domestic arrangements lay a fundamentally civic purpose. Just as admirable features derived from the education of the young person, so, it was believed, the strength and stability of the mature Roman state derived from the admirable habits which had been tried and tested over so many generations. Therefore, each new generation must be brought up to understand, take pride in and abide unquestioningly by the 'custom of the ancestors' (*mos maiorum*). And, of course, civil and religious ceremonies played a dramatic role in reinforcing this process of socialization.

Obviously, the precise nature and effectiveness of the family-based education depended on the aptitude of the parents and the willingness and ability of the father especially to undertake and perform their pedagogical functions. Most of the evidence we have concerns the wealthy and publicly involved citizens, from whose diligent performance of teaching duties it may be hazardous to generalize. For example, Cicero refers in *On the Laws* (*De Legibus*) to a former requirement that all children learn the Twelve Tables by rote – though it had lapsed by the time he was an adult (see Cicero 1928b: II, 59). This is of special interest for us. It confirms the honour accorded to antiquity since these bronze tablets codifying criminal, civil and public law were originally displayed four centuries before Cicero's time. Moreover, their continued memorization reflects the legal tenor of Roman civic education (see Cowell 1948: 152–4). However, to pursue our doubt: did literally *all* Roman children 'learn their Tables'? This assumes very assiduous fathers and offspring. After all, schools did not provide the environment for this learning:

Cicero, in another work, *On the State* (*De Re Publica*), makes this clear. He asserts: 'our people have never wished to have any system of education for the free-born which is either definitely fixed by law, or officially established, or uniform in all cases, though the Greeks have expended much vain labour on this problem' (Cicero 1928a: IV, 3). Yet schools for the '3Rs' certainly did exist by Cicero's time (d. 43 BC). Education in public affairs was part of the father's responsibility. His sons accompanied him to religious ceremonies and public debates in the forum. For the minority of boys destined for public life a transitional year was intercalated between the end of formal education and adulthood: this was called the *tirocinium fori*, novitiate for the forum. An experienced family friend took the youth in hand for this training, akin to the Athenian practice.

With Greek ideas and practices creeping into Roman education from *c*.200 BC, changes took place, notably the increasing use of private tutors, the establishment of more schools and the teaching of rhetoric. And, inevitably, as the Roman Empire expanded, so a Graeco-Roman style of education spread throughout the lands of the Mediterranean basin and western Europe. Furthermore, formal education became more accepted than had been the case in the ancient Roman tradition. In the first century AD Plutarch wrote *The Education of Children* (though some doubt has been cast on his authorship). In this essay he commends a poet for giving the advice, 'Should teach while still a child/The tale of noble deeds' (Plutarch 1960: 17), a point of view as much Roman as Spartan or Platonic Greek. What is Platonic but contrary to Roman educational tradition is Plutarch's conviction of the vital role that philosophy should play: 'it is necessary,' he writes, 'to make philosophy as it were the head and font of all education', for from this study flows all virtuous conduct (Plutarch 1960: 35). The ideal education, in fact, should combine philosophy and politics, because, as he asserts, 'I regard as perfect, so far as men can be, those who are able to combine and mingle political capacity with philosophy'; that is, a practical with a contemplative mode of life (Plutarch 1960: 37).

However, Plutarch did not approve of education in rhetoric, one of the most popular subjects from late Republican into Imperial times (see Gwynne 1964: *passim*). In the first century BC Cicero wrote several works on the subject, notably *On the Orator* (*De Oratore*), and at the end of the first century AD Quintilian wrote the multi-volume *Institutio Oratoria* (*Education of the Orator*). Teachers of rhetoric, from the Sophists and Aristotle to Quintilian, and indeed onwards to at least Vergerio in the fifteenth century, did not speak with one voice on the purpose, structure and style of public oratory. It must be conceded, indeed, that much of what was learned had precious little to do with education for citizenship; even so, enough of it did to justify some commentary here. One of the earliest extant works of Latin prose, dating from *c*.85 BC, is a textbook on rhetoric. It contains, in the usual model speeches of such books, a number drawing upon contemporary political and legal issues. To take two examples: 'Should Scipio be exempted from the legal age for accepting office as consul?'; 'Should the Italians receive the rights of citizenship?' (see Gwynne 1964: 68; on the latter question, the enfranchisement of the whole population of the peninsula and the designation of the frontier with Celtic Gaul were controversial issues at this time).

To proceed, therefore, to Cicero's contribution to the art of oratory as a form of education for citizenship. Cicero was educated soundly in both the Roman and Greek traditions and became an incomparable literary stylist in Latin and the foremost forensic orator of his age. Born in 106 BC, he was a mature, experienced man when he wrote his famous *On the Orator* in 55 – described by one authority as 'a masterpiece which may not unfairly be called the orator's programme of educational reform' (Gwynne 1964: 81). Rather like the Sophists, Cicero holds that the orator must have an education in sufficient breadth to be able to discourse on any topic. At the same time he makes it clear that philosophy, history and law are the most useful. Writing of the need of the orator to understand the whole gamut of human nature, he explains, 'And all this is considered to be the special province of the philosophers, nor will the orator, if he take my advice, resist their claim' (Cicero 1948: I, 54). On the other two disciplines, we may choose this comment: 'no long discussion is needed to explain why I think the orator must also be acquainted with public law, which is exclusively concerned with the State and Empire, and also the records of past events and the precedents of antiquity' (Cicero 1948: I, 201).

Quintilian, a distinguished teacher of the subject, followed in the Ciceronic tradition of expounding the principles of oratory, though he was dubious about the need for a philosophical foundation in the orator's education. We must, furthermore, remember that he published his *Education of the Orator* at the end of the reigns of the Flavian emperors, an age when a lively political citizenship as experienced by Cicero was barely known. Nevertheless, Quintilian would have his student orator taught politics (see Quintilian 1922: XII, 25–6), though he gave precedence to law (see Quintilian 1921: VII, 30–4). Even more, he asserted that:

> The man who can really play his part as a citizen and is capable of meeting the demands of public and private business, the man who can guide a state by his counsels, give it a firm basis by his legislation and purge its vices by his decision as a judge, is assuredly no other than the orator.
>
> (Quintilian 1920: I, 10)

It is evident from passages such as this that Quintilian was striving to restore Cicero's concept of oratory as a live contribution to the citizen's political function. But there is a sad irony in this. While successive emperors (notably Augustus, Claudius and Caracalla) conferred citizenship on increasing numbers throughout the Empire, by concentrating all power in their own hands the emperors drained the Roman citizenship of all political meaning, leaving it as simply a legal status. Moreover, the teaching and practice of oratory lost its civic and moral purpose and decayed into the mere technique of rhetoric for its own sake.

Education for citizenship in the late Republican and Imperial epochs assumed rather the deliberate policy of the Romanization of the provincial upper and urban classes by means of newly created schools. In these establishments the sons of the privileged families learned the Latin language and absorbed Latin culture. A French scholar, taking examples which span a century (79 BC to AD 85) and three provinces, writes:

The Roman procedure began in the same way everywhere: Rome took as hostages the children from all the best families in the newly conquered land, and brought them up in Roman schools. The method adopted in Spain by Sertorius was repeated along the Rhine by Caligula and in Britain by Agricola.

(Marrou 1956: 295)

Consequently, they acquired the basic prerequisites of citizenship.

Legacies of the ancient world

The ancient ideas on and practices of citizenship education did not die with the deaths of the philosophers and the demise of the Greek and Roman states. To provide some indication of the persistence of the classical traditions it will be useful to say a few words about interest in Sparta, revivals of Platonic and Aristotelian ideas and the continuation of Roman-style education in rhetoric, as commentary upon the three main sections of this chapter; and also to give an indication of classical consciousness and content of civic education in the broadest sense from the Renaissance onwards.

The classical revivals of the Renaissance and Enlightenment, not surprisingly, brought about a renewed fascination in Spartan education. In his extraordinarily influential treatise on education, written at the beginning of the fifteenth century, Pier Vergerio, Professor at Padua University, praised the Spartans' tough training of their children. However, in the words of the authority on the Spartan tradition, 'the later eighteenth century in France is the great age of lacomania, gathering together the threads – moral, social, educational, and political – that had usually been separate since the Renaissance' (Rawson 1969: 227). Because the great burgeoning of educational thinking and planning in France during the last forty years of the eighteenth century will be a major feature of Chapter 2, this comment should be recalled in that context.

More pertinent still for civic education specifically are two aspects of German thinking and practice in the twentieth century. One was a fallacious racial interpretation of Spartan superiority, based upon the supposed differences between the Dorian and Ionian Greeks. A brief explanation reads as follows:

From K.O. Müller (1824) to W. Jäger (1932), German scholarship lauded [Spartan education] to the skies as a product of the Nordic spirit possessed by the Dorians – the conscious embodiment of a racial, militarist totalitarian policy – a model . . . of the ideal which . . . never ceased to inspire the German soul.

(Marrou 1956: 23)

Once in power, the Nazis had opportunities to establish boarding-schools for their elite, no doubt with the approval of the Führer (see Rawson 1969: 342–3). One type, the Napolas (National Political Education Institutes), has been described thus:

The programme concentrated on the development of a military spirit, the fusion of Prussian and National Socialist values, the development of courage, dedication and simplicity. Its administrators under the direction of a high-ranking SS officer were members of the SA and SS.

(Bracher 1978: 331)

Little wonder that the term 'Spartan' has come readily to mind in portraying these institutions (see e.g. Shirer 1964: 317).

Comparisons between the Nazi educational objectives and Plato have also been made. One American scholar, for example, commented that 'like Plato they propose a stratified society . . . in which complete harmony obtains so long as the point of view of each and every man in each and every class is controlled through appropriate education and propaganda' (Brady 1937: 123–4). In the same year an English academic published a book, *Plato To-day*, in some parts of which the author imagines fictional or semi-fictional characters in dialogue. 'A philosopher' with overt Nazi sympathies has this to say on the subject of connections between Sparta, Plato, Nazi Germany and education:

> The Spartan education is a wonderful prototype of our Aryan ideals. It subordinates the individual to the State, and the follower to the leader; and it develops those qualities of courage, simplicity, and discipline which are the marks of a warrior – and of a ruling race.
>
> Sparta was Plato's ideal, and it is our German ideal too.
>
> (Crossman 1937: 239)

Such was the academic mood of the time, making simplistic correlations to boost or denigrate the Nazis' supposed classical credentials. Even outside the totalitarian empathy with Plato's *Republic*, no twentieth-century writer in the history or theory of education seems to have considered his own work to be complete without copious reference to that book. Many used Platonic ideas analogously, others dragged in the name of the great philosopher sometimes with scant justification. One example from a passage on Fichte, who, admittedly, like Plato, compounded politics and education, illustrates this second tendency. The authors write that one aspect of the Prussian's work '*suggests* a study of Plato', and they continue, '*Perhaps* from the same source' (Curtis and Boultwood 1956: 353; emphases added).

True, some of the interest in Plato's work avoided elements of its political content – the *Laws* was neglected, for instance. On the other hand, insofar as Aristotle's *Politics* was studied, the political aspect of his thoughts on education could scarcely be avoided. His works became known again in Europe in the thirteenth century. This influence in Italy has been described thus:

> With the translation and dissemination of Aristotle's *Ethics* and more particularly *Politics* – Latin version by William of Moerbeke *c*.1260, potted version for Italian townsmen by Guido Vernari 1320s – ancient Greek political, or *polis*, philosophy began to pervade all parts of Italian culture . . . especially writing on government.
>
> (Jones 1997: 463)

Aristotle's political ideas, in particular his Greek concept of an active, participative citizenry, were widespread throughout the Italian city-states, especially Florence. The Dominican Friars were devoted to popularizing Aristotelian thought through university teaching, pulpit addresses and publications – Moerbeke was a Dominican; and they even established schools in Florence in which they taught about Aristotle's concept of the political nature of man. Moreover, the politically conscious citizens of the city-states had Vernari's digest to read, a work that seems to have sold quite well. Thus Aristotle contributed to citizenship education in the late Middle Ages, not so much by what he wrote on education in Chapters 7 and 8 of the *Politics* as by awakening the Italian public to what citizenship in its fullest sense could really mean.

However, unlike Plato, Aristotle has evoked little interest among writers on education, though we may note three exceptions because these do, in fact, show the much greater pertinence of Aristotle's ideas to present-day liberal societies than Plato's. The first is the American philosopher Dewey (see Chapter 3), who commended the relevance of Aristotle for two main reasons: his distinction between skill training and liberal education, and his thoughts on the most apt form of moral education. 'Aristotle was permanently right,' Dewey argues, 'in assuming the inferiority and subordination of mere skill in performance and mere accumulation of external products to understanding, sympathy of appreciation, and the free play of ideas' (Dewey 1961: 256); though what is needed in a modern industrial democracy is access to both kinds. Dewey also applauds Aristotle's rejection of Plato's thesis that morality is acquired through knowledge in favour of its acquisition through habituation, practice and experience (see Dewey 1961: 355). The English educationist E.B. Castle focuses on a different point made by Aristotle, namely that the citizen should be educated in the spirit of the constitution (see Aristotle 1948: 1310a, 1337aII, and above); so in modern England education should support the democratic polity. Nevertheless, Castle thought that Aristotle's further statement – that 'the system of education in a state must . . . be one and the same for all' (Aristotle 1948: 1337a) – goes too far, and supported the post-1944 tripartite concept of *appropriate* education (see Castle 1961: 201). In contrast, the Canadian academic Eamonn Callan supports both Aristotle's interpretation of moral education and, by implication, though without citation, his advocacy of the same education for all. Callan argues that modern pluralistic societies need the cohesion provided by (using the American term) common schools:

> The Aristotelian thesis would suggest that the growth of reasonableness requires at some stage that reciprocity be practised in dialogical contexts that straddle our social cleavages. Call this the dialogical task of common education. The common school is an obvious way of creating the necessary context for that task prior to assuming the duties of citizen.
>
> (Callan 1997:177)

If Aristotle became the principal guide to politics, Quintilian became the principal guide to education (together with Cicero specifically for rhetoric). Key exponents of Quintilian and, significantly, of the civic purpose of education in post-classical times were Vergerio of Padua (b.1349) and his pupil, Vittorino of Feltre. Vergerio published an exposition of Quintilian's *Education of the Orator*, which promoted his revival. In the words of one historian of education, 'Every educator of the Revival [i.e. Renaissance], whether man of theory or man of practice, whether on Italian or Teutonic soil, steeped himself in the text and in the spirit of this treatise of Quintilian's' (Boyd 1932: 171).

The most pervasive influence, however, derived from the study of Greek and, especially, Latin literature from the Renaissance to the nineteenth century, and from the great respect this learning generated for classical civilization. A portion of this respect was accorded to the classical style of citizenship. There are four particularly significant examples.

The first is Renaissance Italy. Here we find in city-states such as Bologna, Pavia, Milan, Venice and, the exemplar, Florence the most highly developed form of citizenship in that age; and a political theory of civic virtue (*virtù*) to match, for example, in the writings of Bruni and Machiavelli. Each state tried to cultivate an expectation of citizenly virtue and patriotism, and the broadly educative devices used to achieve this objective had a classical resonance in various forms. The cities tried to prove and stress their Roman origins in order to acquire the cachet of a 'Latin city'. In addition, the Church was conscripted as a partner in the civic enterprise, asserting the cardinal importance of community harmony. Clerics purveyed the message in the schoolrooms, from the pulpit and during the magnificent and popular municipal pageants and festivals which were, in all probability, the most effective method of civic propaganda. These festivals, based on a kind of civic religion, are typical of the 'civic' or 'classical republican' style of citizenship as practised in Greece and Rome. Gradually, however, the religious element weakened so that, in Florence, for instance, secular teachers were using the models of Sparta, Athens and Republican Rome to impress upon their pupils the ideals of citizenship. For example, it has been said of Vittorino's teaching of personal honesty and civic responsibility to his pupils that he 'believed that both virtues could be learned from the study of the classics' (quoted Dynneson 2001: 107).

The second and third examples are provided by late eighteenth-century North America and France, where interest in classical writers and commitment to a republican form of government with its classical style of civic virtue supplied a background to educational thinking, as will be shown in Chapter 2.

The fourth example is to be found in eighteenth- and nineteenth-century England. There, the endowed grammar schools and public schools educated the elite citizenry who dominated domestic and colonial government and administration. The curriculum offered by these schools until well into the nineteenth century was almost solely in the Classics – indeed, that is what *grammar* schools were for (see e.g. Barnard 1947: 17–20; also Chapter 3 below). The stock author for Latin prose was Cicero. For example, when Samuel Butler became Headmaster of Shrewsbury School in 1798 he revealed in a letter that Cicero was taught on four separate occasions in the week (see Sylvester 1970: 205–6). And Cicero was a staunch believer in civic virtue.

To sum up succinctly: the classical world exerted an influence on citizenship education for several centuries in three main ways. Through the study of classical literature and Greek and Roman history, youths have learned about ideas concerning citizenship and the various styles in which the Spartans, Athenians and Romans practised that role. The ancient art of rhetoric, with its forensic and political potential, persisted in school curricula, and some educational theorists and politicians have argued that the ancient virtue of civic consciousness should be restored by the broadest educational means for the benefit of modern states. In questioning the absolutism of *ancien régime* monarchy, revolutionaries in the period which came to a climax with the French Revolution were able to look back to the classical traditions of republicanism and citizenship as an attractive alternative. Effecting the change was an educational as well as a political challenge.

2 The ages of rebellions and revolutions

The early nation-states

While politically fragmented Germany and Italy retained into the modern era the ancient and medieval nature of citizenship as a status enjoyed in urban or city-state contexts, England and France in particular were becoming consolidated nation-states. Furthermore, these states were ruled by monarchs who pretended to absolute power by virtue of the authority they held from God. If the monarch was so exalted by divine right above even his most noble subjects, could citizenship exist either in theory or in practice? The short answer is that the concept was so ingrained in political thinking that it could not be discarded even in this apparently uncongenial authoritarian environment. It had to be adapted; and education for this adjusted understanding of the status also had to be adapted. We start this chapter, chronologically, in the sixteenth century and pursue the story to the end of the eighteenth. By entitling the chapter 'The ages of rebellions and revolutions' we intend to highlight characteristics of this time-span which help to explain the nature of civic education in theory and practice over these years.

The argument about what we might call 'the age of rebellions', a condition which existed beneath the superficial power of absolutism, runs along the following lines. Monarchical absolutism was a response to fissiparous tendencies in the European kingdoms, was never truly absolute, and the royal efforts to make it so had to be sustained against the rebelliousness of their politically ambitious or hostile subjects. In England, this threat burst into outright rebellion with the two risings in the North in the sixteenth century and the 'Great Rebellion' of the Civil War in the seventeenth. France suffered the civil wars of religion in the sixteenth century and the Fronde in the seventeenth. In order to strengthen the monarchical regimes, centralized bureaucracies were created, developments associated particularly with the names of Thomas Cromwell and Cardinal Richelieu in England and France respectively. These bureaucratic cadres may be thought of as elite citizens, and required education to prepare them for their functions. Furthermore, although in proper political terms the populations of the kingdoms were *subjects* of the monarchical sovereign, the classical term of 'citizen' still sometimes tended, confusingly, to be used and reworked by political theorists to emphasize the duty of the citizenry to support the authority of the prince. Again, it was recognized that education was needed to bring the 'citizen' to an understanding of this duty.

Because, as a result of the Reformation, religion was an intensified political force, the churches were used as a means of conveying this message in the nation-states just as they were in the Italian city-states (see Chapter 1). Moreover, in an age of religious dispute and conflict, which contributed signally to the mood of rebelliousness, teaching the 'true' religion of the state from the pulpit was itself a form of civic education for consolidating loyalty to the monarchical state. Religion also played a completely contrary role by undermining absolutist monarchy because, in one of its Protestant forms, it helped to mould the cast of mind which argued that sovereignty belongs not to the prince but to the people. A British scholar explains: 'In the course of the English Civil War the individualist element in Calvinist thought was extended from the religious to the political field. . . . Sovereignty was now claimed for the people as "under God the original of all power"' (Cobban 1960: 91). Absolute monarchy was threatened and we are on the brink of the age of revolutions.

A century or so after the English Civil War, Rousseau, in his *Social Contract*, cogently argued that the collectivity of citizens form a people, by means of a social compact they create a body politic, and by so doing show that sovereignty belongs rightly to the people. Later in the century the American and French Revolutions were justified by and were built upon the sovereignty of the people and the nation. The right of George III and Louis XVI respectively to rule over the American colonies and the French nation against their wills was denied, in the case of the Bourbon king, fatally. Consequently, citizenship came fully into its own again; for whereas monarchies have subjects loyal to their prince, republics have citizens loyal to their state. By the same token, citizenship education became revolutionized in theory, and gradually in practice in the nineteenth and twentieth centuries when republican forms of government in nation-states came into being. Secular education replaced religious education; education for identification with the nation and to acquaint pupils with the rights as well as the duties of citizenship came into vogue. But this is to encroach on the next chapter.

Adapting to absolutist monarchy

Having set the scene for the whole chapter, we are now in a position to examine the earlier portion, and also to indicate that in the decades before the eighteenth century hints of post-absolutist civic education were already being suggested. We may discern three main features of citizenship education in practice and in advocacy in Europe in the sixteenth and seventeenth centuries. To recapitulate and expand. First was the principle that the security of the monarch and the security of the state required the subjects of the realm to be taught to help achieve these objectives. The second was the religious context in which these objectives were not only commended but actually practised. The third feature was the concentration on educating 'gentlemen' in order to provide the state with loyal and efficient administrators. The leading political theorists during the unsettled years from the mid-sixteenth to the mid-seventeenth century were Bodin and Hobbes. Bodin published his *Six Books of the Commonwealth* (*Six Livres de la République*) in 1576 in the midst of the generation-long wars of religion in France; and Hobbes published his *Leviathan* in 1651, two years after the execution of Charles I. It is not surprising, therefore, that their purpose was to argue the case for strong central government based upon indivisible sovereignty, and that their views on education should reflect this priority.

Bodin's concern about the political instability of his times, in fact, pre-dates the start of the series of French civil wars: there were plenty of other conflicts in other parts of the continent of which he was only too aware. Thus, in 1559, in an address delivered in Toulouse, he bewailed this condition of bellicosity and argued that a radical change in educational practices was essential if this endemic violence was to end. Children, he asserted, did not learn the virtues and habits of social cohesion when educated privately. To rectify this weakness he urged the establishment of what are today called 'comprehensive' or 'common' schools, and which he described as 'identical' schools. He declared:

> We saw not such a long time ago, waves of civil war endanger neighbouring kingdoms and peoples, who have still not restored peace completely and who will restore it only by introducing an identical education regulated by an organic law, for the children of all citizens.
>
> (Mesnard 1951: 58; author's translation)

Hobbes's prescription for citizenship education flows from two propositions: that the principles whereby a polity may be rendered secure are readily discerned, and that ignorance of them is the result of the powerful and learned preventing their disclosure to protect their selfish interests. He proceeds:

> I conclude therefore, that in the instruction of the people in the Essential Rights (which are the Naturall, and the Fundamentall Lawes) of Sovereignty, there is no difficulty . . . but what proceeds from [the Sovereign's] own fault, or the fault of those whom he trusteth in the administration of the Common-wealth; and consequently, it is his Duty, to cause them so to be instructed; and not onely his Duty, but his Benefit also, and Security, against the danger that may arrive to himselfe in his naturall Person, from Rebellion.
>
> (Hobbes 1914: ch.30: 180)

Hobbes supplies a seven-point programme for 'the People':

> First, that they ought not to be in love with any forme of Government they see in their neighbour Nations, more than in their own, nor . . . to desire change. . . .
>
> Secondly, that they are to be taught, that they ought not to be led with admiration of the vertue of any of their fellow Subjects, how high soever he stand, nor how conspicuously soever he shine in the Common-wealth. . . .
>
> Thirdly, they ought to be informed, how great a fault it is, to speak evill of the Sovereign Representative (whether One man, or an Assembly of men) . . .

whereby he may be brought into Contempt with his People, and their Obedience (in which the safety of the Common-wealth consisteth) slackened. . . .

Fourthly, seeing people cannot be taught this, nor when 'tis taught, remember it . . . without setting a part from their ordinary labour, some certain times . . . wherein they may assemble together, and . . . hear those their Duties told them, and the Positive Lawes . . . read and expounded, and be put in mind of the Authority that maketh them Lawes. . . .

[Fifthly,] because the first instruction of Children, dependeth on the care of their Parents; it is necessary that they should be obedient to them. . . .

[Sixthly,] every Sovereign Ought to cause justice to be taught. . . . Therefore the People are to be taught to abstain from violence to one anothers person . . . and fraudulent surreption [i.e. theft] of one anothers goods. . . .

Lastly, they are to be taught, that not only the unjust facts, but the designes and intentions to do them . . . are Injustice.

(Hobbes 1914: ch.30: 182–3)

This is assuredly a well-conceived prospectus for the generation of good citizens, virtuous and informed, albeit targeted mainly at adult 'classes'. Notice, especially, Hobbes's fourth point, the provision for mandatory civic instruction.

The question naturally arises about how this teaching is to be conducted. This matter leads us into our second feature of civic education in this period, namely the importance of religion, because, as will be explained, Hobbes designated the church as the principal channel for conveying the messages of good citizenship. However, this role of religion is only one of three that helped shape civic education in the period before the revolutions of the late eighteenth century. The others were the significance of Martin Luther and the accepted religious content of civic education.

Not only did Luther's stand effect the schism in the western Christian Church; by denying the Pope's authority he also opened the way to the formation of state Churches. Add to these accomplishments a passionate conviction in the state provision of education for all children so that they might absorb the principles of Christian and civic morality, and we can appreciate the comment of one authority on German education that 'Luther is considered by German educators to have been the founder of civic training' (Kosok 1933:150). Luther launched his campaign in 1524 with the publication of his *Letter to the Burgomasters and Councillors of all the towns in German lands, urging the Establishment and Maintenance of Christian Schools*. Obviously, the destruction of Roman Catholic control of schools in Protestant lands required replacement policies. Nevertheless, Luther's ideal remained only that: the reconstructed school systems paid little attention to the needs of the bulk of the young populations.

The churches themselves were often left to perform the function of civic educators, an arrangement that was most apposite in any case because, in this age of heightened religious consciousness and fearsome disputation, civic education without a solid theological content would have been ineffective, indeed unthinkable. Let us take England as an exemplar of these policies of religious instruction as a form of civic education and the use of the churches as well as the schools to broadcast the approved messages. When Elizabeth I ascended the throne in 1558 her most pressing concern was to enact a religious settlement and end the fanatical horrors of her sister Mary's reign. She also realized that the consolidation of her regime required an educative element. A number of Royal Injunctions, Ecclesiastical Canons and Acts of Parliament ensured a measure of royal control over the schools. The first were the Injunctions of 1559. Only those men with a 'right understanding of God's true religion' were allowed to teach; moreover, the Injunctions required 'that all teachers of children shall stir and move them to the love and due reverence of God's true religion now truly set forth by public authority', i.e. the Acts of Uniformity and Supremacy (Sylvester 1970: 125). The machinations of the Jesuits and the supporters of plots to replace Elizabeth with the Catholic Mary, Queen of Scots, led to an Act of 1585 against the Jesuits, which also included the provision making it unlawful for any English subject 'to send his or her child . . . into any the parts beyond the seas out of her highness's obedience. . . . Upon pain to forfeit and lose for every such their offence the sum of one hundred pounds' (Sylvester 1970: 127–8). No child, therefore, should be allowed to escape education in the 'true' religion, to be indoctrinated into the Catholic faith in France. In addition, civic education of a secular, patriotic tenor was promoted by the Church in Elizabeth's reign. For example, when the Privy Council was apprised (by the author!) of a school textbook, *De Proeliis Anglorum* – a history of English prowess in wars from the Hundred Years War to Elizabeth's accession – it was the bishops who were instructed to ensure that it be read in the schools. To proceed to the next century we need to refer again to Hobbes. He believed that the education he prescribed would be acquired partly by people conversing with their more learned neighbours and acquaintances. However, the knowledge would be obtained 'chiefly from Divines in the Pulpit'. He concludes: 'It is . . . manifest, that the Instruction of the people, dependeth wholly, on the right teaching of Youth in the Universities', for that is where the clergy acquire their learning (Hobbes 1914: ch.30: 183).

The total identification of state and Church in England – the synonymity of membership of the Church of England and the realm of England – was famously propounded at the end of the sixteenth century by Richard Hooker in his *Laws of Ecclesiastical Polity*. It is clear too that Hobbes wished to convey this interpretation in his recommendations on education because each of his seven items is bolstered by biblical justification. Nor was this Church–state interrelationship perceived only by the philosophers. From 1549 a Catechism was in use which expounded the duties required of every Christian, hence of every English, person. It concluded: 'to do my duty in that state of life unto which it shall please God to call me.' A civic message of complaisance. And it was quite thoroughly disseminated, as the following commentary shows:

> After morning prayers on Sundays in every one of the 10,000 parishes of England there gathered, or should have gathered, the group of adolescents from the houses of the gentry and the yeomen, the husbandmen, the tradesmen, the labourers and even the paupers, to learn from the priest what it meant to be a Christian. . . .

The only thing that young people were ever told about obedience, authority and the social and political order was contained in the catechism. Many or most of these youths and maidens, moreover, had no means of confirming or revising what the grave minister had to tell them, for they could not read.

(Laslett 1983: 217–18; see also: 336 n.4)

We turn now to the third feature of civic education in the period under review, namely the education of the gentlemen or gentry. Since it was this class that pre-eminently provided the personnel of all three branches of government – the officers of central government, the judges and justices, and the Members of Parliament – the publicly active men of this class may be thought of as forming an elite citizenry. Their education for this role is therefore of interest to us. One of their number, Sir Thomas Elyot, published the first book on education to be written in English: it is *The Boke named the Governour*, and appeared in 1531. Its main purpose was to indicate the proper education in skills and morality for the budding servants of the state, the 'governours'; and its valued relevance is indicated by the fact that it was in its ninth edition by the end of the century. Moral philosophy, he advised, should be taught to 17-year-olds via the works of Plato and Cicero. Roger Ascham's *The Schoolmaster*, published in 1570, had a similar purpose; that is, to advocate the education suitable for a young gentleman so that he live a life 'in the interest of his country in which he was born and to which he owes his service' (quoted Riesenberg 1992: 213). Moreover, he complains that the laziness of the privileged youth has allowed 'meaner men's children' to secure important government offices (see Sylvester 1970: 139, 140).

By the late seventeenth century, indeed, in many European states, sons of the upper classes were being taught geography, history, jurisprudence and politics with the deliberate aim of preparing them as 'elite citizens' for public service. It was against this background that Locke, in *Some Thoughts Concerning Education*, laid down a gruelling curriculum to meet these needs. The prescribed books by Cicero, Grotius and Pufendorf contribute in a '*general Part of Civil Law* and History . . . which a Gentleman should not barely touch at, but constantly dwell upon, and never have done with'. The young student's reading should also embrace a study of the English law, constitution and government; for, 'whatever station he is in, [the law of his country] is so requisite, that from a Justice of the Peace, to a Minister of State, I know no Place he can well fill without it' (Locke 1989: 239–40). Insofar as he gave any thought to a more democratic form of citizenship and citizenship education, it was in unenthusiastic mood.

Locke's work on education was the most distinguished in a century notable for innovative thinking in this field. The political, religious and social disorders of the English Civil War triggered thinking among the Puritans about the role schools might play in shaping a more virtuous and ordered society. The central figure in this activity was the politician and philanthropist Samuel Hartlib, who persuaded his friend John Dury to write a book, *The Reformed School*, which was published *c*.1650. Hartlib outlined his own concerns in a Preface. He argued that:

from the ordinary schools all magistrates and ministers and officers of state are taken throughout the nations of the world to be set over others, and that the impressions both of vice and virtue which they have received in the schools, are exercised and become effectual for good or evil, afterward, in their places towards the Church and Commonwealth: so that the schools are to be looked upon as the ordinary and natural fountains of a settlement, as of our corruption so of our reformation, if God will bless us with any.

(Sylvester 1970: 157)

The need to ensure the moral quality of the leading citizens of the realm as a starting point for the improvement of society at large reflects the simultaneous views of Hobbes. Furthermore, it was part of Hartlib's credo that the state could and should intervene to ensure that schools actively promoted the betterment of social conditions.

The text of Dury's book includes a detailed curriculum for schools reformed along the lines which he and Hartlib desired. His recommendations for 13- to 20-year-olds offered a most thorough and interesting general education 'to fit them for any employment in Church and Commonwealth'. So pertinent to the needs of this age-group was this curriculum that it provided a model for many of the English dissenting academies into the eighteenth century. Item 5 in his list of ten topics is especially germane to citizenship education:

The doctrine of economics, of civil government, and natural justice and equity in the laws of nations should be offered unto them as the grounds of that jurisprudentia whereof the sum is to be given out of the Institutions of Justinian and Regulae Juris.

He also, in item 10, advocated the study of history for personal social development:

for the attainment of wisdom and prudency in the government of a man's own life, wherewith the directions to observe the ways of others, the rules of judgment, discretion, prudency and civil conversation to order their own ways aright towards all.

(Sylvester 1970: 160–2)

Dury wanted to reform the school system, not revolutionize it. His civic purpose, like that of Elyot, for instance, was still to educate an elite. There was no concern about the civic education of the masses in schools: teaching social morality was the function of the churches. Yet, at the same time, much more radical thoughts were abroad that questioned the whole set of principles for sustaining absolutist monarchy. After all, from 1649 to 1660 Britain had a republican government, the Commonwealth; there was no monarch. Moreover, the revolutionary activities of the mid-century were bound to evoke revolutionary ideas. One of the most radical thinkers and activists of the time was Gerrard Winstanley, who outlined political thoughts that moved far beyond the concepts of absolute monarchy and education subservient to that style of state. In 1652, two years after the collapse of his communist Digger community in Surrey, he wrote a substantial pamphlet, *The Law of Freedom in a Platform, or True Magistracy Restored*. In effect it is a constitution for a communist state, making provision, for example, for manhood suffrage and the election of magistrates. Winstanley was keenly interested in the potential of education for achieving a virtuous and just society, and he devoted a whole chapter to the topic in this pamphlet. He asserts that there are four ages of man. In childhood, 'his parents shall teach him a civil and humble behaviour toward all men'; then they send him to school for more formal education. Youth extends to the age of 40 when employment in productive work would end; and manhood and old age embrace the years from 40 to 80. From these third and fourth 'degrees of manhood' 'shall be chosen all officers and overseers to see the laws of the Commonwealth observed' (Winstanley 1944: 174). Winstanley's plan was that schools should educate young people for a positive and effective civic life before as well as after the age of retirement. What is more – and this is what sets Winstanley apart from other thinkers of his time – all pupils were to be treated equally (though there was to be a separate, domestic curriculum for girls): all, therefore, were prepared for the possibility of active citizenship. He identifies three purposes of school learning:

> First, by being acquainted with the knowledge of the affairs of the world, by their traditional knowledge they may be the better able to govern themselves like rational men.
>
> Secondly, they may become thereby good Commonwealth's men in supporting the government thereof, by being acquainted with the nature of government.
>
> Thirdly, if England have occasion to send ambassadors to any other land, we may have such as are acquainted with their language; or if any ambassador come from other lands, we may have such as can understand their speech.
>
> (Winstanley 1944: 173–4)

The individual would consequently grow up as a citizen in the personal, political and international senses.

However, neither did Winstanley's hypothetical constitution, any more than his Digger community, come to fruition. The Restoration of the Stuart monarchy and the Church of England in 1660 put an end to the Cromwellian interregnum and, despite James II's brief absolutist ambitions, set the country on the path to constitutional monarchy. On the other hand, the concepts of civic virtue and therefore of citizenship in the classical sense flourished in England from the late seventeenth century (see e.g. Burtt 1992), though without any noticeable effect on educational thought. Yet, on the continent the vocabulary of citizenship, similarly revived, did start to percolate into pedagogical thinking. True, this classical revival did not at first question monarchical government. Indeed, since the civic republican form of citizenship has stressed duties over rights, it could be interpreted as sustaining the status quo. For example, in 1673 Samuel von Pufendorf wrote his *Two Books on the Duties of Man and Citizen* in which he declared:

> Teachers appointed to instil knowledge into the minds of the citizens should not teach that which is false or noxious: the truth should be transferred in such a way that those listening assent not from habit, but because they have been given substantial reasons; they should not teach that which tends to disturb civil society, and hold human knowledge redundant, if it provides no gain for the life of man and citizen.
>
> (Clarke 1994: 92)

Writing outside and beyond the context of absolute monarchy, Winstanley, without using the term 'citizen', advocated the state provision of education for all and for the good of the state; Pufendorf did not argue explicitly for such provision, but did use the language of citizenship. They can be interpreted, each in his own way, as figures of transition somewhat before their time, for their ideas lay dormant until their revival in France during the four decades from 1760.

The plethora of French plans

In *ancien régime* France, schoolteaching was in the hands of religious orders, pre-eminently the Jesuits. The politically ambitious institutions at the time were the senior lawcourts, the *parlements*, pre-eminently the *parlement* of Paris. And the *parlements*, posing as the representatives of the French nation and as defenders of its interests, were bitterly hostile to the Society of Jesus as an intrusive foreign body debilitating the French body politic. In 1762, through political ineptitude, the Jesuits presented the Paris *parlement* with an opening to launch a mortal attack. The *parlementaires* decreed that the Society's doctrines were 'injurious to Christian morals, pernicious to civil society, seditious, a challenge to the rights of the nation and royal authority' . . . and more to that effect (quoted Cobban 1957: 86–7). The king had little option but to issue an edict abolishing the Society in France. One of the most significant consequences was that the Jesuit fathers were lost to the teaching profession and their places were taken by members of other Orders, mainly the Oratorians, and some lay teachers. Not that the curriculum suffered any alteration. However, although the dramatic event had little effect on educational practice, it certainly did excite an unprecedented determination to write about the subject: from 1762 to 1765 alone, thirty-two publications are known to have appeared (see Palmer 1985: 48).

As R.R. Palmer has helpfully explained, those engaged in this flurry of publishing were *parlementaires*, *philosophes* and *professeurs* (Palmer 1985, e.g.: 55). Writing from different backgrounds and perspectives, they naturally offered slightly different prescriptions, though the need for a nationally organized state- and not Church-provided system of schooling was a common theme. Nevertheless, whether an overtly citizenship education should appear as part of the proposed reforms was by no means universally agreed. Neither many of the *philosophes* nor the parents of young peasants had any wish to see the country's workforce and the family's new generation of bread-winners diverted from their prime economic function in order to engage in active citizenship (see e.g. Linton 2001: 122). Moreover, the idea of secular education, which the *philosophes* did commend, aroused some disapproval. After the outbreak of the Revolution, this was one of the contributory factors in Burke's passionate hostility to the events of 1789 across the Channel. He inveighed against the 'philosophical fanatics' who were of the opinion that the politically stabilizing strength of religion can be replaced

> by a sort of education they have imagined, founded in a knowledge of the physical wants of men; progressively carried to an enlightened self-interest, which, when well understood, they tell us, will identify with an interest more enlarged and public. The scheme of this education has been long known. Of late they distinguish it . . . by the name of a *Civic Education*.
>
> (Burke 1910: 145; see also: 354n.)

Burke may well have had in mind the comments by Helvétius in his *On the Mind* (*De l'Esprit*). In another work, *On Man* (*De l'Homme*), Helvétius famously announced, '*l'éducation peut tout*' – education can do everything. It was this optimism in the potential of schooling that encouraged the exponents of reform in their chosen task.

We shall shortly ask how far the reforming plans advocated education for citizenship. However, we need first to know what form that kind of teaching already took before the expulsion of the Jesuits – and, indeed, continued, barely changed, to the Revolution. Civic education was confined to the sons of the privileged by means of the teaching about past ages in the *collèges*, which catered for wide ranges of both academic levels and ages. Some modern history was taught, though the staple diet comprised Latin texts. Among politically conscious adults in the eighteenth century a dominating theme was the concept of republican civic virtue as understood from the models of Sparta and Republican Rome. By studying classical history through Plutarch on Sparta and Livy and Tacitus on Rome and Cicero as a master of rhetoric, for example, it can be imagined that these adults, when pupils, would have absorbed the principles of citizenship, principles which could then be transferred to a critical understanding of contemporary France. But was this in fact so? Palmer states that the value of history 'was held to lie in giving concrete examples of moral and political principles. . . . It conveyed a kind of embryonic political science' (Palmer 1985: 18). Marisa Linton, on the other hand, is less certain. She points out that one can discover from the Roman authors themselves how difficult it is to practise the ideal of republican citizenship (Linton 2001: 39); and that:

> One should not exaggerate . . . the extent to which members of the revolutionary generation were being subjected to a diet of republican virtue during their formative years. There was still a preponderance of religious works which downplayed virtue, ignored the idea of social improvement and concentrated on the issue of individual salvation.
>
> (Linton 2001: 183)

Even so, the classical ideals of probity and public service were accepted as lessons to be taught to students in the *collèges*. At the very least these elements of citizenship education were mediated through the classical curriculum.

To return now to the publications following the demise of the Jesuits. These have been summarized in the following words: 'All wanted to produce more useful members of society', which included, in their views, becoming 'a good *citoyen* for *la nation* and *la patrie*' (Palmer 1985: 56). Four authors are of particular interest for our examination of citizenship education: La Chalotais, Navarre, Rousseau and Turgot.

It suits our purpose very well to start with *An Essay on National Education* (*Essai d'éducation nationale*), published in 1763 – for three reasons. Its author, La Chalotais, a leading figure in the *parlement* of Brittany, had vented his choleric temper on the Jesuits and was commissioned by the *parlement* to address the educational problem caused by the expulsion of that Order; through the title of the essay he popularized the notion of a *national* education, which became the leitmotiv of the reforming plans of the 1760s; and, perhaps because of his political prominence, the work became particularly well known. Pursuing his vendetta, he rails at the scandal of teachers owing allegiance to a foreign institution having been allowed to teach French youth, and at the absurdity of their useless curriculum. 'Since education should prepare citizens for the State,' he explains, 'it is evident that it should relate to its constitution and its law' (de la Fontainerie 1932: 49) – precisely what the Jesuits failed to do. Because these men of religion had no knowledge of the world themselves it was inevitable that 'the greatest defect of this education' should be 'the complete lack of instruction in the moral and political virtues' (de la Fontainerie 1932: 55). La Chalotais indicates his remedy:

> young people should be acquainted with the principles of natural law, of ethics and of politics. . . .
>
>   history will serve as the school of ethics; experience and reading will develop the principles, and aid in drawing conclusions. They will teach us to know men: a knowledge which is the foundation of ethics and politics.
>
> (de la Fontainerie 1932: 146)

Notice 'reading' and 'knowledge': La Chalotais put his faith in book-learning in order to achieve his goal of a national education focused on civic understanding. A crucial feature of his proposal was the production of new textbooks, which would 'replace every other method of instruction'; moreover, 'If these books were well made, there would be no need of trained teachers', the only qualifications being that they be 'religious, of good conduct and know how to read well'! (de la Fontainerie 1932: 168).

Our second author was a far less prominent figure. Père Jean Navarre was a member of a religious Order, who won a prize in 1763 for an essay expounding his ideas on the best educational system for France. The following extract could not be more pertinent to our subject:

Why should our children not learn from their teachers to be not only sociable beings and Christians, but also citizens? Why should not literary education serve to multiply the prodigy of political virtues? Why should so many arid and unfruitful studies neglect the sublime study of duties to one's country? Why in France, as at Lacedemon and Athens and in China, should our colleges not become schools of patriotism? *For the king and for France* are two sentiments that education should unite and incorporate, so to speak, in the hearts of French youth as they are in the national constitution.

(quoted Palmer 1985: 56)

From an obscure priest to the most famous of all eighteenth-century writers on politics and education – Jean-Jacques Rousseau. Although Rousseau was a most distinguished and influential theorist of citizenship and education, he had, paradoxically, little in detail to say about the teaching of citizenship. The explanation for this is none the less clear. The reasoning runs along these lines. The person has two, conflicting identities – man and citizen; therefore there are two 'conflicting types of educational systems' – 'One is public and common to many, the other private and domestic' (Rousseau 1911: 8). Clearly, the former is the type to provide the civic education, and, taking his writings as a whole, Rousseau has basically three thoughts on the matter. One is that the current educational institutions – 'our ridiculous colleges' (Rousseau 1911: 8) – were incapable of performing this function. The second is the need for explicit teaching in order to promote a consciousness of national cohesion. The third kind of thought Rousseau had on the matter is that, in an ideal state, as he outlined particularly in the *Social Contract* (*Contrat Social*), the education of the citizenry into an attitude of civic virtue and for performing their civic functions would come about through the broadly educative activities of the state rather than being confined to the schools. Consequently, in spite of Rousseau's failure to write a book or even a chapter of a book specifically on education for citizenship, it is very evident that he gave the issue a fair amount of consideration. It will therefore be instructive to look at what he had to say under these three headings.

Faced with the two types of education, the individual (or, effectively, the parents) must make a choice between one of the two near-ideals: self-fulfilment through personal study in an environment protected from the corrupting influences of society; or a fully-fledged Lycurgan or Platonic state control of young people (see e.g. Shklar 1969: 5, 160). He even argued in his article on political economy for the *Encyclopédie* that the Spartan, Cretan and Persian systems of removing young children from their families so that the state should be able to control their education was to be commended. For, by this device, young people would grow up with a keen understanding and appreciation of the General Will, Rousseau's key concept for ensuring political freedom and stability. 'It is by [education],' he declared, 'that young citizens will be trained early on to lead all their passions to converge in love of the *patrie*, all their wills in the General Will' (quoted Cobban 1964: 112; author's translation). The proper functioning of free institutions and the shaping of a cohering national consciousness are alike dependent on an education system provided and controlled by the state.

Rousseau was especially aware of the role of education in shaping a consciousness of nationhood when, in 1771, he was approached to advise the Poles in their time of crisis on the means for improving their condition. 'It is education that must shape the minds of youth in the national mould', he asserted firmly (quoted Palmer 1985: 52). But this was an urgent remedy for a politically ailing, culturally and socially heterogeneous country. Ideally – and it was ideals Rousseau was interested primarily to expound in the *Social Contract* and his most important essays – he assumed that a state would already enjoy the necessary homogeneity which eighteenth-century Poland lacked. This assumption was due partly to Rousseau's own conviction that the best state is the city-state. We thus come to his third set of views on citizenship education; that is, its transmission through the general educative activities of the state. We may detect four main ways in which he believed this objective could be attained: by political participation, public entertainments, a civil religion and censorship (see e.g. Oldfield 1990: 69–74). So varied is his civic education in this osmotic sense that it cannot but be evident that Rousseau, having little faith in schools and the teaching profession, portrayed these other means for teaching citizenship and sustaining citizens in that role as being preferable.

Participation is education. By attendance at assemblies, citizens learn how to conduct themselves as citizens, both in the sense of knowledge of procedures and in the sense of the feeling of communal as distinct from selfish activity. This is education as heuristic learning. So, the more opportunities for participation, the more thorough the learning. The quality of civic education consequently depends on the quality of the constitution: 'The better the state is constituted, the more does public business take precedence over private in the minds of the citizens. . . . In a well-regulated nation every man hastens to the assemblies' (Rousseau 1968: III, 15).

Yet this is a sober way of learning, hardly conducive to stimulating the interest of the unpolitical person. Most people, however, will respond to spectacles with their hearts; Rousseau therefore advises:

> Plant a stake crowned with flowers in the middle of a square; gather the people together there, and you will have a festival. Do better yet; let the spectators become an entertainment to themselves; do it so that each sees and loves himself in the others so that all will be better united.
>
> (quoted Oldfield 1990: 72)

A citizen should be bonded with his co-citizens; what better method than community entertainment – though, of course, with a civic message. We shall have occasion to return to this idea in most vivid realization when we reach the years of the Revolution.

There is yet a greater potential educative force, persistent, not occasional, to bring citizens to their sense of duty and strengthen their resolve to live by that code. This is religion; not, be it said, an exclusively dogmatic religion, but a civil religion. And it was to this idea that Rousseau devoted the final chapter of his *Social Contract*. There he writes:

> There is . . . a profusion of faith which is purely civil and of which it is
> the sovereign's [i.e. citizenry] function to determine the articles, not strictly
> as religious dogmas, but as sentiments of sociability, without which it is
> impossible to be either a good citizen or a loyal subject.
>
> (Rousseau 1968: IV, 8)

All citizens must learn and abide by the tenets of the civil religion, not for personal
salvation in the hereafter, but for the salvation of the polity in this now and future
world. Moreover, there should be a censorial tribunal (Rousseau 1968: IV, 7)
to prevent the opinions and judgements of citizens from erring. This provision
reflects the very essence of Rousseau's understanding of the nature of citizenship
and how citizens should be brought to honour the status. That essence is civic
virtue, the individual's moral commitment to the community. The heart and mind
of the individual can be attuned effectively to this civic need only by the citizen's
absorption of the lessons and messages transmitted by the state.

Rousseau's *Social Contract* was published in 1762; that is, a year before the
essays of La Chalotais and Navarre. We move on now to 1775. It was probably in
that year that Turgot presented to the new young king, Louis XVI, a memoir on
the organization of municipalities, which contained a tiny section entitled 'On the
Manner of Preparing Individuals and Families to Participate Properly in a Good
Social Organization'. Turgot spent his life in public service and was the most
efficient, intelligently reforming and benevolent of all such *ancien régime* figures.
His collaborator in drafting the memoir was his able secretary, Dupont de Nemours,
who was later to play a useful reforming role during the Revolution. He also retained
his interest in education; for example, having emigrated to the United States, he
struck up a friendship with Jefferson to whom he proposed a scheme for national
education in that young state (see Palmer 1985: 54 n.30, and below).

Because of its brevity, 'On the Manner of Preparing Individuals' is often
disregarded. This is unfortunate, since it contains one of the earliest and most
forthright expressions of the belief that formal citizenship education is of capital
importance. A detailed summary of the pertinent points is therefore warranted (de
la Fontainerie 1932: 179–83). The text starts with a proposal that a Council of
National Education be created, the primary function of which would be to promote
'instruction . . . on the social duties of man'. This function would be discharged
primarily by the production of textbooks which would conform to this curricular
design: 'that the study of the duties of a citizen and of a member of a family and of
the State would be the foundation of all other studies, which would be arranged
in the order of their utility to the country.' Such a national system of education
would make men of all social classes and all intellectual levels 'just in spirit and
pure in heart, zealous citizens'. In other words, the Council would promote a
'uniformity of patriotic ideals'. The objectives of this programme were to make the
youth of France

> clearly understand their obligations to society and to [the king's] authority
> which protects it, the duties which these obligations impose upon them and

the interest which they have in fulfilling these duties, both for the public welfare and for their own.

The text, furthermore, reveals that touching optimism of some *philosophes*, so epigrammatically voiced by Helvétius with regard to education, that man can improve himself. Thus Turgot asserts:

> If Your Majesty approves of this plan. . . . I dare to guarantee that within ten years your Nation would no longer be recognizable, and that for education, good conduct and enlightened zeal for your service and for that of the country it would be infinitely above all other peoples.

The new young generation of men would be

> Prepared for the service of the State, devoted to their country, submissive to authority – not through fear, but through reason – helpful to their fellow-citizens and accustomed to recognize and to respect justice.

How tantalizing, therefore, that we shall never know what the wisdom of Turgot and Dupont would have contrived as detailed syllabuses to effect this civic renovation; their promised full account was not written. Having fallen foul of the *parlement* of Paris, Turgot lost favour with the king and was dismissed from office in 1776. Ironically, the *parlements* were major contributors to the crisis that became the French Revolution, which, in turn, led to the drafting of yet more plans for a national system of education – thirty-two published between 1788 and 1790, coincidentally to match the same number that had been published between 1762 and 1765 (see Palmer 1985: 48).

'Bliss was it in that dawn to be alive', Wordsworth famously wrote in *The Prelude*, looking back on his excited youthful enthusiasm for the new age of happiness and justice which the French Revolution appeared to presage. In that statement he reflected too the conviction of the representatives in the successive Assemblies that they had it in their power to create an utterly reformed and enlightened polity and society. This task involved the transformation of institutions; yet this reforming effort would be otiose if the mind and spirit of the French nation remained lodged in *ancien régime* attitudes and behaviour. Consequently, the people of France had to be educated to be citizens, in the new, active sense. At no other time in modern history has the title of citizen – of *citoyen* and *citoyenne* – resonated with so much potential meaning. Schools, therefore, would shoulder the responsibility of training the rising generation in an understanding of that meaning. But the revolutionaries – as is their wont – were in a hurry; the current adult population also had to be re-educated for its civic role, by means far more various than Rousseau envisaged in his commendation of the civic value of 'spectacles'.

Indeed, the 1791 Constitution guaranteed state provision of schooling and civic occasions in its basic Title I:

Public Instruction shall be created and organized, common to all citizens. . . .
   National *fêtes* shall be established to preserve the memory of the French
constitution, to maintain fraternity among citizens and to bind them to the
constitution, the *patrie* and the laws (author's translation).

Napoleon, too, reckoned that education, effectively organized, had a most important
political function. He declared:

> There will be no fixed political state without a teaching body with fixed prin-
> ciples. So long as one does not learn from childhood whether to be republican
> or monarchist, Catholic or irreligious, etc., the State will not form a nation.
>
> (quoted Palmer 1985: 308)

But, even in the field of education, he revealed his fundamental dictatorial agenda,
so far from the ideals of 1789. In 1806, the year after the above statement, he
explained that, 'In establishing a body of teachers, my principal end is to have the
means of directing political and moral opinion' (Chevallier and Grosperrin 1971:
62; author's translation).

   Before passing on to some of the detail in the revolutionary and Napoleonic
years, we must pause on Napoleon's use of the word 'nation'. It was, indeed, during
this time that it was taking on its modern meaning, especially the idea that a nation
is a group of people whose feeling of unity and potential for united action are made
possible by their speaking a common language. During the Revolution, and in truth,
well beyond, the fact that many French people did not speak French worried those
politicians who were anxious that the country should be a culturally and politically cohesive state. And if there were French children who spoke, for example,
Breton or German or Italian, surely it should be the responsibility of the schools to
ensure that they acquired at least a working knowledge of the French tongue. The
Committee of Public Safety worried about this and Barère, one of its members,
produced a report on the matter in 1794. In this document he explained:

> the first laws of education should be to prepare the individual to be a citizen;
> now, to be a citizen, it is necessary to obey the laws, and in order to obey them,
> it is necessary to know them. You therefore owe it to the people to give them
> a primary education, which allows them to understand the voice of the legislator
> [he lists eight departments where French was not spoken]. The legislator speaks
> a language that those who must execute and obey the law do not understand.
>
> (Baczko 1982: 433; author's translation)

   From these preliminary remarks about the revolutionary and Napoleonic period,
the questions therefore arise: What was planned during these years and what was
in practice put into effect? As with our summary of the post-1762 plans, we shall
examine just a few examples, selected by the criteria of their importance at the time
and for our topic of citizenship education. These are the programmes prepared by
Mirabeau, Talleyrand, Condorcet, Lepeletier and Bouquier.

The Comte de Mirabeau was arguably the most able and level-headed of the revolutionary politicians. With collaborators, he wrote four speeches on public education, which his untimely death in 1791 prevented him from delivering to the Constituent Assembly. They are none the less of significance because they represent one of the most thorough early attempts to think through the issue of education in the new revolutionary context. Mirabeau asked for a complete renovation of the educational system so that the new would reflect the transition from tyranny to liberty. The admirable new French Constitution had to be supported – and 'There is no other means than a good system of public education: by it your edifice will become eternal; without it, anarchy and despotism' will destroy the constitutional structure (Baczko 1982: 72; author's translation). For:

> The learning of liberty is not so simple that it can appear at the first glance. . . . This learning is intimately linked to all the great works of the mind and all the branches of ethics. Now, *messieurs*, it is only with a good public education that you should expect this full regeneration, which will lay the foundations of the people's welfare; and these foundations will be based on the people's virtues, and its virtues on its enlightenment.
>
> (Baczko 1982: 73; author's translation)

Thus does Mirabeau demonstrate the inextricable connection between a liberal polity and a national system of education.

Five months after Mirabeau's death, Talleyrand, the versatile – not to say tergiversating – cleric and politician, presented to the Assembly a lengthy report, which has been judged 'a great document in the history of education' (Palmer 1985: 98). Talleyrand, like Mirabeau, explicitly related educational reform with the political revolution:

> Would the Constitution truly exist [he asked], if it existed only in our law, if from there it did not throw out roots into the hearts of all citizens; if it did not imprint there for ever new sentiments, new customs, new habits? And is it not by the daily and ever growing activity of education that these transformations are preserved?
>
> (Baczko 1982: 111; author's translation)

Moreover, he specifies civic education under four headings. First is knowledge of the Constitution; second is to learn how to defend the Constitution through military training; third, though difficult, is to learn how to improve the Constitution; and fourth, to learn how to become imbued with the moral principles upon which the Constitution is founded (see Baczko 1982: 116–17). The report was received with little enthusiasm and was shelved. Even so, the principles and structures it proposed did become the bases of the post-Revolutionary system.

Following the overthrow of the monarchy and the election of the Convention in 1792 a new impetus was given to the planning of educational reform. Already, earlier in the year, the report of a committee whose leading figure was the distinguished mathematician and philosopher, Condorcet, had been submitted to the Legislative Assembly. This report formed the basis of the Convention's early deliberations on the subject. What, then, does Condorcet say about education for citizenship? Four principles for the educational system underlay this specific aim: 'to establish among all citizens an actual equality, thus rendering real the political equality recognized by the law' (de la Fontainerie 1932: 323); it is the government's duty to provide such a system; that 'all education . . . should be as free as possible from political control' (de la Fontainerie 1932: 325); and the certainty that

> Never will a people enjoy a stable and assured liberty if instruction in the political sciences is not general . . . [and] if you do not prepare for them, by a general education, the means of achieving a more perfect constitution, of making better laws, and of acquiring a more complete liberty.
>
> (de la Fontainerie 1932: 343)

Notice the echo of Talleyrand in the idea that young citizens should learn to improve the Constitution.

Condorcet's specific recommendations for citizenship education fall into two requirements. One is that, although the Constitution and Declaration of Rights should form, as it were, the set texts, appreciation of their inestimable quality should not come about as the result of indoctrination: they are to be taught as the outcome of the employment of reason, the path to eternal truth (see de la Fontainerie 1932: 328–9). The second requirement is for lifelong civic education, not truncated on leaving school. Condorcet is quite precise:

> Every Sunday, the village schoolmaster will deliver a lecture for citizens of all ages. . . . In these lectures, the principles and rules of ethics will be further expounded, as well as those of the laws of the Nation which every citizen must know, or else he would not know his rights and would, therefore, be unable to exercise them.
>
> (de la Fontainerie 1932: 328; see also: 325, 329)

Note, especially, the last sixteen words of this quotation: education in order to *claim* the *rights*, not to be *drilled* in the *duties*, of citizenship. We are tentatively entering a new age, as we shall explain in Chapter 3. One final word about Condorcet's report, namely that national holidays should be used to tell, or refresh the memories of, the citizenry as a whole about the country's traditions, especially of heroism, to confirm the historical foundations of the call for citizens to recognize their duties.

During the debates in the Convention on Condorcet's plan, one of the members, Michel Lepeletier, produced an alternative plan, but he was assassinated before he could publicize it. In the meantime, Robespierre had taken an interest in education and it was he who presented the Lepeletier plan to the Convention. At its heart lay the concept of *l'éducation commune*, a term more bandied about than clearly defined. Lepeletier took it to a quasi-Spartan extreme. He stated:

This law consists in establishing a style of education that is truly national, truly republican, equally and effectively common to all. . . .

I ask you to decree that, from five to twelve years of age for boys and to eleven for girls, all children without distinction and without exception will be brought up in common, at the Republic's expense.

(Baczko 1982: 351; author's translation; see also: 352)

In point of fact, none of the plans or reports presented to the revolutionary Assemblies became law. Until, that is, the end of 1793 when a report proposed by the artist-playwright-politician Gabriel Bouquier did achieve this distinction. The scheme was divided into two parts, which we may characterize as basic education and socialization. The decree specified for the basic level that the Convention's 'education committee [present] to it elementary textbooks with the knowledge absolutely necessary to make citizens and . . . that the first of these books are to be the rights of man, the constitution and the roster of heroic or virtuous actions'. Furthermore, in accord with the mood of the time, teachers were to be strictly monitored and were to be prosecuted if they taught any 'precepts or maxims contrary to the laws and to republican morality' (Chevallier and Grosperrin 1971: 26; author's translation). After completing the basic level, young people need 'to acquire the notions relating to the organization of democratic government' (Baczko 1982: 421; author's translation). This 'last' (i.e. second) stage of education was not, therefore, to be conducted in schools. Quite the contrary:

The true schools of virtue, ways of life and republican laws, are in the popular societies, in the assemblies of the sections [local revolutionary communes], in the ten-day fêtes, in the national and local fêtes, the civic banquets and the theatres. It is there that the youth will acquire, effortlessly so to speak, the knowledge of their rights and duties, from there that they will draw the appropriate sentiments to raise their souls to the height of republican virtues.

(Baczko 1982: 424; author's translation)

There speaks the man alert to the educative power of the visual and the dramatic. An attempt was indeed made to style the theatres as '*écoles de civisme et moeurs républicains*' (schools of republican citizenship and ways of life) (quoted Kennedy 1989: 182) – schools of citizenly behaviour and republican morality. However, although the repertoires of the theatres may have conveyed the appropriate message, the plays were performed to very much a minority audience. A far wider reach was achieved by the various festivals, ceremonies and planned public gatherings.

Some of these were modest affairs, such as the planting of trees of liberty early on in the Revolution and symbolically anti-Church events later. Others were great, highly organized fêtes, the three most spectacular being the Fête of Federation on 14 July 1790, the Fête of 10 August 1793 and the Fête of the Supreme Being on 8 June 1794, all held in Paris, though the first notably drew in crowds from the provinces. The propaganda was manifest: the 1790 celebration was held on the first anniversary of the fall of the Bastille, the second on the first anniversary of the fall of the monarchy, and the third was the occasion for Robespierre to inaugurate his Rousseauesque civic religion. Citizens participated in or were observers of the amazingly theatrical processions and pageants throughout the country, though, naturally, the most elaborate were staged in the capital. For example, the throngs who witnessed the Fête of Federation in Paris alone were estimated at a quarter of a million, apart from those who lined the routes taken by the National Guard contingents marching from the provinces to participate in the metropolitan spectacle.

What, then, was the outcome of this extraordinary half-century of activity in France to promote a consciousness of citizenship by educational means? Very little.

The attempt at adult civic education through fêtes declined steadily after the heady days of 1790–94. For example, the ceremony alone on 10 August 1793 cost 1,200,000 livres, whereas during the whole of the year from September 1794 only one-third of that sum was expended for all national festivals (see Cobban 1957: 225; Palmer 1985: 334). In 1799 Bonaparte, immediately on assuming power, abolished all national fêtes except those commemorating the fall of the Bastille and the pronouncement of the Republic. One may wonder, in any case, how effective these occasions were in converting the populace to the revolutionary cause. People will turn out for spectacles because they are spectacular – for their entertainment, not their pedagogical value.

Nor was the use of schools to teach the youth the principles of citizenship much more successful than the use of public events to teach the adults those same lessons. At the absolutely basic level of the provision of schools and teachers the revolutionaries failed abysmally. Planned new school buildings did not materialize; and the attacks on the Church – from the insistence on an oath of allegiance, which half the clergy refused to swear, to outright de-Christianization – produced a chaotic decline in school places. The early organization of local government involved the creation of districts as subdivisions of the departments. In late 1794 two-thirds of the districts responded to a survey of schools. Less than one-tenth reported that they had the number required for their child populations. In Paris there was but one teacher per 400 pupils (see Kennedy 1989: 160–1). Admittedly, this was a time when the Terror was at its most intense and presents the nadir of education during the decade of revolution; moreover, Napoleon later rectified the situation. The problems in the mid-1790s none the less demonstrate the failure of one of the central ambitions of the revolutionaries.

Even if schools and teachers were available for educating the young generation in the contents of the Declaration of Rights and the Constitution and the telling of heroic deeds as required, many parents were unhappy that their children should undergo such an education. Let us take one tiny example, from the small town of Angerville, some forty miles south of Paris – not, notice, a counter-revolutionary region. The date is the summer of 1795. The teacher was living in the rectory. One day he was faced with a village deputation demanding that he quit the house and hand over the school benches for removal to the church. He refused. He describes the effects of his recalcitrance:

> At eleven in the morning, my class coming to an end, a riot breaks out in my playground and a mob of women and children numbering about 150, roaring and making sharp and offensive menaces . . . such that I believed it was my last hour. I stayed shut in for three hours.

The deputation succeeded in evicting the wretched teacher and persuaded the *curé* to take his place. The mob had acted on the instructions of the local council and were aided by the pupils of the local private school (Chevallier and Grosperrin 1971: 39; author's translation). Resentment of a lay, politically appointed teacher and, by implication, at the replacement of the teaching of religious morality by a civic morality, was evidently strongly held in the community. And we may wonder whether, if the incident had occurred three or four years later, the pupils of the private school would have acted differently; for in 1798 a system of spot inspections of these schools was introduced to ensure that they were teaching about the Constitution and the Declaration of Rights and not counter-revolutionary ideas. The indications are, however, that private schools were not effectively brought into line.

Yet the reader must not be left with the impression that the committed efforts of the 1790s bore no fruit at all. There were three positive effects. The most general point is that the revolutionary principle of citizenship, with its rights and expectation of civic activity, was absorbed and continued as a key element in French political culture. The second point is that the understanding of the interconnection between education and politics which emerged in the *ancien régime* was firmly consolidated in left-wing thinking, despite the post-Revolutionary restoration of clerical domination of the school system. These two achievements of the Revolution, indeed, consciously underlay the educational reforms of Jules Ferry in the Third Republic, when, as we shall see in Chapter 3, citizenship education at last became a permanent reality in French schools. And third, teaching materials specifically for citizenship education were produced under government auspices, thus initiating this practice. The first textbook was entitled *Selection of Heroic and Civic Actions by French Republicans*. This was written by a politically active man, Léonard Bourdon, who took a passionate interest in education. The book went through five impressions in six months in 1794. In addition, to replace the traditional Christian catechisms, republican catechisms were produced. The most widely used was composed by the playwright La Chabeaussière, who also, incidentally, wrote a textbook, *Principles of Republican Morality*. His catechism consists of thirty-seven questions and the responses are set in rhyming quatrains, a number of which relate to citizenship. He appended notes and there, in a tone of admonition, he asserts that, 'The teacher who will not himself give his pupil, when defining the law and speaking of liberty, the measure of enthusiasm the subject requires and the expression that I have tried to put into it, seems to me unworthy of his position' (La Chabeaussière 1794: 16). One of the most vivid quatrains answers the question, 'What is Liberty?: it is 'The finest gift of heaven, our God on earth', and 'he who loses it must die' (La Chabeaussière 1794: 8). The pamphlet was continually reprinted, even as late as the three impressions published from 1879 to 1882, in connection with Ferry's reforms: a vivid little illustration of the continuity of the felt need for citizenship education in France for well over a century.

Diffusion of radical ideas

In the 1960s, considerable excitement – and controversy – were generated among students of late eighteenth-century history by the publication of two works. One was R.R. Palmer's *The Age of Democratic Revolution: A Political History of Europe and America, 1760–1800* (1959, 1964); the other was Jacques Godechot's *France and the Atlantic Revolution of the Eighteenth Century, 1770–1799* (1965). Taken together, these books by American and French scholars argued that the French Revolution was not an episode *sui generis* but was part of a revolutionary movement which had democratic objectives and which stretched geographically from central Europe to the Americas. This thesis is pertinent to our interests because the vocabulary of citizenship and the appreciation that education is essential for the development of the status and the sense of commitment it entails are evident in some other countries beyond Revolutionary France. Germany, England and especially the young United States of America provide compelling examples of the spread of this thinking.

During the generation from the early 1770s to the early 1800s Germany revealed a remarkable efflorescence of educational thinking including considerations on civic education (see Kosok 1933: 151–6). We can detect three phases. Before the French Revolution, Enlightenment ideas about the efficacy of education and the ambitions of the rising middle class for greater participation in and influence over public affairs stimulated this activity. The educational thought of this period is exemplified by the work of F.G. Resewitz and J.B. Basedow. The former wrote a book entitled *The Education of the Citizen*, published in 1773, surely one of the earliest books with a title so explicitly focused on our subject. The latter had an extremely widespread influence as an education reformer throughout Germany. The second period was influenced inevitably by the ideas and events of the French Revolution. The great outpouring of pedagogical writing in these years may be illustrated by H. Stephani's *Outline of the Science of Education* of 1797, C.D. Voss's *Essay on Education for the State* of 1799, and K.A. von Rade's *Education for Civic Training* of 1803. Three years later Prussia, the last German bastion against French imperialism, was defeated by Napoleon, leading to heart-searching about German national identity, Prussian patriotism and the changes in education needed to bolster these sentiments. This is our third period, during which national humiliation persuaded J.G. Fichte and W. von Humboldt to propound their schemes for educational reform, Fichte in theory, notably in his *Reden*, his *Addresses to the German Nation* in 1807–08 and Humboldt as the minister in charge of the Prussian Bureau of Education from 1808–10. By surveying the work of these men it is possible to discover what German educationists meant by citizenship education at this time.

Voss advanced a succinct and cogent case for citizenship education:

> If the concept of the state and its purposes, of the rights and duties of the citizen, of the necessity and the value of the reigning power etc., are more than mere

fancies, if patriotism or the feeling of citizenship is no chimera, then we must be able to teach them and they can surely be imparted only by special instruction, by a specially directed effort in this direction. . . .

Such an education would therefore really be training for the state and would also be the 'business of the state.' In every school there should therefore be a department for instruction in civics.

(quoted Kosok 1933: 155)

The implication is that citizenship should be taught as a direct subject, whereas others favoured the indirect approach through geography, history and law. Humboldt stands out by insisting that inspiration for the regeneration of Prussia would be accomplished most effectively by studying the civilizations of Rome and, in particular, Greece. His conviction, incidentally, persuaded English educationists who developed Classical syllabuses in the public schools. Resewitz had taken the contrary view, musing over an ideal future when Classics-teaching grammar schools would be converted into citizen schools (*Bürgerschulen*). He also advocated the teaching of comparative government (see Kosok 1933: 152).

Not surprisingly, though Voss includes teaching about rights, the main purposes of the proposals of this period were to firm up the related commitment to duty and the sense of patriotism. Napoleon's hegemonic control of central Europe helped the transition from state patriotism to German nationalism. In this process, Fichte is a key figure. In his Ninth Address he stated that 'the majority of citizens must be educated to this sense of fatherland' (quoted Heater 1998: 112); this was in notable contrast to Humboldt, whose faith in the efficacy of a classical education perforce related to a minority of the population. In the first of his Addresses Fichte had placed powerful emphasis on the necessity for a widely available education. He declared that the means of Germany's very salvation consisted in:

The fashioning of an entirely new self . . . and in the education of the nation . . . to completely new life. In a word, it is a total change in the existing system of education that I propose as a sole means of preserving the existence of the German nation.

(quoted Heater 1998: 112)

An emotional call voiced with the express purpose of transforming the hearts of German citizens by the means of education.

But hearts are not always excited easily in the classroom, and both Baselow and Fichte understood this. Baselow therefore advocated the celebration of festivals throughout the year, with school work arranged to reinforce the themes of 'the great examples of patriotic sacrifices, the advantages which flow from civic union in the state, the duties to the fatherland', in the words of one authority (Kosok 1933: 152): echoes of Rousseau's faith in 'spectacles'. Fichte placed his faith in the cohering effect of some adolescents living together. He drew up proposals for mixing students in the Prussian University of Erlangen from all parts of Germany, with the result, he argued, that 'something common remains in which all agree, namely German custom and German national character in general, and this is loved and honored by all' (quoted Heater 1998: 112).

Two extra elements in this thinking must be added as being of especial interest. One is that two of our selected writers include girls/women in their recommendations. These are Stephani and Rade. Rade held that girls should receive civic training 'even though they are, because of their physical disabilities, excluded from all public affairs' (quoted Kosok 1933: 156). The other element is the consideration of the cosmopolitan dimension alongside the state dimension of citizenship – an issue we shall survey in Chapter 5. Strikingly, Baselow, Stephani, Voss, Rade and, famously, Fichte all adjudged this to be a matter of some import. Voss feared that a cosmopolitan strain in civic education would weaken the desired patriotic effect. The others believed that citizens, properly educated, could learn to serve humanity through learning how to serve their fatherland. Stephani distinguished between the individual as a human being and as a citizen; and, through the knowledge and 'capacities' the individual could acquire in both roles, he would carry over what he learned in his civic training to fit him to be a world citizen. Fichte expounded the idea of a synthesis of citizenship and world citizenship in a more mystical way. He forecast the coming of a new era in the history of mankind in which the excellent German nation would lead the rest of the world on to a higher plane of understanding. 'The German alone,' he asserted, 'can be a patriot; he alone can for the sake of his nation encompass entire humanity' (quoted Heater 1998: 107). The implication, detected also in his *Aphorisms*, is that education for citizenship should embrace patriotism, nationhood and cosmopolitanism. However – though this is a matter of dispute – in demanding stern educational adherence to the goal of a human culture shaped by the German's sole grasp of the philosophical road of progress, Fichte's thesis seems to foreshadow the Nazi creed of civic education (see Chapter 4).

This was not the way of thinking about civic education in England, even though the cult of Empire a century later has sometimes, in a mood of some hyperbole, been compared with the German tradition of inculcating the youth with ideas of racial superiority, militarism and global hegemony (see Chapter 3). In the period we are treating here, however, English writing on civic education was in a clearly radical, democratic mode, often suspicious of state control of schools, and, in any case, designed for the benefit of the poor.

Before explaining the Radicals' positions, a brief comment is apt about the view of Adam Smith on the connection between politics and education. In the *Wealth of Nations*, which appeared in 1776, he explained his belief in the need for education of 'the inferior ranks of the people' for political prudence:

> The State . . . derives no inconsiderable advantage from their instruction. The more they are instructed, the less liable they are to the delusions of enthusiasm [i.e. fervency] and superstition, which among ignorant nations frequently occasion the most dreadful disorders. An instructed and intelligent people . . . are more disposed to examine, and are more capable of seeing through, the interested complaints of faction and sedition, and they are, upon that account,

less apt to be misled into any wanton or unnecessary opposition to the measures of government.

(quoted Barnard 1947: 53)

We return, after this conservative interlude, to the radical stream of thought. The 1770s were years of remarkably heightened political consciousness. Demands for parliamentary reform and organizations to campaign for this cause proliferated into the early 1780s. Newspaper readership doubled in the four decades from 1753 to 1792 (see Plumb 1950: 119), enhanced, it goes without saying, by the outbreak of the French Revolution. Inevitably, that momentous event revivified the demands for parliamentary reform and radical political debate relating to liberty and equality – all expressions of a lively citizenly awareness of the political and civil conditions that prevailed in Britain and the shortcomings of those conditions.

This growth of civic awareness in Britain arose, therefore, in two phases, concentrated in the 1770s and 1790s. Although the term 'citizen' was foreign to British constitutional law, the debates and legislation in France changed the vocabulary, so when demands for reform were drafted in Sheffield, for example, the Radicals asserted: 'that equality we claim is, to make the slave a man, the man a citizen, and the citizen an integral part of the state; to make him a joint sovereign and not a subject' (quoted Dickinson 1977: 255).

Furthermore, the wished-for status of citizenship and the availability of education were perceived as being linked. As one historian has succinctly expressed it: 'Since most radicals believed that rational argument and accurate information were essential to political progress, they regarded education as a vital agency' (Dickinson 1977: 261). However, whereas the educational planners in France pinned their hopes on persuading the government to implement programmes incorporating some measure of civic education, their counterparts in England were divided on strategy. One of the proponents of a state system of education was George Dyer. He not only advocated public provision of education for the poor, but also wanted rich and poor to be taught under the same roof. (Compare this proposal with those of Benjamin Rush and other Americans, below.) If all citizens are in theory equal, they should approximate to equality in their schooling. 'Such policy,' he declared, 'would humanize the heart. . . . The principle which equalizes men, dignifies and exalts him' (quoted Dickinson 1977: 261; see also 350 n.78).

In the other camp – those deeply suspicious that state provision of education would mean state control of education – were the two most distinguished English contributors to thinking about citizenship education in the late eighteenth century. These were Joseph Priestley and William Godwin.

Priestley was an Enlightenment equivalent of the Renaissance man, distinguished in so many fields: chemist, theologian, political pamphleteer and educationist. He combined in his thinking the eighteenth-century concepts of the sovereignty of the people and the perfectibility of man. Because he was a nonconformist Unitarian minister and held views akin to the early French revolutionaries, he appeared to the conservative and Francophobe English populace at the time of the French Revolution as a threat to both Church and state. As a consequence, his house was utterly destroyed in riots in Birmingham in 1791. However, it was some years before this that he wrote his educational work in which we are particularly interested. This was *Essay on a Course of Liberal Education for Civil and Active Life*, published in 1765, a most thoughtful little piece, bedded in his own experience as a teacher. His case is that there should be inserted into the curricula of schools and universities, between 'an education for the counting-house' and the study of 'the abstract sciences' (Priestley 1788: 1; references hereafter are given as page numbers only), subjects conducive to an effective life related to affairs touching on the good health of the nation.

He describes the theme he recommends for this purpose as: 'CIVIL HISTORY, and more especially, the important objects of CIVIL POLICY; such as the theory of laws, government, manufactures, commerce, naval forces, &c' and factors that have tended to the strength and happiness of nations (p.10). To expound this theme he suggests three courses of lectures. The first of these he calls the study of history in general, taught in such a manner as 'to contribute to its forming the able statesman, and the intelligent and useful citizen' (pp.11–12). In this course, the topic of commerce would be stressed. The second series of lectures would be devoted to the history of England; and the third, to the present Constitution and laws. Priestley accepts that objections would be raised against his proposals, including the argument that 'these subjects are too deep, and too intricate for [youths'] tender age and weak intellect' (p.14). He efficiently counters all these.

There is, however, a great deal more of interest than this skeleton syllabus. Throughout the essay Priestley adduces a number of reasons for presenting his case. One is that the current content of general education is useless and subject to ridicule. Another is that the topics he lists form the content of intelligent adult conversation, to which the students of such a course could usefully contribute. The third reason is that it is far preferable for an individual to be properly taught about issues of policy and commerce than through random reading or 'from the company he might accidentally keep. . . . For there are subjects, on which almost every writer or speaker is to be suspected; so much has party and interest to do with every thing relating to them' (p.17). The main thrust of Priestley's argument is, indeed, that a programme of civic education would benefit the country at large. He asserts:

> Many of the political evils, under which this, and every country in the world, labour, are not owing to any want of a love for our country, but to an ignorance of its real constitution and interests. . . . [Also, such a course] might, perhaps, contribute more to produce, propagate, and influence, a spirit of patriotism than any other circumstance.
>
> (p.33)

Who would be the recipients of this civic education? Priestley emphasizes those persons who have the power to affect the fortunes of the nation and who have influence in shaping opinion – that class we called 'the elite citizenry'. More than that, he seems to assert adamantly: 'This is not teaching politics to low mechanics and manufacturers' (p.35). Only seems to, because on other pages he takes quite the contrary position. 'The better these subjects are understood by the *bulk* of the nation,' he suggests at one point, 'the more probable it is that the nation will be benefited by such knowledge' (pp.18–19; emphasis added). And as he draws his essay to a close, he reveals his real radical colours, declaring:

> A true friend of liberty will be cautious how he discourages a fondness for that kind of knowledge. . . . Only tyrants, and the friends of arbitrary power, have ever taken umbrage at a turn for political knowledge, and political discourses, among even the lowest of the people.
>
> (pp.36–7)

Priestley's essay was a remarkable analysis of the issues surrounding the matter of civic education, not just as a reflection of his judgement about the needs of his own era, but for the resonance it carries into the discussions that have been taking place in our own age.

Unlike Priestley and other Radicals of his time, William Godwin was more concerned to argue theoretical principles than to present practical schemes of reform. When his works were published they were, even so, no less influential for all their abstract style. He built his arguments on the twin beliefs that man is capable of reason and that justice is the prime objective of human society. His thoughts on this latter belief are contained in his major work, *An Enquiry Concerning Political Justice*, which was published in 1793. There, we may find a chapter entitled 'Of National Education'.

Godwin launches straight into his concern about the proposed need of a publicly provided education. He explains that this suggestion must be examined because 'the idea of this superintendence has obtained the countenance of several of the more zealous advocates of political reform' (Philp 1993: 356). He advances three objections to this view, even though these proponents argue the impossibility 'for patriotism and the love of the public to be made the characteristic of the whole people in any other way successfully, as by rendering the early communication of these virtues a national concern' (ibid.). The first and third of Godwin's objections may be seen to relate to education for citizenship. The first is that nationally imposed education tends to stagnate, to become obsolete, to support prejudices: 'even in the petty institution of Sunday schools,' he claims, 'the chief lessons that are taught, are a superstitious veneration for the church of England, and how to bow to every man in a handsome coat' (Philp 1993: 357). Repeating the splendid Latinate verb 'venerate', he expounds his third objection. He worries that government-controlled education would lead to education for the perpetuation of established institutions:

> It is not true that our youth ought to be instructed to venerate the constitution, however excellent; they should be instructed to venerate truth; and the constitution only in so far as it corresponded with their independent deductions of truth. Had the scheme of a national education been adopted when despotism was most triumphant; it is not to be believed that it could have for ever stifled the voice of truth. . . . Still, in the countries where liberty chiefly prevails, it is

reasonably to be assumed that there are important errors, and a national education has the most direct tendency to perpetuate those errors, and to form all minds upon one model.

(Philp 1993: 359)

This logically wise warning alone must allow Godwin a critical place in the history of citizenship education. The argument derives from his conviction that the individual's capacity for personal reasoning is superior to and leads to greater justice than a civic education directed by the state. The reader is invited to keep this in mind during the course of Chapter 4. But is a light-touch state encouragement of and responsibility for citizenship education possible and even desirable, avoiding Godwin's worries? This was certainly the aim of most of the Founding Fathers of the United States of America.

Founding the American Republic

The American colonies rebelled against British dominion in 1776. They wanted freedom from the Hanoverian Crown and the Westminster Parliament; they wanted a republican style of polity and a relatively democratic form of government; and they wanted their own national identity. The Founding Fathers were keenly aware that these were revolutionary ideals that could not be attained solely by military victory and constitutional enactment. A new mood was also essential: the populace needed to think patriotically, to understand the nature of the infant Republic and their role in it. In short, there was a recognition that 'a new kind of person' was required. Such a renovation in moral and civic character has, indeed, been a common feature of modern revolutions (hence the call after 1917 for 'the new Soviet man', for example (see Chapter 4)). And just as the Founding Fathers were generally agreed on the character they wished their liberated country should display and enjoy, so too they agreed that it would be very hard to approach this ideal without an education system devoted to the same goal. A straightforward, clear, accepted objective for a relatively small population – the first census, taken in 1790, gave a figure of a little over three million whites and 700,000 blacks. Looked at in this superficial light it might appear that the objective was easily attainable. It was not. The divisions, cross-currents and complexities that faced the keenest of would-be educational reformers in the late eighteenth century – the likes of Jefferson, Rush and Webster – proved quite daunting. Education for citizenship presupposes a certain degree of homogeneity in the society into which the young people are to be inducted and, arguably, *pace* much of Athenian and Roman practice, a state provision of education. The USA, even after more than two centuries, has still not fully achieved these requirements.

By the mid-seventeenth century, however, the New England colonies were build- ing a civic consciousness. The Protestants of English origin maintained this sense of common cultural ethnicity, morally strengthened by the Christian ethic expounded – sternly so in the case of the dominant Puritan sects – from the pulpit. Moreover, in addition to the habit of church and home education of the children, the conviction that towns should create their own schools was slowly developing. In 1642 Massachusetts started a trend of government intervention, requiring towns to provide (albeit fee-paying) schools . In combination, home, church, school and local authorities were coming to provide a coherent education with a weighty moral content.

Nevertheless, a century later (the focus of our interest here) this coherence even in New England, let alone the totality of the thirteen colonies, had disintegrated. There were several causes. One was the wave of non-English immigrants, mainly Scotch-Irish and Germans, who arrived during the first half of the eighteenth century between the end of the War of the Spanish Succession and the start of the Seven Years War. Added to the Dutch, the Swedes and the French Huguenots already present, they increased the cosmopolitan character of the colonies. They also added to religious diversity. No longer were the Nonconformist sects of English origin in the north and the Church of England in the south wielding Christian monopolies. At the same time socio-economic diversity became increasingly marked. As towns were founded, urban and rural modes of life became more distinctive. In addition, the aristocratic, slave-owning plantation economy of the southern states as an alternative American society, distinct from the burgeoning commercialism and industrialization of the north, was consolidated by the growth of the Carolinas and Georgia from the late seventeenth century.

These developments had significant impacts on education. Population dispersal, related to the urban–rural divide, severely loosened the incipient regularization of school provision. To quote a leading American authority:

> A distinct sense of localism developed in the outlying districts among families who soon wanted their own schools. . . . Thus a tradition of decentralization of school control grew up. . . . This further weakened the civic solidarity that had marked earlier generations. It was, in a way, a remote forerunner of the later persistent demands for community control.
>
> (Butts 1989: 63)

Moreover, as the economic interests of urban and rural communities diverged, so their considered schooling needs also diverged, and required release from central ties. Farmers resented their children being withdrawn from work on the land; businessmen wanted lessons relevant to a commercial life. The latter, with wealth to be used freely, set up private schools to suit their purposes. The southern plantation owners too had their views about education for social superiority. These different needs were satisfied by the establishment of a wide variety of private schools. So much for the concept of civic education by public schools. Hence the basic dilemma of the Founders:

> If they wanted to build a cohesive republican political community that would embrace and foster a pluralism of religious, economic, and local interests (and most did), could they be satisfied with the disparate, diverse, and contentious models of private education of competing churches, businesses, and private voluntary associations?

In short, and recalling the US motto, 'Could they achieve political *unum* in the light of this educational *pluribus*?' (Butts 1989: 64).

No less a politician than John Adams, who later succeeded Washington as President in 1797, expounded the thoughts on civic education of his fellow Founders when he asserted two years after the Declaration of Independence:

> Children should be educated and instructed in the principles of freedom. . . .
> The instruction of the people in every kind of knowledge that can be of use to them in the practice of their moral duties, as men, as citizens, and Christians, and of their political and civil duties, as members of society and freemen, ought to be the care of the public, and of all who have any share in the conduct of affairs, in a manner that never yet has been practised in any age or nation. The education here intended is . . . [that] of every rank and class of people, down to the lowest and the poorest.
>
> (quoted Pangle and Pangle 1993: 96)

It is interesting to compare Adams's socially comprehensive ideal with Turgot's of three years earlier, though the Frenchman's stress was on loyalty, not freedom.

It is also of interest that, in his advocacy, Adams cites Aristotle's argument that citizenship education should match the style of the polity (see Chapter 1), for the Founding Fathers were much influenced by the Classics and the classical republican concept of citizenship. The question whether they were more committed to this style, stressing duty, or the Lockean liberal form, has generated considerable scholarly debate (see e.g. Lutz 1992: 134–40), but this need not detain us here. Suffice to say that awareness of the character of classical republican polities and thought through an acquaintance with ancient history and modern commentary from Machiavelli onwards occasioned a certain nervousness. Republics had a tendency to instability; the USA was a bold experiment in modern republicanism in a large state; education was therefore crucial to prevent this political weakness from replicating itself in this new endeavour.

But how were the liberty and equality, propounded with such conviction in the Declaration of Independence as fundamental to the just-born state, to be reconciled with the necessity for a firm commitment to order, selfless civic virtue and patriotism to sustain the Republic? And how were these contending ideals to be translated into educational practice? The problem could not with intellectual honesty be side-stepped, even though the simpler issue of recruiting young people into schools so that they could later perform the basic functions of democratic citizenship needed prior solution. A number of politicians, journalists and scholars bent their minds to the matter, and we outline below the ideas of the leading figures.

As President, George Washington used his office to encourage commitment to education for citizenship. In his First Annual Message to Congress he declared that:

> To the security of a free Constitution [education] contributes in various ways: By convincing those who are entrusted with the public administration, that every valuable end of Government is best answered by the enlightened

confidence of the people: and by teaching the people themselves to know and to value their own rights; to discern and provide against invasions of them; to distinguish between oppression and the necessary exercise of lawful authority . . . and uniting a speedy, but temperate vigilance against encroachments, with an inviolable respect for laws.

(quoted Pangle and Pangle 1993: 113)

Exercising this fine balance between thoughtful obedience and critical watchfulness was assuredly sage advice for all teachers of citizenship. However, his military, then political, responsibilities left Washington little time for thinking about education. We must look rather to five men who devoted serious thought to the matter of civic education during the last quarter of the eighteenth century and a little beyond. These were Thomas Jefferson, Benjamin Rush, Noah Webster, Samuel Harrison Smith and Samuel Knox.

Although he made a successful President (1801–09), Jefferson's strengths were intellectual rather than practical. And he wished so to be remembered, devising his own epitaph with the words: 'Here Was Buried Thomas Jefferson Author of the Declaration of Independence Of the Statute of Virginia for Religious Freedom And Father of the University of Virginia.' His persisting interest in education may be discerned as having three main features. One was his exchange of ideas with a wide range of contacts, both American and foreign, among the latter, Dupont de Nemours and Priestley (whose names have appeared already in this chapter). Second, he worked sedulously to develop educational opportunities in his own colony/state of Virginia. Third, he was always keeping in mind the civic necessity for education.

Jefferson was convinced that, in a democracy, politics and education are inextricably intertwined, or, rather, should be. For instance, in a letter to Madison, he wrote that to give 'information to the people . . . is the most certain and the most legitimate engine of government' (quoted Honeywell 1931: 148). However, his fullest and most famous expression of his arguments for citizenship education is to be found in the preamble to his unsuccessful education bill presented to the Virginia legislature, initially, in 1779. Here we find his two key propositions, namely that political institutions, howsoever well wrought, cannot, without the undergirding of an educated citizenry, guarantee good government, and that public financial support is essential to ensure that even the poor enjoy the benefits of schooling. In his own words:

Experience hath shewn, that even under the best forms, those entrusted with power have, in time . . . perverted it into tyranny; and it is believed that the most effectual means of preventing this would be, to illuminate, as far as practicable, the minds of the people at large . . . that . . . they may be . . . prompt to exert their natural powers to defeat its purposes. . . . [And poor] children whom nature hath fitly formed and disposed to become useful instruments for the public, it is better such should be sought for and educated at the common expence of all, than that the happiness of all should be confided to the weak or the wicked.

(quoted Pangle and Pangle 1993: 107–8)

Four decades later, in 1818, Jefferson, again in his local environment, wrote the *Rockfish Gap Report to the Legislature Relative to the University of Virginia*. To set the scene, as it were, he defined the objectives of primary education. These included, for the citizen:

> To understand his duties to his neighbours and country, and to discharge with competence the functions confided to him by either;
>
> To know his rights; to exercise with order and justice those he retains; to choose with discretion the fiduciary of those he delegates; and to notice their conduct with diligence, with candor, and judgement.
>
> (Williams 1971: 193)

This is a splendid, succinct description of the qualities of a good citizen; but to be instilled into pupils at primary school, finishing their education when barely teenagers (if the anachronistic word may be forgiven)? It would have required skilful teaching beyond the competence of most members of the profession at the time.

In terms of organization, Jefferson's especially favoured scheme was to create primary schools in all his proposed new administrative units, which he variously called 'wards' or 'hundreds' (the old Anglo-Saxon term). Each would be, in his design, a little republic, in which children would be taught free and the adults would be involved in their own local affairs. 'I consider the continuance of representative government,' he wrote, 'as absolutely hanging on these two hooks' (quoted Pangle and Pangle 1993: 119). This plan did not come to pass.

Another of Jefferson's ideas was taken up – but not, as we shall see, in the manner he intended. This was his suggestion that the illiterate should be disenfranchised, a recommendation that came to his mind from a similar provision in the famous, liberal and bulky Spanish Cadiz Constitution of 1812. Jefferson conceived a dual purpose: to encourage parents to send their children to school, and to ensure that the voters had at least a basic education. He explained his aim as:

> To strengthen parental excitement by the disfranchisement of his child while uneducated. Society has certainly a right to disavow him whom they offer and are not permitted to qualify for the duties of a citizen. If we do not force instruction, let us at least strengthen the motives to receive it when offered.
>
> (quoted Honeywell 1931: 36)

Both the ward scheme and the disenfranchisement scheme were not so much arrangements for citizenship education as preventatives against citizenship being exercised by the ignorant. (It may be noted that Jefferson set great store by the politically educative value of newspapers, a value that could, of course, not accrue to illiterates.) It is ironic that Jefferson, the slave-owning exponent of liberty and equality, should have proposed a literacy test for the suffrage, which was used later in the century as a reason to deny the vote to legally emancipated black people in the south.

Each colony, and, after independence, each state, defined the right to the suffrage in different ways. Some were quite democratic: for instance, the Pennsylvania Constitution accorded the vote to taxpayers aged over 21, resident in the state for a year. It is not surprising, therefore, that Jefferson concerned himself about the civic competence of the mass of the people. He did not, none the less, neglect what he thought to be the educational needs of the 'elite citizens'. In the Rockfish Gap Report he included in these requirements:

> To expound the principles and structure of government, the laws which regulate the intercourse of nations, those formed municipally for our own government, and a sound spirit of legislation, which, banishing all arbitrary and unnecessary restraint on individual actions, shall leave us free to do whatever does not violate the equal rights of another.
>
> (Williams 1971: 194)

In other words, he sought to ensure that, in classical terms, the magistrates of the republic be educated to discharge their offices with a due sense of civic justice and responsibility.

The core ideas of Jefferson's plan for civic education, despite the ambitious aims written into the Rockfish Gap Report, were simple, indeed simplistic: citizenly attitudes would be inculcated through the teaching of appropriate facts. In the words of one scholar: 'Jefferson wished to diffuse only knowledge which would produce homogeneous – and Whig – political views. Dialectic, the clash of factions, the battle of opinions in the "progressive science" of government had no place in the school-room' (Tyack 1966: 36).

Benjamin Rush held to a similar view about uniformity: indeed taking it further by insisting that freedom is dependent on homogeneity. One of the signatories of the Declaration of Independence and a distinguished physician, Rush was a man of extraordinarily eclectic interests, including a commitment to the abolition of slavery. He is a cardinal figure for us because of an essay he produced in 1786, entitled *A Plan for the Establishment of Public Schools and the Diffusion of Knowledge in Pennsylvania, to Which Are Added Thoughts upon the Mode of Education Proper to a Republic*. But in this work he reveals an eccentrically indoctrinatory temper quite distinct from Jefferson's approach; for Rush drew his inspiration from ancient Sparta, and herein lies much of his importance. The Pangles sum up:

> Rush's essay may be bizarre, but in its moral and political seriousness – in the earnestness with which it looks at the classics, through searching if not welcoming eyes – Rush's discussion brings to the fore the most important dimension of the Founders' concern with classical texts and authors.
>
> (Pangle and Pangle 1993: 35)

The following passage indicates the tone:

> To assist in rendering religious, moral, and political instruction more effectual upon the minds of youth, it will be necessary to subject their bodies to physical

discipline. To obviate the inconveniences of their studious and sedentary life, they should live upon a temperate diet. . . . The black broth of Sparta and the barley broth of Scotland [!] have alike been celebrated for their beneficial effects upon the minds of young people.

(quoted Pangle and Pangle 1993: 33)

Two images – 'republican machines' and 'public property' – are cited frequently to indicate Rush's attempt to translate Lacedaemonian practices to Republican America. 'I consider it as possible to convert men into republican machines,' he wrote. 'This must be done, if we expect them to perform their parts properly, in the great machine of the government of the state.' And:

Let our pupil be taught that he does not belong to himself, but that he is public property. Let him be taught to love his family, but let him be taught, at the same time, that he must forsake and even forget them, when the welfare of his country requires it. He must watch for the state, as if its liberties depend upon his vigilance.

(quoted Tyack 1966: 34)

Moreover, harsh discipline is essential to manufacture these republican machines:

In the education of youth, let the authority of our masters be as *absolute* as possible . . . [and] *arbitrary*. . . . I am satisfied that the most useful citizens have been formed from those youth who have never known or felt their own wills till they were one and twenty years of age.

(quoted Pangle and Pangle 1993: 33)

Yet the pupil 'must be taught that there can be no durable liberty but in a republic' (quoted Tyack 1966: 35). So the young must be taught the incomparable value of liberty by being deprived of their freedom: a paradox scarcely acceptable in citizenship education programmes in democratic states today.

But at least Rush did not fall into the hypocritical position of arguing the teaching of the equality of citizenship in a variety of schools very evidently providing unequal quality of educational experience. He proposed unequivocally 'one general, and uniform system of education' in order to 'render the mass of people more homogeneous, and thereby fit them more easily for uniform and peaceable government' (quoted Tyack 1966: 33). To ensure this peaceableness, indeed, the pupil 'must shun the rage, and acrimony of party spirit' (quoted Tyack 1966: 34).

One final message from Rush to note: without explicit reference, he commends the classical concept of multiple identities and loyalties in concentric circles, rippling out from the self, a notion which received renewed approval in the eighteenth century and again in recent years. The pupil must be taught to love his family; however, also,

He must be taught to love his fellow creatures in every part of the world, but he must cherish with a more intense and peculiar affection, the citizens of

Pennsylvania and of the United States . . . [for it is inadvisable] to require him to embrace, with equal affection, the whole of humankind.

(quoted Tyack 1966: 34; for the history of concentric
thinking see Heater 2002: 44–52)

This work by Rush was the first significant publication on education after the Revolution; the second was *On the Education of the Youth of America*. This was written by Noah Webster, the famed American lexicographer; but his dictionary is not his only claim to distinction. Blessed with inexhaustible energy and, as it proved, longevity (his dates are 1758–1843) and impelled by a widely enquiring mind and burning patriotic zeal, he contributed much to other fields, notably education. He has been dubbed America's 'pioneer of learning' (Shoemaker 1966) and 'school-master to America' (Warfel 1966). One of his biographers has asserted that 'Webster became the first American teacher of civics' and that 'he was first to prepare a system of education, and first to write and teach American history and civics' (Warfel 1966: 92). Indeed, Webster stated quite firmly in the work cited above:

Our national character is not yet formed; and it is an object of vast magnitude that systems of Education should be adapted and pursued, which may not only diffuse a knowledge of the sciences, but may implant, in the minds of the American youth, the principles of virtue and liberty; and inspire them with just and liberal ideas of government, and with an inviolable attachment to their own country.

(quoted Tyack 1966: 33)

The relevance of Webster for our purposes is clear.

Unlike most of the names mentioned so far in this book, Webster actually had experience as a schoolteacher, a fact which gave his writings on education and his textbooks considerable credibility. His school books were mainly readers, spellers and grammars designed for elementary education; however, he deliberately included material with an evident civic purpose. For instance, in some of his readers he produced 'A Federal Catechism, Being a Short and Easy Explanation of the Constitution of the United States'. (Compare La Chabeaussière's secular Catechism in France, above.) This was part of the widely used *The Little Reader's Assistant*, published in 1790, for example. He used a different device in his multi-volume *Grammatical Institute of the English Language*. He entitled the 1787 edition of Part III *An American Selection*, over one-third of which were patriotic texts. He appended a subtitle, part of which reads: 'Calculated to Instruct Them in Geography, History, Politics of the United States.' The quotation he chose for its motto on the title page is especially telling: 'Begin with the Infant in his cradle; let the first word he lisps be Washington' (see Shoemaker 1966: 187). This encouragement of the most insidious form of indoctrination is something of a shock, a tiny foretaste of the Stalinist cult of personality (compare the paean which ends: 'And when the woman I love presents me with a child, the first word it shall utter will be: Stalin' (quoted Wayper 1954: 237)).

But, then, Webster was most firmly dedicated to the task of creating a new American nation of republican patriots, and deeply concerned that the schools at the time of the Revolution – neither the system, nor the teachers, nor the textbooks – were remotely capable of educating the youth to this felt commitment. The educational and political systems were out of kilter. He bemoaned the fact that

> In several states we find . . . no provision is made for instructing the poorer rank of people even in reading and writing. Yet in these same states every citizen who is worth a few shillings annually is entitled to vote for legislators. This appears to me a most glaring solecism in government. The constitutions are *republican* and the laws of education are *monarchical*.
>
> (Pangle and Pangle 1993: 97)

So he campaigned, through his publications and journalism, for the rectification of this absurd condition. And his textbooks revolutionized the teaching materials available to teachers. They were interesting to the children; they were politically relevant to the country's needs; they sold in large numbers; and they provided models for works of a similar nature well into the nineteenth century. Let the following judgement, written in 1921, stand as a statement of Noah Webster's practical importance in the history of citizenship education in the USA:

> The introduction of text-books which were neither imported from English printing houses nor written in close imitation of trans-Atlantic models became a potent factor in Americanizing the school. Of these the works of Noah Webster were perhaps the most influential in molding the ideas of the first generation of children born under the flag of the Republic. . . . There had been not a few text-book writers in the colonies but none had ventured so boldly on innovation nor emphasized the patriotic motive so constantly.
>
> (quoted Shoemaker 1966: 189)

In 1797 the American Philosophical Society offered a prize for an essay outlining a plan for a national system of education. Samuel Knox and Samuel Harrison Smith were joint winners. Knox argued the case for what came to be called the common school (see Chapter 3) on the grounds that America needed homogeneity – that word again – and that bonds of friendship and fellowship tying young people from different backgrounds would have a civically harmonizing effect. Smith went further, urging boarding-schools for the same purpose, citing Spartan practice in support of his case. Moreover, he worried about the incipient peril of the lower orders of society being unaware of the benefits of living in a republic (see Pringle and Pringle 1993: 97). Both prize-winners, indeed, were adamant that children should learn about the Constitution. Smith insisted that it would be the duty of all pupils in his proposed secondary schools 'to *commit to memory* and frequently to repeat the Constitution and the fundamental laws of the United States', while Knox proposed that the Constitution should be an essential part of 'a well-digested, concise *moral catechism*' (quoted Butts 1988: 50).

By focusing on the general principles and objectives of the schemes and arguments that arose in the late eighteenth century, we have passed over two matters of some moment, which we now need to consider.

First, and foremost, are the thoughts relating to the civic case for the education of girls. Jefferson, in expounding his ward system, stated that 'all the free children, male and female . . . shall be entitled to receive tuition gratis' (quoted Pangle and Pangle 1993: 114). But it was Rush and Webster who were particularly emphatic about the importance of female education. Rush, in fact, wrote specifically on the topic: his *Thoughts Upon Female Education* was published in 1787. He declared, on grounds of prudence and convenience, that

> The equal share that every citizen has in the liberty and the possible share he may have in the government of our country make it necessary that our ladies should be qualified to a certain degree, by a peculiar and suitable education, to concur in instructing their sons in the principles of liberty and government.
>
> (quoted Kaestle 1983: 27–8)

Webster too advanced prudential reasons. The positive reason was that mothers should be able to 'implant in the tender mind, such sentiments of virtue, propriety and dignity, as are suited to the freedom of our governments' (quoted Pangle and Pangle 1993: 102). So, the negative reason was that females should be educated, not as a right, not as a preparation for civic participation, but as a means of rendering the male half of the population civically knowledgeable and virtuous.

The other important matter for explanation at this point is the subject-matter that was considered most apt for citizenship education. Insofar as children received an education in the colonial period to fit them for citizenship, this was undertaken through the 4Rs (including religion) and ancient history. Jefferson was opposed to religious education in schools because he believed the Bible to be in essence incomprehensible to children. He pinned his faith much more on the teaching of history, modern English and American as well as Ancient, at all levels (see e.g. Honeywell 1931: 37, 123, 149). Webster, also, advocated the inclusion of history in the curriculum; though, whereas Jefferson hoped the subject would warn against political evils, Webster wished it to be taught to enhance a sense of national identity. Yet both recognized the utility of a broad curriculum. Acknowledging the importance of the New Testament and of spelling (naturally), Webster also stated that 'An acquaintance with ethics and the general principles of law, commerce, money, and government is necessary for the yeomanry of a republican state' (quoted Pangle and Pangle 1993: 97), though notice the social stratum he has in mind for this curriculum. We have already explained that Webster also wished there should be taught, through the medium of his 'Federal Catechism', lessons which are recognizably 'civics', an approach which Jefferson did not commend. Thus we see a division of opinion already opening up on the appropriateness of using traditional subjects or a separate political subject. However, another contentious issue, namely the most effective teaching method for citizenship education, was rarely thought about by the Founders; except that Benjamin Franklin adhered to the classical system of the teaching of oratory.

What did the Founders achieve in the field of citizenship education? They defined the need: 'They began the search for an educational underpinning for democratic republican political institutions. They began to formulate the idea that free, universal, compulsory, common schooling was indeed the necessary underpinning' (Butts 1989: 84). Furthermore, when, in the mid-1780s, two Congressional committees drafted ordinances relating to geographical expansion, Jefferson chaired them both and ensured that the new lands be equipped with schools as 'necessary to good government' (see Butts 1989: 72). We may also add the sterling work of Webster in providing schools with textbooks for citizenship education. Yet that is about all. None of the plans was taken up, not even Jefferson's for Virginia, despite his persistence in presenting and re-presenting his bill from 1779 to 1817. Although the American efforts were conducted on a smaller scale than the French, there was a parallel failure to implement an effective programme of civic education across the Atlantic. How is this to be explained?

We may start our answer by understanding the impact of the War of Independence. Although the very act of victorious rebellion had fostered a feeling of patriotic pride in the soldiery, the schools suffered from neglect in the chaos and priority of the conflict. In 1782, at the effective end of the war, Governor Clinton of New York spoke of the consequent 'chasm in education' (quoted Kaestle 1983: 8). Yet, even without the war, it is unlikely that the efforts at educational reform along civic lines would have met with any success. There were deeper, less contingent reasons, which may be clustered into two main sets of attitudes.

One is the lack of policy agreement among the leading politicians. Some were pessimistic that education could supply the political dividends promised by the exponents of civic learning: lawlessness and self-interest are embedded too firmly in human nature for schools to combat. Thus, John Adams, in pessimistic mood and in contrast to other, positive comments cited above: 'experience has ever shown, that education . . . [is] totally inadequate to the business of restraining the passions of men, of preserving a steady government' (quoted Pangle and Pangle 1993: 4). That young people could be schooled in civic virtue and be taught to use their civil liberty for the general good was a view challenged by those who believed that, if schools had a civic role, it was to impose discipline and order. There was, in addition, another division of opinion, a constitutional issue: Should the provision of schools be a federal, state or local responsibility? Already, in the state constitutions framed during the war, education was included as an obligation of the states. This arrangement was confirmed implicitly by the absence of any reference to the subject in the US Constitution. And so, if individual states failed to take measures to ensure citizenship education for national purposes be undertaken, the national government had little power, beyond advice, to mend this gap in the child's schooling.

The second set of attitudes relates to the hostility of the great majority of parents and politicians to the establishment of schools so that education for the civic purposes of integration, understanding and virtue could be pursued. Jefferson bemoaned the 'ignorance, malice, egoism, fanaticism, religious, political and local perversities' that stymied his own plans for Virginia. To this catalogue may be added indifference to education – except that which had a religious or vocational purpose – and the staunch opposition of the people to pay taxes and of the politicians to attempt to levy them for public schools.

Because even the combined impulses of independence, revolution and committed leadership were of insufficient momentum to create more than a minimal form of citizenship education throughout the nation, the efforts made without such advantages in the nineteenth century before the shock of the Civil War were all the more commendable. By those efforts the USA came to enjoy programmes of citizenship education far in advance of any other country.

During the period of just under three centuries covered in this chapter an extraordinarily rich range of thinking emerged on the topic of education for citizenship. Even though few of the thoughts, recommendations and plans of these generations bore fruit in classrooms, as greater numbers of young people entered schools and the political potential of education became more widely understood, the legacies of this earlier age evidently became very useful in the nineteenth century. We may discern several such inheritances. One related to the education of what we have called 'elite citizens'. As the dispensing of justice, the administration of government and the drafting of legislation burgeoned with the growing size and complexity of the modern state, so an increasing number of personnel were needed to perform these functions, and the appropriate education they should undergo had to be considered. From Elyot to Jefferson, suggestions were readily forthcoming. The political upheavals from the mid-seventeenth to the late eighteenth centuries generated ideas, demands and goals that forced consideration of the civic role of education beyond the narrow stratum of the governing classes. Democracy, republicanism and nationalism all required an extension of political consciousness, loyalty and even involvement of a far greater proportion of a state's population. Mass education was becoming necessary, not so much for the sake of the individual, but for the sake of society and the state – for its renovation or for its strength or for its stability. English reformers from the Civil War to the eighteenth-century Radicals wrote for democracy. French plans focused on national cohesion and adaptation to republicanism. So did the Americans. The Germans, who rejected the individualist purpose of education, wanted education to contribute to the cause of national unification. Yet we must not forget the thread of nervousness, from Bodin to Adams, that education for citizenship must concern itself primarily with social and political quiescence and order.

3 Education for liberal democracy

New dimensions

The age of revolutions revolutionized citizenship and, as a consequence, posed new educational questions. The old citizenship was based upon the assumption of an elite, small in numbers and virtuous in civic conduct. The new citizenship was based on the assumption of the masses endowed with democratic rights and owing loyalty to the nation-state (see e.g. Riesenberg 1992: xv, 272–3). Peter Riesenberg has called this new style of citizenship 'second citizenship', though, in truth, we can identify three phases in its development during the nineteenth and twentieth centuries, which we may label western liberal, totalitarian and post-colonial. In this chapter we shall be examining the educational responses in the first and third of these, postponing the totalitarian phase for separate treatment in Chapter 4. We shall also give separate treatment – in Chapter 5 – to the complication of multiculturalism as it has affected and still affects citizenship education.

The geographical size of modern nation-states, produced by national unification, for example, of the USA, Germany and Italy, and by the decolonization of Africa and large areas of Asia, has presented problems of 'nation-building', a sense of civic cohesion essential for the proper functioning of citizenship. Demographically, the size of the citizen body – and hence electorate – of a modern nation-state has raised the problem of concord founded upon trust. We have lost the mutual knowledge and understanding that was possible in a *polis* and which Aristotle was convinced was the absolutely essential condition for effective citizenship. Today, social scientists refer to 'social capital', the body of trust built up in a community so that citizens have confidence and faith in the good conduct of each other and of the government, and the government has similar, reciprocal confidence and trust.

Both the building of a nation and of a fund of social capital are educational issues in the broadest sense. A more specifically pedagogical issue, related to the growth of mass citizenship, has been voter ignorance; that is, the low levels of even basic literacy in many countries, let alone of political literacy. In the case of the western democracies this matter became an increasingly salient concern as the suffrage was gradually extended; in the case of the former Afro-Asian colonies it became an immediate concern because of the simultaneous concession of independence and universal suffrage against the background of limited – often exceedingly limited – school provision by the imperial powers.

The connection between education and the right to vote is not a simple matter. We may identify three pairs of opposed arguments. The basic opposition, which may be roughly identified with Left and Right political positions, concerns the wisdom of allowing uneducated people full citizenship rights. The Left have argued that a civic right should not be conditional on any other factor, that even the lowliest and most ignorant are capable of assessing what policies are in their best interests, and that a basic intelligence or *nous* and a sense of civic virtue are really all that are needed to cast a vote conscientiously. On the other side, it has seemed ludicrous to entrust the vital duty of choosing a government to the uneducated, especially, as has sometimes been argued, that ignorance and vice are connected features of the lower orders. One of the most persistent and convinced opponents of the extension of the franchise in mid-nineteenth-century England was Robert Lowe. He argued most colourfully that 'venality, ignorance, drunkenness and facility for being intimidated, or impulsive, unreflecting and violent people' are to be found in the lowest strata of society, and that such people would dominate the House of Commons in the event of any further extension of the vote after the First Reform Act of 1832 (quoted Briggs 1959: 499).

The second pair of arguments about the enfranchisement of the uneducated concerns the propensity of such citizens to be politically manipulated. This result could be deplored or celebrated, depending on one's point of view. Each may be illustrated from nineteenth-century France. Guizot, who was responsible for a law in 1833 expanding the number of primary schools, had expressed his worry seventeen years earlier that 'the less enlightened the multitude, the more amenable it is to being misled and diverted' (quoted Vaughan and Archer 1971: 129; for Guizot, see also below). During the revolutionary months of 1848 the election of the Constituent Assembly supplies a clear example of cynical manipulative techniques in the politically unsophisticated rural areas. The government attempted to use primary schoolteachers in a campaign to support approved republican candidates; the Church used the *curés*. The election was arranged for Easter Sunday to weaken the conservative countryside vote; in a number of parishes Mass was said early and the *curés* led their congregations to cast their votes. Clerical manipulation was more effective than pedagogical; many teachers were intimidated (see Cobban 1970: 68–81). French countryside citizens were insufficiently educated to have the knowledge or confidence to think for themselves – and the ministers of the state and of the Church knew it.

Did this extraordinary episode in France show that citizenship education should precede the universal acquisition of the franchise, or vice versa? This was of equally general application, and exercised the minds particularly of the Chartists in England in the 1840s. It is a commonplace that the six-point People's Charter for parliamentary reform (including universal manhood suffrage) was devised and gained support because political change was perceived as a means towards achieving socio-economic change. Part of this change would be substantial improvement in the schooling available to the children of the working classes. However, the leaders of the movement were not at one about tactics or phasing (the educational element of Chartism is explained below).

Those politicians and educationists who, over the past two centuries, have been able to navigate their way through these difficulties to positions where they have had the power to develop educational processes for helping young people to grow into effective democratic citizens, have nevertheless still been faced with complications concerning the methods to be used to achieve their goals. Essentially, three methods have been indispensable. Foremost and utterly basic, it goes without saying, is literacy – a formidable problem in all underdeveloped countries. Until the production of cheap radios, illiterates have been dependent on acquiring information and arguments second- or third-hand, a poor and potentially dangerous means of making the judgements required of citizens. The British writer and publisher Victor Gollancz described a mere basic education without any cultivation of critical thinking as 'the growing pains of democracy' (Gollancz 1953: 327). Second, pupils have needed to learn the elements of their country's traditions, institutions and current issues facing it. Literacy achieved, classes in civics have been commonly organized. However, the third and most difficult strand to arrange and teach has been civic moral commitment. Literacy provides the fundamental tool, civics provides the essential knowledge; but they do not necessarily cultivate good citizenly behaviour: hence attempts in some countries to ensure that the ethos of the school is conducive to this need, arrangements for pupils to participate in the management of the school, and creating opportunities for young people to undertake practical work in the community.

All these introductory remarks relate to the two-century span of time covered by this chapter. However, by any historical yardstick, the arousal of interest in, the increasing concern about and fuller implementation of citizenship education from the final years of the twentieth century have been quite extraordinary (see e.g. Cogan and Derricott 2000; C.L. Hahn 1998; Ichilov 1998a; Torney-Purta *et al*. 1999). This phenomenon needs special commentary. A combination of two major factors may be suggested as explanations. One was the belief that liberal democracy had become the only effective political form – an idea reinforced by the influential but simplistic essay 'The End of History?', which Francis Fukuyama published in 1989. The transformation of former authoritarian regimes, military and, most dramatically, Communist, seemed to support this thesis. The corollary was that the populations of the newly democratized states needed to be taught the principles of democratic citizenship. The other factor was, paradoxically, the fragility of liberal democratic states, both old and new, challenged by sub- and supra-national forces, demands and ideals, and threatened by the cynicism, apathy and egoism of so many of their citizens. Liberal democratic politics allowed citizenship to flourish. But if citizens did not want to be citizens – in allegiance and performance of responsibilities, even though rights were demanded and seized – then people, notably young people, had to be taught about the nature and the inestimable value of that status and about the vital need to live it properly in order to preserve the hard-won prize of liberal democracy.

Awareness of this remarkable spread of citizenship education in a liberal democratic form – and, it must be said, the improved professionalism of its teaching – must not be allowed to obscure the fact that, in historical terms, it has been so far of exceedingly short duration. This observation is by no means intended to suggest that the momentum is likely to slacken: indeed, the evidence suggests quite otherwise; but rather to remind the reader that this book is a work of history. We are therefore interested in the developments since *c*.1990 only insofar as we can place them in the long context. Another reminder, too: with the sudden multiplication of countries in which governments and educationists are taking citizenship education seriously, it is quite impossible to describe what is happening in every state without reducing this chapter to a list of brief encyclopedia-type entries.

Making choices is inevitably difficult. France, England and the USA must be included in order to sustain the historical narrative from the previous chapter. In any case, to omit France and the USA, countries with such lengthy commitments to civic education, or England, with such a long-lived confused approach to the matter, would be perverse. But states beyond the so-called 'western' portion of the world must not be forgotten, so considerable space has been devoted to the experiences of some former Asian and African colonies both before and after decolonization. Other countries, in order to extend the range, will feature in Chapter 5, where they will exemplify the problem of citizenship education in multicultural states (not forgetting, of course, that we all live in multicultural states now, and have always so lived, albeit perhaps unconsciously). Our two groups of states – large 'western' and 'Afro-Asian' – may, by being treated separately, give the impression of there being only two categories, namely the major, western powers of modern history with long traditions of citizenship education, and Afro-Asian states with short traditions determined by the relatively brief proportions of their histories during which they have adopted western ways, including the concept of citizenship and the need for education to prepare for that status. Such an impression would be unfortunate because it would lead to the omission of two important categories of states; that is, small western countries and Latin America. So, short comments will be provided here about these groups of states.

In the first category, the Netherlands and Sweden are of especial interest. Both these small European states started formal civic education relatively early. They reveal in the ways this teaching developed the main issues that have characterized the attempts by liberal democratic states to introduce this work into schools.

In 1857 a Dutch law declared that the object of primary education was 'to develope [*sic*] the reason of the young, and to train them to the exercise of *Christian* [Arnold's emphasis] and social virtues', Christianity understood in a non-theological sense to embrace 'all those ideas which . . . prepare the union of citizens in a common sentiment of mutual goodwill' (quoted Arnold 1962: 195). In Sweden, too, early civic education had a religious tinge, though government legislation came later than in the Netherlands. The 1918 to 1919 school reforms introduced civics as a subject for older pupils, in response to the introduction of universal suffrage (see Englund 1986: 292, 190; for an interpretation of the Swedish experience to the 1980s, see Englund 1986 *passim*).

Although the Dutch government made an early intervention in this field, there was no real central leadership thereafter, until 1963, when the Secondary Education

Act of that year required all schools of this kind to teach *maatschappijleer*, the study of society (its teaching actually started in 1968). Even then, it was left to teachers to interpret the curricular content of this vague term. Their efforts bore fruit in 1983 when a coherent social and political programme for 12- to 16-year-olds was devised (for details, see Hooghoff 1990: 157–71). In contrast, the Swedish School Committees and Commissions reported regularly, as a result of which a new civics subject, *samhällskunskap*, was introduced in 1948, and detailed adaptations to content and objectives were made periodically in subsequent years (for the civics syllabuses see Muñoz 1982: 435). Yet, although the roles of government were so different in these two states, their histories of citizenship education until the end of the twentieth century shared the same unsatisfactory conditions. These conditions were, first, confusion as to the content of civics lessons and the relationship of this subject to allied disciplines, notably history, and, second, and no doubt partly because of this uncertainty, the low status of the subject within the curriculum and teaching profession. For many years Dutch teachers failed to agree among themselves about what they should be teaching (see Hooghoff 1990: 157–8); and in Sweden, advocates of a 'progressive' interpretation were at loggerheads with the advocates of a 'hegemonic' interpretation, that, is quarrelling over whether the focus should be on democratic values or national unity (see Englund 1986: 197). Teachers in the field of citizenship education in many other countries will have been only too familiar with these problems.

To offer a succinct account of how liberal forms of citizenship education evolved in Latin America is impossible; all that may be offered here are a few indicators. First, and obviously, so many Hispanic-American states have been ruled by military juntas since the age of liberation in the early nineteenth century, and so impoverished has the region been, that, until recently, it has not been realistic to expect that coherent programmes of civic education could have been installed. Second, with the remarkable swings to liberal democratic styles of government in many states from the early 1980s, we may expect to find greater efforts to instil a sense of citizenship in school pupils since then.

Perhaps the most interesting history of citizenship education in any Latin American country is to be found in Colombia. As early as the mid-nineteenth century, education for 'good', deferent citizenship was already under way. In the words of one Colombian authority writing in 1999, 'Its strongest model was Carreño's *Manual of Urbanity* (1812–1874), the first canonical model of education for the Latin American citizen. . . . This manual is still [!] used in many schools, and teaching from it is frequently requested by parents and educators' (Rueda 1999: 140; *Urbanity* is a literal translation of *Urbanidades*, politeness or courtesy). From the 1960s to the 1980s to this kind of moral education was added teaching about political institutions by rote learning. From the mid-1980s to the mid-1990s reforms in this sphere were rapidly devised, consolidated by a Resolution in 1994 stating that 'the axis of civic education is "to live democracy" at school and that the student acquires a citizen's "way of being" basically from interpersonal relationships' (Rueda 1999: 141). At the same time the General Law of Education specified nine compulsory areas, including the social sciences, moral education and ethics.

The renovation of citizenship education in Colombia was helped by the introduction of a new, more democratic constitution in 1991. Change in style of government has, after all, been normal in the region. However, the little state of Costa Rica stands as an extraordinary exception to that rule. Its avoidance of phases of strict authoritarianism has been conducive to the development of a liberal style of civic education. It is therefore not surprising to find that in the 1970s a Year 10 course on the country's democratic institutions and the rights and duties of the citizen was available. Moreover, the detailed syllabus of content and activities would have put many other countries to shame at that time (see Muñoz 1982: 440–2).

However, to finish on the experiences of the great majority of Latin American states: because authoritarian governments were so common in the continent's history, the transition to liberal democratic regimes from the end of the twentieth century has not been easy for ordinary citizens to accommodate. Political apathy has been widespread. Hence the interest in citizenship education. Three Argentine scholars have explained the conditions lucidly:

> Since the process of redemocratization in Latin America started in the early 1980s, there has been considerable debate on how to sustain and consolidate democratic institutions in the region. . . . Particular attention is now being paid to citizenship education, as scholars recognize that there is no immediate correspondence between institutional arrangements and political culture. . . . Many of the 'new democracies' of Latin America govern peoples in which there is no widespread norm of political tolerance or democratic participation.
> (Chaffee *et al.* 1998: 149)

They continue: because an anti-democratic mood persists that could threaten the democratic regimes: 'much more is at stake in citizen education in Argentina and similar young democracies than it is in established democracies' (Chaffee *et al.* 1998: 152).

Different as these few states we have surveyed above have been in their educational policies, they illustrate between them the handful of basic issues faced by those attempting to create liberal democratic styles of citizenship education: how conducive is the political regime; how much leadership is provided by the government to the schools; whether the focus should be moral, social or political education, or a balance of all; and what should be the basic objective(s).

We are now ready to examine the histories of the states selected for major treatment. We saw in Chapter 2 how keen were the French Revolutionaries to educate their young for the role of citizen. It is fitting, therefore, to start the body of this chapter with a survey of how progress was made by later generations of French politicians and educationists.

France from Restoration to Fifth Republic

Asked by the English Inspector of Schools Matthew Arnold what the French Revolution contributed to popular education, François Guizot responded: 'A deluge of words, nothing else' (quoted Arnold 1962: 51; author's translation). In the short term and in terms of concrete reforms that was so, but this is to forget the legacy of attitudes, of which Arnold was quick to remind his reader in order to expand on Guizot's neat epigram. Arnold asserted that, 'It made it impossible for any government of France to found a system [of popular instruction] which was not *lay*, and which was not *national*' (Arnold 1962: 52). Somewhat cynically, we may expand the judgement further by noting that one of the most lasting results inherited by nineteenth- and twentieth-century France from the educational debates of its great Revolution was their failure – their failure to resolve the issue raised by the Enlightenment that the Church should be deprived of its grip on the educational system. A completely lay system was not created, and the struggle between Church and state for control over primary education remained not only a controversial matter of educational policy, but the cause, episodically, of fierce political dispute. In the words of one American scholar, *laïcité* has 'been one of the most bitterly contested issues in modern French history' (Talbott 1969: 24). What is more, the struggle was implicitly related to citizenship education because it set the teaching of religious morality against civic morality, and Roman Catholic influence against the reality of a heterogeneous nation that included Protestants, Jews, agnostics and atheists too. The argument for civic morality as preferable to a Church-taught morality was fervently believed by academics and politicians of a republican inclination, exemplified by Edgar Quinet's *The People's Education*, published in 1850 (see Buisson and Farrington 1920: 1–4), and came to the fore in the Third Republic. However, a little background to the establishment of civic education in this atmosphere in the late nineteenth century will be useful.

The clash between Church and state, the latter represented by the schoolmaster, is vividly illustrated by Matthew Arnold's observations:

> 'In what condition is the moral and religious instruction in your school?' one of M. Guizot's inspectors asked a schoolmaster. '*Je n'enseigne pas ces bêtises-là*' [I do not teach those stupidities] was the answer. Another inspector found the schoolmaster parading, at the head of his school, the town where he lived; drums beating, the scholars singing the Marseillaise; and the procession halting before the clergyman's house to shout at the top of their lungs, 'Down with the Jesuits!'
>
> (Arnold 1962: 66)

The surreptitious, albeit strictly illegal, return of the religious Orders banned in the eighteenth century exacerbated the tension. Moreover, although the correlation was certainly not absolute, the Church–state conflict over education tended to deepen the basic fault-line in French politics after the fall of Napoleon I and the Restoration of the monarchy. Republicans were more often severely anticlerical than the monarchists, who tended to view the Church as a mainstay against renewed revolutionary threats (see e.g. Gildea 1983: ch.1).

Even so, republicans as well as monarchists tended to be conservative in their attitudes to and negligent of civic education, except for the brief enthusiasm of the

1848 Revolution, and until the forceful change of policy after 1870. The duty of the schools, especially the primary schools, was to inculcate in their pupils an attitude of acceptance of the status quo and a determination to live useful lives. The tone was set at the Restoration by the Ordinances of 17 February 1815 and 29 February 1816. Article 30 of the latter reads in part: 'The commission of Public Instruction will carefully ensure that, in all schools, primary instruction is based on religion, respect for the laws and the love owed to the sovereign' (Chevallier and Grosperin 1971: 102; author's translation). The conservative theme may be pursued through the various regimes prior to the Third Republic. Guizot, the middle-class academic, Montalembert, a leader of the clerical party, and Duruy, appointed by Napoleon III in 1863 to weaken the clerical hold on the schools, all sang from song-sheets composed to harmonize on the motif of education for the stability of the state. Guizot's law of 1833 established state primary schools and teacher-training institutions (*écoles normales*). In 1850 Montalembert, dismissing the schoolteacher as a force for good order, nominates the priest as representing 'at the same time the moral order, the political order and the material order'. The authors who quote this comment explain that he was 'linking the educational function of the clergy with the defence of property and of citizenship in the secular state' (Vaughan and Archer 1971: 201). Summarizing Duruy's views on adult education, the authority on his tenure of the Ministry of Public Instruction writes:

> The worker who does not possess any transcending understanding of his role in the industrial and agricultural processes becomes frustrated by the superior economic forces that dominate his life. Education is the only protection against socialism and communism . . . [and explains that he ensured that courses] would not be used to promote political doctrines hostile to the state.
>
> (Horvath-Peterson 1984: 109, 111)

All three, by the way, were anxious that schooling should make the pupils become citizens protective of the economic system and themselves economically productive.

Citizenship, as so often observed in this book, depends upon literacy. A useful index of the level is the percentage of army conscripts who are illiterate. In 1830 the number in France was over 50 per cent (see Prost 1968: 96), though this raw figure masks immensely wide variations from the well-educated eastern departments to the poorly educated Midi (see Dupeux 1976: 115). Yet by the end of the nineteenth century the figure had been reduced to about 5 per cent. This improvement was due to a steady persistence by ministers of education, often against opposition on financial grounds, to increase the numbers of primary schools and teachers. The number of primary school pupils rose from 866,000 in 1817 to 5,526,000 in 1887 (Prost 1968: 108), during which time the whole population increased from only about 29 to 38 million (see Dupeux 1976: 36). On the other hand, we should not forget the prudent pinch of salt. Registrations did not necessarily equate with regularity of attendance, particularly in rural areas. In 1879, for instance, one school inspector complained: 'Reality has nothing to do with administrative figures or statistics' (quoted Weber 1976: 310). Though, true, by the 1890s, road improvements and Jules Ferry's legislation introducing free and compulsory education improved actual school attendance.

None of the events and attitudes retailed above reveals any conviction that young people should be afforded anything like a systematic education for citizenship. This casualness in educational policy was called into question by two episodes in Napoleon III's foreign policy: his idealistic decision to intervene in the Piedmontese-led thrust for Italian unification in 1859 to 1860 and his naivety in being lured into the war with Prussia in 1870. The first of these episodes brought the Emperor into conflict with Pope Pius IX. As a consequence, Napoleon decided to undermine the control and influence of the Church over the French educational system. This government policy received more widespread acclamation from 1864, when the Pope issued his encyclical *Syllabus Errorum*, denouncing as errors an extraordinarily comprehensive list of ideas, practices and achievements of the modern western world, such as science, liberalism, the idea of progress and, lest there should be any unfortunate omissions, 'modern civilization'. How could schools in France remain under the authority of those teachers who, as priests, and more particularly as members of religious Orders, owed allegiance to the Vatican? And if education was to be 'laicized', then so too should the teaching of religious morality be replaced by the inculcation of a civic morality – or thus it could now be more cogently argued.

These changing circumstances in the 1860s provided conditions more conducive to the introduction of a coherent form of citizenship education than heretofore. Yet reform in this direction might still have been delayed had it not been for the appalling shock of the Franco-Prussian War. Within six months the French forces had been crushed, the fortress-city of Sedan delivered up to the enemy, Paris besieged and Napoleon III had abdicated. The experience was a bitter humiliation for a proud nation and a proud army. How could this disaster have come to pass? An explanation had to be sought. Blame had to be laid on someone's shoulders. Had the French character been sapped by decadent journalists and atheist writers? Or, was it the body of schoolteachers who were culpable, so inferior to their German counterparts? The slogan was passed around: 'Sedan was the victory of the Prussian schoolmaster' (see Ozouf 1963: 15 23; author's translation).

These two crucial preconditions for the introduction of civic education into French schools – presumed weakness of character and of teaching – were followed by two governmental decisions which made such reform inescapable. One was the determination of the leaders of the new Third Republic (created in 1871, confirmed in 1875) to restore the universal manhood suffrage that had been conceded by the Second Republic in 1848 and been undermined during the Second Empire. This led to the remarkable election of 1877, when the peasantry rebelled against their social superiors and helped return a very substantial republican majority to the Assembly (see e.g. Cobban 1965: 20–1). The other decision was the appointment of Jules Ferry as Minister of Public Instruction for the equivalent of three years in three phases from 1879 to 1883. He was the true progenitor of modern citizenship education in France; yet, without the 1877 electoral outcome and consequent progressive political agenda, the acceptance of his reforms would have been far less assured.

Ferry is a figure of such cardinal importance for us that we should know something about the man and his strength of purpose in initiating and pushing through his legislation. He was born in 1832, developed republican political sympathies and was mayor of Paris during the grim siege of 1870 to 1871. His guiding principle was the achievement of a secular state, the goal of the Revolution of 1789. Indeed, one of his biographers has dubbed him 'the arch-priest of the secular faith' (Guilhaume 1980: 80; author's translation). Moreover, his secular state must incorporate social and political renovations. And so Ferry's overall aim was to use the school as the means of consolidating these improvements, an aim which has been summarized as follows:

> The instrument of social reform, educational policy, must equally give the Republic firm roots. It is the new school which must enable the new generations to be won over to the sentiment of national unity and to the cult of *la patrie*, over and above regional diversities and differences of conditions.
>
> (Guilhaume 1980: 80; author's translation)

Ferry's belief in the great Revolution as his guiding light for educational reform went deeper than outline principles. His inspiration was the detail of Condorcet's report (see Chapter 2). Within a month of taking office Ferry placed before the Assembly two draft laws striking at the influence of the Church in matters pedagogical. His campaign had begun.

One of Ferry's proposals contained a key article – Article 7. It stated: 'No one is allowed to participate in public or private education, at any level at all – primary, secondary or higher – nor to administer an educational establishment, if he belongs to an unauthorized congregation' (quoted Guilhaume 1980: 81–2; author's translation). We have already noticed how formally banned religious Orders had in practice revived their educational activities. Ferry's objective was to end their involvement, most especially the Jesuits. It was a determined attack on Catholic education. Article 7 set off uproar in the Assembly and the Senate, and heated argument throughout the country. Ferry was vilified by the clericals, lauded by the republicans, but he denied vehemently that he was anticlerical, or that the conflict he was engaged in was between Church and state: 'it is between the *Syllabus* and the Revolution' (Robiquet 1895: 353; author's translation; for the Article 7 affair, see Ozouf 1963: 56–65). A compromise was reached. The Jesuits were expelled again, over a century after the initial destruction of their educational power (see Chapter 2); other Orders were permitted to apply for authorization; many Catholic schools survived; so, therefore, did the divisive educational quarrel.

Not that Ferry's ambition was to replace religious morality with a political civic morality. He believed that both moral teaching and the teacher's handling of all controversial matters should be neutral. His aim of a secular system of education was to achieve that neutrality. In spite of his failure to gain his full objective, he is still, none the less, a crucial figure in the whole span of the history of citizenship education because of the civic content of the curriculum he introduced and the desired objectivity with which it could be taught in the state schools – insofar as objectivity was possible in an atmosphere of post-war-heightened republican consciousness. National cohesion in a republican regime was of the highest priority: for instance, in 1879 the *Marseillaise* was declared the national anthem; and already, in 1870, the republican patriot Gambetta had declared, 'It is the school that will breathe into all the French people a common spirit' (quoted Guilhaume 1980: 91; author's translation).

When Ferry launched his programme for citizenship education in 1882, he was not working on a *tabula rasa*. True, one authority complained in 1871 that 'History was ignored and civics absent from the teaching program' (quoted Weber 1976: 334). Yet that was not completely accurate; some civic education was already under way. For example, we know that as early as 1862 a civics textbook was in use. Its approach to the subject-matter is revealed in this summary:

> (1) French society is ruled by just laws, because it is a democratic society. (2) All the French are equal in rights; but there are inequalities between us that stem from nature or from wealth. (3) These inequalities cannot disappear. (4) Man works to become rich; if he lacked this hope, work would cease and France would decline.
>
> (quoted Weber 1976: 331)

Commenting on this excerpt, Weber states: 'Schools' potent lessons of morality focused on duty, effort, and seriousness of purpose' (Weber 1976: 331). Ferry, then, did not inaugurate citizenship education in France; what he did achieve was a fuller, more rounded, less socially directed syllabus and the establishment of that syllabus nation-wide.

He began with the law of 28 March 1882. The following year he circulated a letter of explanation and encouragement to all primary schoolteachers, a document which is a remarkable expression of his educational philosophy. It calls for generous quotation. He starts on a sympathetic note: 'Of the diverse obligations it imposes on you, assuredly the heaviest increase of work and anxiety, is your mission to instruct your pupils in ethics and citizenship' (Buisson and Farrington 1920: 5–6). He continues by explaining that this duty does not require brilliant scholarship:

> No. The family and society merely ask you to help bring up their children well, to make them honest citizens. This is saying that they expect of you not words but acts; not one more subject entered upon your program, but a very practical service that you can render the country rather as a man than as a teacher.
>
> (Buisson and Farrington 1920: 9)

An important message; yet by expressing the point so bluntly, he rather contradicts the earlier comment about the teachers' extra workload and a later passage in the letter in which he soothes the teachers' fears about the task of preparing new subject-matter: he grandiloquently reports that some of 'the greatest authorities of our time and country' had been recruited to the task of preparing textbooks for this new venture. As a consequence,

> For the last few months we have seen the number of textbooks on moral and civic instruction grow almost week by week. Nothing proves better than this the value public opinion attaches to thorough moral training in the primary school.
>
> (Buisson and Farrington 1920: 12)

It showed, too, the determination and efficiency of the Ministry of Public Instruction to make a success of this innovatory work. For he goes on to explain that teachers will be able to choose from a range of texts, and, to that end:

> I am sending you the complete list of treatises on moral and civic instruction adopted this year by teachers in the different academies. The pedagogical library of the principal town in each canton will receive these treatises from the ministry. . . . It is but just that you should have in this matter [of choice of teaching materials] as much liberty as responsibility.
>
> (Buisson and Farrington 1920: 13–14)

This was evidently a splendid and well-organized service. However, Ferry was also careful to stress that this responsibility was a testing duty. He states firmly:

> I cannot too often impress this on your mind: Let it be understood that you place your self-respect, your honor . . . in causing the practical teaching of good rules of conduct and worthy sentiments to penetrate profoundly the rising generation.
>
> (Buisson and Farrington 1920: 14)

Little wonder that Ferry mentioned anxiety at the start of his missive!

The books to which Ferry referred were designed to support the Moral Education portion of the new programme, arranged as two quite detailed syllabuses for the 9- to 11-year-olds and the 11- to 13-year-olds. For the younger of these age-ranges there were lists of general duties including a specific reference to duties towards God. A section is devoted to the fatherland: 'France, her greatness and her misfortune. Duties toward the fatherland and toward society.' The second section of the syllabus includes telling entries on: 'avoidance of debt, evil effects of the passion of gambling'; 'obligation of all men to work; nobility of manual labour'; and 'Little by little alcoholism entails the violation of all duties toward others (laziness, violence, etc.)' (Buisson and Farrington 1920: 28–9). Not surprisingly, the syllabus for the older children lays greater stress on social and political matters. It was an extraordinarily formidable programme for such young people. Ferry's letter denied that he was expecting academic brilliance of the teachers; but was he not expecting academic brilliance of the pupils? A random sample of some of what are surely very demanding concepts: 'Justice, the condition of all society. . . . Probity, equity, loyalty, delicacy. . . . The difference between duty and self-interest even when the two seem to be identified.' On the other hand, much is obvious and sensible material for moral civic education. We may cite: 'Respect for the opinions and beliefs of others. . . . Duties of benevolence, gratitude, tolerance, mercy, etc.' And the list under the heading 'The fatherland' largely comes into this category, listing such duties as 'obedience to law, military service . . . fidelity to the flag . . . personal freedom . . . the right to work, right to organize'; also, the splendidly phrased, 'Taxes (condemnation of fraud toward the State)'; and, naturally, 'Explanation of the motto of the Republic: Liberty, Equality, Fraternity' (Buisson and Farrington 1920: 30–1).

These syllabuses should be understood in the context of other reforms introduced by Ferry. In 1881 primary education fees were abolished; in 1882 attendance for 6- to 13-year-olds was made compulsory; and in 1886 all teachers in state schools were required to be lay persons. Thus secular civic education was henceforth to be made available to all pupils in state primary schools – in effect, for the lower-middle class, urban working class and the peasantry. The wealthier and more socially elevated middle class, in contrast, had ambitions for their children, overwhelmingly for the boys, in the form of the *baccalauréat* examination and the academic and professional doors which the qualification opened. Insofar as the course contained any form of civic education it was indirectly achieved at that time through classical and historical studies.

What was the outcome of Ferry's initiative in practice? Certainly not the neutrality on which he so frequently insisted. A British historian has summed up the effects of the Third Republic's educational policy:

> The State teachers' training colleges – the *écoles normales* – provided the necessary staff of highly indoctrinated teachers, drilled in anti-clerical sentiments. . . . The result was an army of Radical and Socialist sympathizers – lay missionaries – dispersed in strong strategic positions in every Commune, whether village or township, throughout France.
>
> (Thomson 1958: 144–5)

In addition, Eugen Weber, the American authority on the transformation of 'peasants into Frenchmen' during this period, constantly stresses the uses of schools to superimpose a national affiliation over the deeply embedded local and regional senses of identity. He writes, for instance, that, 'A vast programme of indoctrination was plainly called for to persuade people that the fatherland extended beyond its evident limits to something vast and intangible called France' (Weber 1976: 334). Indeed, a summary of the research undertaken by Carlton Hayes (see below) in the early twentieth century concludes that '*La France* emerges from these studies, regnant and supreme' (Bereday 1966: 127).

To offer a little detail, let us now indicate the enthusiasm of some (though, true, by no means all) leading authorities for citizenship education, and the tone of civics and history lessons and textbooks.

To illustrate the keenness of some major figures we take Ernest Lavisse – though more for his exceptional commitment than as an exemplar of the average. He was an extraordinarily productive and energetic historian and educationist, Professor of

History at the Sorbonne and a member of the French Academy. Ferdinand Buisson, Director of Primary Education from 1879 to 1896 and a close associate of Ferry, wrote:

> M. Lavisse has exerted an unprecedented moral influence over the youth of our schools. His pedagogical work is not confined to the three volumes [on Education], but has taken the form of speeches and numerous articles which have attracted widespread attention.
>
> (Buisson and Farrington 1920: 91)

In 'an open letter to the teachers of France on civic education', published in the *General Manual of Primary Education* in 1898, Lavisse identified what he considered the four main issues. First, the political agenda behind the educational task: 'Gentlemen, help us to complete the French Revolution. You can do so by giving special attention to moral and civic instruction.' Second, he naturally emphasized the role of history:

> I would that the history taught the people be above all else the history of the people through the centuries, the history of the immense effort toward justice and liberty, toward right. . . . It would be, as it were, a preface to that civic instruction which deals with the rights and duties of the French citizen such as the history of France has made him.

His third point was to insist that civic *rights* must be taught, despite the current insistence that the teaching of duties had to be given priority; this teaching was to lead to an understanding that 'these rights and honors cannot be free, that [the Frenchman] must merit them by acquitting himself of his duties toward the State'. His fourth recommendation was the practical issue of the time available in class and the young age at which primary schoolchildren left school. He urged, therefore, that:

> It is essential . . . that you make an important place for civic teaching in the 'instruction after school,' which thanks to you is being organized throughout France. . . . [Because] it is my profound conviction that the only means of saving France is to give our young people definite reasons for loving their country and for discharging their duties toward their country.
>
> (Buisson and Farrington 1920: 106, 107, 108)

Lavisse, as well as being one of Ferry's distinguished authorities, was approached to produce classroom materials. Weber describes his collections of tales and history books as 'pugnacious': 'it was the duty of sons to avenge their fathers; it was the duty of children to wreak revenge for past defeats' (Weber 1976: 335). National unity was another of his themes. In his *First Year of French History*, published in 1884, Lavisse tells his young readers: 'you will learn what you owe your fathers and why your first duty is to love above all else your fatherland – that is, the land of your fathers' (quoted Weber 1976: 334). Three years later, in a book of narrative homilies, he identified four obligations to be discharged by the citizen: to ensure his own and his children's education; to perform his military duty and be ready to die for France; to pay his taxes; and to vote for the best political candidates (see Weber 1976: 336).

Note the military slant to the concept of citizenship as conveyed to young pupils. This was by no means confined to Lavisse's books. Geography was also used as a vehicle for this purpose. In 1884 a teacher's journal suggested that an essential part of the subject was to teach about 'the defence of the country's territory, with its defensive works, fortified points and artillery emplacements' (quoted Ozouf 1963: 125; author's translation). Even the very young were taught songs about being a brave soldier, one, indeed, entitled *The Schoolboy Soldier* (see Ozouf 1963: 122, 124). Restoration of the ideals of the French Revolution, national unity (an objective traceable to the Revolution (see Chapter 2)), stalwart defence of France, and determination to exact revenge against her enemies were the powerful lessons which the post-1882 textbooks sought to teach as the major themes of '*l'instruction civique*' and its close companion '*l'enseignement d'histoire*' – civic instruction and the teaching of history. Having examined the school books of this era, Weber gained the impression that 'the patriotism they advocated placed national integration first, revenge only second', though, inevitably, 'the themes are often mingled' (Weber 1976: 335–6).

The timbre of French civic education we have surveyed above clearly owed much to the country's defeat in the Franco-Prussian War. Similarly, the tone between the two World Wars was greatly determined by the ordeal of the Great War. From 1926 to 1928 the American historian Carlton Hayes visited France and provided a vivid picture of the country as a self-aware 'nation of patriots', his word-portrait including the contribution of schools in fashioning this consciousness. Summarizing Hayes's findings, a later American academic wrote:

> The recurrence of the same subjects over and over again in the course of the study – the whole infused with a heavy dose of nationalist rhetoric – was intended to ensure that the rudiments of reading, writing, arithmetic and love of *La Patrie* were drummed into the most obdurate heads.
>
> (Talbott 1969: 26)

Some detail, therefore, from Hayes's study. Compulsory attendance at school spanned the years from 6 to 13. Twelve subjects were taught, seven of which Hayes classified as 'national' subjects; not only the obvious instruction in morals and French citizenship, but also the large proportion of the timetabled time devoted to the French language fell into this category, so political was the content of these exercises (see Hayes 1930: 39, 43). And the balance of the curriculum for those who continued their studies to the age of 16 in higher primary schools was the same. If language teaching was used for patriotic purposes, naturally the moral and citizenship course was used much more blatantly for this objective.

Nor was there much room for individual teachers to adapt, let alone counteract (as some radical members of the profession tried), this overwhelming national-patriotic tinge to the curriculum. The constraint was due partly to the highly detailed prescription of the government-imposed syllabuses, and partly to the content and style of the textbooks, which not only conveyed the same moralizing communication, but upon which the structure and content of the lessons were so heavily dependent. Quotations convey Hayes's overall impression:

> The texts, in general, are even more national than the official programs. Nearly all the texts seem to be written not merely to acquaint boys and girls with the history, language, and institutions of the country in which they live but also to make them love it with emotional pride and religious zeal. . . .
>
> We are impressed most of all by what French textbooks as a whole do not say. By their omissions they make it difficult for a French youth to be critical of French institutions or conduct, or to know of any services rendered to the world by modern foreign nations. . . . By means of simplification and personification, all party-differences, and local differences are omitted or glossed over.
>
> (Hayes 1930: 55)

Another quotation, this time a passage about the First World War from a history textbook, which, by 1926, was in its twenty-fourth edition:

> Little children, women and old men, mutilated, tortured and enslaved; villages destroyed, cities martyred, Arras and Reims razed by incendiary bombs; all our factories pillaged, our trees cut down, our coal mines rendered useless. . . .
> [And yet] our heroic soldiers got the better of German.
>
> (quoted Hayes 1930: 344)

For 6- to 7-year-olds!

Furthermore, adults too lived in an environment of constant patriotic reminders: from the wireless, the newspapers, the cinema, and – the most emotionally wrenching of all – the multitude of ceremonies, rites and memorials (see Hayes 1930: chs 6, 7, 9).

Citizenship construed as being virtually synonymous with patriotism left little room for instilling into young people – or adults for that matter – a sense of duty to participate practically in communal affairs. Developments after the Second World War throw a fascinating light on this shortcoming in French civic education. Discontent with the operation of the secondary school system led to demands to make the structure less elitist and for the relationships between pupils and teachers to be more relaxed, the latter demand being voiced vehemently by the secondary *lycéens* in Paris during the student tumult in 1968 (see e.g. Archer 1977: 117–18; Ardagh 1982: 481–3). These were declarations of a need for and a will to engage in more democratic school practices, and, in fact, the harsh formality of the *lycées* was relaxed considerably as a result of the 1968 *évènements*.

Yet, on the other hand, the stiff conventions of French education remained quite firmly entrenched in other ways. Schools were instructional workshops, not social communities. After 1968 the Education Minister, Edgar Faure, required all *lycées* to have a *'foyer socio-éducatif'*, an area for pupil-organized activities; but little came of this initiative. Nor had social traditions been conducive to such a change of habits. In the words of a British journalist, writing over a decade later:

> Parents look on school as an academic utility, which should not compete with them as a centre of loyalty; and if a school were to attempt training in leadership or civic responsibility, this would be resented as an intrusion into their own sphere. . . . There is still little attempt in schools to help a child to feel part of a living community or to share in responsibility for it.
>
> (Ardagh 1982: 489)

As a consequence, *c.*1980 French civics lessons were even more abstractly remote from the pupils' lives than in England. A French teacher, in conversation with the British journalist cited above, explained:

> We teach them how Parliament and the communes work, but give them little chance to try it all out in practice. *We* tell them about *préfets: you* make them into prefects. Maybe in Britain your school prefects have too much power: here, children aren't given enough.
>
> (quoted Ardagh 1982: 488)

A thought-provoking comparison, even though the contrast is perhaps somewhat too epigrammatic.

In fact, when this comment was made, movement was already under way in France. An indicative start in changing the style of citizenship education in schools was made in 1977 when the term 'civic instruction' was changed to 'civic education'. Ministerial decrees set forth the requirements for these courses in 1985; and detailed guidance followed. In both primary and secondary schools, from Years 1 to 10, one hour per week was allotted to this subject, taught by teachers of history, geography and French (for the syllabuses, see Starkey 1992: 88–96).

The instructions for primary schools include the injunction to teachers that 'They will use daily incidents and behaviour as educational examples, will insist on cooperative behaviour, will help children to practise equal rights and to participate in the national and international campaigns of charities and humanitarian organizations' (quoted Starkey 1992: 87–8). Similar comments are to be found in the syllabuses for courses in the comprehensive lower secondary schools, the *collèges* (see Starkey 1992: 90, 91–2). Indeed, for 15-year-olds we even read that 'because citizenship education is experienced as much as learned formally, there must be flexibility of timetabling to allow visits, surveys and joint projects with other subjects' (quoted Starkey 1992: 93). Parents and central government have become more supportive of citizenship education interpreted in a wider and freer sense than hitherto, and to these we may add the services of voluntary bodies working in this field. What a transformation from the pictures drawn by Hayes and Ardagh! Notice, for instance, the difference between the French teacher's comparison with civic education in England *c.*1980 and the following comment by an English educationist ten years later:

> It is almost certainly fair to assume that the great majority of French people would put civic education among their priorities for schools. In contrast, it is unlikely that most British people would have a clear idea of what education for citizenship entails.
>
> (Starkey 1992: 100)

However, as we shall see below, perhaps after the lapse of another ten years England has caught up.

England: from radicalism to Empire

Unlike France, England had neither the fervent religious challenge nor the revolutionary spur to egg her on to institute a programme of citizenship education on a par with Ferry's achievement. Nor had she the centralized control of education that enabled a French minister to impose his will on the schools. The comment of the historian Taine that a French minister of education could look at his watch and know which page of which book pupils were studying would have been unthinkable in England. The story of citizenship education in the nineteenth and twentieth centuries is in truth confused and vague compared with her neighbour's. None the less, within this apparent muddle we may discern a pattern of five shaping factors (see Heater 2001). One is this lack of central guidance and in consequence the reliance of teachers on private initiatives. Another has been the connected debate about the relationship between the extension of the franchise, the issue of the maturity of young people to understand political matters and the appropriate kind of civic education. The third factor has centred on the related matters of the different kinds of schooling and examinations for the different social levels of pupils, and how these differences have determined the styles of civic education that have been provided. The fourth factor has been the concern of some teachers to teach about the problems of war and peace. And fifth, Britain's imperial expansion has led, in sequence, to a belief that imperial pride should be inculcated into English youth, and, following substantial immigration from former overseas possessions, to the need to adapt civic education to a multicultural population. Although this and the following section will be constructed chronologically rather than by an analysis of these factors, the reader will be introduced to all but one of them as they arise. The exception is war and peace, which will be covered more conveniently in Chapter 5.

This chapter follows on chronologically from the last, and this division of the material, it must be said, is somewhat arbitrary. We can discern three main ways in which civic educational thinking and practice in England in the first generation of the nineteenth century connects back to the eighteenth century.

First, and forming the backdrop to our scene, is the dreadful neglect of schooling. Through the energetic commitment of the Whig politician Lord Brougham, a parliamentary committee was set up in 1816 'to inquire into the Education of the lower Orders'. It collected a mass of statistics, from which Brougham concluded in 1820 that England was the worst educated country in Europe. School provision had not kept pace with the Industrial Revolution and, in any case, it was widely held that education might well make the lower classes discontented with their standard of living. In 1807 a Tory MP declared that it

> Would be prejudicial to their morals and happiness; it would teach them to despise their lot in life. . . . Instead of teaching them subordination, it would render them fractious and refractory. . . . It would enable them to read seditious pamphlets, vicious books and publications against Christianity.
>
> (quoted Brennan 1981: 32)

There was little chance of civic education being developed for the mass of the English population in these circumstances.

On the other hand, and second, reformers like Brougham were of a very different opinion, continuing the Enlightenment and radical traditions. For example, his great friend James Mill adopted, albeit in less exaggerated form, Helvétius's belief in the immense potential of education in the broadest sense of the term for promoting progress. Yet Mill accepted that the social pressures to conform are almost irresistible. He expressed this view in his article 'On Education', which he wrote in 1818 for the *Encyclopaedia Britannica*. He pursued his argument along the following lines. In the essay he calls political education 'the key-stone of the arch' of education (Cavanagh 1931: 72). However, by 'political education' he did not mean learning in schools, but the moulding of character by the tone and expectations of the 'political machine'. (Mill's use of the word 'machine' may be compared with Benjamin Rush's (see Chapter 2).) He wrote in 1835:

> Among the objects which require the attention of reformers Education stands in one of the highest places; though it is never to be forgotten that it is the operation of the political machine which has the greatest effect in forming the minds of men.
>
> (quoted Burston 1973: 226)

Since he was convinced that the Establishment, to use the present-day term, was inimical to good education, it followed that he believed educational reform was dependent on political reform. He was certainly conscious of the potential of schools for purveying a political education in contradiction of the prevailing political ethos of society. His son, John Stuart, records his father's conviction of the good that would ensue:

> If the whole population were taught to read, if all sorts of opinions were allowed to be addressed to them by word and in writing, and if by means of the suffrage they could nominate a legislature to give effect to the opinions they adopted.
>
> (quoted Silver 1975: 26)

The Mills were of the Philosophical Radical school. Our third connection with the eighteenth century is the continuation of the belief of the political Radicals of the likes of Priestley that schools should contribute to the creation of a more democratic polity. This tradition was carried on most significantly by the Chartists, including their sharing with Godwin the belief that the working class should not allow themselves to be indoctrinated by a national, state-provided system of education. The fundamental requirement of a more widespread education for children was expressed, for example, by the fine Chartist orator, Henry Vincent. One of the main planks of his platform when he sought election to Parliament was that, 'the child of the honest poor man should have its mind trained in everything requisite for the promotion of its spiritual, moral, political and social interests' (quoted Briggs 1960: 167).

The decision to draw up the six-point People's Charter for parliamentary reform was occasioned by working-class disappointment with the First Reform Act of 1832. They had campaigned vigorously for the Bill, yet, when it emerged, it is estimated that only about 20 per cent of adult males had the vote. What is interesting for us is that, during the lifetime of the movement (its main years of activity were 1838 to 1848), education for a civic purpose was a significant subsidiary element in their campaign objectives. One historian has stated that 'It was continually kept in mind by the little group of London agitators and taken up with enthusiasm in many sections. . . . *The Reformer* says that "Popular education will occupy a large share of our attention"' (quoted Silver 1975: 77). The most prominent London Chartist leader was the cabinet-maker William Lovett, though he had not merely a metropolitan significance: he was the prime theorist of the movement.

For his pains in campaigning for the Charter in Birmingham, Lovett was incarcerated in Warwick Prison. While serving his sentence, he, with the help of fellow-Chartist John Collins, wrote a book entitled *Chartism: A New Organization of the People Embracing a Plan for the Education and Improvement of the People Politically and Socially* (see Simon 1972: 229–86). Published initially in 1840, this work is both a blueprint for a school system organized by the people themselves and an argued case on social and political grounds for establishing such a system for the middle and working classes. The stress is on an all-round education – for girls as well as boys – not confined to the 3Rs or even the Classics. Women must be included because, in justice, they are citizens and, as mothers, have a crucial influence over children. The proposed curriculum is very full. In the preparatory schools (junior level) non-timetabled time would be devoted to short lectures or explanations on topics not otherwise covered; the list includes 'the nature of government, laws, rights, and obligations – the production of wealth' (Simon 1972: 280). In the high schools (secondary level) the lower classes would read some subject-matter from cards, including the nature of laws and government, while the higher classes would start history.

Of greater interest are Lovett's views on the relationship between education and politics. He follows Godwin's stand against any effective control by governments over schools. Nor does he mince his words:

Judging from the disposition our own government evince to adopt the *liberty-crushing policy* of their continental neighbours, we have every reason to fear that, were they once entrusted with the education of our children, they would pursue the same course to mould them to their purpose. . . . To talk of right or justice, in many of those countries – to read a liberal newspaper, or book inculcating principles of liberty, is to incur the penalty of banishment or the dungeon.

(Simon 1972: 247)

Lovett thus shared with all radicals and revolutionaries at this time the deeply held fear that the kind of citizenship education he envisioned would be utterly condemned and vetoed in a government-controlled mass education. However, he firmly held to the conviction that merely because the masses were currently untutored in public affairs did not justify denying them the vote. At the very opening of this essay Lovett and Collins alert the reader:

Let it not for a moment be supposed that we agree with those 'educationists' who consider the working classes *'too ignorant for the franchise'*. So far from giving countenance to such unjust and liberty-destroying notions, we think the most effectual means to *enlighten* and *improve* them is to place them on a footing of political equality with other classes.

(Simon 1972: 229)

This assertion suggests that Lovett believed the securing of universal (male) franchise (the first point of the Charter) should precede the creation of universal schooling. Yet he was unhappy about this: ideally, political and educational reform should progress side-by-side because the people

Will still have to acquire the knowledge and cultivate the feelings we have described, before they can enjoy the full fruits and blessings of freedom. . . . It must be evident to every reflecting observer, that *true liberty* cannot be conferred by acts of parliament . . . but must spring up with public enlightenment and public virtue.

(Simon 1972: 235; see also 234)

Politics, Lovett adds for good measure, is a dirty business; only mass education in civic morality can counteract this flaw.

It is sometimes suggested that the Chartists were split into two groups: the Physical Force, advocating (and practising) acts of violence, and the Moral Force, relying on argument; that Feargus O'Connor led the one, Lovett, the other; and that the Physical Force group was contemptuous of education as a means to acquiring the movement's political aims, while the Moral Force Chartists believed in its essential value. A simple pattern can be evolved from this interpretation: the Moral Force Chartists advocated that education for the masses should lay the foundation for and justify enfranchisement, and the Physical Force group advocated the reverse order (see e.g. Vaughan and Archer 1971: 90–2).

However, this collection of antitheses is too elementary; as in any large body there was bound to be dispute over tactics. And the choice of priority – mass education to achieve political reform or political reform to achieve mass education – was a widely discussed conundrum, by no means confined to the Chartist movement, as explained at the start of this chapter. True, the fiery O'Connor, through his organ the *Northern Star*, categorically asserted that no effective social reform, including education, could possibly precede the enfranchisement of the masses, and the Marxist Julian Harney, who was of the same mind, expressed himself no less intemperately:

> The lordly aristocrat, the moneyed vampire and the prostituted priest in a word the enemies of the rights, the liberties, and the happiness of millions, will pretendedly acquiesce in the propriety of educating – of moralizing the people; and it will ever be found that so long as the people's political rights are withheld from them, any system of education which meets with the acquiescence of their foes, will have for its object the perpetuation of the people's slavery.
>
> (quoted Vaughan and Archer 1971: 91)

Nevertheless, as we have seen, Lovett's position was more subtle. He denied that universal suffrage could be justified only after universal education had been achieved; rather, that the vote would be used more intelligently and morally if education were more widespread. Consequently, he argued that political pressure and educational reform should be engaged in double harness. He wrote, 'whilst [the members] are labouring to obtain "the Charter" they shall be instructing themselves, so as to realise all its advantages when obtained' (Simon 1970: 234). He strove to avoid solving the chicken-and-egg question, though the practicability of such a position may be questioned: how could a government-financed, popularly administered school system be devised – against the hostility of the ruling classes, as exponents of Physical Force strenuously argued – within a time-span that could satisfy those hungry for the vote? We may add that it was not only the ruling classes, but also the opinion-makers, who were opposed to the concession of the franchise to an uneducated populace. Thus the editor of the *Manchester Guardian* declared in 1838: 'Let the people have a good education and, with the habits it would induce, the bribe of the intoxicating draught would be less powerful. Till then the elective franchise could not with safety be extended' (quoted Briggs 1960: 39).

It was an argument to be heard again a generation later, with the widening of the franchise by the Second Reform Act. Three years after that piece of legislation, what Godwin, James Mill and the Chartists feared did come to pass: after the tentative arrangements of grants and inspection, the 1870 Forster Education Act brought government intervention fully into the elementary school system. Before that, poor and wealthy alike relied on the private provision of education. In terms of civic education, this consisted of facilities for working-class adults to become politically literate; and the sons of the wealthy to be trained as elite citizens. Before moving on to the 1870s and beyond, therefore, we must look beneath the theorizing that has occupied us so far and outline examples of actual practice of civic education in England in the early to mid-nineteenth century.

Self-help education was organized by working-class people to a remarkable degree from the beginning of the century (e.g. Sunday schools, night schools, mechanics' institutes). Not all of these efforts were related to civic education, yet enough were to effect the raising of political consciousness. Furthermore, insofar as they made inroads on the problem of illiteracy, they enabled an increasing number of the working class (especially men) to become politically aware by reading the substantial flow of newspapers and pamphlets published in the nineteenth century. Both adults and children were catered for one way or another by these developments outside the conventional school system. For instance, the Lancashire Radical, Samuel Bamford, judged that Sunday schools 'had produced many working men of sufficient talent to become readers, writers and speakers in the village meetings for parliamentary reform' as the Napoleonic Wars were drawing to a close (quoted Silver 1975: 67). A remarkable, albeit short-lived, experiment was undertaken in the 1830s by the National Union of the Working Classes (NUWC), in which Lovett was a leading light. This was a federal organization dedicated to parliamentary reform; however, each district was required to arrange a class to discuss and learn about political matters.

Thus Lovett did not simply argue the case for popular education for a civic purpose; he was also instrumental in creating the environment for such studies at the adult level before the Chartist movement came into being. Moreover, largely through his inspiration, the Chartists made an extraordinary contribution to civic education, the like of which has rarely been seen in England. In the short life-span of their organization they created a wide range of opportunities for working men to educate themselves, and, given the essentially political purpose of Chartism, the political content of that education was rarely absent. Harriet Martineau, the political economist and author, who wrote an important history of the period from 1816 to 1846, commented that working men in the Chartist age:

> spent their hard earnings, their spare hours, their sleeping hours, their health, their repose, to promote the education the state did not give. By wonderful efforts, they established schools, institutes, lecture and reading rooms, and circulated knowledge among their class in every way they could think of.
>
> (quoted Silver 1975: 85)

Disparate bodies grew up throughout the century to continue this kind of work, until they were consolidated in the Workers Education Association in 1903.

Insofar as children of the lower classes received a school education before the 1870s, this was provided by two religious bodies. In 1833 the government set up annual grants to these societies; in 1839 a special committee of the Privy Council was created to administer the grant; and inspectors (Her Majesty's Inspectors (HMIs)) were appointed to monitor the work of the schools. The most distinguished of these inspectors, who held the post from 1851 to 1886 (and whom we have already come across), was Matthew Arnold, son of Thomas, the Headmaster of Rugby School, and brother-in-law of W.E. Forster, who introduced the famous Education Bill to establish state 'Board schools'.

What we are concerned with here is the relationship of the grant and inspection systems and civic education. We must, for this purpose, introduce the name of Robert Lowe, who in 1859 became Vice-President of the Council; that is, the government minister in charge of education. In 1862 he introduced a 'Revised Code' to bring into effect what came to be called 'payment by results'. This concentrated the testing of pupils in the '3Rs' and provided funds to the schools according to proficiency in these basic skills. Moral instruction and the teaching of history, for example – fields that had provided a modicum of civic education – were consequently dispensed with for the sake of training the children to satisfy the HMI. Arnold condemned this effect (see Arnold 1962: 215). He also reported that even the teaching of reading was so stilted that little understanding accrued. He cited the evidence of one HMI, especially pertinent in this context:

> Where I found a school *much above par in reading* . . . I tested the *first class*
> by giving them a newspaper and telling them to read aloud some paragraphs;
> but in not more than 20 out of 169 schools did I find a class able to read a
> newspaper at sight.
>
> (quoted Arnold 1962: 223)

So much for the effects on civic education of the English government's early interventions in the administration of elementary schools.

At the other end of the social spectrum the Public schools, originally founded for the education of the poor, were, by the mid-nineteenth century, educating the Victorian equivalents of Elyot's 'governours' three centuries earlier (see Chapter 2), the sons of the privileged classes. (For difficulties faced by teachers in these schools who wished to teach political material in an interesting and challenging way, even in the twentieth century, see Gollancz 1953: chs 4–6.) Accepting again, in our nineteenth-century context, that education for citizenship may be interpreted as the education of the highest stratum of society for public service, then the following quotation provides an exact definition of the Victorian version of that form of schooling. It is taken from the Report of the Public Schools Commission, published in 1864.

> Among the services which they have rendered is undoubtedly to be reckoned
> the maintenance of classical literature as the staple of English education. . . .
> A second, and greater still, is the creation of a system of government and
> discipline for boys . . . which is admitted to have been most important in its
> effects on national character and social life. . . . These schools have been the
> chief nurseries of our statesmen.
>
> (quoted Gaus 1929: 148)

Classics and character-building were the constituents in this magic formula, 'the excellence of which has been universally recognised', according to the Commission. Well, not quite universally. There were certainly worries in England. Let us report these with particular reference to citizenship education. The teaching of Greek and

Latin language and literature to the exclusion of other subjects and without reference to their relevance to the contemporary world deprived the pupil of a rounded education and a frame of mind alert to current public affairs. Flogging by masters and prefects and bullying of younger boys by seniors was scarcely conducive to the egalitarianism and social harmony which should be, by classical standards indeed (*pace* the Spartan example), the hallmarks of the relationship of citizen to citizen. Not all schools were disfigured by unspeakable brutality, however, and by the mid-nineteenth century such habits were in any case in decline. An indicator is that the last of the relatively common serious pupils' rebellions against the inhumanity and injustice of the system – itself perhaps a kind of embryonic citizenship! – broke out at Marlborough in 1851.

One of the most famous Public school headmasters was Thomas Arnold. He held that position at Rugby from 1827 until his death in 1842. It has been said of him that 'All the educational ideals propounded by Arnold are underpinned by the two concepts of Christianity and citizenship' (Vaughan and Archer 1971: 110). By citizenship he meant a sense of social duty, conscientious use of the vote and responsible leadership. Moral education, purveyed through the whole ethos of the school, was the proper and effective method of achieving these ends. First and foremost, moral citizenship must be Christian citizenship; for all the young people, he argued, not only those in the Public schools.

In addition, however, Arnold was utterly convinced of the civic purpose of the Classics – if properly taught, that is. Not only in England, but in France too, for example, heated debates were held concerning the teaching of Classics, in the Public and Grammar schools in England and for the *baccalauréat* qualification in the *lycées* in France. In terms of preparation for citizenship, there were three questions. Was the widely held assumption valid that the study of the Classics by itself was the most apposite training for the country's leaders? Should the Classics be supplemented by 'modern' subjects, notably the sciences? And should the Classics be taught with the explicit and overt purpose of illuminating current issues? Arnold made his position clear: the Classics should remain the bedrock of the curriculum but be taught for contemporary pertinence. He wrote in 1834:

> If knowledge of the past be confined wholly to itself, if, instead of being made to bear upon things around us, it be totally isolated from them, and so disguised by vagueness and misapprehension as to appear incapable of illustrating them, then indeed it becomes little better than laborious trifling.
>
> (quoted Bamford 1960: 69)

Greece and Rome should be yardsticks for measuring the quality of our own modern civilization. For, he added,

> Aristotle and Plato and Thucydides and Cicero and Tacitus . . . are our countrymen and contemporaries, but have the advantage . . . that their observation has been exercised in a field out of reach of common men, and that having thus seen

in a manner with our eyes what we cannot see for ourselves, their conclusions are such as bear on our own circumstances.

(quoted Boyd 1932: 397)

He could hardly have chosen a better selection of ancient authors for conveying the principles of classical republican citizenship.

Arnold thought as well about the most desirable structure for schools in England, arguing in favour of state-controlled elementary schools for the lower classes. This did not come about, as we have seen, until the passage of the Forster Act. As this revolutionary measure came three years after the extension of the franchise by the Second Reform Act, the questions inevitably arise, first, as to whether the Education Act was a response to the Reform Act, and second, how the state influenced civic education in the Board schools.

The 1867 Reform Act increased the electorate to about two and a half million; that is, approximately one in three adult males. Robert Lowe, as we saw at the beginning of this chapter, was horrified, neurotically so in the opinion of some of his colleagues: what now, he asked, remained 'to save the Constitution from the hands of a multitude struggling with want and discontent?' (quoted Briggs 1959: 511). More famously, he is said to have declared, 'We must educate our masters'; his exact words were: 'I believe it will be absolutely necessary that you should prevail upon our future masters to learn their letters' (see Stewart 1986: 101). It has frequently and naturally been argued, therefore, that the enactment of the Second Reform Bill was a crucial factor in the Gladstone administration's introduction of their Elementary Education Bill (see e.g. Frazer 2000: 92). Such an assumption is not, however, entirely secure. The Prime Minister himself had limited interest in the measure (see Morley 1903: 298–9); and it was not until 1869 that the pressure group, the National Education League, led by the young Joseph Chamberlain, was founded. Moreover, one historian has taken the contrary case further and asserted on the issue of the supposed connection that:

> There is not enough evidence to sustain this [argument], either along the lines that, having enfranchised a whole lot of new people, politicians then started worrying about their fitness to vote, or along the lines that newly enfranchised voters began to demand action on education. Apart from anything else the interval of time between Reform Act and Education Act seems too short. Instead, the impulse to action on popular education and the impulse towards parliamentary reform seem to have common roots.
>
> (Sutherland 1971: 27)

On the other hand, Forster, whom Gladstone appointed as Vice-President of the Council in 1868 and who was the passionate driving force behind the Bill, declared:

> Upon this speedy provision depends, I fully believe, the good, the safe working of our constitutional system. To its honour, Parliament has lately decided that

England shall in future be governed by popular government. . . . If we had thus given them political power we must not wait any longer to give them education.

(quoted Brennan 1981: 33)

Acceptance of state responsibility to fill the glaring gaps and repair the inefficiencies in the voluntary elementary systems was certainly long overdue. The Reform Act furnished an added justification.

In what sense, apart from Lowe's dictum to teach the pupil's 'their letters', did the Board schools prepare their charges for citizenship? Taking the period up to 1914, there is evidence of some teaching in this field despite the initial adverse effects of the Revised Code. Compare, for instance, the comment of the sociologist Herbert Spencer in the 1850s with the demand for new textbooks from the 1870s. Spencer wrote: 'Of the knowledge commonly imparted in educational courses, very little is of service for guiding a man in his conduct as a citizen' (Spencer 1929: 34). Two textbooks, published a few decades later, were especially successful. One, entitled *The British Constitution and Government*, was adopted by the London School Board; another, entitled *Citizen Reader*, sold a quarter of a million copies between 1885 and 1916 (see Heater 2001: 106).

Notice the positive action of the metropolitan School Board. Central government (from 1899 the department was called the Board of Education) also issued occasional guidelines for teachers. One declared in 1904 that the purpose of elementary schools was to help pupils 'to fit themselves practically as well as intellectually, for the work of life'. Another, published in 1910, contained two informative references. The first concerns the recommendation that citizenly habits should be gleaned from the 'tone' of the school, what has come to be called 'the hidden curriculum':

The high function of the teacher is to prepare the child for the life of the good citizen, create and foster the aptitude for work . . . and to develop those features of character which are most readily influenced by school life, such as loyalty to comrades, loyalty to institutions, unselfishness and an orderly and disciplined habit of mind.

(quoted Brennan 1981: 34)

The second reference is the inordinate amount of space devoted to temperance, a topic interestingly also included in the French syllabus at this time (see above). In other words, the ordinary citizen should be taught to be a healthy worker.

This attitude raises the question of the content that was considered suitable for civics lessons. In 1882 the historian, educationist and social reformer, Arnold Toynbee, recommended a programme of adult instruction in politics, industry and sanitation (see Toynbee 1969: 226–30). The trouble was that the teaching of this kind of material could be deadly dull, as Toynbee himself admitted. Yet there was little consensus about how to improve civics teaching. The dilemma is encapsulated in comments by H.A.L. Fisher (a historian and President of the Board of Education from 1916 to 1922) in a book entitled *The Common Weal*, which he published in

1924. He included in his list of topics 'the hygiene of food and drinks', yet revealed that textbooks written a generation or more earlier which explained 'the role of different functionaries such as the policeman and the rate-collector' had been damned by Graham Wallas, Professor of Political Science at the London School of Economics, as 'perhaps the most worthless collection of printed pages that have ever occupied the same space on a bookshelf', and Fisher concurred with this judgement (quoted Gaus 1929: 146, 165). He commended history, taught with a civic objective in mind, as the most appropriate vehicle.

There was nothing original about this, of course; teaching to instil civic pride and patriotism has often been placed in the hands of Clio. This was the case from the mid-nineteenth century in English state schools: the Revised Code of 1862 laid down a syllabus of English history down to the death of George III in 1820 for the top three standards. Unfortunately, *c.*1900 only about a quarter of elementary schools taught history, though, in the newly developing secondary schools, teaching merely a small minority of children, the subject was by then obligatory. What is more, a reaction at this time against the subject as boringly teaching 'one damned thing after another' led to the transfiguration of the subject and its texts in schools: history should explain the present. The significance of this alteration has been explained in this way: 'It was only through the new technique that history could achieve its proper purpose, which was the inculcation of patriotism and good citizenship as well as the provision of moral training' (MacKenzie 1984: 177; see also Steele 1976: 1–2).

Eventually, in the twentieth century, this 'inculcation of patriotism' in the state schools became the inculcation of imperialist pride. In 1904 the late Queen Victoria's birthday was declared Empire Day and celebrations, especially in schools, were encouraged. But just as the state schools were laggard in the teaching of history, so they were in generating imperial consciousness; though they made up for this tardiness during the two decades between the two World Wars. An American scholar, visiting England in 1925, quoted in his subsequent book that the London County Council reminded teachers that the day should awaken 'in the minds of the children attending the schools a true sense of the responsibilities attaching to their inheritance as children of the Empire, and the close family tie which exists among all British subjects' (quoted Gaus 1929: 178 n.10).

But we have run ahead of ourselves because, well before this time, the Public schools were infusing their pupils with imperial propaganda. Not that it was thought of as propaganda, but rather the truth about Britain's imperial destiny by virtue of her racial (white), religious (Christian) and skilful (administrative) superiority over her colonial subjects. One author has identified 'four interlocking spheres of socio-political consciousness' in the Public schools, namely selfless service to the state, a sense of racial superiority, imperial chauvinism and uncritical conformity to the values of the group (MacKenzie 1986: 116). Both in the late nineteenth and early twentieth centuries and increasingly during the second half of the twentieth century, some commentators have found the Public school ethos of personal and racial superiority and condescension for the 'lower orders' of society and 'lower races' of humanity utterly offensive. None the less, many a headmaster would have associated himself firmly with the sentiments of the (admittedly extremist) head-master of Harrow, who, in 1895, declared:

> The boys of today are the statesmen and administrators of tomorrow. . . . The pluck, the energy, the perseverance, the good temper, the self-control, the discipline, the cooperation, the *esprit de corps*, which merit success in cricket or football, are the very qualities which win the day in peace and war. The men who possessed these qualities, not sedate and faultless citizens, but men of will, spirit, and chivalry, are the men who conquered Plassey and Quebec.
>
> (quoted MacKenzie 1986: 121)

The picture has a decidedly militaristic hue, reminiscent of the Duke of Wellington's oft-cited epigram that 'The battle of Waterloo was won in the playing fields of Eton'. Unhappily for the Public school image, he was referring not to the building of a tenacious team spirit through organized team games, but through organized fights on those open spaces! (see Barnard 1947: 22).

The vogue for encouraging young people to drill and don uniforms was an extra-ordinary phenomenon of the eighty years from the late 1880s (see e.g. MacKenzie 1984: 228–49, the source for the material below). A multitude of military, Church and secular movements flourished, combining with varying emphases military, imperial, patriotic, moral and civic purposes, though the militaristic threads of the civilian youth movements caused some concern. Nevertheless, the popularity of the organizations spreading across all classes cannot be gainsaid. One authority has estimated that 40 per cent of boys and youths belonged to one or other of these movements in the period 1901 to 1920; another estimate is that from about 1900 to 1980 60 per cent of young people were members of a uniformed movement at some time, this latter proportion having included some thirteen million who had belonged to the Boy Scouts or Girl Guides.

Of all these bodies, the Scouting movement was the most popular (extending, indeed, to many other countries – e.g. western Europe, USA, British dominions and colonies). Founded in 1908 by Robert Baden-Powell, who defined its purpose and principles in his book *Scouting for Boys*, the movement bore the stamp of its founder's experience as a senior army officer in many parts of the Empire. Indeed, the book has been described as 'a strongly imperial, patriotic, and Social Darwinian document, from the outset placing the objective of its subtitle, "A Handbook for Instruction in Good Citizenship", in an imperial and military context' (MacKenzie 1984: 243). And if one feature of citizenship is monitoring the policies advocated by one's elected representatives, then Baden-Powell simplified that task by dividing British MPs into 'politicians', who are to be condemned, and 'statesmen', who are to be lauded. The first category consists of those 'who try to make the Army and Navy smaller, so as to save money' and thus become electorally popular, but, as a consequence, weakening the country and putting the colonies at risk. The second category are the 'better men', who care not for popularity, giving priority to keeping the country safe (see MacKenzie 1984: 244–5). Girls as well as boys were influ-enced in this way by the creation by Baden-Powell and his sister Agnes of the Girl Guides in 1910.

The youth organizations, by interpreting good citizenship as, essentially, healthy living and pride in one's imperial state, reinforced these lessons that were also transmitted in the schools. By the 1960s to 1970s, however, both elements were totally obsolete. Positive social and political understanding, by now needed for democratic participation, could not be taught through classes in 'healthy living'; also the racial conceit lying beneath 'imperial pride' was positively antipathetic to the style of citizenship required in a country with a rising population from Commonwealth lands, who could not, in all justice and morality, be treated as subservient people. What, we must now therefore enquire, were the prevailing attitudes towards and practices of citizenship education during the half-century from the First World War? Then, following that, we must record the generation-long struggle to establish effective citizenship studies and experience in school curricula.

England: slow path to the National Curriculum

The Fourth Reform Act of 1918 gave the vote to all men over 21 and all women over 30. Yet this measure made little difference to official attitudes towards civic education: social conformity and political loyalty remained the order of the day. Even government publications in the 1930s and 1940s reveal just how hesitant – not to say nervous – the Establishment was to embrace whole-heartedly any full and direct education for citizenship in schools. Taking five such documents, we can identify several different approaches.

In 1938 the Spens Report on secondary education was published (named, as has been the habit, after the chairman of the Consultative Committee that drafted it). The Report is careful to distance itself from the direct teaching of citizenship, advocating rather the use of recent history particularly for this purpose for pupils under 16:

> It can be taught so as to induce a balanced attitude which recognises differing points of view and sees the good on both sides. . . . It is in this way, by precept or still more by the breadth of their own sympathies, that teachers can best educate pupils to become citizens of a modern democratic society.
>
> (quoted Brennan 1981: 38–9)

Five years later, the Norwood Report expressed this position more stridently, declaring that:

> Nothing but harm can result, in our opinion, from attempts to interest pupils prematurely in matters which imply the experience of an adult – immediate harm to the pupil from forcing interest, harm in the long run to the purpose in view from his unfavourable reaction.
>
> (quoted Brennan 1981: 39)

Yet, the authors of the report do explicitly include education for citizenship with this dire warning:

we regard it as of vital importance that education should give boys and girls a preparation for their life as citizens. . . . Nevertheless lessons devoted to Public Affairs can suitably be given to older boys and girls [of 15/16+].

(quoted Brennan 1981: 39)

The following year the McNair Report on teacher-training was published. It was guardedly ambivalent on the subject, arguing, on the one hand, the advisability of both colleges and schools having 'some teachers who have made a special study of the social services and of the machinery of government', yet, on the other, and severely constricting the nature of citizenship, announcing that it 'has no foundation apart from habits of moral reflection and a high sense of duty' (Board of Education 1944: 218).

Advice issued by the Ministry of Education immediately after the Second World War was contained in a paragraph in the pamphlet *The New Secondary Education*, published in 1947, and the pamphlet *Citizens Growing Up*, which appeared two years later. The former, casting away nervous caution, advocated the teaching of 'Citizenship' or 'Civics', to cover local and national government, taxation, the judicial system, the Commonwealth and the UN. The latter, a whole official pamphlet, was an unprecedented acknowledgement of the importance of citizenship education, and a form of recognition not to be repeated, as we shall see below, until 1990. *Citizens Growing Up* complains that the schools are doing too little, too inefficiently. Yet the prescription outlined, far from fleshing out the list in the 1947 pamphlet, harks back to Spens and McNair. It declares citizenship to be 'a matter of character' and rejoices in the fact that:

There are forward-looking minds in every section of the teaching profession ready to reinterpret the old and simple virtues of humility, service, restraint and respect for personality. If the schools can encourage qualities of this kind in their pupils, we may fulfil the conditions of a healthy democratic society.

(quoted Crick and Heater 1977: 28)

If forward-looking minds could not conceive of balancing the old and simple virtues with the modern need for an understanding of institutions, law, rights and current issues, how were they to be contrasted with traditionalist minds?

The dilemmas and irresolution surrounding the subject of citizenship education in England *c.*1930–1950 is encapsulated in the history of the Association for Education in Citizenship (AEC). Indeed, the story of the life of this body, so ably told by Guy Whitmarsh (Whitmarsh 1972, 1974), says a great deal about the problems that have dogged citizenship education in many countries in modern times. It is appropriate therefore to bide a while to look at this episode in some depth.

The AEC was founded by Sir Ernest Simon and Mrs Eva Hubback in 1934 'To advance the study of and training in citizenship' (Association for Education in Citizenship 1936: 267); and Oliver Stanley, President of the Board of Education (i.e. minister of Education), expounded its self-appointed task as deriving from a belief 'that direct teaching for citizenship is a subject which can and must be taught more generally'. He continued:

> Few people, I imagine, would disagree with this view, if they were convinced of its feasibility and could envisage clearly the form which such teaching could take. . . .
>   The intangible nature of the subject and the fierce controversies which centre round the whole question make the experienced teacher hesitate to undertake such a formidable task.
>
> (Association for Education in Citizenship 1936: v–vi)

The solution devised by the AEC was to be arrived at along two paths. One was to demonstrate through publications just how citizenship could be acceptably and efficiently taught *directly*. Note that last adverb. They wanted citizenship to be taught:

> As though it were one of the important subjects in the curriculum, and taught by means of a progressive pedagogy. They had in mind a sharp contrast with what they termed the 'indirect' mode of education for citizenship which operated through the traditional subjects of the curriculum, and through the general ethos of the school.
>
> (Whitmarsh 1974: 135)

The second path was to act as a pressure group with the object of persuading politicians and other people of influence that their case was both worthy and practicable. It seemed likely that treading this second path would be a relatively painless journey for three reasons. First, the rise of Communism, fascism and Nazism, with their threats to liberal democracy and their own kinds of efficient citizenship education by indoctrination (see Chapter 4), alerted many in Britain to the urgent need for a form of citizenship education that would construct a bulwark for the country's political values, culture and traditions. Second, the leaders of the AEC succeeded in recruiting an extraordinary galaxy of public and educational figures as vice-presidents and members of its Council (see e.g. Association for Education in Citizenship 1936: 265). Third, a number of these, not to mention Simon himself, were experienced and adept in the arts of exerting pressure on the levers of power.

Yet – and this is the moral of the tale – not even this expertise, deployed in the most propitious circumstances, could overcome official suspicion and inertia. The crucial test came with the drafting of the report of the Spens Committee, whose secretary was Permanent Secretary (the senior civil servant) of the Board of Education. Whitmarsh explains:

> The Permanent Secretary, Sir Maurice Holmes, was against politics in schools which brought with it, in his view, the problems of bias and of teachers as agents of political parties. Like his predecessors, he did not wish the Board's

officials to be exposed to the vagaries of a public debate on the content of education. The Chairman, Spens, made it clear that from his point of view insistence on direct education was disastrous to the Association's hopes of influence.

(Whitmarsh 1974: 137)

We have already seen how the report stressed the indirect approach.

Moreover, it must be said, the AEC's Council itself contained many a covert Trojan horse, including Dr Cyril Norwood (see above). In addition, in order to counter the criticism that the AEC had a pinkish political colouring, in 1938 it recruited overtly Conservative figures, including Stanley Baldwin, recently Prime Minister, as President. The result was that 'The Association had in fact been thoroughly penetrated by the government of the day' (Whitmarsh 1974: 138). Whitmarsh's judgement on Simon's attempt to overcome the conservatism of the civil servants – the effective destroyers of his project – is: 'utterly naïve' (Whitmarsh 1974: 139).

The period between 1962 and 1972 bears sufficient informative resemblances to and reveals enough interesting differences in detail from the two decades of the 1930s and 1940s to warrant a comparison. (For the latter period, see Crick and Heater 1977; Davies *et al*. 1999; Fogelman 1991; Harber 1987.) This exercise may be usefully undertaken under four headings.

First, in each age there was a political justification. In the 1930s and 1940s this was supplied by the challenge of totalitarianism; in the later period the much less dramatic lowering of the age of suffrage from 21 to 18 in 1970 seemed to announce the opening of a new electoral era. The colour supplement of the tabloid *Daily Mirror*

> featured on its front cover the caption, 'Who's afraid of the Virgin Vote?' The accompanying picture showed an 18-year old bikini-clad 'baby' in a pram being fondled by a parliamentary candidate whose leer suggested that he would enjoy depriving her of her political maidenhood.
>
> (Crick and Heater 1977. 70)

It was easy to argue that the schools should be responsible for prudent, if not prophylactic, political education.

Second, debate about civic education took place against a background of hoped-for or planned changes in state education. In the 1930s and 1940s a major concern was to provide secondary-level education for all pupils; in the 1960s it was to raise the school-leaving age to 16 – implemented in 1972 to 1973. The argument that even those approaching the end of their compulsory school years were too immature to cope with citizenship education was now seriously weakened, especially when the youngest of leavers were only two years away from the right to vote.

The third element of comparison comprises the authoritative publications produced by government: the reports and pamphlets of the earlier period cited above, and, in the later period, the documents of the government's Central Advisory

Council and the independent Schools Council, which had central and local government professional membership. The first of these bodies produced the Newsom Report in 1963. Entitled *Half Our Future*, it dealt with the education of pupils aged 13 to 16 of average and less than average ability. It continues the tradition of feeble hesitancy, though it commends the teaching of world affairs to render the individual a truly 'free man' (see Crick and Heater 1977: 30). More positive and clear support for citizenship education was to be derived from the Schools Council Working Papers related to the raising of the school-leaving age. The authors of Working Paper No. 2, published in 1965, for example, were living in an utterly different world of assumptions from those authorities who compiled the publications of the 1930s and 1940s. The later generation spurned the belief that adolescents could not cope with political abstractions. They insisted that ideas such as the rule of law, respect for minority views, freedom of speech and action, trust, responsibility and government by consent must be grasped by members of a civilized society and must be taught (see Crick and Heater 1977: 31; Brennan 1981: 43).

By the time the school-leaving age had been raised, the Politics Association had been founded, our fourth comparison, with the AEC. The Politics Association was the outcome of the combined concern and initiative of an educationist and the interest and drive of an academic, Professor Bernard Crick, whose name will recur. The plan was to create a professional association in order to raise the status and efficiency of teaching politics at the non-academic level. It came into existence in 1969 and succeeded in raising consciousness of the need for widespread and improved political literacy. One of its important offshoots was a research project organized by Crick, leading to the publication of *Political Education and Political Literacy* (Crick and Porter 1978). However, since it was able to pull even less weight than the AEC, it could not achieve a breakthrough in consolidating citizenship education in schools. Its work contracted to supporting the teaching of politics at the 16- to 18-year level, worthy in itself, but totally at odds with the objectives of its founders (see Crick and Heater 1977: 63–6; Brennan 1981: 45–8, 53–7).

However – and to move on chronologically – the climate of official opinion was changing gradually; there was less overt hostility to the idea of political education, as long as it was not mediated through peace studies and was focused on cultivating conscientious citizens. One particular issue brought the matter to the fore in the 1980s, namely the problems which beset the country as a multicultural society (see e.g. Lister 1991; for the universal matter of education for a multicultural society, see Chapter 5 (below)). Inner-city riots, notably in Brixton, south London, in 1981, revealed that the country had not yet achieved a sense of cohesive citizenship suited to its post-imperial inheritance. The question had an educational dimension, and a committee under the chairmanship of Lord Swann, appointed to consider this, significantly entitled its report *Education for All*. It stated quite firmly that 'all schools and all teachers have a professional responsibility to prepare their pupils for life in a pluralist society' (DES 1985: 560). Implementation of this report's recommendations has not, however, been easy. Some ethnic minority commentators called for positive anti-racist teaching to counteract prejudice, and by the turn of the century an argument was under way concerning the preferred policy regarding school populations. The number of single-faith schools was increasing, consolidating the cultural differences between, for instance, Church of England, Roman Catholic, Jewish and Muslim children; that is, strengthening the policy of pluralism. Fears that these schools could exacerbate inter-communal tension, as the unhappy history of Northern Ireland has shown, led to vocal support for multi-faith schools.

To return to the mainstream debate about citizenship education in general, interest widened in the late 1980s. Since the political Right had found it more difficult than the Left to trust schools with citizenship education, the sudden adoption of the Conservatives in 1988 of the concept of 'active citizenship' by which to re-brand the Party was an important landmark. Although initially not related to education, it was difficult to deny that responsible citizenship required some foundation of knowledge, understanding and moral commitment, best learned before the age of 18. True, the Party's fad did not last, but the idea of citizenship had been revived. In the same year that the Conservative Party launched their 'active citizenship' project, the Speaker of the House of Commons set up a Commission on Citizenship to consider 'how best to encourage, develop and recognize Active Citizenship'.

The Commission's report included recommendations for the teaching of citizenship in schools (Commission on Citizenship 1990: ix, 101–5). These were sent to the National Curriculum Council (NCC), a body established to help organize for the first time in English history, and at variance with jealously held tradition, a curriculum to be common to all state schools. The requirement to create a National Curriculum was contained in the Education Reform Act of 1988. Moreover, when the outline was produced in 1989, provision was made for the inclusion of citizenship, albeit in a subsidiary form. It was to take another thirteen years before it was to become a mandatory subject at secondary level, and the goal of the AEC was attained. How was this achieved, against what odds and in what form?

The Labour Party came to power in 1997. The Secretary of State for Education and Employment was David Blunkett, who had been a member of the Speaker's Commission and, disappointed by that body, was determined to establish the subject in a strong position in schools. Accordingly, as a matter of priority, he set up an Advisory Group on Citizenship with the following terms of reference:

> To provide advice on effective education for citizenship in schools – to include the nature and practices of participation in democracy; the duties, responsibilities and rights of individuals as citizens; and the value to individuals and society of community activity.
>
> (quoted Advisory Group on Citizenship 1998: 4)

As Chairman of the Group, Blunkett chose a close acquaintance and an academic with an equally passionate conviction, namely Professor Bernard Crick, whose introduction to school-level work has already been noted (see above; Crick 2000, 2002). In some ways the climate was propitious for the success of this initiative (see e.g. Davies *et al.* 1999: 16, 22–3; Crick 2002: 492–5, 503–4 n.15). As we have seen, the Conservative Party had already trailed the concept of 'active citizenship', and there was widespread concern among the populace about crime, and among the politicians, academics and the news media about low voter turn-out. Moreover, the assumption, dating back to Aristotle (see Chapter 1), that young people were incapable of taking an interest in or even comprehending public issues, was being undermined by research and the work of teachers, particularly those assisted by the Citizenship Foundation. This voluntary body was founded in 1989 by Andrew Phillips, who later became a Liberal Democrat peer.

Even so, without the formidable leadership of Blunkett and Crick the goal could not have been reached, for there were still challenging obstacles (see e.g. Kerr 1999: 204–25). Political doubts concerning the prudence of citizenship education lingered in some quarters. Pedagogically, there was little in the way of a foundation to build upon: what was happening in this field was sketchy in content and patchy in the number of schools keen enough to take the task seriously, limitations which were exacerbated by the paucity of thoroughly trained teachers. Indeed, a teaching force, demoralized and overburdened by the unremitting increase in demanded form-filling and examining, might well be daunted by this addition to their workload. Furthermore, citizenship education had to be defined in such a manner as to be academically and educationally respectable while at the same time capable of practical application, especially in the light of the above obstacles.

The Advisory Group fused audacity with pragmatism. Boldness comes early on in the report:

> We aim at no less than a change in the political culture of this country both nationally and locally: for people to think of themselves as active citizens, willing, able and equipped to have an influence in public life and with the critical capacities to weigh evidence before speaking and acting; to build on and to extend radically to young people the best in existing traditions of community and public service, and to make them individually confident in finding new forms of involvement and action among themselves.
>
> (Advisory Group on Citizenship 1998: 1.5)

Pragmatism is encapsulated in Crick's image of the 'strong bare bones' (Crick 2000: 117) of what is laid down for schools to teach: not detailed, prescriptive syllabuses. This skeletal structure for 11- to 16-year-olds is built upon a tripartite framework of moral and social responsibility, community involvement and political literacy; or, expressed somewhat differently, knowledge and understanding about becoming informed citizens, developing skills of enquiry and communication, and learning skills of participation and responsible action. So much more than rote learning about the British Constitution. Moreover, as Crick has written, the implications of including the phrases 'community activity' and 'participation in democracy' 'broadened the concept from political education into citizenship education' (Crick 2002: 497).

From this framework fifteen or sixteen specified topics and learning approaches to them emanate. The topics cover legal, political, religious, social and economic institutions and systems, ranging across the local, national and global dimensions (see DfEE/QCA 1999). Although citizenship is accepted as a subject for teaching at the age-groups below 11 and above 16, this core 11 to 16 group is crucial because, since 2002, the subject has been legally mandatory for them. As Crick notes: 'England (still not Scotland, Wales or Northern Ireland) was the last country in Europe (indeed in the USA and the old Commonwealth too) not to have Citizenship as a subject in a national curriculum' (Crick 2002: 488). He brought the country into line with others – in some respects in advance of the USA.

United States: social complexity and pedagogical uncertainty

The desired pattern for citizenship education that the Founding Fathers left as their legacy was in essence quite simple: children should be brought up with the civic morality of good republicans as a national objective, taught in schools administered at the local and state levels. During the nineteenth century this simple model was overlaid and put under severe strain by the growing pressures of complex social changes. As a consequence, the schools' task of civic education became correspondingly more difficult than the Founders could possibly have envisaged. Our task is, assuredly, not to investigate the social complications in detail, for to do so would overshadow our purpose of surveying what was recommended and undertaken in practice in the schools. None the less, an outline of this background is called for in order to understand the environment in which the teachers had to prepare their charges for the role of citizen (for a fuller analysis see Butts 1989: 91–182). And so, in this section, we shall outline these contextual factors and show how, during the nineteenth century, the work of the schools fluctuated in response; until, at the beginning of the twentieth century, a curricular structure of social studies emerged, taking us into a separate section.

The causes of the phenomenon of growing social complexity were fourfold. They were: industrialization, immigration, democratization and expansion. Together, they transformed the character of the United States, and each affected the approach to civic education.

Economic progress, particularly the Industrial Revolution in the north, unavoidably meant the concentration of the labour force in towns – urbanization, a process starting in the late eighteenth century and accelerating especially in the 1830s. In terms of citizenship education this development produced a paradox: a greater need for this teaching in schools and a reduction in their chances of providing it. The assistance of the schools was felt to be needed for two reasons. The deracination of this new industrial proletariat deprived them of the sense of community provided by rural societies; and an impoverished urban working class, lacking any sense of social bonding, was a potentially destabilizing force. Yet the ability of the schools to compensate for these civically negative trends was weakened in two ways. Partly due to child labour, the percentage of children attending school declined in the early years of the century: of the labour force in the New England mills, half were children. Moreover, the expansion of employment opportunities in various sectors of the urban economy led to demands for vocational education at the expense of any other subjects beyond the 3Rs.

The second cause of social complexity was immigration. Its scale and the 'melting-pot' solution are well known, but the crude numbers should be broken down both chronologically and geographically. Freeman Butts offers a vivid chronological comparison: an additional nine million persons were added to the population from the half-century 1826 to 1876 compared to 27 million during the same time-span, 1876 to 1926 (see Butts 1989: 106); though, of course, the number of immigrants as a *proportion* of the total population is a less startling difference. Geographical analyses reveal a shift from about 1880 to an increasing proportion from southern and eastern compared with northern and western Europe (see e.g. Marquette and Mineshima 2002: 542). The significance of this shift in countries of origin for citizenship education was expressed by the leading educationist Ellwood Cubberley in 1907 in these words:

> These southern and eastern Europeans are of a very different type from northern European who preceded them. Illiterate, docile, lacking in self-reliance and initiative, and not possessing the Anglo-Teutonic conceptions of law, order, and government, their coming has served to dilute tremendously our national stock, and to corrupt our civic life. Our task is . . . to implant in their children, so far as it can be done, the Anglo-Saxon conception of righteousness, law and order, and popular government, and to awaken in them a reverence for our democratic institutions and for those things in our national life which we as a people hold to be of abiding worth.
>
> (quoted Macedo 2000: 91)

Italians and Poles, for instance, added to the earlier Irish and southern German immigrants, increased the numbers of Roman Catholics, and as early as the mid-century the presence of significant numbers of Catholics was a serious problem. During the generation between about 1830 and 1860 the northern states of the union created what they called 'common schools'. Their purpose was to give all children of whatever origin a basic education to form them into good Americans, which meant civically moral, patriotic, English-speaking Protestants (see Kaestle 1983: *passim*). This policy was naturally unacceptable to Catholics. What was to be done? Compromise over the religious tone of the schools proved impossible and the use of public monies for segregated Catholic schools turned to violent controversy – literally so in riots in the 1840s. In this respect the profoundly held belief that common schools would be the quintessential producers of a homogeneous citizenry had to be abandoned. (For a discussion of the problem of multiculturalism see below, Chapter 5. In the United States the dilemma as to whether all citizens should be taught in schools to be Anglophone persisted down to the late twentieth century.)

The reader will have noticed Cubberley's reference to democratic institutions in his list of schools' tasks in absorbing immigrants. This leads us to our third issue of complexity. Was the United States to become a truly democratic polity? The trend during the first half of the century was clear. By 1856 all of the original thirteen states had abolished property qualifications for the suffrage; in the Presidential election of 1840 seven times as many citizens voted as in 1824. The abolition of property qualification was a critical change of circumstance for citizenship education. If the traditional ownership of property as an index of fitness for full citizen rights was discarded, what else could take its place? It could surely only be education. However, the principle that the process of democratization should be based on a system of universal education raised complicating questions. Should it be free and compulsory? Could the system cope with mass immigration? And how should the politically disadvantaged be treated in terms of school provision and curricular content – women, blacks, Mexicans, Chinese and native Americans?

Our final point in this background survey is a relatively minor one. This was the effect of self-conscious, nationalistically inspired territorial expansion, from the doctrine of Manifest Destiny of the mid-century onward. Increasingly and particularly by the end of the century, the schools were being required to reflect this atmosphere by the teaching and expression of intense patriotism.

In order to portray the somewhat confusing course of citizenship education in the United States in the nineteenth century we shall divide the matter into three topics: the expression of attitudes and the publication of recommendations; the relevant subjects taught in schools; and the methods adopted, including the kinds of textbook available to the teachers. By 'attitudes' we mean the moods of the public at large and of those forming opinions on education concerning the desirability of schools discharging a responsibility for the forming of citizens. By 'the publication of recommendations' we mean individuals and groups making available thoughts and suggestions on the issue.

After the enthusiasm of the revolutionary period there followed a period of apathy, even hostility, towards the concept that free, public schooling was the route for achieving a citizenry committed to the Republic. So many separate interests wished to supply private schooling that it was impossible for the ideal of the common school to be realized. By the 1830s, however, educational reformers were making a breakthrough. In the words of an authority on the common school system:

> As the pace of social change quickened in the American North in the 1830s, so did educators' advocacy of free common schooling dedicated to moral education and good citizenship. It was an era of social reform, and common-school reformers were in the forefront.
>
> (Kaestle 1983: 75)

This brief explanation, however, requires several comments for elucidation. First, the educational reformers would have been unable to make such progress in creating these schools with a civic purpose had it not been for the expansion at this time of public support for the enterprise. Second, although, unsurprisingly, the common schools at first taught a very basic curriculum – the civic element being introduced by adjuration rather than through erudition – step by step and 'by popular demand', subjects germane to citizenship were added. Consequently,

> One of the most characteristic notes of educational activity between 1820 and 1860 was for broader coverage. Spelling, geography, history, government,

constitutional law, and a number of other subjects were demanded as 'preparation for citizenship'.

(Butts and Cremin 1953: 213)

Third, outside the schools, but obviously having an influence on young as well
as old, Protestant sects used their services, meetings and camps to propagate the
democratic ideal. In 1839 a Frenchman described American camp meetings as
'festivals of democracy' (see Macedo 2000: 56). Yet, and fourth, all was not positive
and supportive of the aim of education for citizenship in the 1830s. American
industrialization had its hazards. Periodic collapses led to economic crises, which
led to 'Panics'. The Panic of 1837 was severe, and the working-class suffering was
exacerbated by the atrocious weather in the winter of 1837 to 1838. Even basic
education for their children, let alone education for citizenship, was a luxury;
thoughts on and support for this idea were reduced to a middle-class exercise (see
e.g. Smith 1997: 217).

By the 1840s and 1850s common schools were sufficiently firmly established
for the debate on citizenship education to centre on their contribution. And the
fundamental principles were widely accepted that young people should be brought
up to be patriots and be prepared for democracy, despite the limited franchise, so
long as teachers kept to exposition of the Constitution and eschewed controversial
issues. Yet attempts at shaping the common school system in order to improve its
chances of achieving these aims ran up against resistance in two forms.

One was the sensitive issue of how common, common schools should be.
As already indicated, Roman Catholics, especially, wanted their own schools,
and argued in favour of the voluntary provision of heterogeneous institutions and
against state-provided homogeneity. Another aspect of this division in public
opinion (in the north; there could be no debate in the south, of course) was
whether blacks should be taught in the same schools as whites. Opposition to
integration could be found among both blacks and whites. Yet the argument in
favour of integration was compelling. It was presented particularly cogently by
Richard Fletcher, the City Attorney of Salem in Massachusetts, in 1844, and was,
moreover, accepted by the School Committee. His case was that the essence of the
school system was equality and schools for blacks were inferior to those available
to whites; blacks paid taxes and had the vote as well as whites; and taxes could be
used lawfully only for public schools, whereas segregated schools were not public
schools (see Kaestle 1983: 177). Some towns in Massachusetts did introduce
integration in the 1840s and 1850s. Indeed, segregation was made illegal in the
state in 1855, despite a contrary court ruling in 1849 in the case of *Roberts v. Boston*.
This judgment by the Massachusetts Supreme Court set down the principle of
'separate but equal' school provision that dogged the administration of school places
for over a century and to which we shall return below. Needless to say, throughout
the country as a whole, neither religious nor racial integration was widely accepted
in practice; consequently, citizenship education in the sense of equal and communal
experiences was achieved only very partially, leaving the issue as a perennial
problem.

The other controversial matter in the mid-nineteenth century related to the curriculum. The plentiful movements in favour of and proposals for the expansion of the number of subjects taught, and therefore pressure to enrich the pupils' education in both general and civic terms, were opposed on the grounds of uselessness. All that children needed was instruction in – to use the vernacular phrase – 'the Bible and figgers' (see Butts and Cremin 1953: 218).

Partly responding to these debates and partly provoking them was a body of remarkable people campaigning for reform, improvement and progress, sometimes dubbed the 'crusaders' for the common school. Pre-eminent among these, indeed the most distinguished American educational thinker and reformer in the nineteenth century, was Horace Mann.

Mann was Secretary of the State Board of Education of the Commonwealth of Massachusetts from 1837 to 1849; in that capacity he wrote famous reports and edited the *Common School Journal*. Furthermore, for us he is a truly key figure due to the conviction with which he expounded the case for what he bluntly called 'political education'. From his extensive knowledge of both American and European school systems and his understanding of the American political structure and social scene, Mann shaped a social and pedagogical theory which had coherence and relevance for his time. He espoused liberal teaching methods for the purpose of protecting the social fabric against violent dissension, while optimistically believing in the value of political democracy and the vital role of education in preparing for and underpinning that political ideal. It has been well said that 'his philosophy . . . did much to make American education an agency of liberal democracy' (Welter 1962: 98).

Mann's approach to education for citizenship included the realization that, to use modern terminology, both affective and cognitive learning were essential – both development of civic morality and acquisition of knowledge of the Constitution. He also held that it was the government's responsibility to ensure that this learning could take place. In his own words:

> I believe in . . . the duty of every government to see that the means of education are provided for all. . . . Under a republican government, it seems clear that the minimum of . . . this education can never be less than such as is sufficient to qualify each citizen for the civil and social duties he will be called upon to discharge.
>
> (quoted Butts 1989: 104–5)

The religious agitation occasioned by Irish and German Catholic immigrants in New England in the 1830s and 1840s over the issue of public versus private schooling and the social dislocation of industrialization added point and urgency to his adamantine support of common schools and the civic training they could undertake. And he expressed the imperative political need for the arrangement with some eloquence:

> Never will wisdom preside in the halls of legislation and its profound utterances be recorded on the pages of the statute book, until Common Schools . . . shall

create a more far-seeing intelligence and a purer morality than has ever existed among communities of men.

(quoted Marquette and Mineshima 2002: 541)

What, then, did Mann have to say about education for civic morality? We may start by explaining his fundamental belief that the atmosphere in the classroom must be conducive to this undertaking. Just as the political morality of a despotism differs from the political morality of a republic, so young people cannot be prepared for republican morality in a classroom ruled by a tyrannical pedagogue. 'He who has been a serf until the day before he is twenty-one years of age,' Mann declared, 'cannot be an independent citizen the day after' (quoted Welter 1962: 98). Concord, not tension, should reign in the classroom, a mood that could be inspired by music, and singing in particular. With interesting echoes of Aristotle (see Chapter 1), Mann wrote of its 'harmonizing, pacificating tendency', promoting 'peace, hope, affection, generosity, charity, and devotion' (quoted Kaestle 1983: 96).

Nor must sounds of the social and political strife outside the walls of the school be allowed to be heard in the classrooms. Therefore, there should be no presentation of contentious issues that might lead to partisan teaching; not necessarily because it would be pedagogically inadvisable, but because it would put the whole common school system at risk, an outcome he could not bear to contemplate. Referring to the agitation of these years, Mann asks with evident emotion:

> Who shall moderate the fury of these conflicting elements, when they rage against each other; and who shall save the dearest interests of the children from being consumed in the fierce combustion? If parents find that their children are indoctrinated into what they call political heresies, will they not withdraw them from the school; and, if they withdraw them from the school, will they not resist all appropriations to support a school from which they derive no benefit?

(quoted Butts 1988: 53)

No taxation without neutral education.

Mann's solution was to define political education as constitutional study, a sort of civic education lowest common denominator. Between the two poles of schools excluding political education altogether and becoming 'theatres of party politics', he believed, there was, to use a different metaphor, a *via media*, namely what 'all sensible and judicious men, all patriots, and all genuine republicans, must approve' (quoted Butts 1989: 121). The simple approach was that 'the constitution of the United States, and of our own State, should be made a study of our Public Schools'. He especially emphasized that:

> The duty of every citizen, in a government of laws, to appeal to the courts for redress, in all cases of alleged wrong, instead of undertaking to vindicate his own rights by his own arm; and, in a government where the people are the acknowledged sources of power, the duty of changing laws and rulers by an

appeal to the ballot, and not by rebellion, should be taught to all the children until they are fully understood.

(quoted Butts 1988: 52–3)

There is palpable fear of popular upheaval here. The Constitution provides the superior way, to use Mann's word, the 'pacificating' way. Bringing the younger generation to appreciate this truth was the pre-eminent responsibility of the common schools.

An influential writer on teacher-training in the 1830s, J. Orville Taylor, held the common schools in the highest esteem, without which a free citizenship would have been impossible. He declared: 'Within their walls, on this day, are educating four millions of sovereigns, each one to be a citizen king' (quoted Welter 1962: 43). High-flown rhetoric in those dizzy days of exciting reform and hope.

Twenty-two years after Taylor wrote these words the first shots were fired in the Civil War. During those two decades it became increasingly clear that the integrating ambition of the common school system was not coming up to the expectations of the likes of Mann and Taylor. In the north, black and white children became increasingly segregated, in some states the practice being sanctioned by law, in others it just happened, an issue to which we shall return both in this section and the next. Meanwhile, in the south, the common school programme barely got under way even for whites. The racial and geographical divides that lay at the roots of the civil conflict were already evident in the educational setting.

The Civil War, a horrendous and traumatic conflict from 1861 to 1865, shook the United States out of any complacency it had that the formulae of *e pluribus unum*, virtuous civic republican citizenship and the civically harmonizing effects of common schools would easily mould the country into a state of modern citizens. Nevertheless, even during the war, and certainly in the handful of years of reform and rehabilitation known as Reconstruction afterwards, trust in the civically beneficent power of education persisted. In the words of one American scholar, 'The nationalistic liberal republicanism that reigned during the war and early Reconstruction fuelled remarkable educational progress throughout the nation' (Smith 1997: 320). A few figures corroborate this verbal picture of an educational surge. From 1860 to 1870 public expenditure on education rose from $20 million to £62 million p.a. Although the effects were slower to come through in the south than the north because of the wartime devastation and resistance to reform, still the number of children enrolled in the schools of South Carolina, for example, rose markedly between 1869 and 1876 from 12 to 50 per cent for whites and 8 to 41 per cent for blacks (see Smith 1997: 321, 322).

In the light of the fact that the issue of the emancipation of slaves was one of the causes of the Civil War and that their freedom was proclaimed by Lincoln in 1862, it was inevitable that the question of the racial segregation of schools should have been revived after the war. Just as inevitable were the different reactions of the north and south: northern states gradually banned segregation; southern states rapidly passed the Black Codes banning the enforcement of segregation. The American sociologist William Graham Sumner, reflecting Richard Fletcher's arguments of a generation earlier (see above), wrote in 1872 against segregation:

> How impossible it is for a separate school to be equivalent of the common
> school. . . . Such a school is not republican in character. . . . How precious the
> example which teaches that all are equal in rights. But this can be only where
> all co-mingle in the common schools as in common citizenship.
>
> (quoted Butts 1989: 110)

Women, too, benefited, though more as the result of gradual progress. As early as
1819 the renowned educationist Emma Willard had started to campaign for better
women's educational opportunities, especially so that they might enter the teaching
profession (see Pangle and Pangle 1993: 104). As a consequence, by the *post-bellum*
period females in schools, both pupils and teachers, more than equalled males in
number. In parallel with this development, campaigning for female suffrage bore
its first fruits in 1869 when Wyoming territory conceded this civic right.

How far was this growth of educational activity directed consciously to the
improved cultivation of citizens? In short, it was never far from the minds
of politicians and educationists. To give two illustrations. At the beginning of the
Civil War, in 1862, the Superintendent of Public Instruction in Illinois explained
the purpose of publicly provided schools thus: 'The chief end is to make
GOOD CITIZENS. Not to make precocious scholars . . . not to impart the secret of
acquiring wealth . . . not to qualify directly for professional success . . . but simply
to make good citizens' (quoted Kaestle 1983: 98). Five years later, after lengthy
campaigning and with much misgiving in many quarters, a federal Department
of Education was created. In 1874 John Eaton, the second occupant of the post of
Commissioner of the Department, circulated a *Statement of the Theory of Education
in the United States of America*, compiled under his auspices by leading educational
authorities. The thrust of the document was that all American children should attend
school, not so much, as was so often held, to improve the country's productive
industry, but for political purpose. The message was charged with an almost
hysterical urgency, as this summary indicates: 'unless public schools "elevated and
harmonized" the citizenry – especially poor, ignorant blacks and whites in the South,
as well as immigrants – the "existence of a republic" would be an "impossibility"'
(Smith 1997: 322).

Eaton had several causes for this pessimism, for the momentum of reform
soon slowed. In 1869, only two years after its establishment, the Department had
its budget cut and was subordinated to an advisory bureau of the Department of
the Interior; in the north, state education budgets were also diminished; and in the
south by the late 1870s prejudice against both education and blacks reduced both
white and black school attendance. In addition, to proceed to the end of the century,
the issue of 'separate but equal' schools raised its head again in the judgment
of Justice Brown in the *Plessey v. Ferguson* case in 1896. This was not about
schools, but about Brown's comments concerning his belief in natural racial distinc-
tiveness consigning blacks to what was later termed 'second-class citizenship' and
consequently strengthening the position of the segregationists.

Even so, the turn of the century witnessed a reformist revival in the shape of
Progressivism, an era variously dated by historians, but approximately the decade

preceding the start of the First World War. The new mood affected education as much as any other sphere of American life. In the words of one modern authority, 'these were extraordinarily important years in the history of American civic education. Nothing was a more central concern for many progressives' (Smith 1997: 463). The new phase of educational thinking was epitomized by the work of William Torrey Harris, who, after long service as a city School Superintendent, was federal Commissioner of Education from 1889 to 1906. Like Horace Mann, with whose ideas and work Harris's is often compared, his fundamental intention was to bolster American democracy and stability by means of civic education. To cite a British scholar's assessment of his importance:

> The potential reasons Harris advanced to support this position [i.e. for a humane, liberal, as opposed to vocational education] are both interesting and significant. He gave them in a period of increasing industrial unrest when bitter labour strikes were becoming frequent. The broader education was necessary to help the child in his behaviour to others; to prepare him as a citizen with a vote; and to give him the ability to read so as to withstand 'wild schemes of agitation that attack radically all the institutions of civilization'.
>
> (Holmes 1956: 60–1)

It is clear from Harris's concerns when he assumed his post as Commissioner that the goals envisioned by Mann had yet to be achieved. However, two institutional developments show that some progress was being made by the end of the century in areas outside Mann's vision. One was the growth of secondary education for pupils of more mature years than the original common schools catered for and who were perhaps therefore more capable of comprehending the adult status of citizenship. Starting around 1870, by 1900 some fifteen million young people were pursuing the K-8 (kindergarten to grade 8) course.

The other institutional development was the improved professional status and organization of teachers. In 1857 the National Teachers' Association (NTA) was founded. Through amalgamation with other bodies, it was renamed the National Education Association (NEA) in 1870; had become firmly established by 1892, when it appointed its Committee of Ten; and in 1906 boasted a membership of 627,836 (see Callahan 1964: 424–5).

The NEA, through its meetings and the work of its Committee of Ten, became an influential force in the field of curriculum development. However, its position on civic education was somewhat ambivalent. Voices were heard in the 1880s and 1890s urging the NEA to commit itself to education for citizenship. One member proclaimed: 'We take the position, here and now, that the true aim of the public school must be to teach and guide, and if need be compel, its youth to be law-respecting and law-abiding citizens' (quoted Welter 1962: 158). Furthermore, in 1895 the national convention recommended the observance of patriotic ceremonies (of which, more below). Yet in 1893 the report of the Committee of Ten on the secondary school curriculum stressed the importance of raising academic standards, thus teaching history, for example, as a scholarly discipline, not as a means of cultivating good citizenship (an issue to which we shall return below). Nevertheless, by a later act of pedagogical change of mind, in the second decade of the twentieth century the NEA and its Committee of Ten helped to launch the Social Studies programme, in which was firmly encased the objective of citizenship education, and which became standard throughout the country for the rest of the century. But that turning point takes us into the next section of this chapter.

We must now retrace our steps and indicate the subjects that were used as a means of civic education during the nineteenth century. Three subject areas supplied the material for preparing young people for citizenship: moral/religious instruction, history and civics.

Throughout the century the matter of moral instruction as a mode of citizenship education presented its advocates with a severe dilemma, which was particularly troublesome in the middle decades. The problem arose in the following manner. The whole ethos of the American state, accepted by all who influentially thought about the question, and consolidated by colonial and revolutionary traditions, existed as an ethical chain that must be preserved. This chain comprised three links. The first was the political doctrine of republican citizenship, the expectation of loyal commitment and participation. The second was the need for a strong moral component in pupils' education in order to prepare them for this role. The third link was the belief that moral education was inconceivable without a firm religious basis. So far, so obvious, when one considers the unquestioned beliefs of the time. However – and here arises the dilemma – how could moral lessons be taught in a manner virtually indistinguishable from religious education in a land of so many and diverse Christian sects?

We have already seen how Horace Mann tried to circumvent the difficulty by suggesting a non-sectarian form of Christian education in the common schools. The idea could be taken further, to include Jews also. All the monolithic religions believe in certain essential truths, which, in theory, could be taught to all children without offending any parents (see e.g. Macedo 2000: 57–8).

Even so, the numerous Catholics in particular could not be placated. Consequently, as the century wore on, there was nothing for it but to whittle down the religious content and focus moral education more directly on its secular civic purpose. Yet, although the Bible was kept as a key basic 'textbook', this adaptation assuredly weakened the third essential link in the chain. On the other hand, if, because of its divisiveness, the religious link was itself weakening rather than strengthening the process of civic education, then the chain of reasoning had perhaps become obsolete. Or, to put it another way, the religious and civic functions of moral education were becoming recognized as separate priorities. For it was possible to define the religious input to moral education both in non-political and political terms. Take these two quotations from the 1870s. Senator Edmonds defined religious education as teaching, besides theological tenets, 'the duty of man to man, the obligation to truth and personal purity, charity, virtue, intelligence, cleanliness, honor' (quoted Macedo 2000: 65). While James P. Wickersham, Superintendent of the Common Schools of Pennsylvania, asserted that 'religion as an element [in education] is more necessary in a republic than under any other form of government; for without it self-government is impossible' (quoted Marquette and Mineshima

2002: 540). Indeed, for all the dilution of the theologically religious content, the civic value of religious principles was still being upheld at the end of the century (see e.g. Macedo 2000: 74). Meanwhile, secular forms of citizenship were also available through history, teaching about the Constitution and, at the beginning of the twentieth century, the start of more imaginative civics courses.

History was a staple pedagogical diet for citizenship for much of the nineteenth century. The subject was taught as stories of great deeds: of the early immigrants, the War of Independence, founding the Republic, western expansion, for instance – tales, not explanation; narrative, not analysis; to inflame patriotism, not to train objective understanding. Insofar as citizenship includes patriotism, this was citizenship education; insofar as citizenship involves use of a cultivated faculty of critical judgement, it was not. This debasement of history as a discipline started to worry academic historians by the end of the century, especially after the creation of their professional body, the American Historical Association (AHA) in 1884. Therefore professional historians contributed to the work of the NEA (see above) by membership of the Committee of Ten's sub-group on history, civil government and political economy. In these subject-areas, for grades 7 to 12 they rather obviously advised that the bulk of the time should be spent on history. Then, in 1899 and 1909 the AHA itself set up committees to make recommendations on the teaching of the subject at secondary and elementary levels respectively. Also in 1909 they founded a *History Teachers Magazine*. Not surprisingly the scholars started to renovate the teaching of their discipline in school, encouraging the use of primary sources, the critical appraisal of evidence and building an authentic historical understanding from such learning experiences. No synthetic patriotism, no use of history for conscious civic education, but history for history's sake. It did not last long, as we shall see below. In any case, there was a strange ambivalence or tension between two objectives here, because, in the words of a modern American authority, 'The emphasis on citizenship that has been generally accepted by historians . . . at least since the 1880s calls for knowledge about the political milieu within which citizens function' (Morrissett 1981: 48).

Hence citizenship education became especially dependent on the teaching of overtly political material, though with reduced emphasis. In fact, teaching about the Constitution, as Freeman Butts (1988) has shown, was a common practice, albeit interpreted in various ways, throughout the nineteenth century. In line with fairly usual pedagogical practice up until the mid-century, the articles of the Constitution were at first learned parrot-fashion by the question-and-answer catechism method. Structure was learned, not processes: the implementation of the separation of powers doctrine overshadowed the Bill of Rights; and there was certainly no revelation or discussion of the episodic difficulty of relating and balancing federal and states' powers. As Freeman Butts has written,

> A certain amount of information and unswerving loyalty to the Constitution, no matter what diverse opinions might be held about its meaning, seemed to be the major expectations of most citizens, whether early Federalist or Republican, interim Whig, or Democrat or later Republican or Democrat.
>
> (Butts 1988: 52)

Horace Mann was, naturally, a powerful advocate of this sanitized constitutional study, advocating the tactic of the *via media*, as he did for religious education (see above).

The reform of history teaching along more scholarly lines in the late nineteenth to early twentieth centuries affected, and also had its parallels in, teaching about the Constitution. In the process of transforming the secondary school history syllabuses and teaching methodologies, the study of the Constitution, which had often been incorporated into history lessons, was reduced to a much less prominent portion of the whole programme. And even though the social sciences, including political science, were growing in academic respectability, there was a delay in their filling the gap in civic education left by the (temporary) withdrawal of the avowed function of history in this sphere. The American Political Science Association (APSA), founded in 1903, took an immediate interest in the school level, especially after a survey in 1905 by some undergraduate students exposed the extraordinarily woeful ignorance of young people about the system of government (see Butts 1988: 55). The APSA promptly appointed (in accordance with the numerical fashion) a Committee of Five on Instruction in American Government in Secondary Schools. This body reported in 1908, recommending a 'new civics' more in tune with the Progressive era, solid courses on the direct study of American government for grades 8 and 12, thus helping to set the scene for structured citizenship education in the twentieth century.

Subject content and styles of teaching have a symbiotic relationship with text-books. Books are written to provide the tools the teachers want, though innovative books can nudge the teachers to change what and how they teach. Therefore, an indication of the nature of textbooks used for civic education can inform us about what happened in the classrooms. Quotations from two studies undertaken by American writers on nineteenth-century textbooks give us these informative generalizations:

> From Noah Webster in the 1780s to Emma Willard in 1860, the authors of American school textbooks emphatically believed that there was such a thing as national character and that they had duty to help form and pressure it. They set out to create a usable past for republican America – an agreed-upon national myth, we might say now.
>
> (England 1963: 191)

> Unlike many modern textbooks, those of the nineteenth century made no pretence at neutrality. While they evade issues seriously controversial in their day, they take a firm and unanimous stand on matters of basic belief. The value judgment is their stock in trade.
>
> (quoted Butts 1989: 118–19)

Purveying national character and avoiding controversy meant ignoring the differences between north and south and defending the Federalist Constitution. The Civil War could not be ignored, of course. Yet textbooks published in the north were used in southern schools, with the bizarre result that:

A common custom was for southern teachers simply to excise the northern discussion of the Civil War and Reconstruction by pinning the pages together so young readers would presumably skip them in favor of the truth delivered by the teacher.

(Butts 1989: 119)

Two major themes were underscored: liberty and national destiny. For example, in a book published in 1854 entitled *A Pictorial History of the United States for Schools and Families*, the reader is told that in America, 'love of liberty . . . budded and blossomed. . . . Here king-craft and priest-craft never had an abiding place, and their ministers were always weak in the majestic presence of the popular will' (quoted England 1963: 191–2). That it was the destiny of the Americans to settle in and develop the great land as obedience to the will of God or Providence was also learned from textbooks. Emma Willard explained in her history textbook, published in 1860, that the native peoples of New England had been annihilated by plague: 'Thus, Divine Providence prepared the way for another and more civilized race' (quoted England 1963: 196). A confident nationalist tone pervaded the Readers compiled by William McGuffey, the sales of which approached 100 million during the half-century from the late 1830s.

By the 1880s the term 'Civics' was being used and from 1885 to 1900 some twenty-five textbooks were published for this subject at ninth-grade level, after which most pupils left school. Not until such bodies as the AHA, APSA and, later, the NCSS (National Council for the Social Studies) were founded, were textbooks produced that gave teachers the opportunity to avoid both wooden constitutionalism and rhetorical nationalism. The first of these, specifically directed at citizenship education and well received by the teaching profession, was Arthur W. Dunn's *The Community and the Citizen*, published in 1907.

Citizenship education, however, is by no means learning only from textbooks. Ceremonies have been powerful influences since the end of the nineteenth century in the United States. In the late 1880s, flying or showing the flag became a common means by which schools imprinted on their pupils a sense of civic identity, but voicing one's loyalty was soon recognized as being more efficacious. Moreover, this could not be engaged in unless the pupils had command of the English language; consequently, such ceremonies reinforced the widespread pressure at this time that lessons for all pupils of whatever origin should be conducted in English. It was in 1892 that Francis Bellamy, Chairman of the NEA, wrote the famous Pledge of Allegiance to the flag (see Marquette and Mineshima 2002: 544–5). His words were: 'I pledge allegiance to my Flag and the Republic for which it stands, one nation, indivisible, with liberty and justice for all.' Subsequently, 'my Flag' was changed to 'the Flag of the United States of America', and the words 'under God' were added after 'one nation'. The latter alteration was made during the Cold War, taking us well into the period covered in our next section, and during which education for national loyalty became a prime requirement of schools.

United States: structuring civic education

1916 was the turning point in the history of citizenship education in the USA. In that year there were published: the report of the American Political Science Association's Committee of Seven on government instruction in schools, colleges and universities; the report, *Social Studies in Secondary Education*, of the National Education Association's Committee on the Reorganization of Secondary Education; and John Dewey's *Democracy and Education*. The second and third of these were exceptionally influential, though the belief in the crucial contribution of the school to democracy and community, in line with Progressivist political thinking, characterized all three publications.

The NEA report adopted the term 'social studies' and identified this multi-disciplinary field as the means of transmitting civic education. The recommendation was adopted and remained the sturdy structure for this work henceforth, despite detailed worries and adaptations through subsequent decades. *Social Studies in Secondary Education* is therefore owed analysis in some detail (the following matter relies heavily on Butts 1989). The tone and therefore importance of this document may be gleaned from a preliminary working paper written by the Chairman of the Committee:

> Good citizenship should be the aim of social studies in high school. . . . The old civics, almost exclusively a study of Government machinery, must give way to the new civics, a study of all manner of social efforts to improve mankind. It is not so important that the pupil know how the President is elected as that he shall understand the duties of the health officer of his community.

He continues by offering an eclectic and, admittedly, idiosyncratic list, concentrating on local affairs close to the pupil's understanding and appreciation of relevancy, but also including a few broader topics that are, frankly, a strange rag-bag: for example, 'human rights versus property rights, impulsive action of mobs, the selfish conservatism of tradition' (quoted Butts 1989: 126). These themes were incorporated into the civics element for ninth-grade school-leavers.

The report (compiled by Arthur Dunn, author of the 1907 textbook mentioned above) opened the way for high schools across the nation to pursue a social studies curriculum composed of the several pertinent disciplines with emphases on citizenship, relevance and the 'problems approach'. The report declared: 'While all subjects should contribute to good citizenship, the social studies – geography, history, civics and economics – should have this as their dominant aim' (quoted Butts 1989: 127). And all these subjects should be taught, not in an academic style for their own sake, but for their contributions to individuals' understanding of current issues with which their lives are surrounded. This change in teaching objectives inevitably called into question traditional teaching modes; thus, instead of confronting pupils with copious facts and data, they should be presented with problems drawn from the disciplines for them to solve. This revolutionary change is clearly stated in another NEA document, *Cardinal Principles of Secondary*

Education, published two years later in 1918, which commended 'the assignment of projects and problems to groups of pupils for cooperative solution and the socialized recitation whereby a class as a whole develops a sense of collective responsibility' (quoted Butts 1989: 128).

Two further features of the NEA recommendations round off their concept of citizenship education, what we may call intra-mural and extra-mural democratic participation. The *Cardinal Principles* report explains the first of these: 'the demo-cratic organization and administration of the school itself, as well as the cooperative relations of pupil and teacher, pupil and pupil and teacher and teacher, are indis-pensable' (quoted Butts 1989: 128). The extra-mural feature was the recommended application of classroom learning to social action in the local community whereby pupils might advocate, for instance, more parks or railroads or post offices or pure food laws. The issues of transport and health, be it noted, were very salient at this time.

Revolutions, even pedagogical ones, do not happen merely because of the actions of a small number of individuals who are discontented with the status quo. Thus the aims of the teachers of the NEA were supported due to the widespread concerns about the state of American democracy on the eve of the country's involvement in the Great War and by the innovative thinking of educational philosophers, pre-eminent among whom was Professor John Dewey.

Dewey is a cardinal figure in the history of citizenship education, so we must accord him generous space. He was extremely versatile, excelling as philosopher, psychologist and educationist; he was also endowed with prodigious energy, writing numerous books of great originality and travelling the world as an educational adviser – for example, he exerted considerable influence on Lunacharsky, the Soviet Commissar of Education (see Chapter 4). Nor were his powers exhausted by old age: he co-authored his last book when he was 90, three years after he had remarried and started fathering a second family. It has been said that:

> Two outstanding convictions . . . directed the whole course of his educational work – a conviction that traditional methods of schooling were futile and fruitless, and an even firmer conviction that the human contacts of everyday life provide unlimited natural, dynamic 'learning situations'.
>
> (Curtis and Boultwood 1956: 463)

The University Laboratory School, which Dewey founded in Chicago in 1896, enabled him to develop his ideas in practice and brought him considerable fame. Together with his many publications, this work helped revolutionize teaching in elementary schools, liberating children (and teachers) from the traditional dull didactic regime.

We are concerned here mainly with his *Democracy and Education*. However, before giving our attention to this work, we should identify the overall thrust of Dewey's philosophy. His key, related concepts are democracy, community, commu-nication, responsibility and progress.

Democracy, he fervently believed, was by no means only a matter of institutions. 'Democracy,' he asserted in 1927 in *The Public and Its Problems*, 'must begin at home, and its home is the neighbouring community' (quoted Curtis and Boultwood 1956: 492). The school, too, plays a vital role, or should do, if teachers follow his principles of giving young people the experience of the give-and-take of democratic co-operation. By community, Dewey meant not merely the feeling of belonging to the school or locality, but an expansive sense of membership of a great community, embracing many cultures and traditions, a sense that could be cultivated only by means of education. However, community depends on communication; understanding is impossible without verbal intercourse. All this implies a sense of responsibility, a virtue to be nourished in the schools. In his *My Pedagogical Creed* he urges teachers to understand pupils' capacities, interests and habits in order that they might 'be translated into terms of what they are capable of in the way of social service' (quoted Curtis and Boultwood 1956: 481). And then, when adults, as he argues in *The Public and Its Problems*, they will behave as citizens in the full classical sense, as 'officers of the public'. Nevertheless, this pedagogically effected revolution in *moeurs* cannot be achieved unless the pupils' minds are tuned to the future, learning from the faults of the past the need to use the vitality of their youth to regenerate the great community for coming generations.

To turn now to *Democracy and Education*. It is constructed on a thesis that progressive education and democracy (as, in Dewey's mind, truly understood) are inextricably connected. The following sentence from an American academic could not express Dewey's thinking more succinctly: 'The techniques of progressive education, as expounded by Dewey, were intended to produce free men whose intelligences would engage in social reconstruction for democratic ends' (Welter 1962: 279; the analysis here rests heavily upon this work). Democracy requires the capacity to think; schools must cultivate this capacity, and an appreciation of its social purpose. This simple proposition, however, had radical implications: the purpose of schools was primarily reconstruction for democracy, not, as in Mann's thought, stability and harmony (see above). Lest this comparison be misunderstood, it is not intended as a complete antithesis: Dewey had no intention of advocating destabilizing change. A democratic society, he wrote, 'must have a type of education which gives individuals a personal interest in social relationships and control, and the habits of mind which secure social changes without introducing disorder' (Dewey 1961: 99).

How does Dewey, in this seminal work, suggest that schools arrange their curricula to produce young people with this aptitude and frame of mind? First, what the education system should *not* do:

> Democracy cannot flourish where the chief influences in selecting subject matter of instruction are utilitarian ends narrowly conceived for the masses, and, for the higher education of the few, the traditions of a specialized cultivated class. The notion that the 'essentials' of elementary education are the three R's mechanically treated, is based upon ignorance of the essentials needed for the realization of democratic ideals. Unconsciously it assumes that these ideals are unrealizable.
>
> (Dewey 1961: 192)

Second, what the education system *should* do is to cultivate what Dewey calls, alternatively, 'civic efficiency', or 'good citizenship'. He admits that these are vague terms, but, basically, civic efficiency 'calls attention to . . . the fact that the things which most need to be done are things which involve one's relationships with others' (Dewey 1961: 120). Third, the working class should be given a rounded education to prevent their continued subordination, and the curriculum should include 'study of economics, civics, and politics, to bring the future worker into touch with the problems of the day and various methods proposed for its improvement' (Dewey 1961: 318).

Finally, Dewey brings his book to a conclusion with a discussion of the key matter of moral education. He is sharply dismissive – as, indeed, others have been – of lessons in morality which have 'no more influence on character than information about the mountains of Asia'. Except, that is, by authoritarian methods in authoritarian regimes: 'To attempt to get similar results from lessons about morals in a democratic society is to rely on sentimental magic' (Dewey 1961: 354). Morality is learned through living to be good for something, and

> The something for which a man must be good is capacity to live as a social member so that what he gets from living with others balances with what he contributes. . . . And education is not a mere means to such a life. Education is such a life.
>
> (Dewey 1961: 359–60)

But what was happening in practice in the school classrooms at this time? Generalization is difficult because guidelines were loose and were interpreted in different ways. Guidelines themselves reached the teacher in three separate forms.

One was the social studies framework deriving from the work of the NEA and developed by a new professional body consequently specially founded, called the National Council for the Social Studies (NCSS). Several units were particularly germane to citizenship education from grades 3 to 12: community civics, national civics, American history and American government. One of the characteristic features of the programme was its cyclical organization, topics repeated at different levels. The NEA Report of 1916 explained the reasons for this pattern:

> It will be seen that the course of social studies proposed for the years VII–IX constitutes a cycle to be followed by a similar cycle in the years X–XII, and presumably preceded by another similar cycle in the six elementary grades. This grouping coincides roughly with the psychological periods of adolescence, but is based chiefly upon the practical consideration that large numbers of children complete their schooling with the sixth grade and another large contingent in the eighth and ninth grades. The course recommended in this report aims to provide a comprehensive, and in a sense complete, course of social study for each period.
>
> (quoted Morrissett 1981: 39)

The pattern, through inertia, was maintained for many years, even though rendered obsolete by later changes in the school-leaving ages.

Another set of guidelines was provided by state legislation. The entry of the USA into the First World War provoked an intensification of patriotic feeling and a demand that the schools be more assiduous in teaching historical and political topics with the overt purpose of enhancing that sentiment. Slowly, from 1917, the states framed statutes to require schools to teach for citizenship: within ten years all had passed such laws. Thus did citizenship education become universal – for punishment in the event of non-compliance could be severe:

> In cases of a violation a fine of not less than $100 and not more than $500 or imprisonment in the county jail for not less than thirty days nor more than six months, or both, may be the penalty. A teacher is subject to discharge or removal in case of malfeasance, and a college (corporation) is liable to a revocation of its charter.
>
> (Pierce 1930: 231 n.2)

The states had ways of making their children little republicans!

Teaching for citizenship and patriotism having been made mandatory, many of the states' superintendents of public instruction, and many city authorities, issued courses or manuals of study – the third set of guidelines. Bessie Pierce, who examined these documents in the 1920s, describes them as follows:

> The objectives set forth for the teaching of political problems, or civics, have in common the aim of 'good' or 'intelligent citizenship'. Just what these terms mean is generally left unsettled for the teacher, for they are seldom defined. Obviously this might result in as many different concepts for the pupil as there are different interpretations by different teachers.
>
> (Pierce 1930: 243)

The reader may like to compare this quotation with another, taken from a book on social studies teaching published half a century later: 'Course titles can be weak predictors of what is actually taught within a particular course. . . . Probably the most reliable measure of what particular students encounter in a given course is the textbook for the course' (Jarolimek 1981: 4). *Plus ça change.* . . .

To provide the flavour of these manuals, let us take three different examples (quoted Pierce 1930: 244, 246, 249). The first is for the citizenship course in elementary schools in Missouri:

> The great end of government, the service of all the people, should be emphasized at this point. While no attempt should be made to mislead the pupil into the false view that no further improvement can be made in our local and general systems, the whole of democratic government, and the need of loyal co-operation with it are repeatedly demonstrated.

The second excerpt is from Idaho's course on American history:

> Patriotism, the greatest of our national ideals, comprehends all the rest. Love of country is a sentiment common to all peoples and ages; but no land has ever been dearer to its people than our own America. No nation has a history more inspiring, no country has institutions more deserving of patriotic love.

The third example is taken from the city of St Louis, where in the mid-1920s curriculum revision led to the incorporation of the aim 'to develop a sense of membership in the world community'. While the first and third examples show refreshing attempts at avoiding too blinkered an approach to citizenship education, it is likely that Idaho's complacent patriotism was much more common. That is certainly the tone of most textbooks of this period.

Information about titles used in the first quarter of the twentieth century is available in Bessie Pierce's *Civic Attitudes in American School Textbooks*, already drawn upon for the above material. She analysed nearly seventy in the category civics, sociology and economic and political problems, fifteen of which contained the words 'civics' or 'citizenship' in their titles, though there are a few more catchy ones (e.g. *The Boy's Own Book of Politics for Uncle Sam's Young Voters*). It is possible to find in these books admissions of civic vice such as vote-buying and bribe-giving (see Pierce 1930: 146). Nevertheless, it is the virtual perfection of the American traditions and institutions that many of the authors wish to teach (preach?). For instance, in 1920 Sara Cone Bryant's *I Am an American* was published, designed for upper elementary grades. Dipping into this book we find comforting, boastful messages; for example:

> I am an American. My country is the freest, the richest, and the most beautiful land on earth.
>
> My flag is unstained. My navy is unconquered. My army defends the freedom of the world. . . .
>
> One bond binds all races together in her citizenship. It is the bond of loyalty. . . .
>
> I thank God for the privilege of being a child of America. . . . With gratitude and high purpose, for service with the heart, hand, and brain,
> I AM AN AMERICAN
> (quoted Pierce 1930: 171)

Somewhat 'economical with the truth', but so were many textbooks in other countries at this time; and what a peroration! It is scarcely to be wondered that the majority of school books used in social studies courses conveyed patriotic prose when attempts were made to censor them. For instance, in 1923 Oregon passed a law prohibiting the use of any book which 'speaks slightingly of the founders of the republic, or of the men who preserved the union, or which belittles or undervalues their work' (quoted Pierce 1930: 233). However, it is true that these laws soon produced a backlash on the principle of freedom of speech and the press enshrined in Article I of the Bill of Rights. Yet the will had been there.

What we can see from the above is that, by about 1925, citizenship education was entrenched firmly in American schools, by professional guidance, state legislation and the publication of textbooks, in a loose framework which offered teachers freedom to choose precisely what and how to teach; to innovate – or to sink into dull reliance on 'the textbook' that was to hand in the school.

By the mid-1920s, therefore, there can be no doubt that American schools were expected to engage in education for citizenship. One could consequently be led to assume that, from this point on, young Americans effectively learned in their schools what it meant to be a citizen. Yet, if the constant complaints, expressions of concern and projects for improvement that characterize the history of the subject for the rest of the century are anything to go by, that assumption would be seriously misguided. Compare these two statements:

> With many notable exceptions, the teaching of various branches of social science, history, economics, government, leaves much to be desired from the point of view of civic education in regard to attitude, subject-matter and interrelationship. . . .
>
> Defeatism in civic education is responsible for much of our low-level civic behavior.
>
> (Merriam 1934: xiii, xv)

The other commentator argues that 'we [may] presume (and we are convinced that the evidence strongly substantiates it) that civic education has not changed markedly in the 200 years that the United States has been a nation' (Turner 1981: 56). The first quotation is drawn from the report of an investigation of the social studies undertaken for the AHA and published in 1934; the second is the judgement of an authority on social science education, written nearly half a century later.

In surveying the time-span of three-quarters of a century to 2000, it will be helpful to deal with the period in several parts. Our first part covers the generation from about 1930 to 1960. Before looking at the attempts to improve civic education, it is necessary to mention two other, related matters. One is the issue of school racial segregation, and the other is the influence of political events and moods in addition to the race question on the teaching of citizenship.

Two events, thirty years apart, highlight the issue of segregation. The first is the publication in 1924 of Horace Kallen's *Culture and Democracy in the United States*; the second is the judgment of the Supreme Court in 1954 in *Brown v. Board of Education*. Kallen devised the term 'cultural pluralism' in an article which he published in 1915 and developed in the book cited above. He argued that the USA must accept the fact of its peoples being a 'multiplicity in a unity' and that the public schools should reinforce the understanding of this reality by educating all ethnic groups together (see Macedo 2000: 103–7). However, not until the 1954 ruling, following the tense drama in Little Rock, Arkansas, did desegregation of white and black pupils become the law of the land.

The political events and moods of this generation, which could not avoid influencing the nature of citizenship education, are fairly obvious. By the late 1920s the flagrant patriotism of the wartime and post-war years was subsiding; subsequently the Great Depression and the New Deal turned attention to economic and social problems. The Second World War resurrected the atmosphere of patriotism, which became degraded in the McCarthyite anti-Communist hysteria – an episode in the Cold War, which generated a mix of fear and *hubris*. Against this background a vast number of attempts were made to improve the quality of citizenship education. In the words of Freeman Butts,

> The outpouring of proposals and projects to create more effective civic-education programs during the mid-twentieth century would take volumes to relate. The variations of details run to infinitude, yet there is a repetitive sameness to the lists of goals and objectives set forth by one commission after another.
>
> (Butts 1989: 185)

A list of a handful of the organizations engaged in this work indicates the range of this activity: APSA, AHA, AASA, NEA, NCSS, Educational Policies Commission (EPC), Columbia University, US Office of Education. The AHA, funded partly by the Carnegie Corporation, published seventeen volumes on the teaching of social studies between 1932 and 1937, including Charles Merriam's *Civic Education in the United States*, from which we have already quoted. In 1938 the EPC famously identified 'civic responsibility' as one of four objectives of education (see Butts 1989: 190). In 1949 the US Office of Education produced a particularly influential pamphlet, *Life Adjustment Education for Every Youth*. This drew the conclusion:

> The compelling implication then is: In order to develop such knowledge, understanding, and skills on the part of all youth – not just those who will enter the professions or the skilled occupations – it will be necessary for the high school to employ a wider variety of ways and means of developing civic competence than have been generally used.
>
> (quoted Robinson 1976: 33)

The distinguished educationists and political scientists who gave these projects their impetus have been called 'social frontiersmen'. They had some success in persuading the schools of their responsibility to prepare their pupils for citizenship, though it was clearly an uphill task. Yet even that progress had almost ground to a halt by about 1960. The following words paint the picture:

> But the good intentions of the work of the three or so decades preceding the 1960s seemed to have been all but lost in the rapid changes that followed. In the late 50's the emphasis was shifted to science, mathematics and foreign language, with the passage of the National Defense Education Act. . . . Emphasis

upon education for citizenship was reduced to a weak voice in the loud roar of the call for scientific effort.

(Robinson 1976: 34)

Keeping up with – better, overtaking – the Soviet Union in the space and missile races seemed self-evidently so much more urgent priorities than civic education.

The two decades of the 1960s and 1970s were years of dramatic political and curricular activity. The prosecution of the war in Vietnam led to much heart-searching and expressions of heart-felt hostility to government policy. In 1972, a year before that conflict ended, there began the startling events of the Watergate scandal, which led to the humiliating resignation of President Nixon in 1974 and the consequent cynicism about and disillusionment with the political system. At the same time, citizenship education was in chaos. One authority has described the condition with laconic pungency: 'To assert that social studies was in disarray in the early years of the 1970s would be a generous assessment of the situation' (Jarolimek 1981: 9). That this was by no means an unfair judgement may be confirmed by the results of a survey undertaken by the National Assessment of Educational Progress (NAEP) between 1969 and 1976. This revealed, for instance, that one-third of 13-year-olds could not name the Senate as the partner in Congress of the House of Representatives. Moreover, scores declined over the seven-year period. Aware of the dire state of affairs, two private foundations set up a task force to investigate and frame recommendations to rectify the situation. A long section from the report is worthy of quotation here because it gives such a lucid portrayal of the problem:

> Citizenship preparation by the schools has long been a neglected area, but it is now in a serious state of intellectual disrepair. In the elementary schools, this subject has been allowed to disappear behind the façade of more fashionable concerns. Meeting the most vocal demands of the community one at a time, rather than attempting the hard work of building a coherent curriculum, the designers of elementary programs have been compelled to push aside civic education in favor of units on drugs, sex, and social pathology. More recently career education . . . has been fostered on the elementary schools in units that reach as low as the kindergarten.
>
> At the secondary level, the major burden for teaching about citizenship lies in the narrow, lifeless civics courses which comprise the social studies curriculum in grades eight or nine. The weakness is compounded by the fact that too often the civics course is taught by the athletic coach who needs a light teaching schedule because of his after-school coaching responsibilities.

(Brown 1977: 2)

(For a detailed explanation of the decline to this piteous condition, see Butts 1989: 199–202.)

So, there came another surge in activity to improve matters, made even more imperative by the passing of the 26th Amendment to the Constitution in 1971 enfranchising 18-year-olds. There were three difficulties facing the concerned educationists and academics: persuading teachers, parents and school authorities that citizenship education is important; re-creating some form of national coherence in what to teach; and producing new teaching materials to assist this organized revival. The collapse into incoherence, even beyond the tradition of local interpretation, was the core problem. The hard work of the early years of the century was dissipated in the 1960s and 1970s by the havoc of each teacher teaching what he or she felt inclined to do. It took some time to reverse this process of disintegration. One attempt was the 'New social studies' movement advocating teaching the constituent subjects' investigative processes (see Fenton 1966), but this was by no means universally adopted.

More useful was the work of academics to improve textbooks during the 1970s (see e.g. Butts 1989: 200–4). American teachers, as we have seen above, have always been heavily reliant on textbooks. One collaborative effort, begun in 1970, produced a critical survey of available materials (Turner n.d.). This carried an Introduction by John Patrick of Indiana University, who, with Howard Mehlinger, produced a highly successful book entitled *American Political Behavior* (Mehlinger and Patrick 1972). Mehlinger was later to describe the situation as 'The Crisis in Civic Education' (Brown 1977: 69–82). The book evolved from work undertaken by the University's Social Studies Development Center, established in 1966, and was the outcome of the rigorous testing of the material in a large number of schools before publication. Also, it went out of its way to present the subject-matter in an interesting and easily comprehensible manner to secondary-level pupils (see Mehlinger and Patrick 1972: Acknowledgments; Morrissett and Williams 1981: 81–2). This is one example of the serious efforts to rescue civic education by improved teaching materials.

During the last two decades of the twentieth century every component of American society concerned about citizenship education strained to make the schools much more effective institutions for shaping citizens in some true sense of the term – the federal government, state governments, universities, research foundations, publishers (see Butts 1989: 205–25). Most conspicuously, in 1983 the federal Department of Education issued a report entitled *A Nation at Risk*, thereby opening up a long and searching discussion on the desperate need for educational reform. It identified six goals, two of which relate to civic education. One asserts that 'every school in America will ensure that all students learn to use their minds well, so they may be prepared for responsible citizenship, further learning, and productive employment in our modern economy'. The other states that 'every adult American will be literate and possess the knowledge and skills necessary to compete in a global economy and exercise the rights and responsibilities of citizenship' (quoted Cogan and Derricott 2000: 84).

The 1990s saw a number of significant developments. These included the establishment of the Center for Civic Education; the launching of the National Campaign to Promote Civic Education to encourage systematic teaching in this area; and the designing of 'CIVITAS: A Framework for Civic Education' as a model. Even so, the proponents of better citizenship education were still having to struggle against doubting or hostile forces. Uncritical patriotism preferred to a questioning civic mind (see e.g. Janowitz 1983; Turner 1981), and the attempt 'to eliminate [public education's] citizenship function in favor of a narrowly defined labor market perspective' (Giroux 1987: 72) are two obvious examples, though they are by no means confined to this period, as we have seen above.

So much research has been undertaken since around 1990 on how citizenship education is provided in US schools that we have a wealth of information on which to base a general description of the current position. It can be said first that 'most, but not all, students will have had some formal instruction related to democracy, political institutions and rights and responsibilities of citizens by the time they are 14 or 15 years old' (Hahn 1999: 590). Second, the lack of firmly established systematic guidelines continues as a feature precluding detailed generalization. In the words of a leading US researcher, 'Even when teachers in the same school follow a common written curriculum, the way in which it is delivered often varies' leave alone the wide variations between states (Hahn 1999: 589). On the other hand, the same authority has found it possible to provide an outline of fairly common programmes:

> The typical pattern is for primary grade children to learn several patriotic songs, to celebrate national holidays such as Presidents' Day and Thanksgiving with art projects and stories, and to say a daily salute to the flag. Primary grade children often study about 'community helpers,' such as the police and firefighters, and about the need for rules and laws. In grades 4–6, children are usually introduced to United States history and the basic principles of the Bill of Rights and the United States Constitution. Most high school students take a year-long course in United States history and a semester-long course in government. . . . Courses in state history, economics, law, and civics are also prevalent in many states.
>
> (C.L. Hahn 1998:17)

This is not, however, to say that by the turn of the century disputes about the content and teaching styles of citizenship education were contained, or that it was taught at a high level of pedagogical professionalism. Controversies continued concerning multicultural *vs.* national cohesion objectives, national *vs.* world citizenship (see Chapter 5 below), structure of the disciplines *vs.* problems of democracy approaches (see Cogan and Derricott 2000: 81–3), learning about institutions *vs.* learning civic behaviour, academic study *vs.* community service. Even the pledge of allegiance came to be questioned as controversial, as this extract from a British newspaper report reveals:

> All hell broke loose in America yesterday after a court ruled that the pledge of allegiance was unconstitutional.
>   The ninth US circuit court of appeals in San Francisco ruled that asking schoolchildren to make their daily pledge of allegiance to the United States,

'one nation under God', violated the so-called establishment clause in the constitution that requires a separation of church and state.

(Guardian 2002)

The conclusion of one participant in the thorough IEA research, which we have cited in other places in this book, is that many US educators criticize the implementation of citizenship education by the schools as 'being too weak to amount to anything' (Cogan and Derricott 2000: 87). Few countries have enjoyed so much support for citizenship education in principle from politicians and educationists for so long, yet have encountered so many difficulties in making progress in accomplishing it, as has been the experience of the United States.

The colonial experience

The expansionist policy of imperialism conducted by European powers was at root incompatible with the concept of citizenship. The frail and hesitant manner in which the imperial authorities developed educational facilities in their colonies is a clear indicator of this judgement. Furthermore, the difficulties experienced by many African and Asian states since independence in creating meaningful forms of citizenship and citizenship education, let alone of a thoroughly liberal style, have been caused, at least partly, by these weak civic legacies. Another potent factor has been the problem of adapting their own markedly different social and political traditions and hopes to this essentially western ideal and institution. In this section we shall analyse first of all the range of problems that are evident from the histories of the colonies in imperial times. Following this outline we shall briefly compare the limited policies of some of the main imperial powers in promoting the growth of citizenship.

It will be instructive to look at the component arguments for considering the regime of modern imperialism to be basically irreconcilable with the development of citizenship in the full sense by expressing them as pairs of contradictions. To start with the absolutely fundamental, the very practice of imperial rule was erected upon the unquestioned proposition that the colonists were bringing the inestimable benefits of western, including Christian, civilization to the benighted peoples of the Americas (though we shall not be dealing with this continent in this section), the tribes of Africa and the utterly decayed civilizations of Asia. A French authority has explained the mentality thus:

> [To colonize] is not to dispossess, for the colonizer has the duty of taking charge of these 'feeble' populations, also to 'develop' them. He must . . . in short, prepare them to become associated in the management, exploitation and profits of the common domain.

(Grimal 1965: 28)

The colonizer is also the bringer of peace to the incorrigibly bellicose natives; in conscious imitation of the Romans, the British boasted the creation of a *pax*

Britannica. This attitude of mind is a far cry from the notion of citizenship: it is a conviction of superiority, a policy of paternalism, not a belief, certainly not in the foreseeable future, in citizenship as equal participation in a civic enterprise.

But, then, the colonizers could be forgiven for thinking in terms of subjecthood rather than citizenship, because traditions, structures and loyalties were so different in Asia and Africa from the European environment in which citizenship evolved. This is another contradiction. Why should the colonizers feel that they could readily transplant this western tradition, and why should the indigenous peoples want to learn to adapt to this alien idea? With this question we come across another contradiction, or ambiguity. The elite and mass subjects of imperial regimes had different reasons for not wishing to acquire a citizenly status, even through the means of liberation from the imperial power. A French authority, writing about Indochina in 1931, declared that the native elite considered independence from France 'as a pure absurdity, or better still, a nonsense' (quoted Grimal 1965: 29; author's translation). As for the bulk of the populations, the Algerian psychiatrist and revolutionary Franz Fanon, describing them as 'the wretched of the earth', argued that they had been so depressed by colonial control into psychological conditions of inferiority complex and despair that they were bereft of any political expectations (see e.g. Fanon 1967: 74).

Nevertheless, the imperial powers did not totally deny their responsibility for establishing educational institutions in their possessions, though in terms of education for citizenship we have two more pairs of contradictions or priorities. Should these facilities be designed to train an elite native citizenry or to provide a basic schooling for all to understand something about public affairs? And if these forms of education were successful, would the effects be an improved commitment to the empire of which they were part, or an aggravated discontent due to the partiality of their civic status? Since these questions lie at the heart of our concerns, we need to pause longer here for our discussion.

The consciences of the imperialists – of varying sensitivity, and sometimes even indiscernible, as we shall see below – urged them to provide some form of education for their 'backward' subjects. At its most modest this belief has been summed up by an American academic as follows:

> So long as the emphasis in education was mainly on literacy and the idea prevailed that training in the three R's would be accompanied by moral improvement, there was some justification in transplanting to alien civilizations a type of education which was regarded as beneficial under all circumstances.
>
> (Kandel 1960: 139)

At the same time, unease about the consequences of a politically aware populace rendered them irresolute in forging ahead with such a policy. In the elegant words of a Canadian scholar:

> If education remained low among the items on imperial budgets, this was partly because awkward minds had proved to keep company with awkward emotions,

among people who did not think and would not learn that common sense, compromise, and acceptance were obvious virtues. Imperialists delayed dealing with this dilemma as long as they could.

(Thornton 1978: 63)

This trepidation about the politically adverse effects of solid educational programmes was one reason for the generally slow progress indeed of educational standards for the people at large in the colonies. One French commentator on Dutch policy in the East Indies stated flatly that they wished 'to establish their superiority on the ignorance of the natives' (quoted Grimal 1965: 83; author's translation); and even as late as the 1960s, after independence, it is estimated that over 90 per cent of the Indonesian population were illiterate. There were, however, also non-political reasons for the lack of educational progress: the difficulty of transposing a style of education from an alien culture and the problem of language. In each colony it often happened that a babel of languages and dialects were (and are) spoken; to take the example of the Dutch East Indies again, some 300. As well as the objective of 'civilizing' the indigenous peoples, practicalities dictated teaching in the colonists' tongue; yet learning a strange language was itself an impediment to the acquisition of literacy.

Mastery of the imperial lingua franca was, naturally, a *sine qua non* for the creation of an elite indigenous citizenry. And an imperial power had need of elite citizens for the smooth running of the lower strata of its administrative apparatus. Clerks, teachers, lawyers had to be educated to fill these posts, but herein lay the imperialists' dilemma. Their grip on the colonies depended on efficient administration; efficient administration depended on educating the most intelligent and ambitious of the indigenous peoples; these individuals could readily become discontented with their lowly status and, by learning from their masters' own literature the principles of liberty, democracy and national self-determination, use the fruits of their education to demand independence – real citizenship; and thus undermine the very edifice they had been educated to sustain. Having been taught by the schools to read an ABC primer, they could later teach themselves to read Bukharin's *ABC of Communism* – or Mill's *On Liberty*, according to taste. A most pertinent example of this unforeseen consequence of education for stability metamorphosing into education for overthrow may be taken from Tunisia. In 1920 the nationalist party's agenda was:

An assembly consisting of French and Tunisians, with equal rights and universal suffrage; a government responsible to that assembly; a separation of legislature, executive, and judicial powers; the 'Tunisianization' of the public services; equal pay for French and Tunisian workers; elective municipal councils; freedom of the press and of association; and a compulsory system of education.

The historian from whom this summary is taken adds his own comment: 'they were speaking in a language that owed all its concepts to the imperial context from which it sprang' (Thornton 1978: 66).

In most cases such politically conscious and active people had learned what citizenship meant by default. Yet the imperial states did not totally reject the idea that some of their colonial subjects, however small a proportion, could be educated to become citizens in a reasonably full and proper sense. However, if this was to come about, a question of constitutional law had to be decided. Should those qualifying for the status be citizens of the colony or of the whole Empire, of the Gold Coast or of the British Empire, for example? That the matter of citizenship was taken seriously – though by some imperial powers more seriously than others – is evident from the discussions that arose from this question. Two more sets of contradictions now confront us: the arguments for and against imperial citizenship and for and against colonial citizenship.

The idea of an imperial citizenship had the advantages of the precedent of the expanded Roman citizenship and, as we shall see below, of the ideals of a unitary French Republic and a monarchical British Empire. If membership of an empire was to mean anything and attract loyalty, then citizenship should be a status related to that political whole, and education should be shaped to that end. On the other hand, the populations of modern empires were large and impoverished compared with the size and wealth of the metropolitan countries. Therefore, a democratic imperial electoral system would result in the political wishes of the citizens of the metropolitan European state being overwhelmed by the wishes of the citizens in other continents. Furthermore, if citizenship is to include welfare rights, the equalization of the socio-economic features of the status would have been quite impossible in practice. It follows that teaching about these imperial civic expectations would have led to dangerous disappointments. Local, colonial citizenship was by definition a smaller-scale proposition and thus more practicable. Demand for equal citizenship rights in an independent Senegal, to take a possible example, had the powerful attraction of imminent feasibility compared with equal citizenship rights in the French Empire, which sprawled over five continents. However, each colony then became potentially an independent state; consequently, to accord wholesale citizenship rights to the indigenous people, buttressed by supporting education, would encourage more pressing thoughts of national self-determination than would be the case of an imperial citizenship.

We now need to ask what policies the imperial powers did in fact pursue to extend civic rights to their colonial subjects. Three general points may be made. First, there was considerable variation between the approaches of the metropolitan governments. Second, some attempted constitutional arrangements, others did not. Third, and most pertinently for us, education was the key issue in the framing of policies. The reason for this third aspect of imperial policies is that the focus of all governments was on the education of an elite citizenry in the colonial possessions for reasons indicated above: the thrust of these programmes was to mould these men into native replicas of the citizens of the mother-countries – in language, culture and manners. The French and Belgians wished these individuals to go through the process of evolving as Frenchmen and Belgians, to become *évolués*; the Portuguese wished theirs to be assimilated into their culture, to become *assimilados*; the British version, expressed with inelegant brevity, was education of their colonial subjects to become (particularly in India and later most pejoratively) WOGS – westernized oriental gentlemen.

Of the five major imperial powers (after the liberation of Spanish America and leaving aside Russian expansion, both rather different histories), only France and Britain made serious efforts to educate their colonial subjects. Although the question was debated widely in the Netherlands and Portugal and by the administrators, clerics and teachers in their colonies, especially in the early and middle years of the twentieth century, these states achieved very little. We have already cited the abysmal illiteracy rate in the Dutch East Indies. The Portuguese policy was similar to the French in theory (see below), in that the colonies were considered part of a total Portuguese Union. The weakness in practice is well summarized in this passage published thirteen years before the independence of Angola and Mozambique:

> Education in the African colonies has been distinguished by the official stand-point that education is important for promoting assimilation; by the perhaps unconscious sentiment that education for the mass of the population represents an implicit threat to Portuguese interests; and by the inability of both Church and State to create an educational system capable of serving more than a small percentage of the inhabitants of Angola and Moçambique. . . . The Salazar regime dithered and planned for twenty years before anything was done, and only in the last decade has the African illiteracy rate begun to drop slowly from a figure of about ninety-nine per cent.
>
> (Duffy 1962: 173–4)

The Belgian legacy to the Congo when independence was conceded in 1960 was even more dire. The Brussels government's position, as late as 1959, was that independence was inconceivable. Education for or experience of citizenship, even elite citizenship, in the newly independent state was for all intents and purposes non-existent. In the words of a British academic:

> The first [national] elections ever held in the Congo were held a few weeks before the date of independence. At that date the Congo had scarcely any University graduates, no Congolese held any more responsible position than that of clerk or primary schoolteacher, and every commission in the army was held by a Belgian.
>
> (Hanna 1961: 32)

The history of citizenship and citizenship education in the French colonies starts in 1789, and in their doctrinal ardour for clarity, it must be said, the revolutionaries set the scene for a century-and-a-half of hypocritical confusion. The starting points were the principles that France was 'a nation one and indivisible' and that all Frenchmen are citizens, a status rendered achievable and acceptable by the assumption that all would be imbued by socialization and education with the incomparable French culture. Moreover, since the colonies were viewed as merely extensions of metropolitan France – *France d'Outre Mer*, 'Overseas France' – the populations of these territories could not be rated as exceptions to this rule; though true, they would need to be educationally brought up to standard by the *mission civilisatrice*. Accordingly, in 1794:

> The National Convention declares the abolition of Negro slavery in all the colonies; in consequence it decrees that all men, without distinction of color, residing in the colonies, are French citizens and will enjoy all the rights assured by the constitution.
>
> (quoted Hunt 1996: 116)

The persistence of this principle into the twentieth century is proved by the following. In 1921 a French scholar explained the policy of assimilation as 'not separation, but, on the contrary, an increasingly intimate union between the colonial and the metropolitan country. . . . The colonies are theoretically considered to be a simple extension of the mother country' (quoted Betts 1991: 17). The Constitutions of the Fourth and Fifth Republics confirmed this relationship by referring respectively to the French Union and the French Community. Article 77 of the latter states: 'There is only one Community citizenship.'

But what of French practice? It was certainly very different from the ideal design; inevitably so. Hence the common formula: 'Much subjection, very little autonomy, and a dash of assimilation' (quoted Grimal 1965: 64; author's translation). We may identify a number of reasons. The first concerned the Islamic populations of the Sahelian region and the Maghreb, mainly Algeria. Writing of the period from about 1870, a British scholar explains:

> The only indigenous community which could vote was the Jews. . . . It is true that the Arabs could acquire, by naturalization, all the rights of French citizens; all they had to do was abandon their status in Moslem law, adopt monogamy, accept the full principles of the civil code: in short, by their standards, cease to be Moslems.
>
> (Brogan 1940: 222)

Obviously, if a French citizen was a Frenchman by culture, including language, an Algerian Muslim could be taught the French tongue; but, as this comment explains, few members of that faith would submit to being transformed in the full cultural sense, the majority wishing their children to attend Islamic schools.

However, other colonial peoples, such as those in the West Indies and West Africa, were more ready to receive an education in French culture. On the other hand, there were two major obstacles to an effective citizenship education, and opportunities to practise the citizenship thus learned for any except a handful of the colonial subjects of France. One was the dominance of the white colonists in the political system. With reference to the West Indies, it has been said that, 'In the islands, representation merely meant the selling by the coloured electorate of their votes to the highest bidder in a good-humoured and frank fashion' (Brogan 1940: 222). The other obstacle was the lack of enthusiasm in metropolitan France to organize and finance any really effective school systems in the colonies or encourage civic participation, even after the Third Republic restored the limited franchise enjoyed in a few colonies (it had been abolished under the Second Empire) and, in 1885, allotted to the colonies ten seats in the Chamber of Deputies.

It was possible for an educated native of a colony – an *évolué* – to become an active elite citizen, though these were exiguous in number. The two most distinguished examples were Félix Houphouet-Boigny of the Ivory Coast, who was educated in West Africa and became a cabinet minister in the French government from 1956 to 1959; and Léopold Senghor of Senegal, who was educated in Dakar and Paris and became a member of the Chamber of Deputies, having contributed to the framing of the Constitution of the Fourth Republic.

To trace an overall picture of education in French colonies is extremely difficult because there were so many differences in both place and time. First, an indication of the differences related to place. Although the secularization of education had been an objective in France from the eighteenth century and many politicians wished to pursue the same policy overseas, the strength of religious schools in the colonies made this impossible. Thus, missionary schools in sub-Saharan Africa, Koranic schools in the Maghreb and pagoda schools in Indochina survived. We must also take into account differences in the levels and breadth of enjoyment of citizenship rights.

Senegal was the first French African colony and was exceptional. A British historian has explained that 'It might be argued that the civil rights of the Senegalese in the 1780s were more clearly recognized than those of some of their French contemporaries' (Hargreaves 1967: 71); though, perhaps, as this decade pre-dated the French Revolution, this is not saying a great deal – except for its uniqueness in Africa. In addition, the colony stayed ahead politically and educationally.

Changes over time relate mainly to the fluctuations in the commitment of the government in Paris and the colonial governors to press forward with designing and implementing detailed policies. Two phases are particularly significant in the development of education: inter-war and post-Second World War. In 1924 Jules Carde, Governor-General of French West Africa, laid down the principle of a two-tier system – for the elite and for the masses. However, provision remained patchy. In 1935 there were only just over 50,000 children in primary schools in the whole of French West Africa. The quality of the teachers and curricula was also questionable. Again, Senegal, and also Dahomey, were to the fore; though even here the subject-matter was scarcely very apt. Admittedly this example is taken from Senegal in the nineteenth century, but it is too good an illustration of Gallicization not to cite: 'There seems to have been general approval for teaching primary-school children about the Merovingian dynasty and the bishops of France' (Hargreaves 1967: 84). The most striking feature of post-1945 educational provision was the encouragement of higher education in French West Africa and for students to attend this level of study in France. From 1945 to 1960 political consciousness grew rapidly in the French colonies, led by the elite products of the educational systems.

However, we must retrace our steps and examine the principles and objectives that remained constant throughout the generations prior to independence, in spite of the variations we have noted (see e.g. Cowan *et al*. 1965: 8–9; Léon 1991: 305–7). One was the 'civilizing' and 'moral conquest' of the indigenous peoples. A second was the offer of such schooling facilities that would provide employment for both the mass and the elite, the former very basic and of short duration, the latter comparable with that obtaining in France itself. A third universal aim was '*fusioner les races*', to bring together all the ethnic groups. Although a controversial issue, the spread of the French language was the prime method for pursuing this objective, as well as part of the 'civilizing mission'.

As is true of other countries, the content, focus and slant of textbooks offer a fairly accurate insight into the messages conveyed in the classrooms. The clear evidence they provide for us is that, despite the repetition in the prefaces supporting the fusion of races, the texts 'all have in common the presentation of colonial society as a static world, divided, with no significant conflicts and without any real inter-ethnic exchange' (Léon 1991: 262; author's translation). For example, a reading book that went through fourteen editions from 1925 to 1952, *Moussa et Gi-Gla*, tells of a long journey by these two children, from the then Soudan (now Mali) and Dahomey (now Benin). At one point it is explained that whites and blacks have mutually advantageous and compatible skills:

> The Whites are more . . . advanced in civilization than the Blacks and . . . thanks to them, the latter can . . . one day become really useful men. . . . On their side, the Blacks render service to the Whites by helping them with manual work of all kinds.
>
> > (quoted Léon 1991: 260; author's translation)

(This is an appropriate point at which to remind the reader of Fanon's thesis, mentioned above.)

In truth, there was, as already noted, little enthusiasm for a thoroughgoing educational system throughout the empire that would have upgraded the indigenous peoples' hypothetical citizenship to a status on a par with the inhabitants of France itself. Two main reasons, the basic flaws in the whole project, may be identified for this hesitation. One, to repeat in the French context the general point already made, was the overwhelming relative numbers of the overseas population. An effective policy of assimilation, in the stark imagery of the politician and long-time mayor of Lyon, Édouard Herriot, would make metropolitan France 'the colony of the colonies' (quoted Léon 1991: 253; author's translation). The second reason is to be found in the fundamental ambiguities that lay at the heart of colonial educational policy. A modern French authority summarizes:

> The school contributes to making the colonial order wholly acceptable by shaping the person's intellect and moral code, while the same process favours the awakening of national sentiment and a questioning of that order. The school participates in the complete destabilization of the native societies by encouraging the emergence of an elite or a new social class, capable of taking part in the liberation of the countries under foreign rule. On a more individual

level, the pupil ought theoretically to profit from his dual linguistic and cultural upbringing. But he finds . . . [that] the school ignores or devalues [his origins], and refuses him . . . the prospect of becoming a citizen like the others.

(Léon 1991: 305; author's translation)

By the end of the Second World War it was becoming increasingly obvious that as an egalitarian imperial citizenship was unthinkable, the options were polarized. One option was the continuation of a condition for the masses that was effectively closer to subjecthood than citizenship; the other was the emergence of a national citizenship through independence. We know that the latter option prevailed. Yet, despite an attempt by an advisory Commission in 1951 to reform civic education in line with the new Constitution, the education of the colonial peoples had scarcely prepared them for this outcome.

French imperial policy has often been contrasted with the British, even though there were some similarities. Britain, after all, had no tradition of citizenship grounded in the concept of a unitary republican polity. Nor, in spite of British (or English?) arrogance towards its colonial peoples, did it come to have as its ultimate objective their refashioning by education into coloured Britons; rather, their preparation, in the long term, was for autonomous governance, even full independence, in modes adapted to their own traditions. It will be convenient to survey British imperial policy on civic education in three parts: the structure, plans and practice of the whole edifice; those features as related to India; and those features as related to Africa. The reader should also note that education for Empire in Britain itself has been mentioned earlier in this chapter and that Nigeria and Canada are treated in Chapter 5.

British governments only haltingly came to accept that all their colonial possessions should become independent. There were so many different kinds of territories, even though all were coloured pink in the atlases. In 1938 the Dominions and Colonial Secretary, Malcolm MacDonald, made a definitive speech on the policy of variable-paced achievement of self-government:

> The great purpose of the British Empire is the gradual spread of freedom among all His Majesty's subjects in whatever part of the world they live. . . . In some countries it is more rapid than others. In some parts of the Empire, in the Dominions, that evolutionary process has been completed. . . . It may take generations, or even centuries, for some parts of the Colonial Empire to achieve self-government. But it is a major part of our policy, even among the most backward peoples of Africa, to teach them and encourage them always to be able to stand a little more on their own feet.

(quoted Hargreaves 1976: 7)

Progress towards the goal of self-government could be undertaken by two methods, namely direct rule by British administrators, or indirect rule whereby British officials supervised the governing activities of the local princes or chiefs. Both arrangements operated in India where the provinces were distinguished as

British India and Indian states. The most influential figure in the colonial service in the half-century to the end of the Second World War was Frederick (Lord) Lugard. He was the pro-consul of Nigeria for two decades and was firmly convinced from his experience there of the wisdom of what he termed 'Indirect Rule' or 'Dual Mandate'. The implication of the policy of eventual independent statehood was that civic education should be designed in each of the separate colonies, in MacDonald's words, to 'teach them to stand on their own feet'; to be proto-citizens and, in due course, full citizens of their own countries.

There was an alternative, as has been mentioned in the French context, of conceiving of the whole Empire as a political unit and educating for citizenship of that entity. That this should somehow be brought to pass in the British Empire became a topic for debate in the late nineteenth century when the Empire was at its apogee. A variety of laws and conventions existed, in a condition of some confusion except for the general acceptance that all inhabitants born in the Empire were British subjects. This status was officially recognized by the Imperial Act of 1914.

But what of common *citizenship*, as distinct from being a subject of the Imperial Crown, and what would it mean? Two keen supporters of the Empire in the inter-war years were the British politician Leo Amery and the South African statesman Jan Smuts. In 1921 Amery wrote to Smuts on this question, with particular regard to the Dominions. In this letter he argued that:

> These independent political units are composed equally of British subjects and have thus a common and interchangeable citizenship. . . . Nothing could be more typical of this community of citizenship than the fact that you, while a South African Minister, were actually for a time also a member of the British War Cabinet.
>
> (quoted Hall 1971: 376–7)

There were, in fact, prior examples: in the 1890s two Indian men secured election as MPs to the Westminster Parliament, standing for English constituencies. Nevertheless, efforts to define the nature of a British Commonwealth citizenship (the term 'Commonwealth' started to replace or complement 'Empire' at the time of the First World War) led to the increasing legal contortions of the half-dozen British Nationality and Commonwealth Immigration Acts from 1948 to 1981.

The sense of the unity of the Empire was transmitted to and encouraged in the young people of the Dominions and colonies in the inter-war years especially. We have already recorded earlier in this chapter the roles of Empire Day and youth groups, particularly the Scout and Guide movements, in educating about the Empire in Britain itself. These influences were repeated overseas. One British historian has described the celebration of Empire Day thus: 'schoolchildren all over the Empire [were] assembled under the union jack to hear imperialist harangues and to pipe up "Land of Hope and Glory"' (Cross 1968: 186). In addition, the League of Empire, founded in 1901, undertook much work to promote awareness of the constituent members of the Empire, though, it is true, with emphasis on the Dominions. Its central activity was its teacher-exchange scheme. At its 1924 Conference on

Imperial Education held in London for educators from throughout the Commonwealth, one of its recommendations was that teachers should be better trained 'for influencing the standard of public life and culture and arousing in their pupils a sense of the importance of the duties of empire citizenship' (quoted Gauss 1929: 85; see also 97 n.23).

No European colonial possession posed greater problems for government policy, local administration and provision of education than India, because of its size and its own firmly established political and cultural traditions and school systems. During the two centuries of effective British imperium from the end of the Seven Years War to the end of the Second World War a variety of governmental and administrative arrangements were tried and educational institutions created quite unmethodically. Despite the reforming zeal of some Britons and the resigned submissiveness of most Indians, relationships often combined the complacency of the rulers and the complaining of the ruled. To give two typical examples, both taking a broad historical perspective. Lord Curzon, who was Viceroy from 1898 to 1905, when he was an ardent reformer especially in education, had, as a young man, declaimed that, 'There has never been anything so great in the world's history as the British Empire, so great as an instrument for the good of humanity' (Stewart 1986: 44): a commonly held Victorian conviction. A western-educated Indian, writing at the beginning of the Second World War, described the British legacy in education as:

> surely . . . one of the most perverse and irrational in history. Its object was not intellectual development or character building or *training for citizenship* or any other 'ideals' familiar to pedagogues, but solely to impress on middle-class Indian youths the glory and grandeur of Britain and to train them to be competent servants of a foreign bureaucracy.
>
> (Shelvankar 1940: 43; emphasis added)

Generalization about civic education in pre-independence India is difficult for a host of reasons. The provinces differed in the availability of educational facilities and political consciousness; changes inevitably took place over this lengthy period of time; cultural distinctions, especially between Hindus and Muslims, were an important variable; and different influential individuals had different opinions about the policies to be pursued. Concerning this last factor, it should be borne in mind that some British politicians and officials wished to prevent any development of political consciousness among the Indians, others wished to foster a sense of identity with and loyalty to the Empire, while yet others accepted the wisdom and justice of preparing them for independent statehood. Among leading Indians who gave thought to the issue, some were content with the concept of citizenship of the Empire, others looked forward to the reshaping of India as a nation-state in modern westernized style, while others, on the contrary, wanted India to discard western influences and return to its traditional cultures revitalized. Again, of course, these differences varied according to time and place.

In tracing the history of civic education and the political and general educational background, it will be helpful to divide the whole stretch of time into four periods:

to 1858, 1858 to 1898, 1898 to 1921, 1921 to 1947. (For a useful survey of the history of education in India in the nineteenth and twentieth centuries, upon which some of the following paragraphs have depended heavily, see Naik and Nurullah 1974.)

Until 1858 responsibility for the administration of British India remained in the hands of the East India Company, which had been founded in 1600 and which, because of its essentially commercial purpose, had little interest in education. Even so, one of its employees, Charles Grant, put forward the argument at the end of the eighteenth century that:

> It is perfectly in the powers of this country, by degrees to impart to the Hindoos our language; afterwards through that medium to make them acquainted with our easy literary compositions . . . and . . . progressively with the simple elements of our *arts*, our *philosophy* and *religion*. These acquisitions would silently undermine, and at length subvert, the fabric of [their] errors.
>
> (quoted McCully 1966: 12)

This proposition was pregnant with educational and political implications. In 1813, the position of the company was revised in the Charter – or East India – Act, which, *inter alia*, opened up India to missionary educational activity and made the company responsible for educational development (see e.g. Naik and Nurullah 1974: 55–7).

In 1835 the distinguished English historian, Thomas Macaulay, then holding East India Company appointments and having been asked by the Governor-General to report on education, wrote his famous Minute on the subject. He went beyond Grant and, in a remarkable prognostication, suggested:

> That the public mind of India may expand under our system till it has outgrown our system; that by good government we may educate our subjects into a capacity for better government; that, having become instructed in European knowledge, they may, in some future age, demand European institutions.
>
> (quoted Somervell and Harvey 1959: 242)

By now a controversy had arisen between those who argued in favour of Indian education for Indian culture and the 'Anglicists', who favoured Grant's position. Given his political forecast, Macaulay could hardly help but side with the Anglicists. The question of the political and educational effects of his influential Minute has, in fact, been a matter of political, pedagogical and historiographical controversy. In 1854 the document known as the Wood Despatch was published, a most thorough set of recommendations for education in the subcontinent, which recognized that teaching in English, though very important for the small minority who could manage the language, was impractical for the vast majority. None the less, the Despatch repeated the words of Grant quoted above. The East India Company started to implement a few of the recommendations, but in 1858 responsibility for the governance of India was transferred to the Crown.

For the next forty years, our second period, little of moment occurred in the field of education in terms of events or policy because, in truth, neither the metropolitan government in London nor the Indian government in Calcutta was interested in anything but supporting the development of more private schools and cultivating the learning of the English language. What did happen, however, was a steady increase of anti-British political consciousness among the tiny minority of the population who had enjoyed an English-style education. During the last quarter of the nineteenth century a nationalist movement rapidly got under way. The vital events were the foundation of the Indian Association in Calcutta in 1876 and the Indian National Congress in 1885 to campaign for the reform of and greater justice for Indians in the system of administration. Henry Cotton, a British bureaucrat in Calcutta, explained in that latter year the connection between English education and national consciousness:

> It is education, and education according to English methods and on the lines of Western civilization that is already serving to unite the various forces among the Indian population. No other bond of unity was possible . . . now the English language is established as the channel through which . . . [all Indians can] give expression to their common interests and aspirations.
>
> (quoted McCully 1966: 295)

The small book from which this quotation is taken was published fifty years after Macaulay's Minute advocating, as Grant had done, the spread of the English language and voiced this view as well as containing his prediction of its outcome.

Furthermore, the Indian intelligentsia had learned 'the characteristics of English civilization and institutions, the rights of English subjects, and the "humanizing influence" of English citizenship' (McCully 1966: 226, summarizing the views published in a Hindu newspaper in 1877). Thus it has often been said that Indian nationalism was nurtured on the works of Burke, Paine and Mill. On the other hand, by achieving their education and political consciousness through the medium of English, this elite proto-citizenry were detached from the huge majority of the population, who remained largely uneducated, politically unaware and dependent for communication on their vernacular tongues.

Yet the demands, sometimes given extra force by agitation, of the politically literate were starting to cause concern to the British authorities of the *Raj*. The most aware and most determined to react vigorously was Lord Curzon, who, as noted above, arrived in Calcutta to take up his post as Viceroy at the end of 1898. We have thus reached our third phase. The pivotal significance of Curzon has been summarized, with quotations from his own speeches, in the following words:

> The Viceroy believed that education was of vital importance and was 'perhaps the most clamant necessity of all' in India. Because here education was required not primarily as the instrument of culture or the source of learning. . . . 'It is a social and political' even more than an intellectual demand.
>
> (Basu 1974: 6)

Although Curzon tackled the subcontinent's educational needs on a broad front and presented his reforms as education for education's sake, the belief that current political discontent was a consequence of the education, especially higher education, systems was never far from his mind and thus a motive for his programme. He was convinced that 'the first and foremost cause of political unrest in India was "the education we have given to the people of the country"' (Basu 1974: 9). Others were of the same mind. The Secretary of State wrote to Curzon that it was 'impossible to dissociate their ideas and their hatred of England from the course of education and training through which they have passed' (Basu 1974: 9; see also 10–11). Education to cement a conception of citizenship of the Empire was failing; the granting of a citizenship of India, which the education of the upper ranks of society also led them to expect, was too long a-coming.

As has so often happened when governments wish to improve the temper of the people to a stauncher loyalty to the polity, Curzon advocated better moral education. In his *Resolution on Educational Policy* of 1904, having expressed his concerns, he declared that:

> The remedy for the evil tendencies noted above is to be sought, not so much in the formal methods of teaching conduct by means of moral text-books or primers of personal ethics, as in the influence of carefully selected and trained teachers . . . [and] the proper selection of text-books, such as biographies, which teach by example.
>
> (quoted Naik and Nurullah 1974: 266)

In the meantime, during the early years of the twentieth century, agitation for a greater degree of self-rule intensified, leading the government in London to accept that concessions should be made. In 1917 the Secretary of State announced the policy in principle. This statement was followed two years later by a Government of India Act, which inaugurated the system of Diarchy, the constitutional change to a sharing of power. Yet, although this was a major step on the road to independence in political terms, the shift of powers from the provinces to Calcutta, which was part of the new arrangements, involved a retrogression in education. The relatively generous grants to the provincial governments for education, which had started in 1901, were discontinued when these constitutional innovations came into effect.

While political demands were being voiced and being responded to, considerable thought was also given to the need for India to have a national form of education. Both British and Indian educationists advocated this, though the campaign was bedevilled by the perennial problem of interpretation of what this should mean. From the late 1890s the formidable English lady, social reformer and theosophist Mrs Annie Besant, who was later to found the Indian Home Rule League, was an especially persistent advocate of a national, not to say nationalist, education. She declared:

> Nothing can more swiftly emasculate national life, nothing can more surely weaken national character, than allowing the education of the young to be controlled by foreign influences, to be dominated by foreign ideals. . . .

[Our national education] must be controlled by Indians, shaped by Indians, carried on by Indians. *It must hold up Indian ideals of devotion, wisdom and morality. . . .*

National education must live in an atmosphere of proud and glorious patriotism.

(quoted Rai 1966: 6–7)

This excerpt has been taken from a short work written in 1918 by an Indian educationist, who, though admiring Mrs Besant's passionate interest in Indian affairs, disagreed with her focus on Indian traditions. This writer was Lala Lajpat Rai, whose book was believed to be so relevant to India's current education policy in the 1960s that it was republished by the Ministry of Information and Broadcasting forty-six years after its initial appearance (see Rai 1966: i–ii; also Naik and Nurullah 1974: 354). Rai argued the contrary case, for a modernized national education which recognizes that 'The boys and girls of to-day are the citizens of to-morrow', and that 'All life is social' (Rai 1966: 16). Accordingly, what pupils need is not courses in traditional Indian philosophy and literature: quite the opposite:

A study of the modern laws, of civics, of the modern world, of the forms of government prevailing in other countries, of their politics and economics, is a *sine qua non* of future progress on healthy lines. These things ought to be taught to every boy and girl, even in elementary schools. It is only their widespread dissemination that will make us politically self-conscious and alert.

(Rai 1966: 30)

Rai argued thoroughly and persuasively too for the teaching of patriotism (Rai 1966: esp. 57–63).

We have now reached our fourth and final phase in this survey; that is, the years from 1921 to 1947. The political scene during this period was dominated by gradual progress to independence through constitutional reform for the delegation of more powers from London to Delhi (the new capital of India), tense negotiations, local demonstrations, and a growing split between Hindus and Muslims. The diarchical arrangement ended in 1937 as part of the Government of India Act of 1935. Yet despite the lack of interest in and funding for education during these sixteen years, there is a positive feature to report. For, although the *quality* of education declined, *quantity* increased; as an example, the number of pupils in primary schools rose from 61 to 102 million. Among the people there occurred, indeed, a remarkable waxing of enthusiasm for education. This was noticed by the Hartog Committee, set up in 1927 to report on the matter of education:

Our Review of the growth of education reveals many points of fundamental interest for the political future of India. The largely increased enrolment in primary schools indicates that the old time apathy of the masses is breaking down. There has been a social and political awakening of the women of India and an expressed demand on their behalf for education and social reform.

(quoted Naik and Nurullah 1974: 325–6)

Most provinces had, in fact, by this time introduced legislation to try to make primary schooling compulsory.

Even so, if one takes literacy as a basic index of the progress of elementary education, without which civic education cannot evolve fully, the statistics for this period paint a gloomy picture. The figure remained at 7 per cent from 1921 to 1931 and, although this had risen to 12.2 per cent in 1947, this improvement seems scarcely consonant with the increased commitment to primary education among the people. Two comments may help to explain this disappointment. The first relates to the number of primary schools. These rose from 82,916 in 1881 to 1882 to 192,244 in 1936 to 1937, then declined to 167,700 in 1945 to 1946. The other comment is Mahatma Gandhi's: 'Money spent on primary education is a waste of expenditure in as much as what little is taught is soon forgotten and has little or no value in terms of the villages or cities' (quoted Naik and Nurullah 1974: 380; see 375–7 for statistics).

Gandhi gave considerable thought to the problem and came up with the innovative concept of Basic Education, which, in 1937, he applied to the conditions prevailing in India. In that year the First Conference on National Education was convened. This body appointed a committee to draft a detailed syllabus for Basic Education, under the chairmanship of Zakir Hussein (who was later to commend Lajpat Rai's book). The central idea of Basic Education was that pupils should be taught crafts so that the acquired skills would stand them in good stead in later years and that the income from the sale of their products would finance the running of the school. The Committee also saw the civic implications of this approach and included in their report two paragraphs headed 'Ideal of Citizenship Implicit in the Scheme'. These explained that the:

> Close relationship of the work done at school to the work of the community will . . . enable the children to carry the outlook and attitudes acquired in the school environment into the wider world outside. Thus the new scheme which we are advocating will aim at giving the citizens of the future a keen sense of personal worth, dignity and efficiency, and will strengthen in them the desire for self-improvement and social service in a cooperative community.
>
> (quoted Naik and Nurullah 1974: 385)

The onset of war and the intensification of nationalist protests adversely affected the development of Basic Education during the years before independence, and even though its potential was widely recognized, it was not often put into practice.

The problem of adult education was also addressed at this time. For example, in 1939 the Education Minister in Bihar said that the objectives of the adult education 'movement should be (1) to teach the illiterate adult the three R's, and (2) to impart knowledge closely correlated to his working life and give him a good grounding in citizenship' (quoted Naik and Nurullah 1974: 391). And, for good measure, he quoted Lenin's famous statement on the relationship between literacy and politics (see Chapter 4 below). But, again, the war interrupted this activity.

None the less, during the years of war the intense interest in education and the determination to effect improvements brought forth a number of development plans. The most important of these was the *Post-War Educational Development in India* report (the *Sargent Report*) of 1944, the official scheme for a national education system. At the primary and middle levels of schooling an adapted form of Basic Education was recommended, retaining the concept of education for future citizenship. In the academic high schools civics was to be included in the curriculum. Throughout the system the language of instruction was to be the pupils' mother-tongue.

The educational legacy of the era of British rule can be expressed in the features of two unequal chronological spans. One was that 'the educational policies in India between 1813 and 1937 were characteristic of the British genius for "muddling through to success"' (Naik and Nurullah 1974: 406; though, assuredly, that success was very partial). The other was the belated production of plans for a coherent national system during the final decade. When India introduced its Constitution in 1949, this instrument provided for universal adult suffrage and stressed the equality of citizenship for all. In order to give all citizens the opportunities to play their civic roles effectively a huge educational task still lay before the new state.

Whereas the East India Company, followed by the British government, had from the eighteenth century successively encouraged the participation of some Indians in the administration of their country, it was not until the late nineteenth century that Britain had any substantial colonial territories in Africa. Therefore, it was only in the early years of the twentieth century that the government in London started to think seriously about their educational needs and the advisability of supplementing the work of the Mission Societies. In 1923 the Colonial Secretary, the Duke of Devonshire, set up an Advisory Committee on Native Education in the British Tropical African Dependencies. Its report, published two years later, is most instructive on the considered policy to be pursued and the inclusion of some thought to citizenship education in the overall recommendations. The guiding principle was that:

> Education should be adapted to the mentality, aptitudes, occupations and traditions of the various peoples, conserving as far as possible all sound and healthy elements in the fabric of their social life; adapting them where necessary to changed circumstances and progressive ideas. . . . Its aim should be to render the individual more efficient in his or her condition of life, whatever it may be, and to promote the advancement of the community as a whole through . . . [various means including] the inculcation of true ideals of citizenship and service.
>
> (Cowan *et al.* 1965: 46)

This concern to shape the education to African traditions and needs is reflected in the requirement that English geography and history textbooks should be replaced. However, the main area of discussion germane to citizenship education is in the paragraph on religion and character training (Cowan *et al.* 1965: 46–7). Because of the unsettling effects of European intrusion on traditional authority and beliefs, these aspects of the work in teacher-training colleges and schools 'should be accorded an equal standing with secular subjects'. This teaching, the report goes on to say, 'should find expression in habits of self-discipline and loyalty to the community'.

The advice on how to achieve these desirable outcomes is very akin to the English Public school tradition, not surprisingly, since the members of the Committee would have been products of that system. The following sentences reflect this:

> History shows that devotion to some spiritual ideal is the deepest source of inspiration in the discharge of public duty. Such influences should penetrate the whole life of the school. One such influence is the discipline of work. Field games and social recreations and intercourse are influences at least as important as classroom instruction.

The Committee accepted that the Boy Scout and Girl Guide movements could contribute, but the best results would be achieved by imbibing the ethos of the school and exercising monitorial responsibilities in a residential school. Thus the elitist cat was let out of the Colonial Office's bag. Indeed, reference had been made earlier to 'the training of those who are required to fill posts in the administration and technical service as well as those who as chiefs will occupy positions of exceptional trust and responsibility' (Cowan *et al.* 1965: 46–7).

British grip on her possessions in the Middle East and the Indian subcontinent was weakening in the inter-war period and on her African possessions immediately after the Second World War. Yet neither the wartime Coalition government nor the post-war Labour government devised any coherent policy of decolonization. Indeed, during the Second World War, Herbert Morrison, who was to be the Deputy Prime Minister in the post-war Attlee administration, bluntly declared that giving independence to the African colonies would be 'like giving a child of ten a latch key, a bank account and a shot-gun' (quoted Cross 1968: 262). Three days of furious rioting in Accra, capital of the Gold Coast (now Ghana), in 1948, sparked by a panicked small police contingent opening fire on a huge but peaceful demonstration, changed that attitude. Britain, debilitated by six years of total war, had no stomach for repressive imperial rule against nationalist demands for liberation. Within twelve years, her African possessions were independent states.

Meanwhile, accepting that the colonies should, nevertheless and albeit at an extremely leisurely pace, be educated to assume greater autonomy, the Colonial Office and the Advisory Committee on Education in the Colonies decided in 1946 to set up a subcommittee on education for citizenship. Its terms of reference were:

> To study the technique needed to prepare people for responsibility, and examine generally the problem of building up a sense of public responsibility, tolerance, and objectivity in discussion and practice, and an appreciation of political institutions, their evolution and progress.

(Colonial Office 1948: 3)

In the event, the group agreed that their report should be confined to recommendations for Africa, and although the word 'citizenship' was absent from their brief, they were convinced that this was the crucial word to describe their field. In fact, it is clear from the detail in the paragraphs (41–73) on education for citizenship through the schools and the entries in their bibliography that the Subcommittee was influenced by the work of the Association for Education in Citizenship, which has already been mentioned in this chapter.

The report pays tribute to the increase in civic consciousness in the British African colonies since 1919 through the media of schools, the cinema, the wireless and the press. Nevertheless, this progress, they aver, had been too slow for the conditions and expectations prevailing in the post-1945 world. 'The Colonial peoples,' they explain, want democratic self-government, and 'In this matter . . . [they] are setting themselves the task of passing in one generation through a development over which the leading nations of the West have spent two or more leisurely centuries.' Consequently, 'In this period of rapid transition, education becomes of greater importance and urgency than ever before.' A conscious preparation for citizenship was essential 'if political freedom is to benefit all the people and not merely the favoured few' (paras 3, 4).

How, then, to proceed? First, native traditions should as far as possible be honoured and maintained. But new opportunities for assuming responsibilities especially in local government should be made available for adults, because 'the theory learnt in the lecture-room [*sic*]' is of little use if not applied in practice (para. 38). This statement clearly refers to well-educated adults, despite the proclaimed need to 'benefit all the people'.

The pages of suggestions are in many ways very sensible for the advantaged minority and for out-of-class activities. On the other hand, one wonders whether, in the treatment of the contributions of the various classroom subjects (the importance of geography and history is stressed), the Subcommittee lost sight of the severe practical difficulties to which they do nevertheless alert the reader:

> We realise that in many schools there are at present no materials at all for giving the children a glimpse of the outside world – no pictures, no newspapers, no magazines or printed matter of any description beyond the handful of textbooks in the cupboard. In conditions like these, group study must perforce be restricted to materials that can be obtained orally, in the village market for example.
>
> (para. 46)

Another cause for querying the complete helpfulness of the report in light of the scale of the task before them is the scanty space allocated to the difficult but major problem of adult illiterates. Although they identify this as one of their four categories of needed educational provision, they seem to have despaired at the immensity of the problem, and concluded that:

> Since much discussion is needed, education for citizenship can be carried out only with comparatively small groups of leaders. . . . We do not think it possible

to treat the necessarily somewhat abstract material of citizenship with as large numbers of pupils as can profit from a demonstration of poultry, cookery or ploughing.

(para. 80)

Nevertheless, the seriousness of purpose of the Subcommittee cannot be gainsaid. That a whole report of 102 paragraphs should have been devoted to citizenship education in Africa shows a remarkable advance since the 1925 report, a mere thirteen years before. Furthermore, this earnest concern is expressed in the clarion call of their conclusion:

This task of education for citizenship . . . [is] so large and so urgent that everyone will be needed if the Colonies are to be helped to assume their responsibilities in the modern world. One of the most urgent tasks facing Colonial Governments is to rally to their aid all people of any race in their territories who are able to contribute to this high endeavour.

(para. 102)

However, since the process of conceding self-government to the British African colonies started in 1957 (with Ghana), there was scarcely time for much effective reform to take place.

Asian and African states after independence

Depending on one's political standpoint, independence was conceded to or liberation was achieved by most of the colonial lands of the Middle East, Asia and Africa during the one-and-a-half decades between 1945 and 1960 with little time anywhere for the indigenous leaders to plan their own educational systems. Yet there was widespread conviction among these leaders that education and education for citizenship were vital necessities for their new-born nations. For example, Kwame Nkrumah, the future President of Ghana, addressing pupils in an elite school in the then Gold Coast, stated quite bluntly, 'The purpose of all true education is to produce good citizens' (Nkrumah 1961: 57). This interpretation was echoed at greater length by KANU (the Kenya African National Union) in its outline of the education policy it would pursue on independence:

The first aim of that education will be to produce good citizens, inspired with a desire to serve their fellow men. The democracy we shall create is more than a set of laws and institutions. It will depend upon the understanding participation by all the people in the democratic process.

(Cowan *et al.* 1965: 123)

In the effort to make progress in this endeavour, politicians and educationists had both advantages and disadvantages.

The main advantage was the excitement of independence. Many welcomed their political liberation and recognized the importance of more widespread education for making a success of their states. Moreover, some, notably the Arab (and some other Muslim) countries, possessed a cultural coherence that could offer a solid basis for education in national self-awareness and loyalty. This point was made very forcibly by a French scholar:

> Of all the factors which influence education in the Arab countries nationalism is the major ideological factor in the education of children. The Arabic language and its potential are emphasized, the past notably after the coming of Islam is taught. . . . Even when teaching subjects as far removed as biology and psychology the spirit is stamped with this nationalist fervour.
>
> (quoted Szyliowicz 1973: 47)

On the other hand, most new states had no such cultural bonds, apart from the imperial ties which they were engaged in loosening. Large countries such as India (see below), Nigeria (see Chapter 5) and (the former Belgian) Congo are culturally heterogeneous to an extraordinary degree. Then, too, there was the problem of poverty. School buildings, teachers, new textbooks, furniture and equipment required outlays that could barely be afforded, certainly by the more impecunious countries. Perhaps the greatest disadvantage and the most daunting task to be tackled as a priority was illiteracy. We have already made some observations about this in our survey of imperial policies. Wanting in such a fundamental skill, the individual can learn about his or her role as a citizen in only the most primitive way by oral communication. Even banners, posters and leaflets are largely incomprehensible (compare the early Soviet policies in Chapter 4). So it was in many states immediately following decolonization.

Special considerations need to be given to Muslim countries that have had a history of relatively authoritarian rule. Inevitably, they have favoured schools and school curricula that concentrate on Islamic studies – the history of Islam, the study of the Koran, and, therefore, the learning of Arabic (where it is not the mother-tongue) in order properly to construe the Holy texts in their original language. Even where the state and government are secular – and Iran has been the only fully theocratic state in modern times – these school programmes might be some-what neglectful of a civic education devised to comprehend the political and legal structures. Furthermore, where autocratic regimes have existed, such study, which could lead to political criticism, would be discouraged. The histories of Indonesia and Pakistan are interesting exemplars of these conditions.

In Indonesia, during the Presidency of Achmad Sukarno (1945 to 1968), Islamic education was such a force, especially in Java, that a Muslim Teachers' Party (NU) became a significant political movement. On the other hand, the President's policy of 'guided democracy' was designed to restrain independent civic thinking. The effect of this atmosphere on schools is revealed in the following comment by a Javanese in conversation with an Australian academic: 'Our textbooks, especially in politics, economics, sociology and related subjects, are pathetic – Sukarnoism run riot. Our brains need to be refreshed with some real thinking' (Grant 1967: 172).

The provinces of India which on independence became Pakistan were formed into a consciously Muslim state in contrast to the predominantly Hindu state of India. Now, although those reaching university standard in their education had the opportunity to read some of the western political texts in Urdu, by and large, compared with those of a Hindu background, the Muslims were slow to develop a national consciousness. This disparity has been succinctly explained: 'The tardy and sluggish growth of Muslim nationalism was in great part due to a lack of educational progress. . . . Schools and colleges were neither adequate to the needs of Muslims nor good enough for the standards demanded of them' (Aziz 1967: 132–3). Even so, despite this weak legacy, well-developed social studies syllabuses were drafted. For example, the fifth grade have studied the Constitution; the sixth, the autonomous powers of local government and the social services; the ninth, 'the ideological basis of Pakistan', via history and biography (see Muñoz 1982: Annex XVI). Though how far teachers used the syllabuses to encourage critical thought, especially during periods of military rule, is another matter.

Since the creation of the UN, the number of its member-states has quadrupled, and a large majority of the additions were former colonies. It is therefore impossible, indeed undesirable, in a book like this to supply a full coverage. So, in order to illustrate how, after decolonization, the new regimes dealt with the problems of building upon their parsimonious legacies in citizenship education, the activities in the former French West and Central Africa will be traced, and the former British possessions of India and Singapore will be contrasted at one stage in their history.

Three conditions have characterized these Francophone states: the strength of the colonial inheritance, poverty, and the desire to build new nations against a condition, feared or actual, of political instability. All but one of these colonies became independent in 1960 (namely Guinea, in 1958), so have had the same length of time to develop their own educational systems; still, it would be tedious (and difficult) to treat all fourteen here. We shall therefore proceed by analysing the main aspects of civic education in this region with exemplifications from a few of the most interesting.

It has already been shown how determined the French were to subordinate and Gallicize their colonies. Two commentators on these countries after independence may be cited as evidence of the persistence of this influence, thus hindering the development of fresh autonomous national identities. One wrote: 'the myth that the Negroes are inferior to the whites and condemned to obey them has profoundly penetrated into the thinking of many generations of Africans'; the other deemed that 'Most of the schools in the former French colonies still operate on a model inherited from metropolitan France, a model, moreover, that is thoroughly impregnated with French notions of authority' (quoted Harber 1989: 142–3, 139). Now, the second quotation was originally published in 1979, nearly two decades after the independence of these colonies, indicating therefore the tardiness of relieving the populations from the colonial imprint. The wish was there, but only Guinea and Mali possessed the drive – ideologically powered, it must be said – to transform the political culture of their schools.

Before examining the way in which they tackled the problem, however, a few statistics will supply a useful background. At the time of independence, even in the more developed French West Africa, let alone French Equatorial Africa, the proportion of children enrolled in primary schools varied widely. The Ivory Coast, Togo and Dahomey (now Benin) all had nearly one-third, while Mali, Mauritania, Upper Volta (now Burkina Faso) and Niger had under one-tenth (see Hargreaves 1967: 12–13). An indicator of the effects of a firm commitment to education is given by Mali, which increased primary school enrolments from 8 per cent in 1960 to 12 per cent in 1962 to 20 per cent in 1972 (see Toure 1982: 192).

The nationalist political impulse for independence in Mali was refocused on education from 1960 to 1962. The prime consideration was 'the political and cultural decolonisation of the people through the medium of the schools' (Toure 1982: 191) – to put the French policy into reverse. The product of this exertion 'was a Malian school system distinct in character and purpose from the colonial school system. In the post-colonial era education was seen as a sure weapon of nation-building, development and modernisation' (Toure 1982: 191). Immediate reform in Guinea took on a particular style. The new stress was on what we would today call a communitarian mode of education. To quote the same African authority we have cited above on Mali, pupils 'should become integrated into the people's life, its sufferings, its concerns, its struggles and expectations. . . . We must remember that the man dies, the people remain' (quoted Harber 1989: 143). To this end, two practical measures were put in place in 1961: a compulsory course of political education for all secondary pupils, and restriction of scholarships to secondary pupils and post-secondary students to those who showed 'fidelity to the PDG and to the country' (quoted Harber 1989: 143). Since only 1 per cent of the eligible age-group were in secondary education at this time, these regulations clearly affected only a tiny number, though they were, of course, the future elite citizens. A second comment: PDG is the abbreviation for *Parti Democratique de Guinée*, and since this was and continued to be the only legal political party, both the course of political education, in which knowledge of the PDG bulked large, and the criterion for scholarships meant that secondary school pupils were in effect indoctrinated.

In the new states where the leadership was sufficiently determined to slough off French influence (except the language, which could not be dispensed with), nation-building and ideological indoctrination became virtually synonymous. Moreover, partly because this was a revolutionary process and partly because the only assistance that was not French could be obtained from Communist sources, the indoctrination was of a left-wing tone. In Mali, where President Sékou Touré was an ideological driving force for many years, the 'communitarian' aims of education were closely related to a government policy hostile to individualistic capitalism. In Guinea, a subject actually called ideology was introduced as a mandatory course from primary to university levels, and included, in addition to classroom lessons, membership of the party's youth movement, the JDRA (*Jeunesse de la Révolution Africaine*; note the word 'revolution').

On the matter of the construction of syllabuses to achieve the processes of 'mental decolonization' and left-wing renovation, the example of the history schemes of around 1980 in Congo (Congo Brazzaville) is of interest. It should be noted that friendship with the Soviet Union and the deep influence of the trade union movement helped to colour the approach to this subject. This is especially evident in the syllabus for the second level in the primary school, which listed five topics (see Muñoz 1982: 455; author's translation). Even the second and third, dealing with 'Our National Flag' and 'Our National Anthem' cannot help projecting this slant. Teaching about the flag included reference to its 'Evocation of the workers' struggle', as well as its national message of 'Unity, Peace, Friendship'. And the National Anthem reflects, among other topics, 'the trade union' and 'the foundation of the PCT' (the *Parti congolais de travail*, the workers', indeed the sole, political party). The other three topics covered the Pioneer youth movement, the PCT and other popular movements.

An African colony of mainly French background but with a specific problem is Cameroon. The country is composed of regions which, for four decades, had been French and British colonies, the French being by far the larger; so in linguistic terms it has been a kind of equatorial Canada in reverse. In addition, inevitably, it inherited two different school systems. Consequently, the policy of using schools for nation-building had to tackle these two major complications. Three curriculum centres were established to spearhead reforms. They aimed 'at applying the notions of "functionalism" and "practicality" to the whole educational system, thus adapting the educational system to the economic or production system of the country' (Shu 1982: 43).

While some of the former French West and Central African colonies continued the French educational policy based on an adapted liberal republican concept of citizenship, it is clear from the above that those with a more vigorous thrust to shape a new education pursued distinctly radical programmes of reform. (The reader may therefore question the placing of this matter in a chapter on education for liberal democracy, but they emerged from a French background which was decidedly liberal democratic.) All, in some measure, attempted a coalescence of 'traditional' and 'modern' styles (see e.g. Harber (1989: 127, 140 n.1) for detailed interpretations of these terms), but the predominant concern was economic, as the curricular reforms of, for example, Congo Brazzaville and Cameroon so plainly reveal. Since it is now becoming increasingly accepted in liberal democratic states that citizenship education must incorporate education for economic understanding, then the stories of these African states are very relevant to our study.

Although the states which emerged from French West and Equatorial Africa differed in levels of educational and political development, they are not greatly disparate in size and wealth. This is not true of Britain's former Asian possessions. It will therefore be instructive to compare the largest and relatively poor with the very small and very rich: the gargantuan India with the Lilliputian Singapore; by classical analogy, a veritable empire, with a modern city-state. In order to make the comparison we shall home in on the period of the 1970s and 1980s, by which time both countries had had time to devise their own post-independence educational policies (India became independent in 1947, Singapore effectively in 1967).

First, the contrasts in size. The Indian census of 1981 recorded a population of 684 million; the Singaporean figure for 1982 was 2.5 million. The area of India is 3.2 million square kilometres; Singapore's, 618. Because of India's great size its governmental structure is inevitably federal, and educational progress has been noticeably faster in some states than in others; even, indeed, within states, as between urban and rural areas, and between districts. A similar patchwork of levels of political consciousness may also be discerned. In contrast, Singapore, despite its multicultural complexity, became politically a tight-knit state. A Singaporean educationist has commented that:

> Singapore's small size and mass media saturation suggest important roles for . . . [a number of] societal institutions. The government itself is the 'great educator'. For more than two decades government leaders have used the mass media extensively to hector, cajole, persuade and inform. . . . The present commitment to greater openness, the institutionalisation of feedback on government policies, extensive grass-roots involvement in the framing of a national agenda indicate continued education outside the school.
>
> (Gopinathan 1988: 136)

How reminiscent this is of Aristotle's insistence on limiting the size of the *polis*: 'A state composed of too many . . . will not be a true state, for the simple reason that it can hardly have a true constitution. . . . Who can give [the mass of citizens] orders, unless he has a Stentor's voice?' (Aristotle 1948: 1326b). The Singaporean government's use of the mass media, accessible to the whole of its population, has given it a voice that easily carries throughout this modern *polis*.

This ready communication has been made possible because of the island-state's wealth. Its per capita GDP in 1980 was US$6,515. Compare this with India's US$240, an average figure which, in any case, masks the vast gap between the few extremely rich and the mass of impoverished. The people of Singapore have been able to buy the means of communication and to be sufficiently literate to read the printed medium. These conditions are quite unlike so many Indian lower-class families, especially the peasantry, who have been unable to afford to release their children from productive work in order to attend school. In spite of the requirement, written into the Indian Constitution, of universal primary education, a quarter of a century after its inauguration the drop-out rate of those enrolled at the age of 6 was 50 per cent by the end of the school year (see Naik and Nurullah 1974: 455–6). In addition to the factor of indigence in inhibiting the growth of education, popular attitudes to schooling in India have also contributed. Successive governments devoted substantial sums to increase the number of schools, but the quality of the teachers and the curricula left much to be desired. Lower-class parents who could afford to keep their children in school saw that they were bored, were making very slow progress and therefore had little chance of achieving their ambition to rise in the social scale. Comparison with Singapore reveals a marked difference, for there, 'Both at the government and the individual level there is almost complete faith in the value of education to do almost anything' (Gopinathan 1988: 134).

In principle, the governments of both states were of one mind that education for citizenship was of cardinal importance. Where they parted company was in the kind of education that was necessary. Here we come to the heart of their differences, differences which were determined by the disparities in their sizes and wealth. Indian authorities wanted education for literacy; the Singaporeans, for morality.

India has been by far the biggest democracy in the world, with hundreds of millions of enfranchised citizens. But illiteracy has weakened the efficiency and justice of this democratic system. The pre-independence aim of eradicating illiteracy has therefore been of even greater concern since. And yet the policy has been pursued at a languid pace. Writing in 1974, the two Indian educationists who have been frequently cited above regretted that, 'Unfortunately not much progress has been made in the spread of literacy among adults during the past twenty-five years. . . . This does not create the home atmosphere which would encourage children to go to school' (Naik and Nurullah 1974: 455, 457). The plain figures for the proportion of literates show a rise from 29 per cent in 1971 to 36 per cent in 1981. However, because the population increased by 143 million during that decade the actual number of illiterates did not decline. Education had to run to catch up with demography. It continued to be an immense task.

No such problem has faced Singapore: no widespread poverty; no illiteracy to worry about. But wealth brought its own civic problems in the 1970s with the importation of the amoral western youth subculture: 'Official characterization then of the attitudes of Singapore's youths – materialistic, unwilling to sacrifice, to put nation before self, even unfilial – implied that corruption had already taken root' (Gopinathan 1988: 134). Education for a civic morality had become a concern of most pressing urgency. This was the view of Dr Gopinathan, whom we have already quoted, writing in 1988:

> Singapore has wrestled with the issues of moral education for two decades with shifts of emphasis and rationales. It would appear that the view taken of values education in Singapore is that the problem is essentially one of bringing about social integration and consensus, of establishing a set of core values, drawn preferably from the traditions of the ethnic groups represented in Singapore. No less than the survival of the nation is seen as riding on the success of the moral education programme.
>
> (Gopinathan 1988: 130)

Accordingly, a deliberate change of curricular policy in this area was brought about in 1974. In 1967 a fairly conventional civics syllabus had been introduced; this was now replaced by an education for living (EFL) programme. It was designed as a syllabus for moral and social education with a focus on nation-building from the disparate eastern and western traditions infused into Singaporean society. Five years later, a parliamentary committee produced a *Report on Moral Education, 1979*, highly critical of the civics teaching and the lack of interest among both teachers and pupils in moral education. As a consequence, teaching materials for the elementary/lower secondary age-ranges were developed, notably a programme entitled *Being and Becoming*, which was shaped by the Report's insistence on the triad, 'Personal Behaviour, Social Responsibility and Loyalty to Country'. In addition, another programme, entitled *Good Citizen*, was produced specifically for Chinese speakers (the 1980 census showed that 75 per cent of the population were Chinese). Yet very real difficulties of implementation remained (see Gopinathan 1988: 138, 141).

Essentially, during the period under review here, neither the people of Singapore nor of India were particularly interested in political matters in any really active way. In Singapore, *pace* the apparent availability of means of participation mentioned above, Gopinathan has reported that, 'While the trappings of Western-style democracy remain, the population has been largely depoliticised in the belief that political argument, debate and opposition are destabilizing and detract from more pressing issues of economic growth and national unity' (Gopinathan 1988: 132). Concerning India, in 1971 the distinguished Swedish economist Gunnar Myrdal wrote of the country as having:

> A firmly established parliamentary government based on universal suffrage and a comparatively high turnout of the electorate. But in spite of this the masses are more the object of politics than its subject. They remain passive and inert. . . . India's democracy has proved stable, but it is largely the stability of stagnation.
>
> (Myrdal 1977: 125)

So, in their different ways, Singaporeans and Indians were expressing little sense of positive citizenship, the former because of dissuasion, the latter because of a natural passivity. In each of these circumstances, the schools were able to make only limited progress in pursuit of a full and energetic education to prepare their pupils for the role of citizen.

Drawing connections between ancient Greece and the modern world is tempting but misleading. Thus it may be assumed that, in the long perspective of history, the theory and style of citizenship that evolved in the liberal states, becoming democratic in due course, derived from the Athenian model. Yet a truer interpretation lies in the development of consultative, then representative government, epitomized by the Anglo-Saxon Witans and the medieval English Parliament, and, later, admiration for the Roman republican ideal. Similarly, despite some esteem and false history, there was no direct historical connection between ancient Sparta and modern totalitarianism, the subject of our next chapter; totalitarianism derived rather from nineteenth-century nationalism and socialism. And if we wish to draw a simple contrast between the two forms of civic instruction related to these modern forms of polity, they also, despite classical parallels, have in fact been responses to the particular needs of modern states. Liberal citizenship has required education for participation to support its institutions; totalitarianism has required indoctrination for mobilization to support the dictators.

4 Totalitarianism and transitions

Words and reality

The term 'totalitarian citizenship education' comprises three words, each of which, by being brought into juxtaposition, is untrue; the term itself therefore has no validity. Or so it may be argued. Totalitarianism as a political word owes its origin in the 1920s mainly to Mussolini and Giovanni Gentile, who expounded in detail the Italian Fascist ideology (see e.g. Schapiro 1972: 13). It was subsequently extended to define what were believed to be the common features of ideologically driven dictatorial regimes as disparate as fascist Italy, Nazi Germany, the Soviet Union and Maoist China, which sought the *total* control of their populations. But, the promiscuous use of the label ignores the deep differences that separated these states, exaggerates the distinction between the so-called totalitarian and other authoritarian forms of government, and assumes an omnipotent efficiency which they did not necessarily exercise in practice.

On the other hand, even those who have objected to the term could not deny that, individually, at least, Nazi Germany, the Stalinist Soviet Union and Maoist China made ideologically justified attempts at constructing politically directed societies. Yet, if citizenship presupposes the ability to frame personal judgements on social and political affairs and to exert some influence based upon those independent judgements, then citizenship in this proper sense could not have existed in those states, in which terrorist political police, tight censorship and pervasive propaganda constricted both private and public lives and minds.

By the same token, education for the citizenly function could not have obtained. That is, if, again, we accept a proper understanding of the term; if, indeed, we accept that the nature of education is the balanced development of the human personality and, in particular, the cultivation of the pupil's capacity to think and reason objectively. This was assuredly not the required purpose of the schools, youth movements and political parties of those regimes. Their purpose was, in contra-distinction to education, indoctrination. Instruction was devised as ways of trying to get pupils 'to believe that a proposition "p" is true, in such a way that nothing will shake that belief', as an English educational philosopher has defined the process (White 1967: 181). The connection between totalitarianism and the indoctrination of youth has, in fact, been shown to have quite deep historical roots. One British historian has argued that insistence on universal admission to education, from eighteenth-century French thinkers to twentieth-century dictators, had the purpose of mobilizing a populace, schooled to only uncritical standards and indoctrinated to a support for government authority; nineteenth-century liberal belief in education as a path to liberal democracy was naive (see Cobban 1939: 227–9).

On a different tack: is the feeling of citizenship compatible with a feeling of hatred? It cannot be, if citizenship implies a sense of community and mutual respect for one's fellow citizens. Yet there is hate in the very fabric of totalitarian ideologies, which seeps into the expectations they have of the behaviour of citizens and of the education they should receive. There follow two examples. In an approved textbook for Soviet primary schoolteachers (and to continue our metaphor) we find the statement: 'The pupils of the Soviet school must realize that the feeling of Soviet patriotism is saturated with irreconcilable hatred toward the enemies of socialist society' (quoted Counts 1957: 122). And again, at the primary level, a comment on a book published in Germany in the Nazi era: 'It goes on, page after page, with no other purpose than to fill little children with hatred for the "enemies of Germany", aside from the Jews, everyone not in complete accord with the plans and methods of the Führer' (Mann 1939: 54).

We must still, however, take into consideration that 'totalitarian' may be better understood as a relative rather than an absolute term. Compare the following two quotations and consider the light they shed on our problem of the validity of the phrase 'totalitarian citizenship education'.

> The most serious application of the doctrine of the Catholic state is Gentile's reform of public education. The public schools are to teach religion just as they teach anything else. The regular teachers do the teaching and regular text-books are prescribed. The Church may have the privilege of approving the text-books, but otherwise it has no control in the matter. . . .
>
> Religion in schools was, of course, a severe shock to the anti-clericals. Both at home and abroad the general cry was raised that education had been turned over to the Church.
>
> (Schneider 1968: 221)

> As part of the Revolution in Education, Mao's radical lieutenants ordered us to write our own textbooks. . . .
>
> Our ignorance [compared with the ideologically bankrupt professors] was a virtue. To ensure the textbooks would have the correct revolutionary spin, we would show our draft not to our teachers but to the local peasants, the motherlode of political correctness. . . .
>
> Grandly called *A General History of China*, [our textbook] would be printed by People's Publishing House. We were guaranteed a national bestseller; all other history textbooks had been removed from the shelves.
>
> (Wong 1997: 127–8, 144)

The first extract is from a book by an American academic, which derived from his studies in Italy in 1926 to 1927. The second is from a book by a Canadian of

Chinese descent who, with Maoist convictions, went to China in 1972 and enrolled as a student at Beijing University. They demonstrate how different the attitudes were in fascist Italy and Maoist China to textbooks which would affect young people's developing civic attitudes. The evidence of Jan Wong is of a centrally directed ideological distortion of a basic learning aid. The evidence of Herbert Schneider is of a compromise arrangement with the Roman Catholic Church, by which religion was cemented into the school curriculum and the Church had a watching brief over the suitability of the books. State and party manifestly exercised far more unrestrained control in China than in Italy. Pope Pius XI drew a general distinction, in the latter context, between 'subjective' and 'objective' totalitarianism. Subjective totalitarianism was permissible, allowing 'that the totality of the citizen shall be obedient to and dependent on the State for all things which are within the competence of the State'; but objective totalitarianism, seeking the subordination of the whole of the citizen's life, including the spiritual sphere, is a 'manifest absurdity' (quoted Binchy 1941: 330–1).

Having demolished at least partially the very concept upon which the main purpose of this chapter is to be constructed, we must now attempt to reassemble the pieces in a different pattern in order to justify what follows.

First, the notion of totalitarianism. In the 1950s the American political scientist Carl Friedrich (in one work, in association with Zbigniew Brzezinski) did, to many readers' satisfaction, define totalitarianism in such a way as to indicate that the term may be used as a valid analytical tool, that the fascist, Nazi, Stalinist and Maoist states, for all their differences, in fact shared certain characteristics. He wrote of it as a 'syndrome' – suggesting therefore a pathological political condition – comprising six interrelated traits. These were: an official ideology, a single mass party led by one man, a system of terroristic police control, technological control over the mass communications media, control over all means of armed combat, and central control of the economy (see Friedrich and Brzezinski 1956: esp. 3–13). We may add a seventh characteristic; that is, the indoctrination of the youth in schools and youth movements. Furthermore, Friedrich and Brzezinski insisted that totalitarianism was a 'novel kind of government' differing 'from autocracies of the past' (Friedrich and Brzezinski 1956: 3).

Accepting that in the inter-war years totalitarianism was a novel form of government, we need to ask if it generated a novel form of citizenship, and, if so, whether that form can yet warrant the title of 'citizenship' with honesty. On this topic too we can counter the sceptic. We may accomplish this by resisting the temptation to conceptualize citizenship as one particular kind of civic behaviour, namely the ideal designed for a modern liberal parliamentary democracy. Let us remember Aristotle's recommendation of relative citizenship education: 'The education of a citizen in the spirit of his constitution . . . consists in his doing the actions by which an oligarchy, or a democracy, will be enabled to survive' (Aristotle 1948: 1310; note that by 'constitution' Aristotle included social system as well as form of government (see Chapter 1 above)). Substitute 'totalitarian regime' for 'oligarchy' – or recognize with Milovan Djilas that the Communist *apparatchiks* were an oligarchical 'new class' (Djilas 1957) – and one can accept that the indoctrination of young people in fascist Italy, Nazi Germany, late Imperial Japan, the Soviet Union, the People's Democracies of Eastern Europe and the Chinese People's Republic *were* being educated in the spirit of their constitutions and for the purpose of enabling their regimes to survive. Another facet of Aristotle's interpretation of citizenship is the need for *homonoia* – of concord rather than discord in the polity (see Aristotle 1955: IX, 6). And surely, the totalitarian states were passionately determined to suppress discord! No doubt Aristotle, the advocate of mixed government, would have raised more than a worrying eyebrow at the bestial totalitarian political police methods and concentration and labour camps. None the less, insofar as such spectacles as the Nazi mass rallies consolidated the regime, he may well have smiled approvingly at these.

So, if the nature of citizenship must be understood not as an objective mode of behaviour but as one carefully suited to the regime under which the citizen lives, then citizenship may be said to have existed in totalitarian states. Thus, in the Soviet Union, the title of 'citizen' was held with as much dignity as that of 'worker'. For example, in a ceremony for 16-year-olds in 1955, the local Party dignitary declared: 'A Soviet citizen! How proudly and majestically this sounds! An honourable and responsible title' (quoted Counts 1957: 132).

Moreover, if readers of Chapter 1 have accepted that the tightly devised training of the Spartiates may legitimately be called education for citizenship, then they will have little cause to deny that term to the Nazi, Soviet and Japanese programmes described below. Indeed, one could even suggest (albeit with tongue in cheek in deference to the arguments against the notion of totalitarian citizenship education as being anything but malign) that the fascist, Nazi and Communist systems provided a more efficient education for citizenship than did their liberal democratic rivals. For example, writing in 1943 about eastern Europe, an English historian asserted: 'They do not understand the complexities of Parliamentary procedure and Constitutional Law. They dearly need Education in Citizenship' (Seton-Watson 1962: 265). In contrast, the fascist believed in the centrality of politics in schools and was determined not to condone ignorance or apathy. Thus, Gentile asserted in 1925, 'it is impossible to be fascists in politics and non-fascists . . . in schools' (quoted Schapiro 1972: 36).

There is still, none the less, the distinction between education and indoctrination. This is, in fact, a much more complex problem than this simple antithesis might suggest. Subject-matter that can be selected, interpreted and presented in different manners may be handled by teachers in many different ways. The teacher can present the material with varying points of view clearly offered and in a balanced and open way, eschewing any suggestion of his or her own opinion. However, the teacher may feel that such a neutral stance may result in a dereliction of the duty to help pupils to learn right from wrong, moral from immoral beliefs and actions. So the teacher, in these circumstances, would bias the lesson in favour of moral goodness. But good and bad may not be objectively identifiable; moreover, even the conscientious teacher striving for objectivity may find it difficult to avoid bias, through ignorance or lack of time or the weaknesses of textbooks. In any case, bias without the intention of forcing a slanted view upon pupils is not to be equated with deliberate indoctrination, if we follow John White's definition quoted above.

All these nuances occur in citizenship education, and for three main reasons. One is that discussion of contentious issues is part-and-parcel of the subject. Second, the moral requirement relating to good civic behaviour towards one's fellow-citizens involves leading pupils away from selfish and antisocial behaviour. Third, the subject cannot escape the fact of the political context of the nature of the state and of the world in which it is taught. Even in non-totalitarian states utterly unbiased civic education has never been desired or achieved. American children have been taught the virtues of republicanism and the duty to honour the flag; English children have been taught the greatness of the British Empire; and French children have been taught the inestimable values of liberty, equality and fraternity. Have these educational processes been examples of bias; even mild indoctrination? Has totalitarian indoctrination been anything other than a much more thoroughgoing extension and application of these habits? Or has there been a truly qualitative gulf between liberal bias and malign totalitarian indoctrination as tested by intentions and behavioural outcomes? Consideration of these questions will be helped by the following comment by a British scholar about the matter as perceived in the Soviet Union:

> As for the claims of other systems to be non-political in aim, they are dismissed, in Lenin's words, as 'hypocrisy and lies'. Most non-communist countries teach religion in their schools, that is, they indoctrinate the pupils with a particular world outlook; also, they might add, national and patriotic attitudes are taught everywhere, openly or covertly. In the Soviet view, their own kind of indoctrination is franker, more thorough and embraces a wider field of teaching than that of other systems, but they would deny that the process of indoctrination itself is a monopoly of the communist approach to education.
>
> (Grant 1964: 24–5)

The nature of totalitarian civic education will be examined in this chapter by reviewing the histories of the Soviet Union, Germany and Japan. In addition, we will show how the modes of citizenship education were changed when each of these countries (taking just Russia as the successor state of the USSR) changed from totalitarian to liberal democratic states. The experiences of the three countries differ in detail and therefore provide variations on the basic theme of this chapter. Germany had the brief liberal experience of the Weimar Republic from 1919 to 1933 before the creation of the Third Reich, and the post-totalitarian transition to a liberal polity took place in two stages – in the Federal Republic after the Second World War and in the former East Germany after that Communist state was united with the Federal Republic in 1990. The Soviet Union's history was simpler – from the creation of the Communist state in 1917, with Party and government control of variable firmness until the transition to a presidential/parliamentary system in 1991. Japan again is different. Even accepting that 'totalitarianism' is a flexible term, Japan is not usually placed in this category, partly because of its distinct oriental traditions, including the divine status of the Emperor, and the lack of a powerful party structure. Nevertheless, the reign of Emperor Hirohito until the end of the Second World War and especially the premiership of General Tojo from 1941 to 1944 have been characterized as fascist; so there is some justification for including Japan in this chapter. What is more, the change to a liberal form of government from 1945 makes a useful comparison with West Germany's at the same time.

Soviet policy

From the Revolution to the collapse of Communism, Soviet politicians and administrators set great store by education as a key means of progressing towards their form of the Communist ideal. True, they made a slow start, and many detailed changes of policy were enacted throughout this three-quarters of a century. None the less, one set of principles remained firmly embedded in the Party's overall plan. These principles were founded on four basic convictions: that Communism implied the creation of a 'new man' – 'the new soviet man' – a morally and politically superior being; that the Revolution could not be completed without intense concentration on education; that, given the revolutionary and ideological spirit of the Soviet regime, education and politics were inextricably intertwined; and, because of the urgency of the need to transform state and society, that education had to be conducted as indoctrination.

Lenin himself took a keen and continuous personal interest in the restructuring of the educational system (see Fitzpatrick 1970: esp. xiii, 188–203), and declared, 'We do not think of education as outside politics and very frankly subordinate it to our political aims' (quoted Harper 1929: xiii). In addition, the list of policy objectives for education drawn up by the Eighth Congress of the Communist Party in 1918 included the item: 'The development of the propaganda of communist ideas on a wide scale and for that purpose the utilization of state resources and apparatus' (quoted Bereday *et al*. 1960: 54). It could hardly have been otherwise. Apolitical education, in Marxist thinking, would be a contradiction: education was part of the socio-political superstructure determined by the dominant class. Communist education therefore had to be anti-bourgeois, anti-capitalist (see e.g. Short 1947). Furthermore, for the Communists, morality was also interpreted politically; accordingly, moral education, *vospitanie*, literally, 'upbringing', had this overtone. Its importance was pronounced by Lenin in 1920: 'the entire question of education of contemporary youth,' he declared, 'must be education in Communist morality' (quoted Counts 1957: 109). In due course, this became a complex programme virtually synonymous with citizenship education, including love of country, love of labour and respect for others (see Muckle 1987: 2–3).

This fundamental redirection of education, it goes without saying, was an immense task. Moreover, a number of problems hindered its initiation. The obvious and immediate problem was the Civil War, which both dislocated the country and diverted attention from other work until 1921. Samuel Harper, an American Professor of Russian Language and Institutions, in his book published after a visit he paid to the country in 1926, revealed that 1921 was a pivotal date. He wrote:

education and cultural development in general, and civic training and political education in particular, have recently come to be spoken of as the 'third front' of the Revolution . . . the other two fronts – the military and the political – were finally won by 1921. . . .

The danger of the growth of a hostile economic ideology . . . made the question of civic training immediate and important. . . . For the first years after 1921 the Soviet citizen was brought face to face with his 'civic obligations' at every turn and in every phase of his life. There developed one of the most deliberate and extensive efforts to promote and direct civic activity.

(Harper 1929: xii–xiii)

There were other difficulties, too, apart from the Civil War, that delayed a concerted drive on civic indoctrination. We may note five of these. First, Lunacharsky, who was in charge of the People's Commissariat of Education (or Enlightenment) (*Narkompros*) from 1917 to 1929, was an intellectual with but a tepid interest in Marxist-Leninist ideology (see Fitzpatrick 1970: esp. 1–10). Second, the Commissariat staff and many teachers were themselves not yet indoctrinated. Third, the interest in pedagogical theory displayed by a number of influential figures, including Krupskaya (Lenin's wife), favoured experimental forms of learning not necessarily conducive to indoctrination, including activity and project work as advocated by American educationists such as Dalton and Dewey. Krupskaya, incidentally, was a distinguished Marxist interpreter of education (see e.g. Zajda 1980: 26–7). Fourth, the immediate imperative need was to restructure the whole educational system to achieve free universal access at all levels from nursery school to university. Fifth, and finally, the Commissariat was faced with the huge problem of illiteracy.

However, this fifth difficulty led to the vigorous campaign for the 'liquidation of illiteracy' that in fact had a political purpose and was conducted as a method of indoctrination itself. It had a political purpose for the very obvious reason that the people of Russia could not become fully moulded Soviet citizens if a substantial proportion were unable to read. Even posters and banners displaying slogans, the basic units of Soviet propaganda, would be useless if the messages could not be construed. (It should be explained, parenthetically, that the word 'Russia' is used here because the concern was concentrated at first on the Russian Federation to the exclusion of the republics on the rim of this central bulk.) The scheme was inaugurated by a decree issued at the end of 1919 requiring everyone between the ages of 8 and 50 to be able to read and write in either Russian or their own language. A society, a publishing house and a journal, all with the name 'Down with Illiteracy' (*Doloy negramotnost*), were founded. Progress was steady during the two decades 1919 to 1939: by 1939 the Soviet Union claimed 95 per cent and 83 per cent literacy rates for men and women respectively.

Comments by Lenin confirmed the political purpose of the literacy campaign. 'You cannot build a Communist state with an illiterate people'; and 'An illiterate person stands outside; he must first be taught the ABC. Without this, there can be no politics; without this, there are only rumors, gossip, tales, prejudices, but no politics': these are two of his telling statements (quoted Bereday *et al.* 1960: 58. As an aside, it is interesting to compare these comments with Robert Lowe's in England in 1867 and the histories of the European colonial possessions in Asia and Africa; see Chapter 3 above). Furthermore, Harper's observations led him to make the following points about literacy classes for adults:

> In the first place the subject matter used in this work is always political in character, so that these older persons who are being taught to read and write may at the same time be made more conscious and active citizens. In the second place, the liquidation of illiteracy among the national minorities adds to the emphasis on national language, which is one of the means adopted to awaken civic consciousness in these more backward Soviet citizens.
>
> (Harper 1929: 273)

Even illiterates can, of course, absorb some political understanding, for example, from their work-fellows and the political mood of the country. Thus, in 1926, when the liquidation of illiteracy campaign was only just under way and successes were confined largely to the Red Army, Kalinin, the President of the USSR and fully involved in educational matters, declared, 'With respect to political education, political activity of the masses, and political permeation, our Soviet Union very likely stands in front of all European and non-European countries' (quoted Bereday *et al.* 1960: 60).

Harper's use of the terms 'active citizens' and 'civic consciousness' and Kalinin's reference to 'political activity of the masses' raise the question of the meaning of the term 'citizen' in the Soviet Union, especially when functional titles such as 'peasant' and 'worker' were used so commonly. These words, with their class and economic connotations, did indeed underlie the meaning of '*grazhdanin*' (citizen) when that was introduced in 1917 as a title. Only individuals who could prove themselves to be 'productive' in some way were accorded the rights of citizenship and were expected to exercise the functions of citizenship in the context of their form of production. Housework was accepted, and so was 'mental productivity', somewhat reluctantly and reckoned to be of an inferior kind. The categories of peasant, worker and intelligentsia came to be enshrined in the Soviet Constitution, though it was not until the 1936 Constitution that the rights and duties of citizens were spelled out in detail; and even then, the term 'toilers' intruded into the text. Given the character of human nature, it has been a feature of citizenship that some citizens perform their civic functions more assiduously than others. In the Soviet Union, identifying the style of citizenship and the depth of commitment, and consequently examining the educational processes to fit the individual for that status are complicated by the close interconnections between state and Party. Because the Soviet Union rapidly became a totalitarian polity, increasingly so as Stalin tightened his grip on the country, opportunities to be active citizens within the state structure were severely confined, not to say cynically manipulated. Participation in reality had to be channelled through membership of the Party. And since this membership entailed being subjected to indoctrination in the ideology, and since opportunities for civic activity through the agency of the Party required expressed conviction in the 'truth' of the ideology, citizenship of an especially active kind was dependent on knowing one's place in the socialist society and on successful learning of the principles of Marxism.

The totalitarian nature of the Soviet Union, its class ideology and the commanding role of the Party made the style of citizenship more complex and the task of civic education, paradoxically, simpler than these comments would suggest. Citizenship should be pictured rather as a spectrum from the ideal convinced and dedicated Party worker to the counter-revolutionary bourgeois denied all rights of citizenship. So, in teaching, these two stylized persons at the two ends of the spectrum became, respectively, figures to emulate and to hate.

The experimental and ambitious schemes for schools were abandoned or diluted, offering more opportunity for indoctrination, but only gradually. In the words of a British academic, 'the ordinary schools were not politically organized until the late 1920s or even later' (Nettl 1967: 112). However, as Stalin consolidated his personal dictatorship and forged his doctrine of 'Socialism in One Country', the agencies of indoctrination placed increasing stress on the adulation of Stalin himself, on his interpretation of the domestic and international political situations, and on a national, not to say nationalist, history. Take this excerpt from a history textbook published in 1938 and imagine the effect on pupils' minds closed to any other interpretations:

> That contemptible enemy of the people, that fascist agent, Trotsky, and his contemptible friends ... organized in the U.S.S.R. gangs of murderers, wreckers and spies, [and] as long as the U.S.S.R. is surrounded by countries in which capitalism reigns, spies and wreckers will continuously strive to penetrate our country and cause us harm.
>
> (quoted Bereday *et al*. 1960: 75)

The duty of the responsible young citizen was clear. Consequently, during the 1930s and 1940s moral education, particularly its patriotic element, became a prime duty for schools. Indeed, the standard book on educational theory and practice in the 1940s edited by Kairov, later to become Minister of Education, devoted seven chapters to the topic (see Counts 1957: 117; also 117–23). Also at this time, in the mid-1930s, a study of the Constitution of the USSR was introduced into the school curriculum, so that, in Kairov's words, young citizens would be able to 'participate consciously in the socio-political life of the country' (quoted Counts 1957: 95). This insistence on the importance of political *knowledge* was also reflected in directions to the Komsomol and Pioneers in the 1930s (see Counts 1957:106).

After the death of Stalin in 1953 and especially from 1956 when the process of 'de-Stalinization' began, history textbooks were rewritten in order to reduce the prominence of his work and the validity of his interpretation of the Marxist credo. Moreover, during the ten years from 1954 to 1964 there was a noticeable loosening of the indoctrination programmes in schools, due partly to the Soviet Union becoming increasingly pervious to western ways. Symptomatic of this change was the arrival of the *stilyagi* craze. Edward Crankshaw, who first reported this phenomenon in the West, described these 'chasers after style' as 'the bright young things in revolt against their whole environment who have focused all their inarticulate desires on jive and flashy clothes', copied precisely from American 'zoot suits' and English Teddy Boys' sartorial habits (Crankshaw 1959: 133).

More serious was a growing hooliganism. In response, when, in 1961, the Party Programme was revised, that document accorded considerable prominence to the role of schools in building Communism and fostering civic consciousness. Reinvigorating the passionate commitment of youth to the Party and its ideology and to the motherland was made a cardinal commitment for all educational institutions. Commenting on the Programme, an article in the teachers' journal *Sovetskaia Pedagogika* declared:

> Advancing a grand plan for the development of public education in the next twenty years, the Communist Party assigns great tasks to the schools; they must achieve the education and training of communistically and highly educated people, capable both of physical and mental labor, of active work in the different realms of public and governmental life, science and culture.
>
> (Ablin 1963: 18)

Moreover, the Soviet leader Khrushchev stated quite bluntly that understanding of the teaching of Marx, Engels and Lenin was falling short of what was needed (see Ablin 1963: 156). A high-powered inquiry into the school curriculum, launched in 1964, reinforced the message that political education must be strengthened. The determination with which the indoctrinatory purpose of the 1961 Party Programme was pursued may be exemplified by the following. In a work on Soviet education published in Britain a decade after the new Party Programme, we find the judgement: 'Today, the political commitment is not weaker but stronger than it has ever been' (Tomiak 1972: 124). Another, similar though milder, impression is provided by an American journalist in a book published in 1975 and based upon three years' close observation of Soviet society:

> The political content of nursery, kindergarten and school propaganda, especially based on Lenin staggers most Westerners. Russians say it is less oppressive and crude than under Stalin when children used to be instructed to scratch out the eyes or blacken the textbook portraits of high officials as they fell victims of Stalin's purges, used to sing worshipful hymns to the dictator, or, at the peak of the Cold War, learned slogan ditties against the West.
>
> (Smith 1976: 201–2)

During his last years (he died in 1982) Brezhnev reiterated the message that persistence with political education was still essential. At the 25th Party Congress in 1976 he reported that, during the previous five years, 'questions of ideological education, and the problems of the formation of the new man, a worthy builder of communism, have occupied a big place in all our work' (quoted Morison 1983:

145). Yet more needed to be done. Three years later the Party's Central Committee issued a decree instructing the Party and the ministries of education of the USSR to take more effective measures to improve the political knowledge and commitment of young people. Then, in 1981, at the 26th Party Congress, Brezhnev returned to the theme, stressing the need to make indoctrination activities more interesting and less theoretical. One of the major concerns was that, with greater awareness of the world outside the Soviet Union, commitment to the motherland and its own style of Communism was still slackening (for this period see Morison 1983: 144–52). Not to mention that hooliganism was still rife.

The agencies of Soviet policy

A regime founded on a holistic ideology would inevitably not be satisfied with allowing education for citizenship to be undertaken solely by the schools. This truism leads us to the need to identify the various methods that were used and agencies that were engaged in education for citizenship, and to explain their relationship. First, obviously, were the schools, administered by the state. Second was the political education of the soldiers of the Red Army. Third were the various methods of educating adults. Fourth, we may identify the non-direct teaching methods of diffusing propaganda through the various media, brought to a fine art by the Party's activities, directed by *Agitprop* (Agitation and Propaganda Department of the Central Committee). Which brings us, fifth, to the ubiquitous activity of the Party, pre-eminently operating through the youth movements. We shall examine in turn each of these five ways in which Soviet citizens learned what was expected of them in the field of civic knowledge and understanding as transmitted through the filter of Communist ideology.

   However, before embarking on this analysis, the reader's attention should be drawn to two matters. One is that we have constructed these five categories in somewhat artificial, even if convenient form; in practice they very much overlapped. The other matter, arising from the Soviet system of dual power, is the overriding issue of the relationship between state and Party in conducting the task of civic education. From the very beginning, the Party sought to enforce its predominance. Even Lunacharsky, the *state* Commissar of Education, was in no doubt about the imperative necessity for this relative authority and he even suggested that the work of his own Commissariat should be subsumed by the Party. At one point, in 1921, he said that the Central Committee of the Party must 'conquer the whole apparatus. . . . The Party must be everywhere, like the Biblical spirit of God' (quoted Fitzpatrick 1970: 244–5); though his views were too radical to gain acceptance at the time. Nevertheless, the initiative for educational policy did pass to the Party, and the Party did infiltrate its influence into all levels from the Ministry of Education to village schools. In the words of one authority, 'During the thirties the Party began to claim omniscience on all matters pertaining to education' (Zajda 1980: 25). All policy was formulated by the Party's Central Committee and dispatched to the government for executive and legal action (see e.g. Pennar 1960: 45–56).

Let us start our survey of the five contexts of civic education with the schools. However, before engaging with the content of this topic, we should note three points. One is that the involvement of the Party in schools will be treated below, when examining the role of the Party generally. The second is that, again, we must enter the caveat that, just as the Marxist dialectic philosophy pretends to a holistic understanding of life and society, so Soviet pedagogy claimed that the complete range of school subjects and activities should be suffused with the purpose of bringing young people to an unquestioning understanding and appreciation of the ideology. Therefore, any division of the topic of school work for civic education into separate components is in a sense artificial. In particular, academic education, political education and experience of manual work were considered originally as being melded into a single pedagogical process. The school 'outside life and politics was a lie and hypocrisy', Lenin declared (quoted Zajda 1980: 14). The third point is that generalization is rendered difficult because of the frequent changes in the structure of the school system and curricular organization over the span of time we are outlining. Despite the proviso of the second point, we will succumb to the convenient device of presenting the Soviet schools' contribution to citizenship education under six notional headings. These are: the organization of the curriculum as a whole; the teaching of history; the teaching of social studies (including politics); the teaching of Marxist theory; military training; and the inculcation of patriotism.

In the early years following the Revolution, concerted efforts were made to connect schools with their economic environments, as, indeed, Marx himself had commended (see e.g. Zajda 1980: 202). Excursions, visits and manual work became integral parts of the pupil's school life. Harper's observations provide concise examples:

> Children are taken to regular meetings of workmen's clubs or committees. The older children may take an actual part in the life of the neighbouring factory, workshop, or state farm by helping to spread literacy or by establishing nurseries . . . the emphasis on labour implies not only study of the labour processes and methods of organization but actual participation in them so far as the physical and mental attainments of each particular age permits.
>
> (Harper 1929: 254–5)

By the late 1920s 'polytechnic schools', favoured especially by Krupskaya, were being organized, with wood and metal workshops. These declined with Stalin's instructions to improve academic standards, but were revived in the 1950s by Khrushchev, who also encouraged renewing the contacts between schools and their working environments.

The two decades from 1966 was a period of intensive curricular reform, during which four principles that had been continual themes in Soviet educational history were re-emphasized. These were: that the whole experience of school should contribute to the shaping of the Communist person; that the primary school years were fundamental in this process; that all timetabled subjects have contributions to make to this process (see e.g. Morison 1983: 157; Zajda 1980: 139–42); and that history and social studies can make the most powerful contributions. Leaving aside this last, and obvious, point for treatment below, one observation each about the elementary (primary) and secondary levels in this period may be of interest. At the elementary level (7 to 11), inculcating Communist morality was one requirement: 'the notions of justice, honesty, friendship, loyalty, patriotism and internationalism' were taught to 7-year-olds by means of stories (Zajda 1980: 135; see generally 131–8). For the example from the secondary level, let us take the Statutes of the Secondary General Education School issued in 1970. These listed three main tasks, the second of which was:

> to mould the marxist-leninist world outlook in the young generation and to instil in pupils the feelings of Soviet patriotism, love for homeland, for its people and for the Communist Party of the Soviet Union as well as readiness to defend the socialist fatherland.
>
> (quoted Tomiak 1972: 59)

One of the key subjects for citizenship education in any state is history. The Soviet Union was no exception. Indeed, as Marxism is itself grounded in a philosophy of history, it would be strange indeed if Soviet educationists did not make the best of the opportunity for using this subject for their civic education purposes.

After the Bolshevik take-over of power, and due to the further disruption of civil war and the constraints of impoverishment, the replacement of 'bourgeois' history textbooks was considerably delayed. The solution? History classes could be conducted as exercises in the criticism and demolition of these 'biased' versions of the past. The standard replacement text was *Outlines of the Study of Society* by M.B. Volfson, which was already in its tenth edition by 1926. In his Introduction, the author declares that he would be 'happy if the book supplies the weapon of a Marxian, proletarian world-outlook to the younger generation' (quoted Harper 1929: 260), and by page 17 the concept of the class struggle has already been introduced. The explicitly political purpose of history as a school subject was made obvious by two decrees, in 1934 and 1959. The latter required substantial syllabus changes, including the introduction of a course on the history of the USSR and extra-European history. Moreover, simultaneously, a new course on 'Principles of political knowledge' was also introduced to complement the revised history programme.

Commentary by two Soviet educationists in the journal *Problems of History* at the time reveals the clear ideological purpose of these curricular reforms. These brief quotations are an indication:

> The teaching of history is not an end in itself. It should help form the character of the builder of communism. . . .
>
> The course [on the history of the USSR] will show the spiritual wealth and lofty moral make-up of the builder of communism and characterize the moral traits of the Soviet people. . . .

The main feature of the new syllabus in history and the principles of political knowledge is that they are expected to play a major role in preparing the younger generation for a conscious, active part in the country's productive and social life.
(Ablin 1963: 147, 148, 150)

New textbooks, it goes without saying, had to be written to support the revamped history syllabuses. The content of these and commentary by Soviet academics provide an illuminating picture of the strong civic purpose of the subject when these changes were consolidated (for the position *c*.1980, see Morison 1983: 158–60; Zajda 1980: 142–4). In particular, the books show a slant towards more recent history at the expense of earlier periods. In addition, some of the material may seem to be intellectually quite demanding. For example, understanding was required of the works of the expounders of Communism from Marx to Brezhnev, and a grasp of terms such as 'capitalist', 'exploitation' – though in fact, the rote-learning of definitions of the keywords in the Communist vocabulary had already been common practice.

Another common practice, naturally, had been the teaching of Communist theory, by means of history, and other subjects as well. Indeed, Harper observed in 1926 that it had become 'a habit for the pupil or student to start an answer to all questions with the phrase: "From the Marxist viewpoint"'; and the American academic was treated by a prominent Soviet educationist to the pronouncement that 'The future Soviet citizen . . . must be a dialectical materialist' (Harper 1929: 268). A generation later, the authors of the *Problems of History* article, cited above, declared that 'The teaching of history is aimed at tireless propaganda of Marxist-Leninist theory' (Ablin 1963: 147). Nevertheless, because of the difficulty of learning about the doctrine, emphasis upon the more theoretical aspects was inevitably postponed to the older classes.

In addition to history, the social sciences, notably politics, when these were added to school curricula, provided material for the direct teaching of citizenship. In the early years of the Soviet regime courses at the secondary level entitled 'Study of society' or 'Social and historical sciences' incorporated the social studies disciplines, including law. However, the introduction of the course 'Principles of political knowledge' in 1960 to 1961, mentioned above, was a vital development. The course was designed to draw upon a number of disciplines and to involve practical activity. As the curricular reforms of the 1960s got under way, a consolidated course of social sciences was developed for Grade 10 pupils. This consisted of the teaching of Marxist-Leninist theory, politics and current affairs. Then, by about 1980, social studies were making an even fuller and more varied contribution to civic education (see Morison 1983: *passim*). For instance, a course was introduced on 'The fundamental principles of the Soviet state and law', and the promulgation of the new Constitution in 1977 provided an apposite text for political study. Young children learned their politics, particularly the immense virtue and unremitting work of the Party, as personified through the life of Lenin. It was at this time, too (around 1980), that teachers of biology and geography were encouraged to make their pupils aware of global ecological issues. This development therefore injected a very different perspective into education for world citizenship, which had hitherto been concentrated on the teaching of the Leninist and Cold War interpretations of the planetary clash between capitalist imperialism on the one hand, and Communist revolutionary liberation from these shackles and exploitation on the other.

This confrontational element in Soviet doctrine made its appearance as the existence of two mutually antagonistic camps in Leninist terminology, and as the USSR being threatened by 'capitalist encirclement' in Stalinist terminology. It followed that, in addition to teaching pupils this 'correct' interpretation of world affairs, the schools had the twin responsibilities of instilling patriotism in and providing initial military training for their pupils. In any case, commitment of one's heart to the state and the acquired skill to protect it have been age-old features of the concept and status of citizenship. Little wonder, then, that the cultivation and sustaining of patriotism is a constant theme in programmes of and commentary upon Soviet education: the word *Rodina* (Motherland) echoes throughout. Patriotic education and moral education very fully overlapped. As one specialist in moral education in the late 1950s expressed it, 'We desire future citizens of the Soviet state who will act from a sense of public duty and will possess a feeling of responsibility before the Motherland' (quoted Bereday *et al*. 1960: 410). And, inevitably, in history lessons, Communist patriotism – displayed in its unparalleled form in the Civil War and the Great Patriotic War – was shown to be far superior to patriotism as displayed in Tsarist Russia or bourgeois states. Nevertheless, Russian history and literature were used to show that Russians, even in the pre-Communist age, had a fine tradition of selfless patriotism; for had not the heroic Russian people fended off hostile incursions for centuries?

Patriotism and a consciousness of the need of and preparedness for military duties may, obviously and most especially among boys, be closely linked in educational programmes. And so they were in the Soviet Union. Discussion of this feature of school curricula is, in fact, best treated in association with our second context, namely the armed services, to which we now turn. Because of the great size of the Red Army, the importance of teaching for citizenship through the agency of the army should not be underestimated. Many millions of young men undertook compulsory military training and service, the civic purpose and style of which were indicated as early as the creation of the Red Army by dubbing the soldiers 'citizen-fighters'. The interrelationship in the Red Army of the three elements – citizenly consciousness and activity, political education, and the role of the Party – may be shown in several ways. Military training was introduced into the curricula of schools and the activities of the Komsomols so that military service became an expected part of a male Soviet citizen's life. During the period of service the soldier was exposed to a particularly well-organized programme of political education classes, and, in the early years of the regime, was expected to engage in informed evening discussions in his unit's club and 'Lenin Corner'. Soldiers were also encouraged to participate in the affairs of the local community where their barracks were sited, and they were actively recruited into membership of the Komsomol or Party, depending on their age.

The army additionally became a vital institution to cope with two particularly crucial problems in Soviet history. One was the multicultural composition of the USSR. In 1938 the former practice of structuring army units in nationally homogeneous regiments was discarded, and, as a consequence, in the words of a French sociologist, 'the army has become a kind of melting-pot and an instrument of Russification, transcending particularism' (Kerblay 1983: 168). The second problem was the horrendous crisis of the Second World War. In 1942 two decrees were enacted to improve military training and patriotic sentiment in schools. These decrees were prompted by the realization that the schools had failed in their duty to inculcate in their pupils the 'strong will, perseverance, stability, and other moral qualities necessary to the future warrior on the battlefield' (quoted Bereday *et al.* 1960: 82). In other words, the crisis of the German invasion highlighted the lack of a Spartan-type military citizenship, which would have served the Soviet Union so well in what came to be called 'the Patriotic War': the schools had not performed their function in this respect with sufficient zeal and efficiency. This kind of policy was reiterated a generation later, in about 1970. In 1968 all boys from the age of 15 were required to undergo military training preparatory to their compulsory national service in the armed forces, and a series of directives instructed schools to perform their duties in this regard. For example, one decree included as aims: 'To prepare the pupils for defence of the motherland' and 'To strengthen friendly relations between the school and the armed forces' (quoted Zajda 1980: 209).

Civic education while serving in the army was a form of adult education – our third agency of civic education. There was also a parallel drive to induct civilian adults into their civic duties from the very early days of the Soviet Union. We have already mentioned the recruitment of people beyond school age into the liquidation of illiteracy campaign. However, as Harper explained, these centres 'represent only the introduction to outside-school educational work among adults. In the large cities are being organized Schools for the Semi-Literate, Schools for the Adults of Higher Grade, and finally Workmen's Universities, functioning evenings and Sundays.' In these institutions particular emphasis was placed on 'social-political and literary' subjects, dealing with, *inter alia*, the history of the class struggle and of the Communist Party, and Marxist and Leninist theory (Harper 1929: 273). Half a century later there were even greater opportunities for post-school education, including provisions made by the Party and trade unions. It has been explained that one of the aims 'of educational-cultural work for adults is to increase communist consciousness and political activity in the mass of the population' (Tomiak 1972: 103).

Universities in the USSR were also a means of civic education. Indeed, courses in politics and economics became compulsory for all students, whatever their specialist subject (for typical time allocations in 1961, see Tomiak 1972: 95, 99). For instance, a Basic Law on Education, implemented in 1974, and following earlier policy statements, included these tasks in its list of purposes:

> Preparation of highly qualified specialists who are trained in Marxist-Leninist doctrine. . . .

Inculcating the students with high moral qualities, communist awareness, culture, socialist internationalism, Soviet patriotism, readiness to defend the Motherland, and physical training of students.

(quoted Zajda 1980: 94)

Let us now pass on to our fourth context in which citizenship education was conducted in the Soviet Union – or set of contexts, for a miscellaneous collection will now be briefly outlined, embracing extra-curricular activities for pupils and students, excursions, ceremonies and the role of the mass media. Since the Soviet Union was a totalitarian society, one may expect that the maximum range of opportunities was offered to encourage citizens of all ages to enhance their civic consciousness. Schools, state institutions of various kinds and the Party all contributed to offer such myriad schemes for participation, learning and propaganda that only the barest indication can be provided here (for the early 1920s see Harper 1929: chs 5, 7, 8, 9, 11, 14 and 15 for a mine of information). Newspapers, journals, radio, theatre, cinema, museums, trade unions, the co-operative movement gave out inexhaustible supplies of information, messages of inspiration and inducements to conform. Perhaps the most remarkable development in the 1920s was the widespread organization of excursions, particularly to museums. Parties of peasants, factory workers, soldiers and schoolchildren provided constant flows of visitors to view exhibits, most of which had a civic/ideological purpose.

Excursions for schoolchildren were but one form of extra-curricular activity, arranged both by the schools themselves and by sundry institutions outside the school system. These arrangements were steadily built into a most comprehensive programme. Moreover, as one American observer has written, 'the major goal of the entire extracurricular enterprise is "the Communist upbringing of children in the spirit of patriotism, mutual help in learning, labour, and social activities"' (Mareuil 1960: 133). Notice the word 'labour'. Throughout Soviet history one of the expected virtues of the citizen was to engage in 'labour', preferably manual work, partly as a form of group discipline (as suggested in Article 60 of the 1977 Constitution). Inside schools, 'circles' (clubs) provided for many interests; and outside, there were 'stations' (sites) for outdoor activities, while many attended camps in the summer holidays. Of special relevance for our purposes was the body called the Red Scouts. They engaged in conservationist activities and helped on farms, but were involved primarily in keeping alive the Soviet Union's heroic traditions. For instance, in 1977, the sixtieth anniversary of the Revolution, their fourteen million members 'launched more than 40,000 historical museums and rooms of military glory. They had erected and taken under their care almost 25,000 war memorials' (Zajda 1980: 214).

However, the most influential provider of extra-curricular civic education was the Party. Indeed, from pre-revolutionary times the Party believed that one of its most vital tasks was to educate the whole population in Communist doctrine and to the Communist style of life. And so we come to our fifth channel through which citizenship education was provided. Although we tend to use the word 'propaganda' for this activity, in fact Plekhanov and Lenin distinguished between 'propaganda' for the Party elite and 'agitation' for the populace at large. The combined task was known as 'Agitprop'. A standard Russian dictionary defined 'agitation' as: 'Oral and written activity among the broad masses which aims at inculcating certain ideas and slogans for their political education and for attracting them to the solution of the more important social and political tasks' (quoted Carew Hunt 1957: 3). In Communist terms, quite a good definition of citizenship education in the wide sense.

One of the most powerful engines for the civic education of adults in the Soviet Union was the press. In the Brezhnev era the Party's Central Committee, in fact, described one of the crucial roles of newspapers as 'to educate tirelessly in all Soviet people a conscientious, creative attitude to work, a feeling of being master of the country and a high sense of responsibility to society' (quoted Kaiser 1977: 207–8). And the newspaper with the largest circulation was *Pravda*, produced by the Central Committee.

On the principle that the conditioning of minds is achieved most efficiently by teaching and influencing individuals when they are young, the Communist Party both ensured that it exercised supreme influence over the schools and created youth movements. We have already explained that the Party came to have more power than the Ministry of Education in fashioning what and how subjects were taught. By the late 1950s one American specialist in Soviet affairs referred to 'a maze of Party controls' and assessed that 'the Soviet educational system is permeated with Communist Party members' (Pennar 1960: 45, 47). Party Central Committees throughout the USSR had their own education departments, whose functions were essentially to ensure the effective and 'correct' teaching of the principles of Communism in all educational institutions. This watching brief naturally included keeping a sharp eye on the content of textbooks. The social science subjects were inevitably a particularly sensitive area, and it would have been difficult to obtain a teaching post in that field without being a Party member. Instructions were quite blatant. An example of such a command issued in 1957 in an *oblast* (region) on the lower Volga read in part, 'The oblast, city, and district Party committees should increase their control over the ideological content of instruction in the social sciences' (quoted Pennar 1960: 52). Party control of the schools was also exercised on the spot by members of the Komsomols.

Throughout the existence of the USSR hundreds of millions of young people were coached in the principles of Communism and expected Communist behaviour through membership of the three Party youth movements, structured in units usually based on schools for those of school age. The Komsomols, for the age-range 15 to 28, were the first to be founded, in 1918. To cater for the age-group immediately below that (10 to 15), the Young Pioneers were set up in 1922. Two years later 7- to 10-year-olds were furnished with their own organization, the Octobrists. (Age-ranges varied over the years: these are the ones that obtained from 1957.)

To start with the two youngest groups. The Octobrists were instituted for two main reasons: to teach children social morality (with an increasing political content) and to provide a pool of recruits for the Young Pioneers. Indeed, the first of their five rules announced that 'Octobrists are future Pioneers'; though each child had to prove him- or herself worthy of membership of that more senior movement (see Zajda 1980: 148–54). On admission to the Pioneers the entrant made the following pledge:

> I, a Young Pioneer of the Soviet Union, in the presence of my comrades solemnly promise to love my Soviet Motherland with all my heart and to live, learn and struggle as the great Lenin bade us and the Communist Party teaches us.
>
> (quoted Tomiak 1972: 86)

Although a voluntary organization, social pressure and the lure of the facilities which were on offer meant that only a small minority refrained from joining. For instance, in 1970 the population of that age-group was 29.7 million (see Kerblay 1983: 29), about 24 million of whom were members (see Tomiak 1972: 85). The prime attractions enjoyed by the Pioneers were their 'palaces' and 'houses'. The largest and most modern buildings were splendidly and generously appointed for the widest possible range of extra-curricular activities. Not all of these had a directly civic purpose, it is true; nevertheless, the underlying socialization function of the movement was always very much in evidence (see Zajda 1980: 154–63).

The Komsomol (the All-Union Lenin Communist League of Youth) was the keystone of this organizational construction for youth, though a smaller proportion of their age-group compared with the Pioneers was enrolled into membership. There were two main reasons for this: the constant factor was the use of more stringent admission criteria than for the Pioneers; the variable factor was the fluctuation in the adolescents' ideological zeal and their willingness to commit themselves to the league's strict regime, affected by the social and political conditions and mood at any given period. The Komsomols' involvement in civic education (and they had a number of other functions) was double-faceted: educating themselves and educating others. The Party, in Leninist terminology, was the vanguard of the proletariat. If they were to provide correct leadership on the road to the Communist utopia, they had to be especially well versed in Marxist philosophy. Therefore, the Komsomol, the cadet member of the Party, needed to acquire a robust basis of its principles, as well as experiencing and learning from the practice of socially and civically useful work. When Lenin addressed the 1920 Congress of the Komsomol his message was: 'Study, study, and keep on studying' (quoted Harper 1929: 44). The Komsomol Charter, indeed, included the item, 'To study Marxism-Leninism attentively'. It also included the precept, 'To explain the policies of the party to the "broad masses of young people"' (quoted Bereday *et al.* 1960: 397).

The Komsomol, then, learned and propagated the Communist creed. Indeed, in 1971 Brezhnev described this latter purpose as its 'central task' (quoted Tomiak 1972: 87). How did it discharge this duty? In three main ways: through publications, its Congress and the presence of its members in educational institutions. It published a number of books for young people and newspapers for both the Pioneers and Komsomols, most notably *Komsomolskaya Pravda*, a junior equivalent of the Party's prime organ. The Congress of Komsomol representatives discussed educational issues, and transmitted their decisions and guidance down the line. Their political influence in schools is aptly summarized in this quotation: 'School branches . . . elect committees to help with clubs and societies, they run debates and meetings, they discuss problems of discipline, moral education . . . and act as

Pioneer leaders' (Grant 1964: 72). In all these contexts they were purveying the Communist, in particular the Party, doctrine of acceptable, collaborative behaviour. Their active presence in institutions of higher education carried even greater authority (see Zajda 1980: 163–74).

In the process of citizenship education the youth organizations played a cardinal role. One authority has written, 'As Soviet children progress from the Octobrists to the Pioneers and the Komosmol, political socialization proceeds in a series of well-defined stages' with the object of making the young people 'completely devoted to the communist regime' (Zajda 1980: 176). However, with the disintegration of the USSR and the outburst of hostility against Communism and the Party in the new Russia from about 1990 there was no room for these organizations.

The new Russian style

In truth, however, the mood for change was already evident from the mid-1980s, the Gorbachev era. In 1984 Gorbachev became Chairman of the School Reform Commission, and from 1985 to 1991 he was General Secretary of the CPSU. The thrust of the recommendations of his Commission was to strengthen labour training and work experience, but not, note, at the expense of weakening the teaching of the Marxist-Leninist creed (see Morison 1987: 24). This new Soviet Education Reform became law in 1985. The following year, the 27th Congress of the CPSU approved a definitive statement of eight main objectives of political education. It provided a most comprehensive picture of the nature of Soviet citizenship education: Marxist-Leninist teaching; work for the common good; Communist morality; patriotism and Communist internationalism; respect for law; atheist-materialist philosophy; combating hostile ideologies; and understanding of the Soviet role against bourgeois ideology (see Morison 1987: 26–7).

When Gorbachev became General Secretary he launched into a programme of reforms signalled by the words '*glasnost*' and '*perestroika*' (openness and restructuring). This agenda of relaxing government and Party control affected education as well as other aspects of life; indeed, in 1987 he declared in his book entitled *Perestroika* that 'a maximum amount of attention has to be paid to the young and the Komsomol' (Gorbachev 1987: 115). Unfortunately, relaxation (as the history of the preludes to revolutions so often reveals) led to collapse; the country plunged into chaos and, by 1992, actual crisis. The USSR disintegrated, leaving the Russian Federation separated from the former Soviet republics, now independent states, on its periphery. Communist power collapsed; the economy collapsed; and political commitment and morality gave way to apathy and crime. In the words of one Russian émigré academic, 'Feelings of citizenship, involvement in public affairs, have not increased following the fall of the Soviet system with its repressive apparatus, as many had taken for granted, but have diminished drastically' (Shlapentokh 1998: 28). Although discontent and disillusionment with the Soviet regime had been building up from around 1980, it was the suddenness of the changes that had such deleterious effects. Rebuilding a sense of civic consciousness, but of an utterly different design, would have been difficult enough in propitious circumstances, let alone in the conditions of the overwhelming problems Russia was facing.

In education, the process of change included the removal of government and Party influence from schools and institutions of higher education, required, in fact, by Article 14 of the 1992 Law on Education. This programme introduced terms which have, unfortunately, usually been rendered literally into English as 'depoliti-cization' and even 'deideologization' (terms from which the reader will be protected henceforth in this book). Yet this was essentially a negative process, resulting in a most unhappy hiatus until liberal democratic modes of citizenship education could be installed. Some of the main features of this dismantling of the Communist ideological edifice in schools, colleges and universities included the obvious moves of banning the youth organizations from schools, the abolition of examinations in Marxist-Leninist thought and the rewriting of history textbooks (see Sutherland 1999: 137–40; Webber 2000: 33–7). What worried most Russian educationists was the consequent loss of a framework for moral education, so that it became exceedingly difficult for teachers to help stem the terrible collapse of civic standards throughout the country. The Rector of the Institute of Youth Studies in Moscow explained in 1993:

> The youth of Russia, like society as a whole, is undergoing a crisis of values. The demise of totalitarianism brought with it the destruction of former ideals and values . . . which were part of people's inner world. . . . A *spiritual vacuum* has formed.
>
> (quoted Sutherland 1999: 140–1)

In schools, the Octobrists, Pioneers and Komsomol had contributed so much to the Soviet style of *vospitanie* (moral upbringing) that their demise created serious lacunae in the civic learning activities both inside school and in extra-curricular provision.

The introduction of new syllabuses, textbooks, teachers' guides and teaching style was a slow and halting process – inevitably, given the confusion. A group of educationists referred in 1999 to the 'great difficulty' encountered in making the transition, including 'the fact that elements of the past continue to linger. For instance, the "soviet" and "imperial" mentality of some of those working in the field of education continues to have an influence' (Bogolubov *et al.* 1999: 524). This should occasion little surprise when we remember that a large proportion of teachers recruited for work in the area of civic education were members of the Communist Party. During the 1990s new programmes under the name *grazhdanovedenie* were introduced, the term sometimes rendered as 'civic studies', though, since '*grazhdanin*' means 'citizen', 'citizenship education' might be a better translation. A professional association of teachers in this field was created, and the Russian Academy of Education drafted a nine-point list of objectives for the social science subjects (see Bogolubov *et al.* 1999: 527–8). The production of new textbooks in history, social studies and the specifically citizenship-oriented courses naturally required time and money. Nevertheless, by the mid-1990s teachers were starting to receive the help they needed with the publication of books such as *Politics and Law*, *Introduction to the Social Sciences*, *Human Being and Society* and *Civics*; not to mention the weekly supplement on citizenship education in *Teachers Newspaper* (see Bogolubov *et al*. 1999: 534–8, 531). But even then, the acquisition of the books was not necessarily trouble-free. A British academic relates the following anecdote:

> One headteacher . . . told me of a visit she had made to the bookshop of a major publishing house in the capital where she had been surprised to see large numbers of copies of textbooks which she had been informed could not be delivered to her school since they had not been published. . . . It transpired that the publisher . . . had put some on sale at high prices to the public, but was meanwhile hoarding large numbers of the book in anticipation that the high inflation rate would guarantee a greater profit margin when it was decided to distribute the books to the schools.
>
> (Webber 2000: 124)

Indeed, all the while Russia lacks a strong civil society foundation and a civic consciousness among the adult population, the teaching of the new citizenship will remain an uphill task, for the pupils have been living in an environment of apathy and alienation. To change the metaphor, by the end of the twentieth century Russian teachers desperately needed the evolution of a virtuous civic circle: citizenship education of the younger generation would improve the mood of the country, which, in turn, would render the pupils more receptive to their citizenship education. As teaching for this purpose steadily improved at the turn of the century, the profession deserved such reciprocity.

The Nazi system and its background

The history of the oscillations to and from the totalitarian and liberal modes of citizenship in Germany was more complicated than the Soviet/Russian transformation. The reason for this difference is simply explained by the more complex history of Germany in the twentieth century. The basic facts are these. From 1918 to 1933 Germany was a liberal polity, the Weimar Republic; from 1933 to 1945 it was a totalitarian dictatorship, the Nazi Third Reich; from 1945 to 1949 with reduced frontiers, the country was administered as four zones of occupation; from 1949 to 1990 two Germanies existed: the 'western' liberal FRG (Federal Republic of Germany) and the Communist totalitarian GDR (German Democratic Republic); since 1990 those two entities have been united into an enlarged liberal FRG.

Before investigating this liberal–totalitarian pattern in twentieth-century German civic education, it will be useful to make some brief comments about nineteenth-century developments. Starting in 1815 (following the period we have surveyed in Chapter 2), we shall proceed to the First World War. During the years until around 1890 the attitude of German governments was one of hostility to any teaching of political affairs at all. This kind of education smacked of revolutionary potential and consequently suffered from the clamp-down of the Metternich era. Even teaching about recent history and constitutional systems was actually forbidden. Perhaps the authorities were right: during the uprisings of 1830 and 1848 demands for civic education resurfaced. Inevitably, the status quo was restored in the post-revolutionary reactions. The effect of this nervousness was illustrated by an article in the French newspaper *Le Figaro* as late as 1906, in which the writer declared: 'I was at first astounded at the almost absolute ignorance of the German middle class (artisans, businessmen and shopkeepers), in regard to the political institutions of Germany or even of their local communities' (quoted Kosok 1933: 131). As the Frenchman's visit to Germany took place over two decades after Ferry's law making civic instruction obligatory in France (see Chapter 3 above), the contrast must have been striking.

One of the prime reasons for the persistent prohibition of civic education in Germany into the post-1871 Imperial regime was the growth of the challenge to the established socio-political structure in the form of the Social Democratic movement and party (*SPD*). Suspicions were aired that many teachers were becoming convinced of the justice of the socialists' demands for reforms; if civics lessons were permitted, therefore, they could be dangerously polluted with the left-wing doctrine. Ironically, however, it was precisely because of the strength of the *SPD* – there were already thirty-five deputies in the Reichstag by 1890 – that Wilhelm II decided to reverse the entrenched policy. He issued an order in 1889 requiring that schools should be used to stem this burgeoning movement by warning pupils about the evil of the socialist teaching, diffused through their organizational network. The Kaiser also revealed a positive motive, namely that schools should teach a patriotic commitment to the Empire and its Hohenzollern dynasty through the careful teaching of Prussian and German history.

At the same time, another form of pressure was propelling the issue of civic education to the fore. Both educational thinking and the business community were recognizing the need for young people to take a more active part in the community. We may cite a few indicators of this trend from each of these two arenas.

In 1901 the Bavarian educationist Georg Kerschensteiner received a prize for an essay entitled 'How can we best educate our young men for citizenship in the years between the end of elementary school and conscription?' What is more, in published form, it became very influential. Kerschensteiner argued that citizenship education was of capital importance, the civic competence as well as fitness for manual work of young men being crucial to the health of the state. In other words, Kerschensteiner was linking a political with the vocational element in education, a connection so commonly advocated at the time. The following fragments from his essay provide an indication of the thrust of his thesis. He argued that the individual should be:

> *able* and *willing* to take up his place in the state organism according to his capabilities. . . . [this is a matter of] clearly and convincingly explaining to the pupil that his own economic and social occupational interests are dependent on the interests of every other citizen and of his country. . . . Elementary virtues [should be fostered]: conscientiousness, diligence, perseverance, a sense of responsibility, willpower, and devotion to a life of industry.
>
> (quoted Englund 1986: 133)

Joining the political concept of citizenship with the economic concept of labour, it is of interest to note, has parallels with similar interpretations in the Soviet Union and the Nazi era in Germany. The encouragement by businessmen in this field led to the foundation in 1909 of a body which came to be named the Association for Civic Training and Education, and, in the following year, of the Business Committee for Introducing Civic Training into Schools.

All this activity produced results. In 1911 the Prussian Ministry of Education issued instructions for civics (*Staatsbürgerkunde*) in the secondary schools, both classroom lessons and visits to public institutions and meetings; and in the following year introduced teacher-training courses. Bavaria followed suit but in a less prescriptive way. The tone of this work was, however, as the Kaiser wished: duties rather than rights; loyalty to the sovereign rather than the cultivation of a questioning frame of mind.

The patriotic theme of civic education was inevitably further strengthened through the war years. Indeed, in the words of one authority writing in the final years of the Weimar Republic, 'During the war the entire school system of Germany became one of the most active agents for the dissemination of patriotic propaganda.' Moreover, he continued, 'The generation whose school life was thus saturated with patriotic training and experience has now grown to manhood, and is a contributing factor in giving a definitely nationalistic color to German political life' (Kosok 1933: 167–8). Even though Thomas Mann was able to write in 1918 that 'German humanity is fundamentally opposed to any politicisation, the German concept of education has no political element' (quoted H.-J. Hahn 1998: 27). It depends, of course, on what you mean by 'political'.

The Weimar Republic, established in reaction against the Imperial regime and in response to the post-war confusion, famously and sadly failed to arouse any enthusiastic commitment to itself. And yet it did endeavour to use the schools to bolster a less stridently nationalistic civic loyalty than the imperial style. Even the Constitution, a copy of which was given to every school-leaver, set down these provisions in Article 148:

> Section 1. In all schools an effort shall be made to develop civic sentiment, personal and vocational activity and the spirit of the German national character and of international conciliation. . . .
> Section 2. Civic and vocational instruction is to be given in the schools. Every pupil shall receive a copy of the Constitution at the conclusion of his compulsory schooling.
>
> (quoted Kosok 1933: 172)

To incorporate these statements into a constitution was an extraordinary decision – perhaps unique in the history of constitutional law. Certainly, the present German constitution (the Basic Law) has no comparable Article, nor has the present South African instrument, one of the most comprehensive ever framed.

But a constitution does not will the means to implement its intention. Two threats to the Republic – its attempted overthrow in 1920 (the Kapp Putsch) and the

assassination of Foreign Minister Rathenau by anti-Semitic nationalists in 1922 –
shocked the government into action, so that by the mid-1920s most teacher-training
courses contained civics as an obligatory subject, and a majority of states of the
federation had issued curricular directions, the most detailed of which were those
promulgated in Prussia for secondary schools. These covered a number of subjects,
history and civics (bracketed together) naturally making the greatest contribution.
There is little to cause surprise in these documents except for the phrases stressed
in the following sentences, the first taken from the general statement on history and
civics; the second from the Prussian statement on biology:

> The history of the German people (*including border and foreign Germans*)
> organizes its material according to its different phases as a representation of
> the development of the political, social, economic and *spiritual life of the
> German race* (quoted Kosok 1933: 174).
>
> If the plant and animal production of colonial countries is discussed in
> connection with their economic value, *the necessity of German colonial
> possessions becomes clear* (quoted Kosok 1933: 177).

The idea that the German *Volk* has a 'spirit' or 'transcendental essence', shared
by members of the *Volk* living outside the frontiers of the German state as prescribed
by the Versailles peace settlement, was a concept that Hitler was expounding in his
denunciations of the treaty. Likewise, he railed against Germany being stripped of
its colonial possessions. Indeed, Hitler's growing popularity and the presence
of these two items in the outline syllabuses provide evidence of the intensity of
resentment against the territorial provisions of the Versailles Treaty. Further,
as new textbooks were published, the same message was purveyed, as we shall
see below.

However, apart from the distribution of the constitutional document, none of
these developments was designed to connect young people to the Weimar Republic
specifically. Until, that is, 1927, when a conscious effort was made to render
Constitution Day an occasion of great popular celebrations. Yet, since few members
of the teaching profession felt inclined to afford the regime any keen support, the
message of loyalty to Weimar was inevitably sung with muted voice.

During the Weimar years young people also acquired some kinds of civic training
and feeling through membership of youth organizations, movements which
proliferated rapidly from the early years of the century. A boost was given to this
trend by the upheaval of the revolutionary period (1918 to 1919) and the lowering
of the age of suffrage from 25 to 21 by the Weimar Constitution. By the end of the
Weimar period there were about a hundred of these organizations with a total
membership of approximately five million, and with a variety of core interests from
the churches to the trade unions. They generally – nevertheless in their own, indirect,
ways – encouraged loyalty to the state. Of cardinal importance was the veritable
institution of the hike, often to a place with a patriotic resonance, the walkers singing
patriotic songs *en route*. Insofar as there was a consciously political youth
movement, this was the youth section of the Social Democratic Party. However, as

disillusionment with the way the government was dealing with political, and especially economic, problems grew, so adult membership of the Communist and Nazi parties swelled, and, with them, membership of their youth offshoots. But, of course, these movements were dedicated to undermining the Weimar regime – scarcely a citizenly objective.

Since the Nazi Hitler Youth movement became such a sturdy support of the Third Reich, its origins under the Weimar Republic are especially pertinent to the theme of this chapter. It was in 1922 that Hitler founded what was then called the National Socialist Youth League (*N.S.-Jugenbund*). After various vicissitudes the movement was renamed the Hitler Youth (*Hitlerjugend*, abbreviated to *HJ*) and emerged fully organized in 1929. Two years later Hitler placed the young Baldur von Schirach in charge. When Hitler formed his government in 1933 he arranged that youth activities should be the responsibility of the Ministry of Education; though three years later he made Schirach personally answerable to himself as Führer by a law which also made membership of the movement the only way of participating in youth activities – all other leagues being subsumed or abolished. Detaching adults and youth from whatever allegiance they felt to the Weimar liberal mode of politics and attaching them to the National Socialist mode of totalitarian politics was a task to which Hitler gave high priority. In addition to Schirach's work with the *HJ*, Hitler required Bernhard Rust's Ministry for Science, Education and National Culture to transform the character of civic education in its areas of responsibility. And although, typically of the Nazi system, these two areas failed to work in harmony, Schirach did voice the ideal aim that 'The youth leader and educator of the future will be a priest of the National Socialist creed and an officer in the National Socialist service' (quoted Bracher 1978: 330). Furthermore, adult minds were reached through the manipulations of Goebbels' Ministry of Propaganda and People's Enlightenment and the control exercised by Hans Kerrl's Ministry of Ecclesiastical Affairs. Nor was the family as an institution exempt from the duty of conditioning the attitudes of the young. A decree issued in 1934 made this clear: 'When Home, School, and Hitler Youth League,' it declared, 'each in its own sphere, assume their proper share of responsibility, they will . . . be able to watch the progress which is being made by the threefold arrangement' (quoted Brady 1937: 108).

Let us, therefore, examine the role of the school in this overall pattern. The pace of the radical changes was amazing, indicative of the Nazis' determination to brook no resistance. The schools were deluged with a cascade of pamphlets directly the National Socialists came to power. In the words of a contemporary observer, 'the National Socialist *Weltanschauung* . . . soon forced itself into the schools, changing them, making rules, interdicting, innovating, and completely changing their character within a few months' (Mann 1939: 38). Every aspect of learning was adapted to achieve maximum support for the regime. A historian, quoting Frick, the Minister of the Interior, explains: 'Schools were now empowered with the education of the politically conscious young German . . . "whose every thought and action is rooted in the service and sacrifice of his people and who is inalienably and inseparably bound to the history and destiny of his state"' (H.-J. Hahn 1998: 79). Since the Weimar Constitution was becoming effectively meaningless, except as a reminder of the liberal democratic mode of government, the distribution of copies to school-leavers was discontinued for both of these reasons. Teachers were again, as in imperial times, classified as civil servants; those who were recruited could therefore be selected according to their political 'desirability', and in any case, the whole profession was encouraged with some pressure to join the Nazi Party. Curricula were subjected to wholesale revision. New textbooks were compiled – indeed, by 1941, textbook production was controlled more easily than before by being confined to only one publisher.

Three themes predominated in the school curricula and textbooks in the Nazi era. These were: the importance of and pride in military strength; admiration of and reverence for the Führer; and the fundamental importance of 'race' as an explanatory factor in some subjects, notably biology and history, and as a motive for feelings of superiority of the 'self' and hatred of the threatening 'other'. Even the lessons and primers for quite young children reiterated these messages. A 1940 directive to elementary schools underlined the essentially political purpose of these institutions in the following manner:

> the elementary school . . . has to develop and harness all physical and mental powers of youth for the service of the people and the state. Therefore, the only subject that has any place in the school curriculum is that which is necessary to attain this aim. All other subjects, springing from obsolete educational ideas, must be discarded.
>
> (quoted Samuel and Hinton Thomas 1949: 83)

For the secondary school, history, narrated to display the valiant deeds of the German race and the incomparably crucial role of the Nazi Party in bringing the story to a heroic climax, was a pivotal subject.

In addition to schools for the mass of German children, the National Socialists founded three kinds of institutions for the training of a Nazi elite. These were Order Castles, National Political Education Institutes (Napolas) and Adolf Hitler Schools, each in their own ways providing indoctrination and military training, reminiscent of the Spartiates' *agogē*, though without its callous brutality (for Nazi interest in Sparta, see Chapter 1).

For the ordinary run of young people the potent cohering experience of communal indoctrination was provided by the Hitler Youth (*HJ*) and its female equivalent, the League of German Maidens (*Bund Deutscher Maedel* (*BDM*)). From ages 6 to 10, then 10 to 14, a boy undertook two kinds of novitiate for the *HJ* proper, as a member of the strangely named *Pimpf*, followed by the *Jungvolk* (Young Folk). The transition was marked by the swearing of an oath 'to the saviour of our country, Adolf Hitler' (quoted Shirer 1964: 315). From the age of 14 to 18 the German adolescent would be a fully fledged member of the *HJ*, after pledging himself again to the Führer, though the oath was now broadened to include God as witness and a commitment 'to fulfil my duty for the common weal of the German people' (quoted Mann 1939: 114). This last clause, at least, provided a citizenly element. The girls' organizations were divided by age between the *Jungmaedel* and the older *BDM*, the leaving age being 21. The social and psychological incentives to join the Hitler youth movement in its various sections, prior to membership being made compulsory, is indicated by the following approximate membership figures: 1933, 100,000; 1934, 3.5 million; 1938, 7.75 million.

The activities undertaken by the *HJ* comprised a combination of political indoctrination, physical training, an unremitting insistence on the absolute necessity and virtue of disciplined collective comradeship, and, above all, military training. Soldierly exercises undertaken by these adolescents may indeed be seen as the zenith of a childhood dominated, initially through warlike nursery rhymes and toys, by the message that the very nature of full manhood is readiness to fight for the fatherland, the *Volk* and the Führer.

The significance of the male Nazi youth movement in the history of citizenship education lies, therefore, in its powerful reinforcement of the determination to indoctrinate and militarize the younger generation. Nothing very complicated about that, but for our purposes the participation of the female half of the population in the *BDM* is of greater interest. This league also provided members with physical training and infused into them a sense of duty, emphasizing all the while the importance of a healthy life-style. Yet, did this experience give young German women less or more of a civic identity (see Reese 1997: 102–20)? Under the Empire, although women were denied the vote, the question came to be raised whether they should be required to undertake community social service as a duty parallel to men's compulsory military service and as a *quid pro quo* for enjoying the civil rights to which they were entitled. By participating in the activities of the *BDM* and, particularly during the Second World War, being recruited to essential agricultural, industrial and military work, a later generation of women, it could be argued, did become the equals of men in their citizenly responsibilities, often deploying the experiences and skills they learned in the *BDM*. They also learned the life of comradeship. On the other hand, this conscription deprived them of the personal freedom their forebears had enjoyed in their domestic environment. Moreover, the constant Nazi command that the woman's vital duty was to bear as many children as possible was an extraordinarily sexually divisive interpretation of the nature of citizenship. And although the *BDM* leaders did not necessarily accord great weight to this idea, the institution of combined *HJ* and *BDM* summer camps certainly provided opportunities for its practice.

This survey of Nazi totalitarian civic education raises two vital questions. One is: How far was it radically different from the Weimar arrangements? The other is: Was the Nazi programme really education for *citizenship*?

Given the rapidity and breadth of the changes we have reported, it may seem strange to ask the first question at all. Yet continuities can be identified. It is possible to interpret the Nazi programme of an ardently nationalist-*völkisch* tone of education as lineally connected with nineteenth-century advocates from Fichte onward (see Chapter 2). Moreover, it is likely that many teachers who grew up in this atmosphere were themselves still transmitting these convictions in the Weimar era. In addition, the feeling of humiliation and injustice at the terms of the Versailles Treaty was widespread, and by no means confined to members of the Nazi Party. History and civics textbooks used in the 1920s contained clear lessons. For example, one civics book glorified war as 'the only *just judgment, the natural selection*, through which healthy and sound nations defeat the weak and inferior ones and provide space and prosperity for themselves' (quoted Samuel and Hinton Thomas 1949: 78), and was free with its resentment of Versailles and scorn of Weimar. The authors of the work which draws attention to textbooks written in this vein conclude that:

> It was these books, embodying reactionary social and political ideals and often deliberately fostering the spirit of war and revenge, of hatred and racial arrogance, which helped to mould the outlook of the generation that reached maturity about the time that Hitler came to power.
>
> (Samuel and Hinton Thomas 1949: 82)

We shall return to the matter of Weimar era textbooks later. Meanwhile, it must be understood that these observations are not intended to dispute the dogmatic intensity with which the Nazis imposed their ideological demands upon the schools. Rather, it is to suggest that their view of civic education did not involve a sweeping reversal of what had obtained before.

A particular distinction between the Weimar and Nazi modes of civic education was the all-embracing – indeed the totalitarian – manner of reinforcing school learning with youth movement experience. The purpose was to indoctrinate young people unquestioningly to accept that their lives were devoted essentially to their being members of a community, the *Volk*. But does a sense of community equate with a sense of citizenship? This is our second question. And the issue is nicely balanced.

On the one hand, citizenship has as one of its functions the promotion of a sense of identity and belonging, both – to use the jargon words – vertically to the state and horizontally to one's fellow-citizens. True, the communitarian slant of citizenship theory stresses this feature more than the liberal; none the less, it is not absent from that latter interpretation. Now, throughout the history of educational theory two schools of thought have vied for implementation, namely education for personal development and education for functioning as a member of society. From around 1800 these two objectives, exemplified by the views of Humboldt and Fichte respectively, were in tension in German educational thinking and practice. Frick, to cite him again, drew attention to this problem from the Nazi point of view. He declared:

> The individualistic concept of education has been the main contributor to the destruction of national life within society and state and in particular its unrestrained application in the post-war era has demonstrated its utter inadequacy as a guiding principle for German education.
>
> (quoted H.-J. Hahn 1998: 74)

The contrary view, namely that the *völkisch* sense of community was antipathetic to citizenship, was expressed epigrammatically by a German educationist in 1939 by describing Nazi policy as the 'taking away of citizenship and the giving of comradeship' (quoted Schiedeck and Stahlmann 1997: 72). For the sake of Aryan purity and integrity Jews were stripped of their citizenship. For the sake of the dictatorial power of the Führer and the Party, the personifications of the *Volk*, the political rights of citizenship were extinguished. To fashion young people into conforming members of the *Volk*, in particular through their Hitler Youth units as microcosms of the *Volk,* they were denied the citizenly right to learn and exercise free judgement on social and political affairs. Moreover, the idea that young people should learn in a community in order to become utterly convinced of the inestimable value of the community was expounded in emotionally mystical mood by one of the most influential Nazi educational theorists, Ernst Krieck, especially in his books *National Political Education* and *National Socialist Education*, published respectively in 1932 and 1933. In the former, Krieck wrote of pursuing this educational purpose through the 'underworld of the soul' and the 'national socialist art of mass arousal and mass movement', noting that 'the many in an assembled group melt into a psychic unit, to unity of feeling, to community' (quoted Schiedeck and Stahlmann 1997: 70). This is irrational community, not reasoning citizenship.

German systems since 1945

There is validity therefore in the ideas that Nazi civic education was both a continuation in exaggerated form of trends originating at the dawn of the previous century and that that barbaric distortion of the tradition was in effect an education designed to produce a deformed style of citizenship. If we accept this argument, then it would seem evident that the controlling powers in the four zones of occupation after the Second World War, from 1945 to 1949, had an incomparable opportunity to clear away these distortions and to create systems of more authentic citizenship education. Indeed, plans for the post-war 'educational reconstruction' or 're-education' of Germany were started during the war (see e.g. Schmidt-Sinns 2000: 15–16); and at the Potsdam conference of the Allied Powers held in the summer of 1945 it was agreed that 'German education shall be so controlled as completely to eliminate Nazi and militarist doctrines and to make possible the successful developments of democratic ideas' (quoted Hearnden 1974: 29; for the period 1945 to 2002 see Roberts 2002). About the initial tasks the US, UK, French and Soviet authorities were agreed: first, that, as part of the overall political policy of denazification, teachers whose backgrounds were tainted with allegiance to the Nazi party should be dismissed, though in practice the numbers varied in the zones. For example, the Russians removed half, the British only a quarter. The second major task of the denazification programme was to destroy the ideologically biased textbooks. The reverse side of this policy was positive 're-education' – the recruitment and training of more suitable teachers and the production of more suitable textbooks.

These vast needs, difficult enough to fulfil in themselves in a short time, were complicated by bitter quarrelling among the four allied authorities, and, especially, between each of the occupying powers in the western zones and German officials, teachers, churches and parents. One of the fundamental issues was resistance to any substantial changes to the traditional German form of education. Many who opposed the American, British and French efforts resented their attempts to expunge the militaristic and nationalistic colouring of school teaching, which had been a constant feature from the Wilhelmine, through the Weimar, to the Nazi eras; and any thought of comprehensive schools was anathema to the many middle-class people brought up in an anti-democratic tradition. In the Soviet zone there was less overt antagonism, as we shall see below.

The difficulties facing the allies are illustrated vividly by the obvious necessity to replace the old indoctrinatory textbooks. The problem was especially acute in history. All books in this subject were withdrawn so that for a time not a single textbook was available in the schools for teaching history, a discipline so crucial to citizenship education. There were two possible solutions. One was to commission new books, but these took time to write, monitor and publish; the other was to reprint textbooks from the Weimar period, at least to tide the schools over until the new works were available. The pursuit of each of these policies threw up graphic evidence of the mind-set of many Germans in the first half of the twentieth century. For were not the German character and school ethos engrained with authoritarian, not democratic preferences? The following comments are taken from experiences in the British zone. There a check-list was drawn up of seven features that might appear in a school book and which would preclude publication. These included: 'Glorifies nationalism', 'Is hostile to the United Nations, or tends to sow discord among them' (quoted Hearnden 1978: 114). Yet when nearly 400 books used in schools before 1933 were examined, only eight were deemed suitable for use in primary classes, so blatantly militaristic and nationalistic were their contents (see Hearnden 1978: 108). Even more worrying were some manuscripts submitted for new books. A proposed post-Nazi history of the Church, for instance, contained this sentence about the Jews: 'Never since the world began was a race so prolific in crime' (quoted Hearnden 1978: 117).

Given all these currents flowing against a ready implementation of a citizenship education along democratic lines in the western zones, which in 1949 were amalgamated into the Federal German Republic, it is hardly surprising that 'a genuinely serious commitment to democracy and a meaningful debate on education under the Nazis did not begin until the mid-1960s' (H.-J. Hahn 1998: 105). Furthermore, as many educationists pondered, the mutation of the German frame of mind to that required of a democratic citizen was a chicken-and-egg conundrum: could the schools effect the change in society, or would they be powerless unless there was a change of attitude in the population at large? In the light of all these hindrances to the aims of the western allies, this comment by a German authority on political education is especially instructive:

> The concept of re-education itself may be questionable as it contains the notion of returning to a former state, whereas the German translation '*Umerziehung*' – '*turning through education*' – seems to be a more appropriate term, because the Weimar democracy before 1933 was not the form of democratic culture the Germans intended to revive . . . after the foundation of the Federal Republic of Germany in 1949, scarcely any means of Allied influence remained effective in the cultural domain.
>
> (Schmidt-Sinns 2000: 15)

However, before examining the halting and convoluted story of the development of citizenship education in the FRG, we need to say a few words about the Soviet zone/GDR. The transition to a style of education favoured by the Soviet authorities was somewhat smoother than that experienced by the western allies. There were several reasons for this. One was the writing of new history textbooks by German prisoners-of-war before the end of hostilities. Second was the ability of the Russians to draft in expatriate members of the former German Communist Party as replacement teachers. A third reason was that these teachers and the occupying personnel were more willing and able to override the kinds of objection which the western allies found embarrassingly unexpected. And a fourth reason was the Soviet wish to retain the militaristic theme in civic education. By the summer of 1946 a new Law for the Democratization of the German School System had been adopted by all the *Länder* of the Soviet zone. Its overall purpose was to provide a system that would educate personnel 'able and willing to put themselves at the service of the community of the people' (quoted Samuel and Hinton Thomas 1949: 171), thus underlining the primacy of its civic aim, and to achieve this objective a comprehensive form of schooling (*Einheitsschule*) was to be established. Accordingly, the East Germans boasted that they were implementing the Potsdam requirement for democratic schooling more precisely than the provisions being made in the western zones. However, and inevitably, 'democracy' was interpreted in terms of Marxist-Leninist ideology, which was broadcast through the new history textbooks, coming more speedily and in greater numbers from the presses of the centrally controlled publishing house Volk und Wissen.

Apart from the Soviet-style insistence on citizens honouring labour, recognizing the virtues of socialist economics and understanding the basics of Marxist-Leninism, programmes of civic education in the GDR, when it became a sovereign state in 1949, had to manage two problems. These derived from the co-existence of two Germanies and concerned the issues of democracy and nationhood. Both German states claimed to be true democracies, and teachers in the GDR clearly had to insist that the socialist form was the authentic version. And if the Germans formed a nation in the cultural sense, how could there be two authentic Germanies? Should pupils be taught that unification as a single People's Democracy was to be commended; or that the People's Democracies of central and eastern Europe represented a new, distinct type of nation-state?

In spite of the central control of ideologically approved curricula by the Ministry of National Education and the German Central Institute of Education, the history of citizenship education during the GDR's forty years of existence was not, in fact, as simple as it appeared from the vantage-point of a comparison between the former zones of occupation. There was no straightforward move to a comprehensive school system; the weight of ideology in teaching varied; and there were difficulties in drafting lasting curricula and syllabuses. It was not until 1957 that the new subject of civics was introduced featuring a study of political economy, Marxist-Leninist philosophy, the theory of the socialist state and the patriotic duty to defend the state. This would have gone some way to meeting the criticism expressed by an education official in 1958 that, 'Although from 1952 on the socialist educational aim was laid down for school work, in the years that followed there was no purposeful realisation of it' (quoted Hearden 1974: 131). In 1958 to 1959 new school syllabuses were introduced, but even the new civics programme was not thought to be satisfactory: therefore in the early 1960s it was extended by two years to a six-year course, with a stress on the superiority of the GDR over the FRG. Moreover, by 1968, with revived concentration on ideological demands, a new principle was being put into effect, namely the use of every subject for politico-ideological education. For example, the study of the chemical industry, declared the chemistry syllabus, was 'to be used for education both for patriotism and for friendship with the Soviet Union and other socialist countries' (quoted Hearnden 1974: 200).

However, conveying political messages via different subjects, especially when ideological stances change, can be a tricky business. For instance, when new curricula were introduced in 1974, the official line was that German reunification was not desirable – indeed, the very term 'German nation' had been expunged from the Constitution in 1968. Loyalty to and pride in the GDR, the socialist state newly created in 1949, was the order of the day and was incorporated into the new civics textbooks so that the pupils were taught this interpretation. Even so, as a German educationist has pointed out, 'the history textbook for grade 10 contained a lot of activities undertaken by the government of the GDR in the 1950s towards a reunification of Germany'. Not until 1977 were 'The former lines of reasoning, all events and all names that could remind pupils' of the previous policy 'eliminated' (Waterkamp 1990: 328; for history teaching, see e.g. H.-J. Hahn 1998: 150–2). In 1983 yet newer syllabuses were issued for civics and history, emphasizing the nature and economic policy of the GDR. Nevertheless, none of these curricular changes had the desired effect of generating ingrained commitment. Most young people revealed deep political apathy. Accordingly, other strategies were devised – including, for example, during the last decade or so of the state, a tripling of the membership of the Free German Youth organization. One illuminating result of investigations carried out at the Leipzig Central Institute for Youth Research in the late 1970s has been summed up thus:

> Identification with the state is not always based on ideology . . . but is often founded on general humanism, i.e. antifascism, and on a general love for the native environment or the native country. Both motives fail to satisfy the educationists because they do not reflect a conviction of the GDR's historical mission.
>
> (Waterkamp 1990: 331)

Scarcely an endorsement of totalitarian education for citizenship grounded in ideology. And the collapse of the state and reunification in 1989 to 1990 told the same story. What one authority has dubbed the East Germans' 'schizophrenic relationship' to the socialist nation and the cultural nation was resolved in favour of the latter (see Führ 1997: 25).

In contrast to the direction of curricular matters by the GDR Ministry of National Education down to the issuing of detailed syllabuses, the Federal government in

Bonn had virtually no influence because, in the words of Article 7(1) of the Basic Law, 'The entire school system shall be under the supervision of the state' (i.e. the *Land*). The autonomy and power of the *Länder* had in fact been confirmed by the western occupying powers in reaction to the centralized authority wielded by the Nazis. Indeed, paradoxically, some western *Länder* had constitutions before the creation of the Federal state. Moreover, these instruments were more specific than Article 7 of the Federal document on the purpose of education. Thus, Article 56 of the Hesse Constitution includes the statement that:

> The objective of education is to fashion youngsters as moral personalities, preparing the way for vocational competence and political responsibility with autonomous and trustworthy service of the nation and humanity through reverence and neighbourly love, respect for tolerance, honesty and truthfulness. History lessons must be directed towards faithful, unfalsified depiction of the past. . . . Views that endanger the foundations of the democratic state are not to be tolerated.
>
> (quoted Führ 1997: 20)

Consequently, it was left to the *Länder* to devise and implement their own school policies, an arrangement which has been described as creating 'chaos and confusion' and 'more of a bane than a blessing' by hindering reform (H.-J. Hahn 1998: 115, 117). This inevitably raises difficulties when trying to generalize about civic education, especially as the political complexion of a *Land* government could colour the guidelines it sent to schools. To make matters worse, quarrels developed over a number of issues, concerning selective *vs.* comprehensive schooling, teaching methodologies and curricular content. All had implications for citizenship education. The first raised the question of the proper form of education for democracy. The second, the most effective means of generating citizenly attitudes and behaviour. The third reflected, for example, the problems of coming to terms politically with and therefore teaching about the Third Reich and the Cold War. The differences of opinion caused serious wrangling. A former member of the Federal Centre for Political Education has judged that 'it was the political climate that, in the Federal Republic more than elsewhere, led to the formation of didactic camps which often argued against one another more fiercely than political parties' (Schmidt-Sinns 2000: 67). Even related subjects in the field of civic education, namely the social sciences and history, sometimes put forward conflicting interpretations to pupils. The *Länder*, it is true, have attempted to provide professional guidance by creating Centres for Political Education.

Efforts have also been made to organize some federal co-ordination. In addition to the regional Centres, the Federal Centre (or Agency) for Political Education (*Bundeszentrale für politische Bildung*) was established. Also, the Standing Conference of Education Ministers has occasionally met to issue guidelines in this field, and professional specialists have distributed statements for nation-wide application. A few examples: in 1961, the Standing Conference issued guidelines on the teaching of contemporary history; in 1976, the Beutelsbacher Consensus gave guidelines on the teaching of controversial issues; and in 1995 the Darmstadt Appeal encouraged teachers to update their courses by incorporating new topics such as globalization and political extremism (see Roberts 2002: 561–3).

Moving now from this analysis of the FRG's institutional background to a chronological survey, we may usefully divide these years into four phases; that is, from 1949 to the mid-1950s, the mid-1950s to the mid-1960s, the mid-1960s to 1990, and since 1990.

The early years of the Federal Republic were dominated by the need for economic reconstruction and a disillusionment with politics, an activity that had led to the catastrophe of 1943 to 1945. Civic education mirrored this mood. In 1951 Friedrich Oertinger published *Partnership: the Task of Political Education*. This book became very influential, the concept of partnership being taken up in textbooks and guidelines. Pupils were taught the importance of community, social partnership, not of political dispute and activity. Many schools used a textbook entitled *With One Another – For One Another* – so widely used, in fact, that, by 1967, it had reached its twelfth edition. The title itself reflects the kind of teaching. This placid form of civic education did, however, arouse criticism; even so, Oertinger's initiative in raising the issue of political education in the new Federal Republic led to a universal acceptance that 'education for good citizenship' was absolutely essential (see Duczek 1977: 5–7).

By the second period, the decade from the mid-1950s, the FRG had gained self-confidence, and teaching about the institutions and democratic processes of this stable state, far from being considered hazardous, was generally encouraged as educationally and politically healthy. Yet these years of assumed and taught social and political concord were not to last.

Schools could not be unaffected by rising political emotions. By the late 1950s anti-Communist teaching in the classrooms mirrored the Cold War tensions, and outbursts of neo-Nazi anti-Semitism provided shocking reminders of the country's immediate past. This latter experience stirred politicians to urge greater attention to political education of a kind that would cultivate a conscientious citizenship. With the 1960s, and entering our third period, came the famous shifts in social mores and political consciousness of seismic magnitude. In its own way, no more than France and the USA in their more violent ways, did Germany manage to escape these tremors. Civics courses which portrayed socio-political harmony and the citizen's functions of mere passive neighbourliness as reflections of reality clearly had to be challenged and transformed. Many new approaches were tried: for example, conveying a sense of national identity independent of antipathy towards Communism, the teaching of social science analysis, the introduction in the 1970s and 1980s of environmental studies. Teachers engaged in this experimental activity were supported by the creation of the *DVPB* (Association for Civic Education) in 1965. In addition, the radical mood of the 1960s produced angry criticism of the persistence of the 'undemocratic' system of selective secondary schools. A key concept in the 1970s and 1980s was the linking of judgement and participation. A quotation from a book published in 1979 indicates this line of argument: 'The aim of political education is to create critical consciousness and the ability to form an independent opinion. Both should result in political engagement' (quoted Meyenberg 1990: 216). Greater realism and dynamism hence resulted from these newly generated ideas. But it was all too much for the schools to digest. Consequently, by 1990, one political scientist was driven to comment: 'Political education is believed to be in a crisis . . . the didactics of political education have passed the phases of turbulence . . . [but] The present situation of political education does not look too bright' (Meyenberg 1990: 216, 218).

The same year in which these pessimistic words were published, West and East Germany were unified, thus presenting more problems to be solved. First, foremost and most obvious was the issue of the Communist tradition in civic education in what had now become the new *Länder* of the enlarged FRG. As with all the transitions covered in this chapter, this was a threefold matter of who was to teach, what was to be taught and in what kind of schools. In all these respects the process was not a unification; it was a virtual annexation of the GDR by the FRG. To take each of the three questions in turn.

> Following unification, 20 per cent of all teachers and most scholars who worked on issues related to politics or policy-making . . . were dismissed. Civics education teachers usually were denied the opportunity to teach this subject any longer. Instead, teachers who were educated in other subjects were trained to teach civic education.
>
> (Händle *et al.* 1999: 261)

Subject-matter was 'westernized' by the simple expedient of delivering to the eastern *Länder* school textbooks already in use in the west. And the GDR comprehensive school system was dismantled, replaced by the FRG selective tripartite system.

Also imposed upon the east, inevitably, was the FRG's devolution of responsibility for education (with the above provisos), so that the variations across now fifteen *Länder* render the framing of generalizations even more difficult than hitherto. A few common themes may, nevertheless, be discerned. First, all secondary schools have had explicit civics lessons in some form or other, usually in grades 7 and 8 (see C.L. Hahn 1998: 12; Händle *et al.* 1999: 260–1). Second (though this quotation is taken from research undertaken only in the western *Länder*), 'social studies/science lessons were usually based on a teacher-led recitation reviewing a photocopied article. Also prevalent was the practice of having a class discussion in which students identified opposing arguments on an issue' (C.L. Hahn 1998: 13). Third, 'civics' has been interpreted extremely broadly. Fourth, in response to an important research project, it was discovered that 'To 90 per cent of the experts, the knowledge of formal democratic functions (the right to express opinions freely, the right to vote freely, the separation of powers) is a central goal of civic education' (Händle *et al.* 1999: 264). There was at least that measure of agreement after a century of vertiginous change in citizenship education in Germany.

Japan

The political histories of Germany and Japan in the period *c*.1870 to 1950 reveal fascinating parallels. We may discern oscillations from imperial autocracy to post-Great War political liberalization, to authoritarian fascism intensified by war, to liberal democracy imposed by the Allied victors after the Second World War. However, Japan's oriental traditions, still pervasive despite the introduction of occidental ways from the mid-nineteenth century, inevitably lent the Japanese experience of civic education its own particular characteristics.

The accession of the Emperor Meiji and the restoration of imperial power in 1867 to 1868 inaugurated a period of extraordinary change in Japan, though not without misgivings. The balance that should properly be struck between traditionalism and westernization in political, social and educational matters became an issue of heated dispute. Insofar as it is possible to speak of civic education in a traditional Japanese sense, it related to the Confucian and samurai codes of living. The samurai warrior-bureaucrats learned moral principles and political skills through a Confucian curriculum and from their families' expectations of courage and loyalty. Accordingly, when, in the late nineteenth century, schools became available to the offspring of the populace at large and constitutional reform introduced an elected Diet, it was natural for educationists who wished to have moral-civic education widely provided to think in terms of an adapted samurai style of learning.

The speed of political and educational change during the Meiji (1867 to 1912) and Taisho (1912 to 1926) eras may be indicated by the following landmarks. In 1871 a Ministry of Education was established with responsibility for state-provided education. From the mid-1870s to the mid-1880s a vigorous civil rights movement, although eventually crushed, not only demanded greater political rights, but also set up as many as a thousand of their own schools to provide political education and produced their own textbooks. The need for alternative textbooks came about because the campaigners objected to the 'naked Confucianism and nationalism' of the texts compiled under state direction and the withdrawal of the more acceptable works written by the likes of Yukichi Fukuzawa (see Aso and Amano 1972: 12). The extremely versatile Fukuzawa was the most distinguished educational thinker of the Meiji era. He was keenly aware of the potential connection between education and politics and of the vital importance of an educated public opinion (see Passin 1965: 208). In 1872 he published a book entitled *Encouragement of Learning*. In this work he expressed the following radical ideas:

> If [the people] have the slightest complaint against the government, they should . . . seek a proper channel to present the case calmly and frankly. If the case is in accord with Heaven's Reason and with Humanity, one should fight for it even at the risk of one's life. Such is the duty of the man who calls himself a citizen of a civilized nation. . . . If we do not wish harsh government, we must see to it that the people are educated.
>
> (quoted Passin 1965: 209)

Equally important was Arinori Mori, though in a complementary way, as a politician. The Emperor reacted to the ferment of the 1870s and 1880s by appointing a cabinet in 1885, issuing a written Constitution, with provisions for an elected Diet, in 1889, and publishing an Imperial Rescript on Education 1890. He appointed as Minister of Education in his cabinet the extremely able Mori, who fervently believed in the civic function of schools. The purpose of education at the school level, he declared, was to 'train the people so that each individual person may fully understand his duty as a Japanese subject, practice ethics and become qualified to enjoy welfare' (quoted Aso and Amano 1972: 20). Moreover, he consciously drew upon the samurai code as his model for educating all the people to a sense of moral civic duty (see Cummings 1987: 16–17). His epigram became famous: 'what is to be done is not for the sake of the pupils, but for the sake of the country' (quoted Passin 1965: 150). Furthermore, the educational system Mori created lasted until the end of the Second World War. Its philosophy was enshrined in the 1890 Imperial Rescript, which contained what amounted to an official statement on citizenship and citizenship education, albeit in a very limited sense. The Emperor adjured his subjects to

> Advance public good and promote common interests; always respect the Constitution and observe the laws; should emergency arise, offer yourselves courageously to the State; and thus guard and maintain the prosperity of our Imperial Throne coeval with heaven and earth.
>
> (quoted Passin 1965: 151)

But neither the Emperor nor prevailing public opinion would countenance any teaching that might approach the kind of citizenship education being pioneered at this time in the USA and France, despite the close contacts which Mori and other Japanese educationists had with these countries. On the contrary, conservative signs of a veritable totalitarian, extremist nationalist mood were already evident. For all his stress on patriotism, Mori was considered insufficiently nationalist by many, and, for this reason, he was assassinated in 1889. In the same year portraits of the Emperor were sent to schools for teachers and pupils to revere, and two years later copies of the Rescript were provided to be displayed in an equally sacred way. The presence of the royal portrait, it may be noted, was part of the civic ethos in English as well as Japanese schools, and honouring the flag was similarly introduced in the USA and Japan. However, the atmosphere in Japanese schools was incomparably more devotional, as the following description reveals:

> The reading of the Imperial Rescript was more a religious incantation than the recitation of a secular document. . . . So sacred were these symbols [i.e. also the royal portrait] that in case of fire they were to be saved before everything else, even at the risk of life. There have been dramatic cases where teachers or principals of schools, accidentally responsible for some impropriety – for example, dropping the Imperial Rescript, or making a mistake in its reading – committing suicide.
>
> (Passin 1965: 155)

In the classroom moral education with a nationalist slant pervaded the curriculum, akin to what was to become the Soviet practice; not only was it taught as a discrete subject, but it coloured many other disciplines, notably history.

During the brief reign of Emperor Yoshihito, political reforms were introduced of such significance that the term 'Taisho democracy' has been coined to describe this era. (*Taisho*, 'great righteousness', was the Emperor's description of his reign.) A Reform Act of 1919 doubled the electorate and six years later universal manhood suffrage was introduced.

Nevertheless, although during these years of reform teachers were given greater classroom freedom and some new textbooks reflected this modernization and liberalization, significantly, history books still held to a firm nationalist narrative. What is more, any hope of moderating the extreme nationalistic interpretation of the Imperial Rescript was shattered by the effective take-over of power from Emperor Hirohito in 1931 by the military and extreme nationalistic politicians. Reformers walked fearfully between the fascist government to their right and the incipient revolutionary tendencies to their left: hence the name for the decade from the invasion of Manchuria in 1931 to the attack on Pearl Harbor in 1941, *Kurai tanima* – 'dark valley' (see Storry 1961: 182). In 1932 the Ministry of Education set up an Institute for the Study of Moral Culture in order to exert ideological control; and two years later the Orwellian-named Bureau of Thought was formed within the Ministry. The intensification of chauvinist education proceeded apace under the impetus of a new Education Council from 1937. One of its recommendations was to make attendance at youth schools compulsory up to the age of 19, with courses which included military training (see Kobayashi 1976: 38–9).

In 1941 General Sadeo was appointed Minister of Education. Indoctrination in schools was now imposed by the military authorities, and textbooks became more and more nationalistic. At the same time, citizens' schools were established offering education beyond the minimum compulsory six years. Article 2 of the Regulations governing these institutions stated, in part:

> Citizenship studies will teach the morals, language, history, and geography of our nation, and in particular will clarify the essence of our national polity in order to cultivate the national spirit. The pupils will be happy that they were born in our Empire, and they will acquire the spirit of reverence and service.
>
> 'Citizenship' will make them understand the features of our history and land that have brought forth a superior national character.
>
> (quoted Passin 1965: 267)

The first paragraph would not have seemed out of place in England, for example; the second, however, has louder echoes of Nazi Germany. Moreover, as the Americans turned the tide in the Pacific theatre, the war effort took precedence over any other aspect of life. But to no avail. And with the American occupation in 1945, fundamental changes were imposed in order to transform the character of Japanese education.

Only two months after the Japanese surrender, the Supreme Commander of the Allied Powers issued a Memorandum on Education. Paragraphs germane to our subject include the following:

> Dissemination of militaristic and ultranationalistic ideology will be prohibited and all military education and drill will be discontinued. . . .
>
> Teachers and educational officials . . . who have been active exponents of militarism and ultranationalism, and those actively antagonistic to the policies of the Occupation will be removed. . . .
>
> New curricula, textbooks, teaching manuals, and instructional materials designed to produce an educated, peaceful, and responsible citizenry will be prepared . . . as rapidly as possible.
>
> (quoted Passin 1965: 270–2)

In addition, on the last day of the year, a peremptory order was circulated with the core message that 'All courses in Morals . . . Japanese History, and Geography . . . shall be suspended immediately' (quoted Passin 1965: 273). The weight of American determination to create a democratic Japan in its own image by political and educational means could not be resisted. Thus, the Fundamental Law of Education of 1947 stated that the ideal of building a new democratic state 'shall depend fundamentally on the power of education' and incorporated, as Article VIII, the following requirement:

> Political Education. The political knowledge necessary for intelligent citizen-ship shall be valued in education. The schools prescribed by law shall refrain from political education or other political activities for or against any specific party.
>
> (quoted Passin 1965: 301–2, 303)

Although decisive efforts were made to alter Japanese political and educational culture after the Second World War and to use citizenship education (under whatever label) as a vital adjunct to this policy, all has by no means been well in its implementation. In the first place there have been many changes in the ways the subject-matter should be taught as defined by the courses of study which are issued periodically by central government. Initially, social studies was introduced as a core curriculum subject. In 1955 and again in 1960 the subject was subdivided into component disciplines, and in 1958 moral education was made a separate subject (see Cummings *et al.* 1988: 82); then, in 1968, social studies was renamed civics. However, by this time the Central Council of the Ministry of Education had issued in 1966 a statement defining 'The Image of the Ideal Japanese', which formed an important reference point for yet more curriculum reforms in 1971 to 1972. Still more adaptations followed in later years. On the other hand, the basic purposes of citizenship education were set down by the Ministry of Education in 1970 and have remained unaltered as guidelines. These covered: Japanese national sover-eignty; local community; national culture, economics and international relations;

understanding of individual's rights and responsibilities; and ability to act in relation to them (see Cogan and Derricott 2000: 68). By the turn of the century elementary schools taught social studies (geography/history) in grades 3–6, and junior high schools taught civics (contemporary social life, improvement of national life and economy, democratic government and international community) in grade 3. High schools taught contemporary society or ethics and politics/economy (see Cogan and Derricott 2000: 69–70).

However, behind all these changes of content and subject relationships lay two rather more unfortunate features of citizenship education in the second half of the twentieth century. One was the wooden style of teaching centred on factual memorization, rendering some of the courses unpopular with the pupils. The second was the gradual increase, under government direction, of traditionalist and nationalistic content and interpretation, which caused divisions within the country and resentment in other countries, notably China and Korea, for what they believed to be distortions in history textbooks. As we have seen, there was nothing objectionable about the 1970 guidelines in outline; it was their interpretation, especially in history, that caused offence and controversy.

The problem has had its origins in the system for licensing books and the arrangement for issuing 'courses of study'. The first of these devices, intended to be a temporary measure after the war, has been used to censor and introduce bias into school textbooks; moreover, the arrangement was tightened up by the Textbook State Control Law of 1966. The second device has also been used gradually to slant the advice to teachers. Two British authorities commented in 1973 that the history course of study 'has undergone continuous, retrogressive revision, democratic, pacifistic and scientific elements being gradually whittled away from it' (Halliday and McCormack 1973: 187). The most famous example of government interference in the content of textbooks concerned a history book written by Professor Saburo Ienaga. Incensed by the amendments demanded, he took the government to court, denying the validity of the 320 changes he was required to make. The case was pursued for years through the courts with a torpor akin to the English Victorian civil law procedures (see Cummings 1986: 22; Halliday and McCormack 1973: 187, 189). As an indication of what Ienaga was up against, we may cite comments made in 1970 by the senior Ministry of Education official responsible for textbook certification. All current textbooks, he declared, were 'biased and ignorant'; and, revealing the underlying reason for his judgement, he explained, 'I prefer to be called rightist. I am an ultra-nationalist' (quoted Halliday and McCormack 1973: 190).

Japan, more than either the Soviet Union/Russia or Germany, illustrates the difficulties of making the transition from a totalitarian to a liberal style of citizenship education, though teachers in all of these states have faced formidable difficulties. The young have been politically apathetic, more interested in youth 'culture' than in public affairs. Adults have been more interested in their standard of living and careers than in civic responsibilities. And memories of past conditions, greatness and humiliations have fostered suspicion and resentment of liberal and tolerant interpretations of citizenship. For some Germans, in the face of immigration, neo-Nazism has seemed attractive and the defeat of 1945, a calamity. For some Russians, in the face of economic collapse and burgeoning crime, Communism has seemed not such a bad system in retrospect. The Japanese case is slightly different. Their problem has been one of a clash of cultures: the difficulties of reconciling traditional Nipponese with western values, experienced since the Meiji initiation of the enterprise, have still not been resolved. All three countries we have examined are committed to citizenship education of a liberal style which has become virtually universal. Nevertheless, there is a limit to what the schools can achieve against social backgrounds with such retrogressive features.

In the meantime, the Russian feeling and understanding of citizenship are having to take account of the existence of ethnic, especially Muslim, minorities, the Germans must incorporate citizenship of the European Union into their citizenly understanding, and all three countries must learn to relate to the growing consciousness of world citizenship.

5   Multiple citizenship education

Inadequacy of the state–citizen model

Whether in city-state or nation-state, republic, principality or empire, citizenship has throughout history been a legal and political status accorded by the state to the individual and a bond of loyalty owed by the individual to the state. Citizenship education has accordingly sought to induct the individual into that status and to clinch that bond. Indeed, so self-evident has the relationship seemed to be that, in both theory and practice, it has often been thought natural, prudent and necessary for the state to make provision for a form of citizenship education in its own image. As the ages have passed, and with increasing acceleration since the eighteenth century, more elements have been added to complicate the citizenly idea and practice. Yet the state–citizen nexus held. Until relatively recently, that is. If the state demands that the moral and psychological ties take precedence over other social and ethical connections, then, in the event of intense consciousness of other relationships and allegiances, the monopoly of the state on the citizen's fealty will be queried. The state can then be interpreted as merely one unit in the social–moral–political strata of human groupings; then arguments can be marshalled to suggest that citizens should share their allegiances to ideals, groups or institutions both below and above the state. In short, citizenship must be conceived as a multiple, not a unitary concept and status (see Heater 1990: ch. 9). In this event, citizenship education becomes more complex.

The challenges to sole state citizenship from below come from ethnically or culturally distinct minorities in the state who wish for recognition by the state of their own identities. Where the minority is geographically compact, the response may be political in the form of devolution or federalism. Where the minority is geographically dispersed, legal and communal rights may be conceded. The challenges to a sole state citizenship from above can come either from the creation of transnational institutions offering a citizenship status, as is the case with the European Union; or from the consciousness of or belief in the concept of world citizenship with a moral code that transcends the obligations of state law and, even, with pretensions to cosmopolitan legal and political institutions. The idea that there is a complementary world citizenship was first effectively formulated by the ancient Stoics. The challenge from below to the assumption that the state alone can confer and determine the nature of citizenship has been more recent. It derives from the conflation of state and nation. Because the assertion that the political state must be synonymous with the cultural nation is an impossibility in practice, cultural minorities have become increasingly discontented with the implication that citizenship must be shaped by this falsehood.

However, these complications raise difficulties for the theory of citizenship. It can and has been cogently argued that to stretch the term 'citizenship' to include 'world citizenship' is a semantic confusion. The very meaning of citizenship entails an individual–state relationship; there is no world state; ergo, there can be no world citizens. Even the status of citizen of the European Union, despite its enshrinement in international law, is an unfortunate dilution of the term, again, because there is no European state. The objection to the adaptation of citizenship to accommodate the divisions within a multicultural state involves important practicalities. To adopt a federal solution is acceptable because by constitutional definition the component states of a union are states, with the essential legal and political institutions which define that political status. But to concede separate legal, even political, rights to minorities in a constitutionally unitary state is to undermine the status of citizenship, which should, at least ideally, be founded on the fundamental equality of all citizens. Leaving aside the constitutional device of federalism (and the quasi-federal nature of EU citizenship), the above complications have arisen because it is recognized that citizenship is a matter not just of status, rights and duties legally defined, but also of commitment, loyalty and responsibility – of being a 'good citizen'. If the concept of world citizenship carries any validity, it is largely in this sense of global civic virtue. And the issue of multiculturalism in a state has ramifications for citizenship, again, because of feelings of attachment – for reasons of tradition, language or religion – that make the minority distinct from the majority population. When these feelings – be they cosmopolitan or cultural – are sufficiently firmly embedded, they can inevitably challenge the character of citizenship as a monolithic status.

This derangement of the simple notion of citizenship in its original, Greek, sense cannot but have implications for citizenship education. The purpose of this chapter is to explain these implications in their historical contexts. Here it will be helpful to outline the main complications. Let us begin by accepting that it is not too much of a caricature to depict traditional citizenship education as a process of learning about and understanding the legal and, particularly, political workings of one's own state, and in such a manner as to inculcate an allegiance to that state; both cognitive and affective learning have been involved, the objectives of which, and even the methodologies, have been reasonably straightforward and clear. Adding the extra dimensions of multicultural education, education for European citizenship (in member-countries) and global/world education has increased the amount of material to be taught and raised the issue of teaching for multiple identities and allegiances.

Problems unavoidably arise in the construction of syllabuses and in the ways in which the subject-matter is presented. The more potential subject-matter that can have a claim for inclusion, the more difficult the task of selection becomes. This problem is exacerbated in global education because of the uncertainty of defining with any precision what world citizenship means. But sheer quantity is only one of the problems. There is also the question of the proper balance to be struck across the various kinds of citizenship material. The task of teaching for multiple citizenship also becomes hazardous because no solution to these problems can be perfect, and syllabus outlines on paper and teachers in classrooms can be subject to the criticism that teaching for state citizenship is diluted and/or the selected material or the manner of its delivery is biased. Moreover, the topic of multicultural education has its own special political as distinct from pedagogical difficulty, which governments have needed to resolve. This is: whether schools should be so ordered as to preserve or destroy the minority cultures of which the state is composed; to accept a mosaic citizenry, or attempt to meld the variations into a culturally coherent citizenry. On the other hand, whether one is considering multicultural education, education for European citizenship or global education, one development is clear: that all these approaches have heightened the awareness of educationists that education for citizenship must give a high priority to learning tolerance and teaching about the nature of human rights.

Citizenship, culture and ethnicity

Originally, citizenship was barely related to ethnicity. Although the Greeks were wont to distinguish themselves from 'barbarians', citizens were not citizens by virtue of their Hellenic culture, but by virtue of their membership of a particular *polis*. Similarly, citizenship of Italian city-states was Florentine or Venetian citizenship, for example, not Italian. And the Roman citizenship was accorded to non-Latins increasingly from the time of Augustus, even if the donation of the status to Greeks, Gauls, Spaniards and Britons by Claudius did produce a sniffy comment from Seneca (himself Hispanic!) (see Sherwin-White 1973: 237 and *passim*).

We must, none the less, in the context of city-states and the Roman Empire, distinguish between ethnicity and culture. Athenian citizens could not have been citizens without an upbringing in Hellenic culture, nor could Florentines be citizens without Italian culture. The Roman policy, admittedly fluctuating and exceedingly complex, illustrates this distinction admirably. We have seen in Chapter 1 how schools to teach the Latin language and culture became agents of a positive policy of Romanization of the provincial elite. There was also a process of what Sherwin-White calls 'self-Romanization', in the interest of advancement in life (Sherwin-White 1973: 222). The necessity to have a command of the Latin language in order to be a Roman citizen may be shown by two examples. One is the reported view of Claudius that 'it was not proper for a man to be a Roman who had no knowledge of the Roman tongue' (quoted Sherwin-White 1973: 246); the other is the comment by Libanius, a fourth-century professor of rhetoric, that it was the policy of Diocletian (d.306) and his successors to supplant Greek with Latin in the east (even though Greek soon resumed its dominance) (see Marrou 1956: 257). On the other hand, Caracalla's *Antonine Constitution* had already, in 212, extended the Roman citizenship to all free inhabitants of the Empire, irrespective of their educational background. Prior to the modern era, then, citizenship education was designed to fit young men to participate in the life of their *state* – not of their people or nation.

At the dawn of the age of nationalism, however, a new idea arose, namely that young people should be educated to a consciousness of nationhood; even if the nation and state did not coincide. We have seen in Chapter 2 how Fichte strove to connect the Prussian state with the German nation by educational means. Moreover, by the end of the nineteenth century international law was coming to accept 'nationality' and 'citizenship' as synonymous terms, and they were defined thus notably in 1930 in the judgement of the United States–Mexico General Claims Commission:

> A man's nationality *is a continuing legal relationship between the sovereign State on the one hand and the citizen on the other. The fundamental basis of a man's nationality is his membership of an independent political community.* This legal relationship involves rights and corresponding duties upon both – on the part of the citizen no less than the part of the State.
>
> (quoted Starke 1947: 180)

Parallel with this development in jurisprudence came the conviction that a state should be a 'nation' in both senses: a sovereign political entity and an ethnically and culturally homogeneous community. And since so few states, if any, conformed to the latter definition, it became virtually universally accepted that steps should be taken to achieve this necessary homogeneity. These steps were primarily educational, the schools used especially to teach the children of minority groups the language, and also the traditions, of the majority people. Apart from the ideological assumption that a state should be a nation in the cultural sense, there were two other motives informing this educational policy. One was the belief that cultural cohesion was necessary to guarantee the patriotic loyalty of all the state's citizens and thus the security of the state. The other was the argument that, in a democratic society, individuals would be incapable of enjoying their rights of citizenship and discharging their concomitant duties if they had no command of the official language of the state of which they were members. (As we are taking a historical perspective here the past tense has been used, yet these observations are still currently true.) We may briefly illustrate each of these two motives. In the nineteenth century, policies of Russification and the less forceful Germanization were introduced by those two countries in order to absorb their Polish subjects. For example, following the Polish insurrection against the Tsarist government in 1863,

> The [Polish] language was completely banished from the schools, administration and public life and even the use of the Latin script or the Polish method of driving a carriage [!] forbidden. In Poland proper, all schools were Russified and the pupils forbidden to speak their mother language within the walls of the schools.
>
> (Macartney 1934: 132)

On the practical issue of participation, the classic exposition of the case is J.S. Mill's:

> Free institutions are next to impossible in a country made up of different nationalities. Among a people without fellow-feeling, especially if they read and speak different languages, the united public opinion, necessary to the working of representative government, cannot exist.
>
> (Mill 1910: 361)

Ernest Gellner has gone further, insisting on the necessarily tight relationship of citizenship, linguistic nationality and education in the modern world. He argues along the following lines. Literacy is the minimum requirement for the exercise of citizenship; only a nation-state can marshal the resources required for a fully developed educational system; and education has to be conducted in a language comprehensible to all citizens. He concludes: 'only education makes a full man and citizen, and that education must be in some linguistic medium. It explains why nationalism can and does move such broad masses of humanity' (Gellner 1983: 48).

One can push the argument to an even more comprehensive analysis and identify five conditions under which the nation-state will make a special effort to promote education with a national civic purpose. The first occurs during a process of secularization. It is generally accepted that education should have a moral purpose; if that is not provided by religion, the alternative is, to use an awkward word, 'civism' – the atheist policy of the Soviet Union, for example (see Chapter 4). The second condition occurs after a revolution, when the new regime uses education to consolidate its position and purpose. Nazi Germany is an illustration of this (see Chapter 4). The third condition is revealed in newly founded states, especially after independence from imperial rule. African states provide good examples (see Chapter 3). The fourth condition is present when the so-called nation-state is in fact composed of more than one culturally or ethnically identifiable and conscious group, which the state feels it prudent to weld into a coherent 'nation'. France after 1789 exemplifies this condition (see Chapters 2 and 3). Fifth, there is the experience of immigration. The history of the USA demonstrates this condition (see Chapter 3). It is evident, however, that more than one of these conditions can prevail in any given state to determine its educational policy.

The formula of state educational systems constructing a culturally homogeneous national citizenry, so widely accepted in the nineteenth and twentieth centuries, has recently been seen to be too simplistic, even undesirable and impractical. The symbolic clash of cultures in the attempts in France and Singapore in recent years to forbid Muslim girls to wear headscarves in school epitomizes the dilemma. The simplicity of this old pattern has been widely queried for both theoretical and practical reasons (see e.g. Delanty 2000), so just an indication of the main points of particular pertinence for our purpose must suffice here. The theoretical issue arises from analyses of the nature of citizenship. Three main schools of thought co-exist, namely the anciently based civic republican concept, which stresses duty; the modern liberal concept, which stresses rights; and the recently propounded communitarian concept, which, while sharing much of the civic republican school, stresses commitment to and identification with one's community. The practical issue arises from the failure of the state-nationalist proposition. The ideal nation-state, insofar as it ever properly existed, is now seen to be crumbling under the pressures exerted by burgeoning sub-state, provincial ethnic and cultural consciousness and the immigration of sizeable numbers of alien peoples.

Citizenship theory and demographic diversity interact in the following way. Liberal citizenship presupposes citizens as equal individuals living as members of a political state; civic republicanism presupposes citizens as forming a population patriotically attached to the state; and communitarianism presupposes citizens as being members associated in different groups. The problems arise, therefore, in the typical twenty-first-century state, which is so clearly culturally heterogeneous, as to whether an integrated theory of citizenship can be devised, whether a workable inter-communal social policy can be framed, and whether the educational system can cope with the new demands. The core issue lies in the wisdom of politicians in selecting one of the three possible basic models for designing their policy (see e.g. Delanty 2000: 103–4; though some sociologists favour more complex analyses: see e.g. Esser 1991: 45–9). The first is assimilation or integration – the nineteenth-century American 'melting-pot' and Russification policies are instances, whereby minorities have been led or forced into cultural conformity with the dominant population. The second option is marginalization; that is, the policy of keeping the minority population(s) in a condition of second-class citizenship – the position of the blacks in the USA at least until the 1950s and, more recently, of the Christians in the Sudan, for example. The third model is pluralism, or multiculturalism; that is, the toleration of multiple ethnicities in a state, in the belief that loyalty and stability are best achieved in the contemporary world by this light-handed approach. British policy towards their Jewish, black, Asian and Muslim citizens is an example of this policy.

It is obvious that the role of schools will be required by the state to be different depending on which model is adopted. Even so, if a pluralist political policy is pursued, the question remains to be answered whether schools should be organized as common institutions catering for all children of the multicultural community, so that they grow up understanding about and tolerant of members of groups other than their own; or as segregated institutions, so that the children of each group are able to retain intact their separate cultural identities. It is a problem that is discussed most learnedly by Eamonn Callan (1997), who comes down in favour of the common school. To trace Callan's complex thesis on this matter in unfairly sketchy form, then: A society based upon liberal virtues is faced with the difficulty of reconciling the rights of the parents to shape their children's education and the children's rights as prospective citizens. This issue connects to the tension between the claims of separate and common schools; because the former can exist to honour parental and minority rights, while the latter, being more heterogeneous in composition, give their pupils better grounding for operating in a pluralist society. He is pessimistic about resolving such problems, but civic morality indicates the priority of the case for common schools.

Because, as has been indicated, an ethnically pure and culturally coherent state is something of a myth, very many countries could be chosen as case studies. We have selected as illustrations mainly of assimilation and marginalization Hungary and Israel, and mainly of pluralism, Canada and Nigeria, as thus supplying broad geographical coverage, though Hungary alone provides a reasonable chronological span. However, other countries' policies have already been alluded to above and in other chapters in order to give a fuller impression of their experiences and a broader spread of examples.

Policies of some multicultural states

It is fitting to start with Hungary because of the length of time over which it has been engaged with the ethnic dimension of civic education. Observing its political history during the past one-and-a-half centuries, we notice four main phases which determined that country's policies on education for citizenship. These were the Habsburg Imperial regime, the Horthy Regency and right-wing movements of the inter-war and Second World War periods, the Communist system and the post-Communist polity.

The Hungarian uprising of 1848 under the leadership of Kossuth was prompted by a double nationalist purpose: to free Hungary from Habsburg Austrian hegemony, and to impose Hungarian hegemony over its own minority nationalities. For the Hungarian half of the Austrian Empire was itself an extraordinary medley of peoples – Magyars, Romanians, Ruthenes, Slovaks, Croats and Germans; a kingdom of far greater extent than the present-day republic. In 1867 an *Ausgleich* (Compromise) was implemented, whereby the Empire became the Dual Monarchy of Austria-Hungary, restoring to Hungary its former internal sovereignty. Prior to this agreement opinion was divided on how to tackle the nationalities problem: in today's terminology, should the kingdom's policy be one of assimilation or pluralism? The tendency between 1848 and 1867 had been more in favour of the former, namely Magyarization, the domination of the Hungarian people, language and culture. Then, with the *Ausgleich* came an opportunity for the Budapest government to define its position. In the following year a Nationalities Law was passed recognizing minorities' rights. It was very soon ignored. The governing classes were adamant that Hungary should become a cohesive nation-state, just as nineteenth-century nationalist ideology specified. The obsessive strength of this ambition is acutely summed up by one authority in the following manner:

> All the moral and spiritual energies of the state were devoted to this unique aim of national assimilation, centralization, and consolidation. The entire educational system of the state served, almost with religious fervor, this supreme dogma of national unity.
>
> (Jászi 1961: 440)

Hence, we arrive at the educational implication of the foregoing tracing of Hungary's national problem: civic education was nationalist education.

The policy of Magyarization as it affected schools was an attempt to force all children to learn about the greatness of, and be proud to be members of, Hungary, defined as the Magyar nation. This policy was pursued by specific legislation and regional pressure. The main milestones were as follows (see e.g. Macartney 1937: 24–5). In 1874 the three Slovak secondary schools were closed down. In 1879 a law was introduced making a knowledge of Magyar mandatory for every teacher and enforcing the teaching of Magyar in every primary school. In 1883 the fourteen remaining non-Magyar secondary schools were placed under strict control and the teaching language in all state secondary schools became Magyar. As a climax came the Education Acts introduced in 1907 by the minister, Count Apponyi, a fervent nationalist. These even extended state control into the Church schools and exerted further leverage on teachers by requiring of them an oath of loyalty and threatening with dismissal any teachers whose pupils were ignorant of the Magyar language. True, these laws were not fully implemented, and in Ruthenia the carrot of a 100-crown bonus for teachers whose pupils spoke Magyar was introduced (see Macartney 1937: 211 n.2); nevertheless, the authoritarian intention is clear.

Let us now add a little detail about the practical effects of this Magyarization programme. First, a small matter. In 1909 Apponyi issued a decree requiring that all textbooks, maps and globes should show and refer to the Austro-Hungarian monarchy or Austria-Hungary as 'Hungary and Austria'! History, as so often in nationalistically inspired education, became, together with the use of the Magyar language, the main vehicle for creating and boosting a Magyar civic consciousness. But, of course, it was a history simplified and distorted into a nationalist mythology of past unified valiant struggles. One senior local authority administrator described the effects:

> A kind of romantic symbolism permeated all the instruction. . . . Generally speaking, the whole elementary and secondary education was characterized by the fact the child's face was turned backward, he could look only upon the past. He could never see himself in relation to the present. And the past was an artificially constructed picture in the center of which stood the heroic Magyar nation, surrounded by a few friends and many enemies. No wonder, therefore, that the student . . . did not know anything concerning the real cultural and economic forces of his country and the opposite historical traditions of the various nations.
>
> (quoted Jászi 1961: 442)

Thus, if citizenship education in a multi-ethnic state should include the cultivation of an empathetic understanding of this social variegation, nineteenth-century Hungary was adhering to a quite contrary agenda. Statistics, too, tell the same tale, even though different sources give slightly different figures and there are problems of definition. Two sets of figures are nevertheless clearly indicative of the trend. The number of schools teaching in Slovak in 1874 was 1,971, and in 1919, 327; the number of schools teaching in Ruthene Russian in 1871 was 353, and in 1915, zero (see Macartney 1937: 90, 90n., 221n.).

But was this programme of forcible Magyarization through the schools successful? The effort certainly wrought changes, particularly in the urban schools. Yet it was patchy; in some respects, superficial, and in others, produced results other than those intended. Of the elementary schools especially, Jászi wrote in 1927, 'Where the nationalities lived in compact masses and where intercourse with the Magyars was rare, the Magyarizing drill of the elementary schools was only good for learning patriotic verses and songs by rote' (Jászi 1961: 330). Moreover, the time devoted in school to learning this difficult language robbed the pupils of adequate education in other subjects, so that Jászi had concluded in 1912 that 'The forcible Magyarization in the schools is one of the chief causes of the pitiful cultural backwardness of the non-Magyar peoples' (quoted Jászi 1961: 330). Nor was his by any means a lone complaining voice. For example, in 1908 there was published in Budapest a book entitled *The Crimes of our Popular Education*, written by Sigismund Kunfi, who became Minister of Public Instruction immediately after the First World War. Furthermore, Magyarization in the secondary schools backfired in a different way. Some students grew resentful and became supporters of nationalist movements, an outcome which contributed to the disintegration of Greater Hungary in 1918 to 1919. One wonders how many knew the epigram, 'A realm of one tongue and one set of customs is feeble and unstable' (quoted Macartney 1934: iii). It was written by St Stephen, the effective founder of the Hungarian kingdom in the early eleventh century.

However, before passing on to the 1918 to 1945 period, a few words are necessary about the attempts at cultivating a Magyar national civic consciousness outside the school environment. Festivals and literary events and social institutions were all used to that end. So, too, naturally, was the press: the Magyar newspapers became virulently nationalist; the non-Magyar papers which dared utter an independent view were persecuted.

The boundaries of Hungary as set down in the 1919 Treaty of Trianon reduced the state so drastically that 90 per cent of its population was Magyar, and thus it has continued, except for the temporary reacquisition of Transylvania during the Second World War. Yet citizenship education remained nationalist and was provided through history lessons precisely because of the loss of so much territory. The schools had the function of helping to compensate for the humiliation of Trianon by preserving the proud memories of past glories. Evidence for the intensity of that felt shame is provided by the growth of political organizations. In the words of one authority, 'Of all states in interwar Europe, Hungary probably took the prize for the largest assortment per capita of various fascist-type, semi-fascist, right radical, or simply authoritarian nationalist groups and movements' (Payne 1980: 110). Even so, as to the minority communities still inside Hungary, the government passed laws in 1923 and 1935 which conceded the right for some instruction in their mother-tongues (see Macartney 1937: 448–9, 454–5).

Since the Second World War, more conscious efforts have been made to develop all-embracing and agreed civic education programmes. None the less, these have enjoyed only partial success, for three main reasons. One is the change of political climate from Stalinist communism (1949 to 1956) to relaxed national Communism (1956 to 1989) and to parliamentary democracy (since 1989). Second, confusion has reigned concerning the most appropriate subject-vehicle for the task – history, civics, social studies – and the consequent oscillations of official policy, until the introduction of the National Core Curriculum in 1996. Third, there has been little enthusiasm for the idea of citizenship, in any case, and therefore for citizenship education (see Békés 1990; Čsepeli 1990; Mátrai 1998, 1999; Cogan and Derricott 2000). What concerns us is how the matter of nationhood has continued to colour Hungarian education for citizenship. Recently published textbooks accord little weight to this element and the teaching approach is generally 'flat': 'The teaching of nation-related topics and education in national identity,' says one authority, 'are carried out in a kind of descriptive-homogeneous approach' (Mátrai 1999: 356). On the other hand, an opinion poll conducted in 1996 showed that 65 per cent of teachers believed that history and literature should remain as compulsory final examination subjects, so that the influence of the nationalistic themes in the teaching matter of these two disciplines could be sustained. Furthermore, the National Core Curriculum provides for a generous time allocation for what Mátrai calls 'nation-related topics' throughout the whole ten-year span of compulsory schooling (see Mátrai 1999: 356).

Unlike Hungary's slow evolution, of extraordinarily erratic territorial elasticity, Israel was created *de novo* in Palestine in 1948, and, apart from the 1948 to 1949 and 1967 conquests, has remained territorially relatively static. Since the indigenous population had been overwhelmingly Arab, Israel was unavoidably a multinational state from the beginning, and one where the two major communities, Muslim and Jewish, have lived in tension. However, because of the flight and expulsion of large numbers of the Palestinian Arabs from the land of what became the state of Israel, the population in 1949 was overwhelmingly Jewish, fewer than one-twentieth being Muslim. Nevertheless, occupation of Arab lands in the Six-Day War of 1967 shifted the balance dramatically, despite substantial Jewish immigration in the interim: another million Arab Palestinians came effectively within the state of Israel. Thereafter, especially in the early 1990s, further Jewish immigration boosted the proportion of the adherents of Judaism. Yet these migrant waves posed another multicultural issue, because they came from a variety of geographical, cultural, political and linguistic backgrounds. Although in principle all groups have enjoyed equal rights of citizenship, the difficulties of organizing citizenship education for pupils with such a diversity of native countries of origin can be imagined. Furthermore, because of the variegated nature of the Israeli population, there evolved a variety of schools – for the tiny Druze minority, for Arabs (with classes conducted in Arabic) and for Jews (with a stress on learning the Hebrew language and about Hebrew culture); and because of the divisions within the Jewish portion of the population, three Jewish systems have also evolved: state education, state education with a strong religious content and independent schools for the ultra-orthodox (see e.g. Iram 2001: 214–15).

We should, however, start from the beginning, and with a paradox. Some Jews received citizenship education before there was a state for them to be citizens of. During the nineteenth and early twentieth centuries, the period known as the *Yishuv* era (the Hebrew word for settlement), 'education for Zionist citizenship' in Palestine had the function of making young people conscious of national symbols in order 'to amalgamate Jewish immigrants from all over the globe into one nation' (Ichilov 1998b: 70; this survey is heavily dependent on Ichilov 1998b and 1999). The pupils were taught that they were 'pioneers' of the forthcoming Zionist state, but should this teaching be directed towards the heart or the head, the emotions or the intellect? Educational opinion was split. The advocates of educating the emotions won. Consequently, by the time the state of Israel was created, all disciplines were contributing to Zionist indoctrination, so that 'each school subject opens its pages and hours to the Zionist enterprise. Each reader today contains a selection of the legacy of the founders, leaders, and dreamers of Zionism' with the objective of formulating in young minds 'deeply rooted and undisputed Zionist convictions' (quoted Ichilov 1998b: 71). Moreover, this national consciousness was ingrained into young people not just in the classroom, but by their participation in Zionist celebrations and work-camps, and many other civic activities.

The establishment of the state of Israel made possible the regularization of these civic education processes, and the concomitant influx of new citizens from different backgrounds made that regularization imperative. However, in essence, the kind of education outlined above continued after 1948: what was required to prepare for statehood was required to consolidate statehood. Yet here we encounter another paradox. The civic education of the *Yishuv* period was provided by a number of unco-ordinated bodies, each with its own particular, often partisan, aims and interpretations of the task. The continuation of the pre-1948 arrangements therefore hindered the very cohesiveness that citizenship education should have provided and which the Israeli government wanted. Change was, even so, achieved. In the words of Orit Ichilov:

> Gradually, however, 'politics' became banned, and civic education came to focus solely on the structural and legal characteristics of state institutions. Furthermore, the emotional components which were dominant in education during the Yishuv period became marginal and cognitive, and evaluative components became pre-eminent. Citizenship education came to rely mainly on concepts rooted in the social sciences, and Jewish heritage lost its hegemony as a source of both national and universal ideas.
>
> (Ichilov 1998b: 74)

Restricting ourselves for the moment to the 1948 to 1967 years, the Israeli Arabs were an anomaly. They were citizens of Israel, theoretically on a par with the Jews. Yet, they were subject to serious restrictions curbing their civil rights, they were a religiously distinct minority, and they were suspected, for good reason, of resenting the Jews who were occupying and governing their land. In a multiplicity of ways, the Arabs were discriminated against as second-class, marginalized citizens, whom many Jews both despised and feared. Relations were marked by mutual antipathy. There was virtually no likelihood that any but a small minority of the Israeli Arabs could come to think of themselves as real Israeli citizens; *pari passu*, there was effectively no chance of Arab children learning in their schools to be Israeli citizens.

The immediate and long-term effects of the Six-Day War worsened even this civically and educationally uneasy co-existence. The rump Arab lands of Gaza and the West Bank outside Israel were occupied, though together they eventually achieved a measure of self-rule in the form of the Palestinian Authority; Jewish settlers began to infiltrate these territories; and political animosities polarized and violence inevitably erupted in the guerrilla terrorism of the Palestinian *intifadas* (uprisings, literally 'shaking off') and the state terrorism of Israeli retaliation. The Israeli Arabs could scarcely be unaffected by these happenings, nor their children, nor the children in the Occupied Territories, nor the Jewish children. Indeed, the most forceful impact on children's minds occurred in the Gaza Strip and the West Bank, where they participated by stone-throwing in the Palestinians' desperate intransigence. This experience provided their most indelible civic learning: hatred of the occupying Jews (see e.g. Mazawi 1998).

How could teachers, Jewish or Arab, conduct citizenship lessons in anything but a religious-nationalist divisive manner and retain credibility with their pupils and their pupils' parents? The post-1967 conditions, in other words, 'rendered pre-1967 "neutral" civic education irrelevant' (Ichilov 1998b: 77). Nevertheless, in Jewish schools learning about current contentious issues was sanctioned by the Ministry of Education and Culture in 1983; and two years later, the Ministry issued a directive on education for democracy, which laid down that both Jewish-Zionist and universal human values should be taught. Moreover, the document asserted that human values were more important than the values of particular peoples and that both Jewish and Arab children should be taught mutual respect. In order to counter prevailing attitudes contrary to these civic values, the Ministry asked schools to make a special effort in 1986 and 1987 to press home these messages, and, rather belatedly, issued guidance to teachers in 1988. These initiatives had little effect. It has been left to small-scale private attempts at using education to promote civic harmony. Two examples may be used to illustrate this. One was called 'The Rules of the Game', cross-curricular materials produced in both Hebrew and Arabic in the late 1980s (see Felsenthal and Rubinstein 1991). Another has been a series of workshops for student-teachers in a programme called 'Education Toward Democracy and Tolerance' at a university with a multicultural intake (see Iram 2001: 221–5).

These have been noble efforts at positive citizenship education in a bitterly divided state. None the less, they have not materially affected the overall picture. By the end of the twentieth century, in neither Jewish state schools nor the Arab schools were there satisfactory programmes of civics teaching or teaching materials of good quality (despite the quantity available). In the words of an Israeli scholar who investigated the topic in the late 1990s: 'The formal curriculum seems to offer unsystematic and sporadic treatment of citizenship education. Civics as a school subject is marginal.' And in the traditional disciplines it is common for textbooks to 'portray stereotypical images of Arabs and neglect the rich cultural traditions of many Jewish and non-Jewish communities which reside in Israel' (Ichilov 1999: 390). But, in a country with such intractable political problems and in a society so sharply polarized, despair must surely supervene to question whether any real educational effort, however widespread and of whatever quality, can have any effect on civic attitudes and behaviour.

In sharp contrast to the experience of Israel, apart from a violent incident in 1970 perpetrated by the *Front de Libération du Québec* (FLQ), a terrorist organization demanding the secession of Quebec from Canada, the history of the relations between the various cultural groups in that country has been remarkably peaceful. Canada has an even more variegated population than Israel, containing Native peoples (Inuits and several Amerindian nations), descendants of early European settlers (mainly British and French) and more recent immigrants (from Asia, Latin America and the Caribbean). Most importantly, however, Canada is a sufficiently big country to have an effective federal system of government, and is peopled by a largely tolerant citizenry, whose patriotism avoids stridency (see e.g. Sears *et al.* 1999: 114–15).

Canada's constitutional arrangements have affected citizenship and citizenship education in two ways. First, the creation of the Dominion in 1867 brought into existence a federation of provinces. As in its southern neighbour, education was retained as a provincial, not a federal, responsibility. Accordingly, the central government in Ottawa has been able to influence citizenship education only indirectly and by encouragement, though it is true that in the second half of the twentieth century this influence was exercised helpfully and vigorously (see Sears *et al.* 1999: 120–4). The other constitutional arrangement affecting civic education has been Canada's position as a group of British colonies and, from 1867 to 1982, as a Dominion of the British Empire and Commonwealth. Until 1947 the people were subjects of the British Crown; from 1947 they were both Canadian citizens and British subjects, until 1976 when the British subjecthood was removed. By a combination of tolerance and federalism the issues of Québécois and Inuit cultural identities were accommodated peacefully in the late twentieth century, though Amerindians remained marginalized. The French Canadians were placated by a declaration in 1971 that the state was officially bilingual and multicultural (a character confirmed by the Canadian Multicultural Act of 1988); and the province achieved a 'Quiet Revolution' of accepted diversity (see e.g. Kymlicka 1997: 87–8). The Inuits' distinct way of life was recognized in 1999 by organizing their Arctic region as a separate, new province of the federation. The status and feeling of multiple citizenship – at province/cultural group, as well as at national level – came to be an accepted feature of Canadian political life, a factor that could not but help to shape citizenship education.

How, we are now ready to ask, has citizenship education evolved against this background? Because the Dominion of Canada was a member of the British Empire and people of British origin were the dominant group, schools, outside Francophone Quebec, inevitably purveyed a sense of Britishness in the nineteenth and early twentieth centuries. Thus it has been stated that:

> English speaking children were raised with the historical myths of British nationalism, as conveyed by adapted editions of the Irish National Reader and authors as diverse as Macaulay and G.A. Henty. What mere Canadian citizenship could compete with the claims of an empire that spanned the known universe?

(quoted Sears *et al.* 1999: 116)

However, from the early years of the Dominion there was widespread acceptance that the schools bore a major responsibility for creating a pan-Canadian and a citizenly consciousness. Thus the School Board of Winnipeg, capital of Manitoba, declared in 1913 that 'the development of a sense of social and civic duty, the stimulation of national and patriotic spirit, the promotion of public health and direct preparation for the occupations of life' should be undertaken in schools (quoted Cogan and Derricott 2000: 57–8). It is interesting to compare the inclusion of public health with the concern about this topic in England at the same time (see Chapter 3).

Even so, the quality and efficacy of Canadian citizenship education left much to be desired. Its function as a means of 'Canadianization' (a word not worthy of losing its inverted commas) was not successful. To cite one authority:

> Public school education, while compulsory, did little to crack ethnic exclusiveness. The singing of 'God Save the King,' 'Rule Britannia,' and 'The Maple Leaf Forever,' and the reciting of patriotic poetry, could do little in and of themselves to teach the values of the wider Canadian community.
>
> (quoted Sears *et al*. 1999: 119)

Nor did courses achieve much in preparing Canadians for effective democratic citizenship. Their objective was elitist, not raising the civic level of the masses:

> From the earliest years of public schooling in Canada West (Ontario) in the 19th Century, 'education was centrally concerned with the making of political subjects. . . . They were to be made by their governors after the image of an easily governed population'.
>
> (quoted Sears *et al*. 1999: 125)

During the years 1968 to 1971 two events caused the adaptation of Canadian education for citizenship. In 1968 the National History Project's seminal work, *What is Culture? What is Heritage? A Study of Civic Education in Canada*, was published, written by the Director of the research, A.B. Hodgetts. In 1971, as noted above, the House of Commons announced the policy of multiculturalism. The first event shook those responsible for citizenship education from their complacent acceptance of mediocre work; the second encouraged the development of multi-cultural and human rights education as components in reformed syllabuses. Hodgetts's report was damning. The bulk of history teaching was found to consist of learning about political and military affairs in a dull manner. He commented with acidity about the 'bland consensus version of history' and the rote-learning of 'nice, neat little acts of parliament' (quoted Sears *et al*. 1999: 125). Teachers engaging pupils in discussion was a rare occurrence. Even worse, he noted that English- and French-Canadian pupils were taught discrepant, even mutually contradictory, versions of their country's history. The effects, he declared, were most regrettable:

> The lack of understanding between our two linguistic communities is in part
> the direct result of what young people have been taught in school. . . .
> Successive generations of young English- and French-speaking Canadians
> raised on such conflicting views of our history cannot possibly understand each
> other or the country in which they live.
>
> (quoted Hodgetts and Gallagher 1978: 1)

In this respect, the teaching was potentially dangerous. The more widespread
problem was sheer boredom, the effect, Hodgetts judged, of the failure of history
teachers to connect their material to contemporary issues, contrary to common
curricular guidelines. The overall conclusion of the report was that the teaching
surveyed was 'a national disgrace' (Hodgetts and Gallagher 1978: 1).

As a direct result of Hodgetts's condemnatory report there was established the
privately financed Canada Studies Foundation, whose work, devoted to improving
teaching about the country, lasted from 1970 to 1986. As a result, the federal
government funded 'surrogate organizations' to improve civic education (see Sears
et al. 1999: 122–3), and the broad range of citizenship 'sub-topics' that became
common in the 1970s (e.g. political, environmental, global education) was
introduced into classrooms (see Cogan and Derricott 2000: 60–3). Two questions
immediately spring to mind. One is: How far was multicultural education developed
in recognition of the pluralistic character of the country? The other is: How effective
were the post-1968 reforms?

The allied curricular dimensions of multicultural education and human rights
education received considerable attention in Canada during the last quarter of the
twentieth century (see McLeod 1991: 164–88). Approaches to these themes may
be classified into four main policies:

1   Programmes for the newcomer to acquire fluency in one of the official
    languages.
2   Cultural maintenance programmes. . . .
3   Multicultural education as an antidote to the conventional portrayal of
    ethnic groups. . . . The acknowledgement of valued diversity is sought.
4   Anti-racism education.

(Moodley 1986: 59)

In the process of implementing these policies, agreed curricular criteria gradually
gelled. One Canadian academic has identified seven such criteria. Briefly, these
are: the requirement to integrate multiculturalism into the whole curriculum; the
importance of balancing the portrayal of similarities and distinctions between
different ethnic groups; avoidance or sensitive handling of bias in teaching
materials; special days should be integrated into the schools' regular programmes;
the subject-matter must be suited to the pupils' intellectual and moral reasoning
levels; both cognitive and affective learning must be included; and teaching methods
must relate cognitive and affective learning (see McLeod 1991: 175). This is all
fairly obvious, but it is indicative of the problems of securing agreement in this

field across all the provinces that it took time for these guidelines to be universally identified and accepted.

This observation brings us to our second question: Have the reforms been successful? It goes without saying that success is a relative term; nevertheless, it is somewhat surprising to learn that there were diverse judgements. Hodgetts was quite content with the impact of his report. He wrote ten years after its publication: 'It is apparent that many of the findings documented in *What Culture? What Heritage?* are no longer applicable to Canadian education' (Hodgetts and Gallagher 1978: 2). And ten years after this assessment, another leading authority wrote about work in the area of political education that 'the renewed interest and activity . . . has begun to transform political education in recent years' (Osborne 1988: 291). Perhaps these judgements were too optimistic or too precipitate, because, by the end of the century, the most carefully designed and authoritative research into civic education concluded that:

> There is often a considerable gap between official policy and actual practice.
> . . . Despite curricular emphasis on the pluralist ideal, critical inquiry, the discussion of contemporary issues and getting students involved in community action, classroom practice seems not to have changed much since Hodgetts' report.
>
> (Sears *et al.* 1999: 128, 130)

Canada has been a simple, coherent country compared with Nigeria's ethnic, linguistic and religious divisions. Towards the end of the twentieth century, in about 1980, it was estimated that Nigeria, with a population more than thrice that of Canada, contained 235 ethnic groups, speaking some 400 different languages. The notorious artificiality of the boundaries drawn on the map of Africa by the imperial powers in the nineteenth century was nowhere more evident than in this British colony (for British imperial policy in general, see Chapter 3). Tribes traditionally in bellicose collision found themselves, on the achievement of independence from Britain in 1960, belonging to the same 'nation'-state. In addition, the Islamic north had resisted the modernization and Christianization processes that had at least partially modified the life-styles and expectations of the southern portion of the country. However, British administration was lightly imposed, so that chieftain rule, duty to kith and kin and expectation of favours dispensed to tribal and family members persisted as socially acceptable, even virtuous, habits. Yet these were incompatible with western political styles and became degraded into corruption and nepotism after independence (see e.g. Arikpo 1967: 114–17).

Since citizenship education involves the use of schools to supply the adhesive of national unity and to instil the virtue of good civic habits, it is evident that the Nigerian education system has had an exceedingly difficult task in meeting these demands. The lack of a powerful cohering central government and a diversity of providers of schooling exacerbated the problem. The British set the pattern by creating separate structures, first for the northern and southern provinces, then the northern, eastern and western regions, the latter arrangement being basically retained after independence from 1960 to 1978, in a constitution of a loose federal nature. As to schools, by about 1900 there were three main kinds: the Koranic for the Muslim children of the north, the Christian founded by missionaries in the south, and some government schools, just starting up. Not until 1930, however, was a Director of Education appointed for the whole of Nigeria. In what senses did this patchwork provide education for citizenship? We must first understand that there was a major constraint on its evolution during the colonial period: the nervousness of the ruling power. A Nigerian educationist has explained. Even after the Second World War,

> There were still these fundamental assumptions, overt or covert, of British colonial power in Nigeria: that it would be many years before the Nigerians were able to rule themselves; that, of course, educational progress was important for such self-rule; but, thirdly, that if you quickened the tempo of education then you were providing a quick dissolution of the British empire in general and British rule in Nigeria in particular.
>
> (Okeke 1964: 13)

We may detect three aspects of civic education in the colonial period against this discouraging background. First was the fashioning of a kind of English Public school ethos (see Chapter 3) for training good – that is, compliant – citizens through discipline, moral instruction and ensuring that schools had the 'right tone' (see Peshkin 1967: 324–5; see also Okeke 1964: 10). Second was the interpretation of civic identity as subjecthood of the British Crown. For example, the history syllabus laid down in 1932 listed the history of Nigeria and the British Empire for the senior pupils in the primary school for developing 'respect for authority and good citizenship' (quoted Peshkin 1964: 325). Writing nearly two decades after independence, a Nigerian educationist conceded:

> We must accept that whatever the defects of the early mission/government schools may have been – and we are all its products – they succeeded in awakening our allegiance to the British Queen. Empire Day Celebrations found us singing 'Rule Britannia, Britannia rule the waves' and 'The British Empire shall never perish again'. They taught us the fear of God, respect for our elders and for authority.
>
> (Adeyoyin 1979: 165)

The third feature of early civic education was the concentration on educating an elite, to participate loyally in administration in accordance with the British style and requirements.

By the late 1940s, with the expansion of nationalist movements, conditions started to change. The leaders were utterly convinced that a massive increase in the numbers of educated people and a huge improvement in the quality of teaching was imperative if an independent state of Nigeria was to be a success. The Ministry of Education for the Western Region declared that 'Educational development . . . must be treated as a national emergency' (quoted Ukeje and Aisiku 1982: 210). In any case, the people had a great hunger for education, if only it could be made widely available. In 1955 the project known as universal primary education (UPE) was inaugurated, making schooling at this level non-fee-paying as a means of achieving the goal of 100 per cent school attendance.

Insofar as this policy had a civic purpose, it both raised a consequent question and backfired. The question was how the curriculum could be reformed to become characteristically African and Nigerian, not British. A simple task. The other question was more serious and virtually impossible of resolution. Primary school enrolments did indeed speedily increase, but far from becoming civically conscious,

> The majority [of school-leavers] were drifting into the towns and fast becoming a solid unemployable community there, to provide fodder for political thuggery and lawlessness. . . . The dangers inherent in the growth of a large class of semi-literate, idle and dissatisfied young people cannot be exaggerated.
>
> (Arikpo 1967:106)

To use an Americanism, the Nigerians were in a Catch-22 situation. In order to prepare themselves to be a twentieth-century parliamentary democracy, they needed a politically conscious electorate; such a body had to be literate in the only lingua franca such an extraordinarily polyglottic country had, namely English; this requirement involved massive expenditure on education; economic development to provide employment was therefore sacrificed; hence the discontent of primary school-leavers, whose schooling, confined to the 3Rs, did not educate them to understand the larger, long-term civic purpose of the education policy, let alone make them willing to submit themselves to the degradation of poverty for this political purpose (see Arikpo 1967: 106).

When inter-tribal conflict reached flashpoint in 1967 and sparked a grisly civil war (quite without comparison in the other countries we have taken as case studies in this section), there was therefore an insufficient body of educated young men committed to the concept of pan-Nigerian nationhood to stave off this conflict. The war, in which the Ibos of the south-east tried to secede as a new state of Biafra, lasted until 1970. They failed. And *post-bellum* reconstruction (the US parallel is interesting – see Chapter 3) included educational programmes with a strengthened civic content and purpose.

The history of Nigeria in the 1970s is replete with plans (see e.g. Mehlinger 1981: 304–11). A number of constitutional changes took place. These included an attempt to mitigate the divisive effects of tribalism by reorganizing the country into nineteen states and creating the Second Republic in 1976. In addition, in 1972 the federal government assumed greater control of education. In the document announcing this change there may also be found this succinct statement so relevant to our subject:

> Through common education, law, policy and curricula, all Nigerian children through the length and breadth of this country shall be taught from the day they

enter primary school to be Nigerians, to value their citizenship, and to be proud of their country.

(quoted Oyovbaire 1985: 149)

In 1976 two other key documents were published. One, the *National Policy on Education* issued by the Ministry of Information, tried, admittedly without success, to use secondary schools to reduce the ugly effects of tribal antagonisms by encouraging multi-tribal recruitment. The other was the Ministry of Education's *Federal Republic of Nigeria Policy on Education*. Education for national unity was a clear strand. A British specialist in African education explains:

> Section 1, on the philosophy of Nigerian education, talks of '. . . the inculcation of national consciousness and unity'. Section 4, on secondary education, suggests education should '. . . foster Nigerian unity, with an emphasis on the common ties that unite us in our diversity'. This section continues, 'Education should help develop in our young a sense of unity, patriotism and love of country. It is essential that everything possible be done to foster in them a sense of national belonging.'

(Harber 1989: 16)

Conviction by sheer repetition.

What was actually achieved in the 1970s? In 1969, even before the end of the war, a National Curriculum Conference was convened, described as 'the first national effort to change the colonial orientation of the Nigerian educational system'. Its report stated that one of the seven objectives of primary education should be 'to promote effective citizenship through civic responsibility', and twelve years later two authorities reckoned that 'These views are gradually permeating the primary school curriculum' (Ukeje and Aisiku 1982: 230). This progress was assisted by the production in 1971 of primary school guidelines by the Nigerian Educational Research Council, which included in its section on social studies the need to 'develop in children a positive attitude to citizenship' (quoted Bray and Cooper 1979: 35).

Citizenship education is more than book-learning. And after the civil war especially the Nigerians increased the number of ceremonies in which school-children were engaged, so that, by 1976, when saluting the flag and the recitation of the national pledge were introduced, the following pattern was established. These ceremonies and the singing of the National Anthem have marked the start and end of the school day. The pledge is:

> I pledge to Nigeria my country,
> To be faithful, loyal and honest,
> To serve Nigeria with all my strength,
> To defend her unity
> And uphold her honour and glory;
> So help me God.
>   (quoted Bray and Cooper 1979: 36)

In addition, certain days of the year, notably Independence Day and National Children's Day, have been celebrated with various patriotic events. At university level, from 1973 graduates were required to spend a year of community work in the National Youth Service Corps (NYSC) in order 'to develop common ties among our youth and promote national unity' (quoted Bray and Cooper 1979: 36).

But have all these efforts met with success? Given the scale of the task, it would be surprising indeed if one could answer this question with positive conviction. Bray and Cooper (1979: 37–9), writing at the end of the 1970s, provide a catalogue of failures: the UPE, accorded prominence in government plans in 1976, was weak because of insufficient funding and the poor quality of the teaching force; the policy of tribal mixing in colleges and secondary schools was resisted; and the pledge was a fiasco – ignored in many schools and probably meaningless to those children who chanted it by rote. Indeed, political instability and outbursts of inter-ethnic violence intermittently marred the history of the country during the last two decades of the twentieth century, and the north–south cultural divide was exacerbated by the consolidation of Islam in the northern states, including the imposition of the stern Sharia law.

Even so, attempts to improve elementary education were still being made at the end of the century. The adult literacy rate had risen to 62.6 per cent by 1999 and a universal Basic Education scheme was introduced, aimed at providing free and compulsory education for all 6- to 15-year-olds; though the beneficial effects of these progressive trends on the feeling of national cohesion and citizenly responsibility remained exceedingly problematic. Successive Nigerian governments have tried the policy of ethnic and cultural pluralism – indeed, neither of the other options explained above (integration or marginalization) would have been at all feasible – but the modicum of social and political unity that the policy presupposes has in large measure eluded them.

Meanwhile, in Europe, its own continental civil wars of 1914 to 1918 and 1939 to 1945 had forced a determination not to allow such cataclysms to recur. The European Union is being constructed; but although internecine conflict is almost certainly a habit of the past, creating a sense of common, supranational citizenship has been proving a slow process.

The European Union

The term 'education for European citizenship' is not easy to pin down. It is possible to distinguish three main, distinct usages. One of these has sometimes been referred to as encouraging 'European awareness' or, more usually, giving education 'a European dimension', the latter term having been first used, in the European Community, in 1976. This approach has no sharp focus, and 'Europe' is not necessarily confined to the countries which have been or are members of the European Community (EC)/European Union (EU). The second usage is also this kind of learning, but is specifically related to the member-states of the EC/EU. The third use of the term is education for citizenship of the European Union in a precise sense; that is, preparation of young people for that legal status, which was introduced when in 1993 the European Union, as a name and a body, in most senses superseded the European Community, which had been the usual name since 1967.

Education with a European dimension has involved the arrangement of school trips to various countries and ensuring a generous allocation of time in syllabuses to subject-matter related to the continent in, primarily, geography and history, but also to the teaching of interdisciplinary courses in European studies. This kind of learning about Europe has been cultivated, for example, by the distinguished activities of the Council of Europe, founded in 1949, and the European Association of Teachers (*Association Européene des Enseignants*), founded in 1956. It is true that these bodies in the 1980s, when the term 'citizenship education' came into fashion, claimed to be working to promote European citizenship. In 1983 the Council of Europe issued a Recommendation which stated that, 'Our education programmes should encourage all young Europeans to see themselves not only as citizens of their own regions and countries, but also as citizens of Europe and the wider world' (quoted Ross 2000: 183). And in 1989 the European Association of Teachers published a brochure defining its recommended handling of the teaching of European citizenship. Even so, what these bodies were both engaged in was really providing a foundation for a consciousness of being 'European', a valuable contribution to the cluster of elements that are needed to build a European citizenship, but certainly not its entirety.

For this we must turn to teaching about the EC/EU; because, although membership of the EU, even at the start of the twenty-first century, has not yet embraced all the peoples and states of the continent, at least citizens of the member-states have come to be citizens of that Union in various ways. However, even in this context, we need to distinguish two uses of the term 'education for European citizenship'. These are: education for understanding that, as a citizen of a member-state, one is also a member of the EU, and learning the meaning of the status of citizen of the Union as set down in the Maastricht Treaty of 1993 (the, admittedly limited, rights of the status are set down in Article 8 of that instrument). Yet, even in this teaching, it must be conceded that much of the work in the former sense has scarcely been distinguishable from our first usage; indeed, the EU has been a prominent popularizer of the term 'a European dimension'.

While focusing on the EU context, it is useful to distinguish between the activities of the institutions on the one hand, and the member-states on the other, in promoting education for citizenship of the Union in both the informal and legal senses (see Davies 1997: 97–113).

Although the idea of creating some form of European collaborative structure has a venerable lineage, it was not until after the Second World War that the building of such a framework began. By the 1960s and certainly the 1970s politicians who favoured this enterprise came increasingly to recognize that popular support was essential for its success. The catch-phrase was, to create 'a People's Europe' – more pointedly in French, '*Europe des Citoyens*'. Moreover, that popular support entailed education from a pre-adult age. In 1976 the European Council (i.e. the meetings of ministers of the constituent states) adopted a Resolution to stimulate action programmes for education, including encouragement to enhance the European content of school syllabuses.

From the early 1980s numerous documents emanated from the Council and the Commission to reinforce the EC/EU's bidding. In 1982 a booklet was published, which asserted:

> At school the evocation of the European idea in textbooks, the study of contemporary European history, the learning of foreign languages and visits abroad while at school or as a student are all factors which determine the future attitude of the adult citizen towards the Community and the European idea.
>
> (quoted Heater 1992: 55)

This was an official recommendation and the word 'citizen' does appear, even though it was a statement of the obvious and was really about teaching a European dimension rather than precisely for European citizenship.

Indeed, the crucial document, which was issued in 1988, refers to the European dimension in education. This statement was presented in the form of a Resolution of the Council, the purpose and background of which are instructive:

> Reaffirming their resolve to strengthen the European dimension in education in accordance with the 'solemn declaration of the European Union' of Stuttgart (June 1983), the conclusions of the European Council in Fontainebleau (June 1984) and the 'People's Europe' report adopted at the European Council in Milan (June 1985);
>
> Considering enhanced treatment of the European dimension in education to be an element contributing to the development of the Community and achievement of creating a unified internal market in 1993.
>
> (European Council and Ministers of Education 1988)

It announced measures to 'strengthen in young people a sense of European identity' and 'improve their knowledge of the Community and its Member States'. Although there is no overt mention of European citizenship, we are getting closer, and in the following year the Commission took the plunge in a document of education guidelines presented to the Council. One of its objectives was to:

> Promote the shared democratic values of the Member States, and increase understanding of the multicultural characteristics of the Community and of the importance of preparing young people for citizenship which involves the Community dimension in addition to their national, regional and local affiliations.
>
> (quoted Heater 1992: 56)

In practice, the EC/EU has achieved little in the way of promoting education for European citizenship, as distinct from other educational initiatives, except in the indirect methods of facilitating student exchanges and language-learning. In the 1990s these schemes, primarily Erasmus for higher education, Lingua for languages and Comenius for schools, were brought together as the Socrates programme. However, what is significant for us is that the guidelines for applicants state that 'The objectives of the Socrates programme include to develop the European dimension in education at all levels so as to strengthen the spirit of European citizenship' (quoted Ross 2000: 184).

There is, in truth, a compelling case for thinking that a vague commitment to education for European citizenship appropriately matched the vagueness of the nature of that citizenship during the years of the European Community. The concept, scarcely a status, may be said to have consisted of four components. The one giving most precision was the right to vote for members of the European Parliament from 1979. The second was the building up of a body of Directives and case law concerning, principally, employment rights. The third was the argument that all citizens of member-states have in common a shared cultural tradition and the enjoyment of living in liberal democratic societies. The fourth component has been unrelated to the EC/EU, that is, the existence of the Council of Europe's Convention of Human Rights and its associated legal procedures. It is these features – mainly, it is true, the third – that teachers have concentrated upon. And in this endeavour they have been assisted, notably in the teaching of history, by the Council of Europe (see Osler *et al.* 1995: 149–60).

A transformation to less hesitancy and greater precision in teaching about European citizenship might have been expected after the Maastricht Treaty came into force in 1993. Any educationist expecting support from the Treaty itself would, however, have been disappointed. It established the European Union, signalling a movement from the Community to tighter binding of the member-states (Article A). Yet its provisions on education (Article 126), despite the proclamation of Union citizenship as a legal status, continue the irresolute tradition of avoiding the term 'education for European citizenship', reaffirming instead the aims of 'developing the European dimension in education, particularly through' language-teaching, and 'encouraging mobility of students and teachers'. The clue to the lack of more positive aims lies in Article 3b, which confirms the EU's acceptance of the principle of subsidiarity; this proclaims that action should be taken at the lowest appropriate level of the political and administrative pyramid. Consequently, the EU must fully respect 'the responsibility of the Member States for the content of teaching and the organization of education systems' (Article 126).

The question therefore naturally arises: how have member-states responded? It should be noted that the 1988 Resolution required all member-states to compile a document explaining their policies regarding the incorporation of the European dimension into education and to circulate it to all their educational institutions. Few adhered to this injunction. Germany was a notable exception, the Ministers of the *Länder* collectively drafting a most explicit document (see Davies and Sobisch 1997: 225–7; it should be remembered that in the federal structure, education is the responsibility of the *Länder*, not the central government (see Chapter 4)). It refers, for example, to awareness of the integration process and of European identity, knowledge of the European institutions, and respect for European laws and human rights.

In contrast, replies to enquiries made by a British educationist in the mid-1990s reveal the bigger picture. He concluded from his survey:

> It is clear that, despite the rhetoric of Europeanism and the range of initiatives which have emerged from the European Union, this area is not receiving a great deal of attention by national bodies. Some countries sent no material at all and when pressed by telephone calls to government offices usually replied that no documentation on education for European citizenship was yet available.
>
> (Davies 1997: 106)

Another British researcher reported in 1994:

> It was significant that senior officials at the French Department of Education were not at all discommoded at being unable to report any particular ways in which the 1988 Resolution had prompted any changes in their education system.
>
> (quoted Davies 1997: 108)

In addition, the authoritative research project by the IEA in the late 1990s (Torney-Purta *et al*. 1999) included eight member-states of the EU. While most contributions refer to their country's membership, few considered that this investigation into civic education should include European citizenship. The main exceptions are Portugal and the Netherlands. Conscious of the weaknesses, the Commission launched a new initiative in 1996, under the name Children's Identity in Europe (CiCe) as an Erasmus thematic network of university education departments. Two years later, it published its recommendation, *Education for Active Citizenship in the European Union*.

Summarized survey evidence, however, does not necessarily reveal governmental as distinct from non-governmental pedagogical assistance. Although it is clear that these latter have been disadvantaged to some extent by lack of official guidelines, there is evidence of some enthusiastic work. Let us take just four examples of different kinds undertaken by different institutions in order to demonstrate the variety of approaches to the topic.

The first, confirming the commitment of the German *Länder*, is a project of the *Land* government of Hesse (see Bell 1997: 223–51). Here, a 'European Schools' programme was started in 1992 involving, initially, five schools plus a network of fourteen associated schools. The European Schools have been a courageous experiment in innovative learning methods stressing collaborative contacts with other schools and the promotion of the European dimension in their work. The second example relates to the activities of official institutes for promoting political education. In 1995 the Dutch *Instituut voor Publiek en Politiek* (Centre for Political Education and Communication) and the German *Bundeszentrale für politische Bildung* (Federal Agency for Civic Education) combined to launch a project called 'Political education towards a European democracy'. Our third example is another collaborative project, this one funded through the EU Erasmus programme,

'Education for citizenship in a new Europe: learning democracy, social justice, global responsibility and respect for human rights', designed for student-teachers. The case study, which is freely available, concerns the use in the 1990s by students of a college associated with the University of Oxford of a small rural school linked with a group of village schools in Italy (see Halocha 1995: 189–99). The European aspect of the project was provided by the exchange of materials and limited teacher-exchange with the objective of developing empathy in the pupils of another European mode of life in some ways different from England. The prime purpose, of course, was the opportunity provided to the students to learn about this style of teaching so that they could adapt it to their own schools once appointed. The fourth example brings us up to date with the use of modern methods of communication. This is the 'Speak Out! On European citizenship' website (www.citizen.org.uk/speakout). The project, started in 2000 in the UK by the Institute for Citizenship and including also Germany, Italy and Sweden, has been a method for involving students in Europe to learn about and discuss issues related to European citizenship.

We have concentrated on the relative lack of interest about defining education for European citizenship with a precise meaning attached to the word 'citizenship'. There are two reasons for stressing this in our survey. One is the obvious matter that if teaching in this field is confined to cultivating a sense of European identity in the person and transmitting an understanding of the collective cultural identity of the European peoples, then a great deal more is missing from the total notion of citizenship – for example, status, rights, duties, responsibilities – which the pupil should be learning. The second reason is that the focus on common traditions skirts difficult questions of the relationship to other kinds of identity. This problem expresses itself in several ways. For instance, what is the meaning of European citizenship to European citizens in the Maastricht, legal sense, whose origins and family traditions are different from some of the core European culture, for example, Muslims? How can individuals handle the dual status of being both a national and a European citizen? Some educationists are starting to look at the implications of issues such as these, accepting that the injunction to teach a European dimension is too simplistic. The 1983 Council of Europe Recommendation, cited above, at least reveals a recognition that education for a multiple citizenship is essential, including also education for world citizenship.

World citizenship: theoretical origins

In common parlance the use of the terms 'citizen of the world' and 'cosmopolitan' has been as widespread as the meanings attached to them have been imprecise. So much of an aura of vague naive utopianism has surrounded the notion that many hard-headed political philosophers have ignored it with disdain or repudiated it with contempt. Yet the conviction that the world citizenship ideal has both practical validity and moral worth has been extraordinarily persistent, welling up in western political thinking episodically over the past two and a half millennia: during the Old, Middle and Late Stoa periods in the ancient world, the Neostoicism of the Renaissance and Enlightenment, and in phases during the twentieth century.

Not all of this thinking, it must be conceded, has been accompanied by related pedagogical considerations. Furthermore, when attempts have been made to work through the educational implications of the basic idea – a process mainly confined to the twentieth century – the committed educationists have been impeded by that imprecision of meaning we have already noted. In this regard, education for world citizenship has suffered in a similar manner to education for European citizenship, though in the case of the world dimension the impediments have been more forbidding. World citizenship as a legal status cannot be taught because, unlike citizenship of the European Union, it has never existed in any proper sense; a feeling of global identity in our culturally variegated world is so much more difficult to teach than the requirements of 'a European dimension'; and since, as has often been the case, education for world citizenship has involved teaching a cosmopolitan morality and the ethic of peace, teachers engaged in global education have been subject to the charge of controverting the state's pressing civic demand of its schools, namely, the inculcation of patriotism.

The reader will have noticed that two different terms have already been used, namely 'education for world citizenship' and 'global education'; 'global studies', 'world studies' and 'education for international understanding' have also been used in English-language literature on the subject, and we shall come across these below. However – and to use the analogy again – just as we have distinguished between teaching with a European dimension and for European citizenship in the full and precise sense, so we must guard against assuming that all these labels are synonymous. What became a condition of some confusion in the twentieth century shrouded the basic duality of the cosmopolitan ideal in both its political-philosophical and pedagogical realizations. We may call these the Stoic and Comenian schools of thought, grounded respectively in the belief in the oneness of humankind and in the absolute need for universal peace, the former expounded by the Graeco-Roman Stoic philosophers, the latter deriving from the ideas of the seventeenth-century Bohemian educationist, Comenius.

We must start our narration, again, in ancient Greece; and, again, in Athens. In 310 BC, twenty-five years after Aristotle founded his Lyceum, Zeno of Citium established the Stoic school in his *Stoa Poikilē* (painted porch), hence the name of his philosophy. Zeno migrated to Athens from his home town in Cyprus, and several of the later developers and exponents of Stoicism came from Asia Minor. Chrysippus, who systematized the Stoic philosophy in the late third century, came from Cilicia, the chief town of which was Tarsus, the home of the Christian apostle Paul, who adapted Stoicism to a Christian context. Indeed, by his time, the educational institution in that city had become a flourishing centre of Stoic teaching. Stoicism spanned many departments of learning, one of which was the development of the concept of *kosmopolis*, the city of the universe, or the universe as a state. The basic concept was that all human beings, and the gods, are subject to a universal moral law. Now, since a cardinal feature of citizenship of a *polis* was the subjection of all citizens to the laws of the *polis*, the Stoics argued analogously that the universe, by virtue of its law, could be likened on a much vaster scale to a *polis*; all are consequently *kosmopolitēs*, citizens of the universe. As such, humans should live moral lives, recognizing all others as their kin. It was but a short step to delete the gods and the whole cosmos from the design, and so refer to this ideal as world citizenship – that is, confined to the human race and this planet. The educational corollary is clear: young people should be imbued with this interpretation of the good, that is, ethical life.

A particularly famous exposition of this guideline for teaching comes from the pen of that most distinguished and elegant essayist, Montaigne. In his 'On the Education of Children' he wrote:

> Mixing with the world has a marvellously clarifying effect on a man's judgement. We are all confined and pent up within ourselves, and our sight has contracted to the length of our noses. When someone asked Socrates of what country he was, he did not reply, 'of Athens', but 'of the world'. His was a fuller and wider imagination; he embraced the whole world as his city, and extended his acquaintance, his society, and his affections to all mankind; unlike us, who look only under our feet. . . .
>
> This great world . . . is the mirror into which we must look if we are to behold ourselves from the proper standpoint. In fact, I would have this my pupil's book. So many dispositions, sects, judgements, opinions, laws, and customs teach us to judge sanely of our own, and teach our understanding how to recognize its imperfections and natural weaknesses; which is no trivial lesson.
>
> (Montaigne 1958: 63–4)

With these words the ancient Stoic cosmopolitan philosophy was being translated at the end of the sixteenth century AD into educational objectives.

Furthermore, Montaigne's essays were read not only in his native France but in other countries too, notably England, where the extraordinarily versatile Francis Bacon was also expressing his thoughts through the essay genre. In one of these, 'Of Goodness, and Goodness of Nature', he propounded the idea that, 'If a man be gracious and courteous to strangers, it shows he is a citizen of the world, and that his heart is no island cut off from other lands, but a continent that joins them' (Bacon 1906: 39). In his utopia, *New Atlantis*, published thirty years later, in 1627, he put forward the notion of an institute of advanced studies with a cosmopolitan staff. Samuel Hartlib, an MP with keen educational interests (see Chapter 2 above), conceived the ambition of founding such an institution in England. As a prospective principal, in 1641 he invited to London a bishop of the Moravian Church who was an admirer of Bacon's work and was developing his own ideas along similar lines. This person was John Amos Comenius. And so, although Bacon's college was never established and he wrote little on education, we may interpret his plan as suggesting that Bacon forms a link between our twin strands of cosmopolitan educational thought, the Stoic and the Comenian.

Comenius is the Latinized version of the name Komensky; he was born in 1592. The defeat of the Protestants in Bohemia in the Thirty Years War forced him, as pastor of the Unity of Moravian Brethren, into a life of exile. He then started to write educational books, including textbooks, an activity which brought him considerable fame throughout Europe. For instance, his *Gateway to Language Unlocked*, first published in 1633, went into some hundred editions, and his *Great Didactic*, published in 1657, according to Piaget, 'is regarded as the classic work upon which every type of systematic teaching is based' (Piaget 1967: 66). Our interest is centred on his major work, the seven-volume *General Consultation concerning the Improvement of Human Affairs*, uncompleted at the time of his death in 1670, and not fully published until the twentieth century. His purpose was to design institutions which would undertake the moral regeneration of the world by deeply embedding Christian principles. Concord would replace war, and education would ensure the success of the enterprise. Little wonder that he felt passionately about his hopes and dreams, because the Thirty Years War spread horror throughout great tracts of the continent. Comenius's own experience personified the conflict: the death of his wife and two children from the consequent pestilence and his own life as a refugee. Inevitably, given his clerical background, his whole thought is suffused with a deep religious faith. Thus he concluded one of his works, *Via Lucis* (*The Way of Light*), with the following passage:

> May Thy will be done even now in the whole earth as it is in the whole heaven! Through the whole of Europe, of Asia, of Africa, of America, through the land of the Magallanes, and through all the islands of the sea, may thy kingdom come!
>
> (quoted Sadler 1969: 196)

But naturally, it is the specifically educational plans in his *Consultation* that concern us. One chapter of Part VI, *Panorthosia*, or *Universal Reform*, and the whole of Part IV, *Pampaedia*, or *Universal Education*, are the relevant texts. Comenius's key idea is 'universal education', a term carrying much meaning, including the proposition, in the *Pampaedia*, that 'all men . . . should walk in the paths of concord . . . and that they may restore dissidents to unity' (Piaget 1967: 119).

Furthermore, education must spread wisdom and benevolence to all peoples for clearly cosmopolitan reasons, as a key passage in the *Pampaedia* indicates. Comenius argues that:

> Whoever then does not wish to show something of foolishness or ill will, must wish good to all men, and not only to himself, a few of his near ones, or his own nation. For it cannot even go well with all its members together and singly. . . . He then who would seriously not wish well to the whole human race, injures the whole human race.
>
> (Piaget 1967: 126)

And just as the world should be the moral measure of people's lives, so should the world be their teacher. Following Montaigne, Comenius declares: 'the whole world is a school for the whole of the human race' (Piaget 1967: 184).

How does Comenius propose that the human race be educated in this manner? He imagines a triad of global institutions: the Dicastery for government, the

Consistery for religion, the College of Light for education. This college (or, these colleges: he lapses into the plural) would oversee all the schools, which would be established at public expense, throughout the world. Light is the light of wisdom, of which Christ is the fountain. And the entire educational edifice, described in Chapter 16 of the *Panorthosia* (see Comenius 1995: 223–30), ensures that all human minds are illuminated to an understanding of universal wisdom. The Colleges of Light would monitor all matters related to education – the schools, teaching methods, book production – and use every means to spread the enlightenment of wisdom throughout the world.

But is this a formula for the education of human beings to become world citizens? It can be interpreted so, in both the weak and strong senses. In the weak, non-political sense, all of humankind would receive the same education and would become aware that the morality of God's wisdom is a universal morality. In addition, the cosmopolitan way of thinking would be consolidated by Comenius's further recommendation that a universal language should be devised. Moreover, he also reveals a Stoic sense of the notion of a cosmopolis when he writes: 'Since . . . we are all co-citizens (*concives*) of one world, who shall prevent us from joining in one republic, under the same laws' (quoted Heater 1996: 62).

That Comenius had a conception of world citizenship in the political sense is attested by the close relationship he envisaged between the College of Light and the Dicastery which would oversee what he calls a new universal political system (see Comenius 1995: 186–93), linked by the acquisition and practice of wisdom. He suggests in the *Panorthosia* that in all the component states of the new world community 'it would be a good idea for all the wise men . . . as a general rule to hold some office, taking it in turn to be guardians and inspectors to see that order and justice are maintained everywhere' (Comenius 1995: 189): an amalgam, as it were, of Plato's elitist citizenship of philosopher-kings and Aristotle's citizenship of ruling and being ruled in turn. However, Comenius's body of political citizens might not be that restricted, for he envisages the new universal political system as 'a world where the Prince of Peace is in supreme command of human affairs . . . where the subjects have the knowledge, the will, and the power to govern themselves . . . and to teach and enlighten themselves and their fellow-men' (Comenius 1995: 193). Through the acquisition of universal wisdom all have the opportunity to become citizens of the universe.

How should we judge Comenius's contribution to education for world citizenship? He can be dismissed in this area of his work as too mystical and impractical for even the most idealistic of today's tastes. In 1960 the Regius Professor of History at Oxford University, the late Hugh Trevor-Roper, chose the epithet 'dotty' as the most apposite word to poison his scholarly barb (quoted Sadler 1969a: 123). Yet a more sensitive understanding of historical context can offer a kinder and more appreciative judgement. The seventeenth century was an age when the desperate need for peace in Europe turned men's minds to the drafting of plans for a confederal solution – Sully, Penn and Crucé are the most famous, the last incorporating non-European countries into his scheme. This stream of thinking, idealistic, if not as utopian as Comenius's, bifurcated and turned eventually into the institutional realities of the United Nations and the European Union. These other seventeenth-century thinkers – dreamers indeed – gave no thought to an educational underpinning for their political constructions. This crucial feature of Comenius's scheme was, however, revived in the global dimension, as we shall see below, by the designers of the League of Nations and the United Nations Organization, against the equally hideous background of what has aptly been called the second Thirty Years War. When UNESCO, the UN's specialized agency for education, was created, its Constitution declared: 'that since wars begin in the minds of men, it is in the minds of men that the defences of peace must be constructed.' This proclamation could have been Comenius's motto, so it is not surprising that UNESCO celebrated his work on the occasion of the tercentenary of his death in 1970.

After Comenius, no thinkers of any note paid attention to the idea of education for a cosmopolitan purpose until the turn of the eighteenth century. Yet by this age the force of nationalism and the perceived need of education to be provided by the state to satisfy its own interests were in tension with education for world citizenship. The most renowned philosopher of the Enlightenment ideal of cosmopolitanism was Kant. So committed was he to this line of thinking that the younger generation of the German Romantics, developing their nationalist creed, renounced, indeed denounced, his philosophy. Moreover, Kant himself expressed pessimistic views concerning the political and moral potential of education. In 1798 he wrote:

> To expect that the education of young people in intellectual and moral culture
> . . . firstly through domestic instruction and then through a series of schools . . .
> will eventually not only make them good citizens, but will also bring them up
> to practise a kind of goodness which can continually progress and maintain
> itself, is a plan which is scarcely likely to achieve the desired success.
>
> (Reiss 1991: 188–9)

Any attempt, therefore, to connect Kant with the intellectual process of relating the cosmopolitan and nationalist purposes of education might therefore seem futile. Yet a reading of his essay entitled *Pädagogik* (*Education*), which he published in 1803, is very worthwhile. He presents here his positive thoughts concerning education for both state citizenship and world citizenship. In the essay he distinguishes between 'home' and 'public' education, the latter meaning schools, though not state provided. On the whole, he says public education is the best 'as a preparation for the duties of a citizen' (Kant 1960: 25). He expands on this:

> Under such a system, we learn to measure our powers with those of others, and
> to know the limits imposed upon us by the rights of others. Thus we can have
> no preference shown us, because we meet with opposition everywhere, and
> we can only make our mark and obtain an advantage over others by real merit.
> Public education is the best school for future citizens.
>
> (Kant 1960: 29)

However, he has already implied earlier in his text that a focused education for state citizenship misses the point about how education really should be designed:

> Children ought to be educated, not for the present, but for a possibly improved condition of man in the future; that is, in a manner which is adapted to the *idea of humanity* and the whole destiny of man . . . the basis of a scheme of education must be cosmopolitan.
>
> (Kant 1960: 14–15)

It therefore follows that, because rulers 'have not the universal good so much in view, as the well-being of the state' (Kant 1960: 16–17), schools should not be provided by the state, as the likes of Basedow recommended (see Kant 1960: 16; for Basedow, see Chapter 2 above). Unfortunately, Kant makes no effort to suggest how the practice of citizenship education and the ideal of cosmopolitan education could be brought together.

His younger compatriot, Fichte, did make such an attempt. A leading exponent of the German ideology of nationalism, which Kant deplored, Fichte broke away from his early adherence to Kant's teaching; yet he retained such a commitment to the cosmopolitan ideal that, in his political and educational philosophy, he strove to blend these apparently polar ideas. There are plenty of references in Fichte's works to education for a patriotic or nationalistic purpose and arguments for state schools (see Chapter 2). However, it was in an address to a Berlin Masonic lodge in 1800 that he revealed his image of the ideal. This was a style of moral education to form a single human spiritual union with a compatible world political union of like-minded states (there are echoes of Kant here). And so, 'the completely educated man . . . becomes the most complete and useful citizen' (quoted Engelbrecht 1968: 74). Both elements are essential: cosmopolitanism without patriotism is cold, useless and absurd; patriotism without cosmopolitanism is narrow and selfish. He portrays the individual thus fully and properly educated in the following way: '*In his mind love of country and cosmopolitanism are intimately united*, and both stand in a very definite relationship. *Love of country is his activity, cosmopolitanism is his thought*' (quoted Engelbrecht 1968: 74). Nevertheless, he does not trust the state to supply such an education; it must be left to enlightened private societies such as the Freemasons.

The struggle to keep cosmopolitanism and patriotism/nationalism compatible was reasonably common in the 1790s and 1800s, but not thereafter. The Italian patriot Mazzini, who held to the same objective in his essays *The Duties of Man*, written in the mid-nineteenth century, is therefore something of an anachronism. However, unlike Fichte, he does not try to fuse them together. On the one hand, he asserts that, 'Without National Education common to all the citizens, equality of *duties* and of *rights* is a formula devoid of meaning; the knowledge of duties and the capacity of exercising rights are left to the chance of fortune' (Mazzini 1907: 87). On the other hand, addressing the Italian working men, he declares:

> It is important to you that [your sons] should feel themselves from their earliest years united in the spirit of equality and of love for a common aim, with the millions of brothers that God has given them.

The Education which shall give your children this sort of teaching can come only from the Nation.

(Mazzini 1907: 87)

Using our dual classification, we may characterize Kant, despite his acquaintance with Stoic philosophy, as essentially a Comenian – his aim was peace. We may characterize Fichte, despite his dislike of the Stoics because he believed them to be atheists, as essentially a Stoic – his aim was to ensure the recognition of all humans as rational, moral beings. And we may characterize Mazzini as a Stoic, despite not acknowledging that philosophy, because his cosmopolitanism is grounded in the fervent belief that God's will is that mankind should live in harmonious brotherhood.

World citizenship: practice and return to theory

The eruption and spread of nationalism in the nineteenth and twentieth centuries had an ambivalent effect on education for world citizenship. In the first place, its ideological appeal and force severely enfeebled the idealistic hopes of the likes of Fichte and Mazzini of running education for nationalist and cosmopolitan purposes in double harness. Indeed, as we have seen in Chapters 3 and 4, by far and away the major function of schooling during these centuries was to serve the needs of the state. Yet, at the same time, nationalism, in its several guises, so exacerbated inter-state and inter-communal rivalries and hatreds that wars became more persistent and intense. As a reaction, thoughts again turned to the possibility that schools might become the agents of pacification and conscious human harmony. To this basic pattern there must be added the horrors of vicious Nazism and subsequently the threat of thermonuclear exchange between the USA and USSR, the injustice of Third World poverty and man's undermining of the ecosystem, all of which seemed to many to give undeniable potency to the cosmopolitans' case.

How was education for world citizenship to be introduced into the schools? Citizenship education has usually been firmly established in practice when the state sees an advantage to itself in cultivating a knowledgeable citizenry. To repeat the point made in the last section, there has never been a world state to foster education for itself, and attempts to introduce this dimension of civic learning can easily raise the objection that it tends to weaken civic education for the state that does exist. Consequently, the history of education for world citizenship in schools has evolved as but a frail companion to education for state citizenship. It has been dependent upon the commitment of members of the teaching profession, educational institutions with a global reach, and transnational political institutions, organizations and movements willing to assist teachers in their cosmopolitan endeavours. It may be cogently argued that what has been achieved in these ways is merely education for world-mindedness – to employ the useful expression – not fully or truly education for world citizenship. By stating this position we have no intention of denying the importance of this kind of teaching, rather to clarify the nature of the objectives, which, in any case, are not so dissimilar to the Stoics' and Kant's.

Since education for citizenship is education for living and operating in a state, education for world citizenship, it has been strongly and logically asserted, may be said to be taking place only when teachers are explaining to pupils the case for a world state – a rare and probably undesirable activity. In fact, this issue of the validity of the term 'education for world citizenship' has been no more than a pre-echo in the pedagogical sphere of the current, belated academic debate on the validity of the term 'world' or 'cosmopolitan citizenship itself' (see Hutchings and Dannreuther 1999; Heater 2002).

The most constant incentive during the past century for introducing a global perspective into teaching has been the Comenian desire to educate for world peace. We may in fact date the effective origins of the modern movements to use education for transnational eirenic purposes to the two decades leading up to the First World War. The growth of German power and the consequent arms race fuelled fears of an Armageddon, prompting the development of popular peace movements and the convening of the Hague Peace Conferences in 1899 and 1907. Educationists could scarcely have remained unaffected by this mood (see e.g. Scanlon 1960: 7–13). School Peace Leagues were founded in Britain, France, the Netherlands and the USA. A portion of a description of the aims of the British body reveals, from today's perspective, how up-to-date it was:

> To promote through the schools, international peace, arbitration, and friendship; to study, in meetings and conferences, the problems of racial relationships and the best means of eliminating prejudice; to study the history of the international peace movement; to promote, through lessons in civics, the development of a rational and humane national life and patriotism, and a sense of the corresponding duties to humanity.
>
> (Scanlon 1960: 7–8)

The greatest energy and enthusiasm for education for peace were displayed in the USA. The School Peace League there pursued its work through state and local branches, helping schools to pursue this kind of teaching with such skill that in 1912 the National Education Association commended its 'excellent work' to all teachers. The leading light was Fannie Fern Andrews. She soon came to believe that if teachers were to teach for an international purpose, there should be an international organization to bring them together. This was by no means a novel ideal. Europeans from post-Napoleonic times onwards, notably Marc-Antoine Jullien, Hermann Molkenboer and Francis Kemeny, had already canvassed such a proposal. Miss Andrews gradually expanded her plans to a much more ambitious scale: to create an international education bureau for research and interchange of information and ideas on a par with the Hague Tribunal for the arbitration of international disputes. She struggled, with US government support, but with hesitant and lukewarm interest from other states, until her initiative was overwhelmed by the outbreak of war.

During the Great War, powerful lobbies advocated that at its conclusion an international body should be created to preclude the recurrence of such horrific conflict. Educationists, including Miss Andrews and Léon Bourgeois of France, argued the case that the putative organization should include education in its brief. The body was established: the League of Nations. Its Covenant was silent on the subject of education. Not until 1925 were the modest wishes of the pioneers partially realized by the setting up of the International Bureau of Education, a *private* organization with its headquarters in Geneva.

Meanwhile, some teachers in a few countries were giving international and global perspectives to their teaching in schools, mainly for the age-range 16 to 18. In a study undertaken in the 1930s, an English scholar, commenting on the teaching of international relations in secondary schools, judged that 'The overwhelming majority of pupils continue to leave secondary school without having been presented with a systematic and objective survey of the nature of the world in which they live' (Bailey 1938: 141). He cites Denmark, the Netherlands, Norway, Sweden and the United Kingdom as partial exceptions to this generalization. In some countries the marking of a special day of transnational significance was an important occasion. For example, in Czechoslovakia, from 1926, on 6 March, the anniversary of the birth of Comenius was celebrated by a lesson on the peace movement – taking half an hour! (see Bailey 1938: 107n.). Following the establishment of the League of Nations, several countries created associations to support its work (even in the USA, which did not join the League).

Nevertheless, it was only in the United Kingdom that such a body, there called the League of Nations Union (LNU), became firmly established, and, through its Education Committee, with some success cultivated learning about the League and international affairs generally. Moreover, by the mid-1920s this kind of school work in Britain was being termed 'teaching for world citizenship' – the title of an address given in 1926 by a distinguished professor of international politics, who used the occasion to plead for more systematic teaching in this field; though, in all conscience, his proposals suggested a very weak interpretation of world citizenship (Webster 1926). Nevertheless, the LNU Education Committee undertook sterling work for the schools, albeit following the League's guidance as expressed through its Assembly's resolutions in 1923 to 1924:

> In view of the resolutions adopted by the Assembly at its fourth ordinary session [1923] regarding the encouragement of contact between young people of different nationalities and concerning the instruction of youth in the ideals of the League of Nations Union. . . .
>
> Instructs the Secretariat to investigate the means by which efforts to promote contact and to educate the youth of all countries in the ideals of world peace and solidarity may be further developed and co-ordinated.
>
> (quoted League of Nations Union 1937: 133)

Note the reference to world peace and the title of the publication in which this is quoted – *Teachers and World Peace*: the Comenian concept of education for world citizenship persists. Along these lines, 'In the 1920s the Union's work in schools went splendidly. . . . In 1927 some 600 representatives of local education authorities met at a national conference and considered how to further instruction on the league in schools' (Birn 1981: 139).

However, by the late 1930s, for political reasons, schools and local education authorities were becoming agitated about this educational activity being related so directly to the League. It was therefore arranged in 1939 that this teaching assistance should be hived off to an independent body, though still retaining close links with the LNU. Accordingly, a new name was needed. After some discussion, 'the Council for Education in World Citizenship' was adopted (soon abbreviated to 'CEWC'). Thus the concept of citizenship with a global meaning was boldly seized. It caused trouble. (For the history of CEWC, see Heater 1984.) 'World citizenship', a notoriously slippery term, had to be defined and could be easily misconstrued as utopian, indoctrinatory, almost treasonous in the dangerous and patriotically tense times of the opening of the Second World War. Politicians, civil servants and the press reacted to the inauguration of the Council with heated hostility. Even as late as 1944, the most renowned figure in its creation, Gilbert Murray, wrote, 'About "world citizenship". . . . I do not quite like the phrase. It seems to profess too much' (quoted Heater 1984: 47). CEWC was caught in the ambiguity of the term as having either a loose, moral meaning or a precise, political meaning. The drafters of their Articles of Constitution, it must be confessed, appeared to be trying to ride both horses, while protesting, in defence against their detractors, that they were only in the saddle of the unpolitical mount; for they declared:

> The main purpose of the Council is to promote throughout the educational system such studies and teaching as may best contribute to mutual under-standing, peace, co-operation and goodwill between all peoples and *lead to the building of a world commonwealth*.
>
> (quoted Heater 1984: 195; emphasis added)

Nevertheless, the organization went on to undertake invaluable work and to earn the gratitude of countless thousands of young people for over half a century.

CEWC also played a leading role during the war in the creation of the institution which came to be called the United Nations Educational, Scientific and Cultural Organization (UNESCO), which brought to fruition the seeds of Fannie Fern Andrews's thinking. Since its foundation in 1945 it has become a truly global organ for education for international understanding (EIU), to use its favoured, abbreviated term. Eschewing the label 'education for world citizenship' and recognizing the increasing number of approaches to global studies, in 1974 it adopted the port-manteau phrase 'Education for International Understanding, Co-operation and Peace and Education relating to Human Rights and Fundamental Freedoms'. In 1995 the formula was again altered to 'Education for Peace, Human Rights and Democracy'; and although this brief catalogue may seem to reduce the world citizenship implications of UNESCO's educational activities, the Declaration that launched the new wording does include such phrases as 'a sense of universal values and types of behaviour' and 'education for citizenship which includes an inter-national dimension'. The tone of the Declaration is nevertheless somewhat pessimistic: it lists the dreadful, mounting global problems and effectively admits that the kind of education advocated by UNESCO has either failed or failed to be adopted, so that the situation 'calls for the transformation of the traditional styles of educational action' (see Reardon 1997: Appendix 2).

One of the main channels through which UNESCO has assisted schools has been the Associated Schools Project (ASPRO), launched in 1953. Originally operating in fifteen countries, within a decade the numbers had increased to forty-three and by 1993 to 114, in all continents, though, admittedly, with varying degrees of enthusiasm and involving only a tiny number of schools. A statement by a senior UNESCO official makes interesting commentary on this last phrase:

> What must be kept in mind is that the Associated Schools Project was never intended as an end in itself. The end was to have an effect upon education generally, through the work of the institutions in this international network. That is having the effect and it is nowhere demonstrated more strikingly than in India.
>
> (Indian National Commission for UNESCO 1965: 12)

On the matter of the small number of schools, the UNESCO policy has been that, once the ASPRO work has been 'evaluated as effective and innovative [the schemes] are to be introduced into the mainstream of the educational system, so that [ASPRO] has a multiplying effect for the benefit of other schools in the country' (UNESCO 1993: 52).

Initially, the ASPRO participating institutions (by 1964 teacher-training institutions, secondary and primary schools) were required to teach about one or more of three topics, namely the work of the UN, human rights or another country/other countries, extended later by the addition of the environment. Indeed, the development of the project, both in number of institutions involved and in diversity of pupils' involvement in cosmopolitan understanding, is illustrated by this description of work in Germany in the mid-1990s:

> 100 UNESCO model schools exist in around 90 towns and cities spread throughout the Federal Republic. These schools . . . participate in school twinnings, interdisciplinary teaching, and international seminars, camps and exchange programmes. Their voluntary donations support worldwide programmes for combating poverty and implementing human rights for all.
>
> (Führ 1997: 237–8)

The extension of the range of topics fostered by UNESCO was a reflection of the growing complexity of global studies in schools. By the 1970s it was possible to identify at least seven themes or approaches: World Studies, Education for International Understanding, Peace Studies, Third World and Development Studies, Multicultural Studies, Human Rights Education, Environmental Studies (see e.g. Heater 1984: 26). Some approaches were especially favoured in some countries, others in different ones, though inter-national education (note the hyphen – teaching about other countries and relations between them) has been fairly common. A brief indication of this generalization, then. Peace studies were particularly favoured in Norway, where a peace teachers group, the strongest in western Europe, was founded in 1952. In 1984 they succeeded in creating an optional course in this field for fourth-year secondary pupils, the first nationally approved syllabus in Europe (see Rathenow 1987). French teachers, in contrast, have taken little interest in peace studies, but have been very committed to human rights education (see Rathenow 1987; Starkey 1992). England has taken multicultural education especially seriously; for example, as early as 1967 the National Council for Commonwealth Immigrants published a pamphlet on the subject (NCCI 1967; see also, DES 1985 and Chapter 3 above). In the Soviet Union, by about 1980 environmental studies were being increasingly taught. Thus one authority on Russian affairs wrote in 1983:

> Hitherto environmental education was carried out mainly in pioneer and Komsomol summer camps, in young naturalists' circles and in the course of other out-of-school activities. Now, it is being introduced into science and literature lessons and lessons in productive labour.
>
> (Koutaissoff 1983: 92)

As to development studies, we may quote the following comment: 'A UNICEF discussion paper of 1977 claimed that a development perspective had become the "yeast of the dough" of the Dutch curriculum' (Wilson 1986: 106). The reasons behind these examples are clear. Norway alone of NATO countries shared a common frontier with the Soviet Union during the Cold War; France has been proud of her revolutionary initiative in declaring that human rights are a natural endowment; Britain received an increasing number of coloured immigrants from Commonwealth countries from the 1960s; ecological problems became indisputably severe in the USSR when, for instance, the shrinking of the Aral Sea and the poisoning of Lake Baikal became well known; and Dutch governments have tended to support the cause of overseas aid, partly because of the Netherlands' imperial past.

Some teachers in a few countries, however, came to favour the more holistic approach of world or global studies – an interest that has recently become more widespread – despite the difficulties of selection of material and design of syllabuses these courses presented. Perhaps the two most distinguished, and often reprinted, attempts to resolve these problems have been *An Attainable Global Perspective* by Robert G. Hanvey (1976) and *Global Teacher, Global Learner* by Graham Pike and David Selby (1988), though Pike and Selby admit to virtually repeating Hanvey's five dimensions of perspective consciousness, state of the planet awareness, cross-cultural awareness, knowledge of global dynamics and awareness of human choices as the very foundation of the modern holistic approach. However, they strike a much more assertive pose:

> Hanvey's work is seminal but, in our view, insufficiently forceful in its promotion of the need for a global perspective. Our global perspective we call *irreducible* rather than *attainable*. It is irreducible in two senses. First, each of

the five dimensions must be present in a school that lays claim to offering a global perspective. Secondly, if the school is not offering the five dimensions then it is not preparing its students adequately for participation in an interdependent and fast-changing world.

(Pike and Selby 1988: 37)

Both lists stress consciousness and awareness, which should also be attributes of citizenship. But Hanvey's list, unlike Pike and Selby's, stops short there, not progressing to teaching in order to 'develop the social and action skills necessary for becoming effective participants in democratic decision-making at a variety of levels, grassroots to global' (Pike and Selby 1988: 35), a crucial additional feature of citizenship. This closer approximation to world citizenship as compared with the looser world-mindedness may be attributable to the differences in dates and/or geographical provenance of these two publications, namely the USA and England.

It cannot, however, be denied that since about 1960 commitment to education for world citizenship in the comprehensive form, despite setbacks and disappointments, has been sturdier and more persistent in the USA than in any other country. The scale and diversity of this commitment has been summarized as follows:

Colleges and universities, academic associations and educational organizations, and local school districts and nonprofit community organizations launched hundreds of projects and programs. . . . Curriculum writers developed thousands of supplemental materials and several 'global' textbooks. . . . National education organizations issued publications and sponsored conferences [etc.].

(Smith 1991: 224)

Yet the outcome of so much help has not been commensurate with the effort expended. Evidence, especially from the mid-1980s, shows that relatively few teachers were according much of a global dimension to their social studies courses, and, in addition, some hostility to the very principle of global education was quite vitriolic. For example, the National Council for Social Studies wrote into their curriculum guidelines in 1979 that the aim of such courses should be 'to prepare students to be rational, humane, participating citizens in a world that is increasingly interdependent' (quoted Hahn 1984: 240); even so, the President of that body complained in 1983 that 'The belief that one should train young people to be good citizens by giving them lots of information about their own country is everywhere' (though she added that 'the United States is not alone') (Hahn 1984: 240, 242). Three years after this address a report entitled 'Blowing the Whistle on Global Education' denounced this work as biased and unpatriotic. It was widely distributed, stimulating other statements in like vein and much angry criticism of global studies among the ultra-conservative elements of the population (see Heater 2002: 160).

Objections to education for world citizenship, under whatever title and not just in the USA, have been based on a number of arguments, but in essence they boil down to two: the political and the educational. The political case has been voiced mainly by those on the Right of the doctrinal spectrum, arguing the essential priority of the political function of the school as being to undergird the stability, strength and security of the state. Teaching the cosmopolitan concepts of the oneness of humankind, the interdependence of nations, the need to conserve the planetary environment, for example – in short, to teach a cosmopolitan ethic – it is asserted, dangerously drains away the pupils' loyalty to the state. This had been felt with particular acuteness during the crucial years of the Second World War and the Cold War. The educational objections have again been aired loudly by those of a conservative cast of mind, and for two not necessarily related reasons. In the first place is the belief that teaching facts about the world presents huge problems of selection, so that it can only be undertaken at the most superficial level with consequent sacrifice of scholarly standards. If the approach through, for instance, world history instead of national history is bad enough, integrated world studies is much worse, because intellectually valuable, respectable and recognized disciplines are pounded into an undifferentiated porridge. There is, second, worse still. Many advocates of education for world citizenship have believed that educating for feelings is more important than teaching facts. Affective learning should be given due weight, even priority over cognitive learning. Educationists, and lay commentators, of a conservative stripe cannot abide this dilution of 'hard' learning. The two sides in this quarrel collided with particularly shuddering effect in the 1970s and 1980s.

The political issue – whether patriotic and cosmopolitan attitudes and feelings can be held simultaneously and in balance – is a core problem that exercised the minds of philosophers in the distant past (see Heater 2002: 37–52) and has exercised the minds of social and educational psychologists in much more recent times. Many exponents of education for world citizenship have believed that the capital means of achieving this resolution is to bring together young people from different cultural and ethnic backgrounds to live and learn a while together in order to come to understand the fundamental unity in human diversity. International camps have been arranged and international schools founded in pursuit of this ideal. A few examples may be listed. In 1933 the British League of Nations Union started what they called Nansen Pioneer Camps, named after the famous Norwegian League official Fridtjof Nansen. These were arranged for pupils aged 12 to 16. 'Boys and girls from other countries take part, and the programme provides training in campcraft and games of all nations, as well as camp fire talks on foreign countries and the work of the League', to quote from the LNU teachers' handbook (LNU 1937: 130–1). Several decades later a bold initiative led to the creation of several United World Colleges, at first, in the 1970s, in Vancouver, South Wales and Singapore. Students from many countries have been recruited: the 1977 entry to the United World College of the Atlantic in Wales, for example, comprised young people from forty-two countries.

We have pointed to the difference between 'weak' education for world-mindedness and 'strong' education for world citizenship; and it will be reasonably clear that, whatever terms may have been used, the latter teaching, in content, methodology and objectives, has, strictly speaking, been quite rare. One reason for this rarity may well be that no attempt has been made seriously to connect a clear and deep understanding of cosmopolitan political thinking with comparable pedagogical thinking. Not until the 1990s, that is, when the American philosopher Martha Nussbaum wrote on this issue (see especially Nussbaum *et al.* 1996), prompting leading intellectuals to bend their minds to the matter. However, the responses might not have been so readily forthcoming had it not been for the immense academic interest in the phenomenon of globalization, including the demographic fluidity of recent times. This development, too, has supplied education for world citizenship with an urgent relevance in the eyes of teachers and pupils and thus given this dimension to civic education a noticeable fillip.

The essence of Nussbaum's case for world citizenship education is to be found in what she calls three capacities and four arguments. The capacities are: a 'critical examination of oneself and one's traditions'; the ability of citizens 'to see them-selves not simply as citizens of some local region but also, and above all, as human beings bound to all other human beings by ties of recognition and concern'; and 'the narrative imagination', by which she means 'the ability to think what it might be like to be in the shoes of a person different from oneself' (Nussbaum 1997: 9–11). The four arguments are: 'Through cosmopolitan education, we learn more about ourselves'; 'We make headway solving problems that require international cooperation'; 'We recognize moral obligations to the rest of the world that are real and that otherwise would go unrecognized'; and 'We make a consistent and coherent argument based on distinctions we are prepared to defend' (Nussbaum *et al.* 1996: 11–15). Teaching the three capacities, she asserts, is essential to the cultivation of humanity, which she equates with cosmopolitanism. And we must assume, though she does not make the explicit connection, that, by learning these capacities, we shall become equipped with the desiderata of the four arguments. Nussbaum bases these educational propositions firmly on principles expounded in classical philosophy, namely the Socratic injunction to pursue self-knowledge and the Stoic presentation of the concept of world citizenship. From Socrates she derives the first two of the world citizen's essential capacities – contextual understanding; from Marcus Aurelius and his Stoic predecessors she derives the third capacity – empathy. Her concern is to present a tightly argued case, not to advocate curricular details, though she is at pains to stress three crucial features that should appear in teaching programmes. First, this style of education should start as soon as the child enters school (see Nussbaum 1997: 69). Second, as many subjects as possible should be taught with a multicultural content (see Nussbaum 1997: 68). And third, that, far from a world dimension obliterating the local, teaching for world citizenship requires a thorough grasp of one's local society and culture, only through which can the individual conveniently act for the cosmopolitan good (see Nussbaum *et al.* 1996: 135–6; Nussbaum 1997: 68).

Nussbaum's position can and has been challenged, mainly on the political issue of the relationship between cosmopolitanism and patriotism (Nussbaum *et al.* 1996). But what we are interested in here is the value of her cosmopolitan arguments for education. She can, in fact, be criticized on three grounds. In the first place, she reveals no evidence of an understanding or indeed knowledge of the huge amount of work undertaken in this field even in her own country (with the exception of a reference to one advanced-level course (see Nussbaum 1997: 81–3)). In the light of that work her recommendations do not seem all that original. Second, she effectively writes about world-mindedness as opposed to world *citizenship*, showing herself too dismissive of her critics who want citizenship to mean something precise (see e.g. Nussbaum *et al* 1996: 125). Third, her claims to base an education for world citizenship on cosmopolitan ethical and political theory are undermined by the weaknesses in her interpretation of the latter. A Cypriot scholar has identified a number of these weaknesses (see Papastephanou 2002), advancing criticisms that vary in strength. Perhaps the most cogent relates to the cosmopolitan case of the essential oneness of humankind. She explains:

> If there is a definable human nature in which all of us participate despite contingent differences, we are only one step away from evaluating cultures on the basis of how close they are to that 'original design of humanity'.
>
> (Papastephanou 2002: 74)

At least Nussbaum was sufficiently courageous to make an attempt at supplying global education with a solid foundation in cosmopolitan philosophy. Specialists in education could profitably build on her ideas, introducing the added ingredient of the concept of 'cosmopolitan democracy' (see e.g. Held 1995) in order to arrive at the sorely needed coherent definition of education for world citizenship. Yet that formulation gives a false impression that the task would be relatively straightforward. Far from it. As the earlier sections of this chapter have shown, other, relatively recent political and social developments demand to be given attention in programmes of civic education. Nussbaum refers to the Stoic idea of living in, as it were, concentric circles (see Nussbaum *et al.* 1996: 9). In truth, it has been an extraordinarily popular image down to our own day (see Heater 2002: 44–52). The idea is, roughly, that we have multiple identities and loyalties from the close relationship of the family to the distant one of the whole of humankind. In modern terms, locality, state, European Union (where this applies), religious affiliation and the world may be conceived of in this geometrical pattern. Tightening up and modernizing this age-old concept and translating it into educational terms, while tackling the psychological problems involved (see e.g. Torney 1979), would build on similar ideas expounded by educationists in the twentieth century to the end of constructing a truly comprehensive and coherent citizenship education for generations to come. Thus will a consciousness of history connect the past to the future.

References

Ablin, F. (ed.) (1963) *Education in the USSR: A Collection of Readings from Soviet Journals, Vol.2*, n.p., International Arts and Science Press.

Adeyoyin, F.A. (1979) 'The Role of the School as a Politicizing Agent Through Citizenship Education', *International Journal of Political Education*, 2.

Advisory Group on Citizenship (1998) *Education for Citizenship and the Teaching of Democracy in Schools* (Crick Report), London: Qualifications and Curriculum Agency.

Archer, M.S. (1977) 'Education', in J.E. Flower, *France Today*.

Ardagh, J. (1982) *France in the 1980s*, Harmondsworth: Penguin.

Arikpo, O. (1967) *The Development of Modern Nigeria*, Harmondsworth: Penguin.

Aristotle (trans. and ed. E. Barker) (1948) *Politics*, Oxford: Clarendon Press.

Aristotle (trans. J.A.K. Thomson) (1955) *The Ethics of Aristotle*, Harmondsworth: Penguin.

Aristotle (trans. H.G. Apostle) (1975) *The Nicomachean Ethics*, Dordrecht: Reidel.

Aristotle (trans. P.J. Rhodes) (1984) *The Athenian Constitution*, Harmondsworth: Penguin.

Arnold, M. (1962) *Democratic Education*, Ann Arbor, MI: University of Michigan Press.

Aso, M. and Amano, I. (1972) *Education and Japan's Modernization*, Tokyo: Ministry of Foreign Affairs, Japan.

Association for Education in Citizenship (1936) *Education for Citizenship in Secondary Schools*, London: Oxford University Press.

Avis, G. (ed.) (1987) *The Making of the Soviet Citizen*, London: Croom Helm.

Aziz, K.K. (1967) *The Making of Pakistan: A Study in Nationalism*, London: Chatto & Windus.

Bacon, F. (1906) *Essays*, London: Dent.

Baczko, B. (ed.) (1982) *Une Éducation pour la Démocratie: Textes et Projets de l'Époque Révolutionnaire*, Paris: Éditions Garnier.

Baglin Jones, E. and Jones, N. (eds) (1992) *Education for Citizenship*, London: Kogan Page.

Bailey, S.H. (1938) *International Studies in Modern Education*, London: Oxford University Press.

Bamford, T.W. (1960) *Thomas Arnold*, London: Cresset Press.

Banks, J.A. and Lynch, J. (eds) (1986) *Multicultural Education in Western Societies*, London: Holt, Rinehart & Winston.

Barnard, H.C. (1947) *A Short History of English Education from 1760 to 1944*, London: University of London Press.

Basu, A. (1974) *The Growth of Education and Political Development in India, 1898–1920*, Delhi: Oxford University Press.

Becker, J.M. (ed.) (1979) *Schooling for a Global Age*, New York: McGraw-Hill.

Békés, Z. (1990) 'Some Results of Hungarian Youth Research and Dilemmas of Political Education', in B. Claussen and H. Mueller, *Political Socialization of the Young in East and West*.

Bell, G.H. (1997) 'Towards the European School: Educating European Citizens Through Whole School Development', in I. Davies and A. Sobisch, *Developing European Citizens*.

Bereday, G.Z.F. (ed.) (1966) *Charles E, Merriam's The Making of Citizens*, New York: Columbia University Teachers College Press.

Bereday, G.Z.F. and Pennar, J. (eds) (1960) *The Politics of Soviet Education*, New York: Praeger, and London: Stevens.

Bereday, G.Z.F., Brickman, W.W. and Read, G.H. (eds) (1960) *The Changing Soviet School*, Cambridge, MA: Riverside Press.

Betts, R.F. (1991) *France and Decolonisation 1900–1960*, Basingstoke: Macmillan.

Bicât, A. (1970) 'Fifties Children: Sixties People', in V. Bogdanor and R. Skidelsky, *The Age of Affluence*.

Binchy, D.A. (1941) *Church and State in Fascist Italy*, London: Oxford University Press.

Birn, D.S. (1981) *The League of Nations Union 1918–1945*, Oxford: Clarendon Press.

Board of Education (1944) *Teachers and Youth Leaders* (McNair Report), London: HMSO.

Bogdanor, V. and Skidelsky, R. (eds) *The Age of Affluence 1951–1964*, London: Macmillan.

Bogolubov, L.N., Klokova, G.V., Kovalyova, G.S. and Poltorak, D.I. (1999) 'The Challenge of Civic Education in the New Russia', in J. Torney-Purta *et al.*, *Civic Education Across Countries*.

Boyd, W. (1932) *The History of Western Education* (3rd edn), London: A. & C. Black.

Bracher, K.D. (trans. J. Steinberg) (1978) *The German Dictatorship*, Harmondsworth: Penguin.

Brady, R.A. (1937) *The Spirit and Structure of German Fascism*, London: Left Book Club.

Bray, T.M. and Cooper, G.R. (1979) 'Education and Nation Building in Nigeria since the Civil War', *Comparative Education*, 15.

Brennan, T. (1981) *Political Education and Democracy*, Cambridge: Cambridge University Press.

Briggs, A. (1959) *The Age of Improvement*, London: Longmans.

Briggs, A. (1960) *Chartist Studies*, London: Macmillan.

Brogan, D. (1940) *The Development of Modern France (1870–1939)*, London: Hamish Hamilton.

Brown, B.F. (ed.) (1977) *Education for Responsible Citizenship: The Report of the National Task Force on Citizenship Education*, New York: McGraw-Hill.

Buisson, F. and Farrington, F.E. (eds) (1920) *French Educational Ideals of Today*, London: Harrap.

Burke, E. (1910) *Reflections on the French Revolution*, London: Dent.

Burston, W.H. (1973) *James Mill on Philosophy and Education*, London: Athlone Press.

Burtt, S. (1992) *Virtue Transformed: Political Argument in England, 1688–1740*, Cambridge: Cambridge University Press.

Butts, R.F. (1988) *The Morality of Democratic Citizenship: Goals for Civic Education in the Republic's Third Century*, Calabasas, CA: Center for Civic Education.

Butts, R.F. (1989) *The Civic Mission in Educational Reform: Perspectives for the Public and the Profession*, Stanford, CA: Hoover Institution Press, Stanford University.

Butts, R.F. and Cremin, L.A. (1953) *A History of Education in American Culture*, New York: Holt, Rinehart & Winston.

Callahan, R.E. (1964) *An Introduction to Education in American Society: A Text with Readings*, New York: Knopf.

Callan, E. (1997) *Creating Citizens: Political Education and a Liberal Democracy*, Oxford: Clarendon Press.

Calliess, J. and Lob, R. (eds) (1987) *Handbuch Praxis der Umwelt- und Friedenserziehung*, Düsseldorf: Schwann.

Carew Hunt, R.N. (1957) *A Guide to Communist Jargon*, London: Bles.

Castle, E.B. (1961) *Ancient Education and Today*, Harmondsworth: Penguin.

Cavanagh, F.A. (ed.) (1931) *James and John Stuart Mill on Education*, Cambridge: Cambridge University Press.

Chaffee, S.H., Morduchowicz, R. and Galperin, H. (1998) 'Education in Democracy in Argentina: Effects of a Newspaper-in-School Program', in O. Ichilov, *Citizenship and Citizenship Education in a Changing World*.

Chevallier, P. and Grosperrin, B. (eds) (1971) *L'Enseignement Français de la Révolution à nos Jours, II: Documents*, Paris: Mouton.

Cicero (trans. C.W. Keyes) (1928) (a) *De Re Publica*, (b) *De Legibus*, London: Heinemann, and Cambridge, MA: Harvard University Press.

Cicero (trans. E.W. Sutton) (1948) *De Oratore*, London: Heinemann, and Cambridge, MA: Harvard University Press.

Clarke, P.B. (1994) *Citizenship*, London: Pluto.

Claussen, B. and Mueller, H. (eds) (1990) *Political Socialization of the Young in East and West*, Frankfurt am Main: Peter Lang.

Cobban, A. (1939) *Dictatorship: In History and Theory*, London: Cape.

Cobban, A. (1957) *A History of Modern France*, Vol.1, Harmondsworth: Penguin.

Cobban, A. (1960) *In Search of Humanity*, London: Cape.

Cobban, A. (1964) *Rousseau and the Modern State* (2nd edn), London: Allen & Unwin.

Cobban, A. (1965) *A History of Modern France, Vol. 3: 1871–1962*, Harmondsworth: Penguin.

Cobban, A. (1970) *France Since the Revolution and Other Aspects of Modern History*, London: Cape.

Cogan, J.J. and Derricott, R. (eds) (2000) *Citizenship for the 21st Century* (2nd edn), London: Kogan Page.

Colonial Office and Advisory Committee on Education in the Colonies (1948) *Education for Citizenship in Africa*, London: HMSO.

Comenius, J.A. (trans. A.M.O. Dobbie) (1995) *Panorthosia or Universal Reform*, Sheffield: Sheffield Academic Press.

Commission on Citizenship (1990) *Encouraging Citizenship*, London: HMSO.

Counts, G.S. (1957) *The Challenge of Soviet Education*, New York: McGraw-Hill.

Cowan, L.G., O'Connell, J. and Scanlon, D.G. (eds) (1965) *Education and Nation-Building in Africa*, New York: Praeger.

Cowell, F.R. (1948) *Cicero and the Roman Republic*, London: Pitman.

Crankshaw, E. (1959) *Khrushchev's Russia*, Harmondsworth: Penguin.

Crick, B. (2000) *Essays on Citizenship*, London: Continuum.

Crick, B. (2002) 'Education for Citizenship: The Citizenship Order', *Parliamentary Affairs*, 55.3.

Crick, B. and Heater, D. (1977) *Essays on Political Education*, Lewes: Falmer.

Crick, B. and Porter, A. (eds) (1978) *Political Education and Political Literacy*, Harlow: Longman.

Cross, C. (1968) *The Fall of the British Empire 1918–1968*, London: Hodder & Stoughton.

Crossman, R.H.S. (1937) *Plato To-day*, London: Allen & Unwin.

Čsepeli, G. (1990) 'Political Socialization of Hungarian Youth', in B. Claussen and H. Mueller, *Political Socialization of the Young in East and West*.

Cummings, W.K. (1987) 'Samurai Without Swords: The Making of the Modern Japanese', in E.B. Gumbert, *In the Nation's Image*.

Cummings, W.K., Gopinathan, S. and Tomoda, Y. (eds) (1988) *The Revival of Values Education in Asia and the West*, Oxford: Pergamon.

Curtis, S.J. and Boultwood, M.E.A. (1956) *A Short History of Educational Ideas* (2nd edn), London: University Tutorial Press.

Davies, I. (1997) 'Education for European Citizenship: Review of Relevant Documentation', in I. Davies and A. Sobisch, *Developing European Citizens*.

Davies, I. and Sobisch, A. (eds) (1997) *Developing European Citizens*, Sheffield: Sheffield Hallam University Press.

Davies, I., Gregory, I. and Riley, S.C. (1999) *Good Citizenship and Educational Provision*, London: Falmer.

de la Fontainerie, F. (ed. and trans.) (1932) *French Liberalism and Education in the Eighteenth Century*, New York: Burt Franklin.

Delanty, G. (2000) *Citizenship in a Global Age: Society, Culture, Politics*, Buckingham: Open University Press.

DES (1985) *Education for All* (Swann Report), London: HMSO.

Dewey, J. (1961) *Democracy and Education*, New York: Macmillan.

DfEE/QCA (1999) *The National Curriculum: Citizenship*, London: DfEE/QCA.

Dickinson, H.T. (1977) *Liberty and Property*, London: Methuen.

Djilas, M. (1957) *The New Class*, London: Thames & Hudson.

Duczek, S. (1977) *Political Education in Germany* (unpublished mimeo), York: University of York Political Education Unit.

Duffy, J. (1962) *Portugal in Africa*, Harmondsworth: Penguin.

Dupeux, G. (trans. P. Wait) (1976) *French Society 1789–1970*, London: Methuen.

Dynneson, T.L. (2001) *Civism: Cultivating Citizenship in European History*, New York: Peter Lang.

Edmonds, J.M. (trans.) (1961) *Elegy and Iambus*, London: Heinemann, and Cambridge, MA: Harvard University Press.

Engelbrecht, H.C. (1968) *Johann Gottlieb Fichte: A Study of his Political Writings with Special Reference to his Nationalism*, New York: AMS Press.

England, J.M. (1963) 'The Democratic Faith in American Schoolbooks, 1783–1860', *American Quarterly*, 15.

Englund, T. (1986) *Curriculum as a Political Problem*, Uppsala and Lund: Chartwell-Bratt.

Esser, H. (1991) 'The Integration of Second Generation Immigrants in Germany: An Explanation of "Cultural" Differences', in R.S. Sigel and M. Hoskin, *Education for Democratic Citizenship*.

European Council and Ministers of Education (1988) *Resolution on the European Dimension in Education* (88/C177/02).

Fafunwa, A.B. and Aisika, J.U. (eds) (1982) *Education in Africa: A Comparative Study*, London: Allen & Unwin.

Fanon, F. (1967) *The Wretched of the Earth*, Harmondsworth: Penguin.

Felsenthal, I. and Rubinstein, I. (1991) 'Democracy, School and Curriculum Reform: "The Rules of the Game" in Israel', in R.S. Sigel and M. Hoskin, *Education for Democratic Citizenship*.

Fenton, E. (ed.) (1966) *Teaching the New Social Studies: An Inductive Approach*, New York: Holt, Rinehart & Winston.

Fitzpatrick, S. (1970) *The Commissariat of Enlightenment*, Cambridge: Cambridge University Press.

Flower, J.E. (ed.) (1977) *France Today: Introductory Studies* (3rd edn), London: Methuen.

Fogelman, K. (ed.) (1991) *Citizenship in Schools*, London: David Fulton.

Frazer, E. (2000) 'Citizenship Education: Anti-political Culture and Political Education in Britain', *Political Studies*, 48.

Friedrich, C.J. and Brzezinski, Z.K. (1956) *Totalitarian Dictatorship and Autocracy*, Cambridge, MA: Harvard University Press.

Führ, C. (1997) *The German Education System since 1945*, Bonn: Inter Nationes.

Gaus, J.M. (1929) *Great Britain: A Study of Civic Loyalty*, Chicago, IL: University of Chicago Press.

Gellner, E. (1983) *Nations and Nationalism* (4th edn), Oxford: Blackwell.

Gildea, R. (1983) *Education in Provincial France 1800–1914*, Oxford: Clarendon Press.

Giroux, H.A. (1987) 'Citizenship, Public Philosophy, and the Retreat from Democracy in the United States', in E.B. Gumbert, *In the Nation's Image*.

Godechot, J. (trans. H.H. Rowen) (1965) *France and the Atlantic Revolution of the Eighteenth Century, 1770–1799*, New York: Free Press, Collier-Macmillan.

Gollancz, V. (1953) *More for Timothy*, London: Gollancz.

Gopinathan, S. (1988) 'Being and Becoming: Education for Values in Singapore', in W.K. Cummings *et al.*, *The Revival of Values Education in Asia and the West*.

Gorbachev, M.S. (1987) *Perestroika: New Thinking for Our Country and the World*, London: Collins.

Grant, B. (1967) *Indonesia*, Harmondsworth: Penguin.

Grant, N. (1964) *Soviet Education*, Harmondsworth: Penguin.

Grimal, H. (1965) *La Décolonisation 1919–1963*, Paris: Armand Colin.

Gross, R.E. and Dynneson, T.L. (eds) (1991) *Social Science Perspectives on Citizenship Education*, New York: Teachers College, Columbia University.

Guardian (2002) 27 June.

Guilhaume, P. (1980) *Jules Ferry*, Paris: Encre.

Gumbert, E.B. (ed.) (1987) *In the Nation's Image*, Atlanta, GA: Georgia State University.

Gwynn, A. (1964) *Roman Education: From Cicero to Quintilian*, New York: Russell & Russell.

Hahn, C.L. (1984) 'Promise and Paradox: Challenges to Global Citizenship', *Social Citizenship*, April.

Hahn, C.L. (1998) *Becoming Political: Comparative Perspectives on Citizenship Education*, New York: State University of New York Press.

Hahn, C.L. (1999) 'Challenges in Civic Education in the United States', in J. Torney-Purta *et al.*, *Civic Education Across Countries*.

Hahn, H.-J. (1998) *Education and Society in Germany*, Oxford: Berg.

Hall, H.D. (1971) *Commonwealth: A History of the British Commonwealth of Nations*, London: Van Nostrand Reinhold.

Halliday, J. and McCormack, G. (1973) *Japanese Imperialism Today*, Harmondsworth: Penguin.

Halocha, J. (1995) 'Promoting Citizenship through International College–School Links', in A. Osler *et al.*, *Teaching for Citizenship in Europe*.

Händle, C., Oesterreich, D. and Trommer, L. (1999) 'Concepts of Civic Education in Germany Based on a Survey of Expert Opinion', in J. Torney-Purta *et al.*, *Civic Education Across Countries*.

Hanna, A.J. (1961) *European Rule in Africa*, London: Historical Association.

Hanvey, R.G. (1976) *An Attainable Global Perspective*, New York: Center for Global Perspectives.

Harber, C. (ed.) (1987) *Political Education in Britain*, London: Falmer.

Harber, C. (1989) *Politics in African Education*, London: Macmillan.

Hargreaves, J.D. (1967) *West Africa: The Former French States*, Englewood Cliffs, NJ: Prentice Hall.

Hargreaves, J.D. (1976) *The End of Colonial Rule in West Africa*, London: Historical Association.

Harper, S.N. (1929) *Civic Training in Soviet Russia*, Chicago, IL: University of Chicago Press.

Hayes, C.J.H. (1930) *France: A Nation of Patriots*, New York: Columbia University Press.

Hearnden, A. (1974) *Education in the Two Germanies*, Oxford: Blackwell.

Hearnden, A. (ed.) (1978) *The British in Germany: Educational Reconstruction after 1945*, London: Hamish Hamilton.

Heater, D. (1984) *Peace Through Education: The Contribution of the Council for Education in World Citizenship*, Lewes: Falmer.

Heater, D. (1990) *Citizenship: The Civic Ideal in World History, Politics and Education*, Harlow: Longman.

Heater, D. (1992) 'Education for European Citizenship', *Westminster Studies in Education*, 15.

Heater, D. (1996) *World Citizenship and Government: Cosmopolitan Ideas in the History of Western Political Thought*, Basingstoke: Macmillan.

Heater, D. (1998) *The Theory of Nationhood: a Platonic Symposium*, Basingstoke: Macmillan.

Heater, D. (2001) 'The History of Citizenship Education in England', *The Curriculum Journal*, 12.

Heater, D. (2002) *World Citizenship: Cosmopolitan Thinking and its Opponents*, London: Continuum.

Heater, D. and Gillespie, J.A. (eds) (1981) *Political Education in Flux*, London: Sage.

Held, D. (1995) *Democracy and the Global Order: From the Modern State to Cosmopolitan Governance*, Cambridge: Polity.

Hobbes, T. (1914) *Leviathan*, London: Dent.

Hodgetts, A.B. and Gallagher, P. (1978) *Teaching Canada for the 80s*, Toronto: The Ontario Institute for Studies in Education.

Holmes, B. (1956) 'Some Writings of William Torrey Harris', *British Journal of Educational Studies*, 5.

Honeywell, R.J. (1931) *The Educational Work of Thomas Jefferson*, Cambridge, MA: Harvard University Press.

Hooghoff, H. (1990) 'Curriculum Development for Political Education in the Netherlands', in B. Claussen and H. Mueller, *Political Socialization of the Young in East and West*.

Hornblower, S. and Spaworth, A. (1998) *The Oxford Companion to Classical Civilization*, Oxford: Oxford University Press.

Horvath-Peterson, S. (1984) *Victor Duruy & French Education*, Baton Rouge, LA: Louisiana State University Press.

Hunt, L. (ed.) (1996) *The French Revolution and Human Rights: A Brief Documentary History*, Boston, MA: St Martin's.

Hutchings, K. and Dannreuther, R. (eds) (1999) *Cosmopolitan Citizenship*, Basingstoke: Macmillan.

Ichilov, O. (ed.) (1998a) *Citizenship and Citizenship Education in a Changing World*, London: Woburn.

Ichilov, O. (1998b) 'Nation-Building, Collective Identities, Democracy and Citizenship Education in Israel', in O. Ichilov, *Citizenship and Citizenship Education in a Changing World*.

Ichilov, O. (1999) 'Citizenship Education in a Divided Society: The Case of Israel', in J. Torney-Purta *et al.*, *Civic Education Across Countries*.

Ikejiani, O. (ed.) (1964) *Nigerian Education*, Ikeja: Longmans of Nigeria.

Indian National Commission for UNESCO (1965) *Report of the National Seminar on International Understanding (Education for International Understanding)*, Delhi: Indian National Commission for UNESCO.

Iram, Y. (2001) 'Education for Democracy in Pluralistic Societies: The Case of Israel', in L.J. Limage, *Democratizing Education and Educating Democratic Citizens*.

Janowitz, M. (1983) *The Reconstruction of Patriotism: Education for Civic Consciousness*, Chicago, IL: University of Chicago Press.

Jarolimek, J. (1981) 'The Social Studies: An Overview', in H.D. Mehlinger and O.L. Davis, *The Social Studies*.

Jászi, O. (1961) *The Dissolution of the Habsburg Monarchy*, Chicago, IL: Chicago University Press.

Jones, P. (1997) *The Italian City-State: From Commune to Signoria*, Oxford: Clarendon Press.

Kaestle, C.F. (1983) *Pillars of the Republic: Common Schools and American Society, 1780–1860*, New York: Hill & Wang.

Kaiser, R.G. (1977) *Russia: The People and the Power*, Harmondsworth: Penguin.

Kandel, I.L. (1960) 'Education and Colonial Dependencies', in D.G. Scanlon, *International Education*.

Kant, I. (trans. A. Churton) (1960) *Education*, Ann Arbor, MI: University of Michigan Press.

Kennedy, E. (1989) *A Cultural History of the French Revolution*, New Haven, CT: Yale University Press.

Kerblay, B. (trans. R. Swyer) (1983) *Modern Soviet Society*, London: Methuen.

Kerr, D. (1999) 'Re-examining Citizenship Education in England', in J. Torney *et al.*, *Civic Education Across Countries*.

Kitto, H.D.F. (1951) *The Greeks*, Harmondsworth: Penguin.

Kobayashi, T. (1976) *Society, Schools and Progress in Japan*, Oxford: Pergamon.

Kosok, P. (1933) *Modern Germany: A Study of Conflicting Loyalties*, Chicago, IL: Chicago University Press.

Koutaissoff, E. (1983) 'Environmental Education in the USSR', in J.J. Tomiak, *Soviet Education in the 1980s*.

Kymlicka, W. (1997) *Multicultural Citizenship: A Liberal Theory of Minority Rights*, Oxford: Clarendon Press.

La Chabeaussière, P. (1794) *Catéchisme Républicain, Philosophique et Moral*, in *Du Culte Religieux en France, Recueil 1791–94*.

Lang, P.H. (1942) *Music in Western Civilization*, London: Dent.

Laslett, P. (1983) *The World We Have Lost – Further Explored*, London: Methuen.

Lawton, D., Cairns, J. and Gardner, R. (eds) (2000) *Education for Citizenship*, London: Continuum.

League of Nations Union (LNU) (1937) *Teachers and World Peace* (5th edn), London: LNU.

Léon, A. (1991) *Colonisation, Enseignement et Éducation: Étude Historique et Comparative*, Paris: Éditions L'Harmattan.

Limage, L.J. (ed.) (2001) *Democratizing Education and Educating Democratic Citizens: International and Historical Perspectives*, New York: RoutledgeFalmer.

Linton, M. (2001) *The Politics of Virtue in Enlightenment France*, Basingstoke: Palgrave.

Lister, I. (1991) 'Civic Education for Positive Pluralism in Great Britain', in R.S. Sigal and M. Hoskin, *Education for Democratic Citizenship*.

Locke, J. (ed. J.W. and J.S. Yolton) (1989) *Some Thoughts Concerning Education*, Oxford: Clarendon Press.

Lutz, D.S. (1992) *A Preface to American Political Theory*, Lawrence, KS: University Press of Kansas.

Macartney, C.A. (1934) *National States and National Minorities*, London: Oxford University Press.

Macartney, C.A. (1937) *Hungary and Her Successors: The Treaty of Trianon and its Consequences 1919–1937*, London: Oxford University Press.

McCully, B.T. (1966) *English Education and the Origins of Indian Nationalism*, Gloucester, MA: Peter Smith.

Macedo, S. (2000) *Diversity and Distrust: Civic Education in a Multicultural Society*, Cambridge, MA: Harvard University Press.

MacKenzie, J.M. (1984) *Propaganda and Empire: The Manipulation of British Public Opinion, 1880–1960*, Manchester: Manchester University Press.

MacKenzie, J.M. (ed.) (1986) *Imperialism and Popular Culture*, Manchester: Manchester University Press.

McLeod, K. (1991) 'Human Rights and Multiculturalism in Canadian Schools', in H. Starkey, *The Challenge of Human Rights Education*.

Mann, E. (1939) *School for Barbarians: Education under the Nazis*, London: Lindsay Drummond.

Mareuil, I. (1960) 'Extracurricular and Extrascholastic Activities for Soviet School Children', in G.Z.F. Bereday and J. Pennar, *The Politics of Soviet Education*.

Marquette, H. and Mineshima, D. (2002) 'Civic Education in the United States: Lessons for the UK', *Parliamentary Affairs*, 55.

Marrou, H.I. (trans. G. Lamb) (1956) *A History of Education in Antiquity*, London: Sheed & Ward.

Mátrai, Z. (1998) 'Citizenship Education in Hungary: Ideals and Reality', in O. Ichilov, *Citizenship and Citizenship Education in a Changing World*.

Mátrai, Z. (1999) 'In Transit: Civic Education in Hungary', in J.Torney-Purta *et al.*, *Civic Education Across Countries*.

Mazawi, A.E. (1998) 'Contested Regimes, Civic Dissent, and the Political Socialization of Children and Adolescents: The Case of the Palestinian Uprising', in O. Ichilov, *Citizenship and Citizenship Education in a Changing World*.

Mazzini, J. (1907) *The Duties of Man and Other Essays*, London: Dent.

Mehlinger, H.D. (ed.) (1981) *UNESCO Handbook for the Teaching of Social Studies*, London: Croom Helm, and Paris: UNESCO.

Mehlinger, H.D. and Davis, O.L. (eds) (1981) *The Social Studies: Eightieth Yearbook of the National Society for the Study of Education, Part II*, Chicago, IL: University of Chicago Press.

Mehlinger, H.D. and Patrick, J.J. (1972) *American Political Behavior*, Lexington, MA: Ginn.

Merriam, C.E. (1934) *Civic Education in the United States*, New York: Scribner's.

Mesnard, P. (ed.) (1951) *Oeuvres Philosophiques de Jean Bodin*, Paris: Presses Universitaires de France.

Meyenberg, R. (1990) 'Political Socialization of Juveniles and Political Education in Schools of the Federal Republic of Germany', in B. Claussen and H. Mueller, *Political Socialization of the Young in East and West*.

Mill, J.S. (1910) *Considerations on Representative Government* in *Utilitarianism, On Liberty, and Considerations on Representative Government*, London: Dent.

Montaigne, M. de (trans. J.M. Cohen) (1958) *Essays*, Harmondsworth: Penguin.

Moodley, K.A. (1986) 'Canadian Multicultural Education: Promises and Practice', in J.A. Banks and J. Lynch, *Multicultural Education in Western Societies*.

Morison, J. (1983) 'The Political Content of Education in the USSR', in J.J. Tomiak, *Soviet Education in the 1980s*.

Morison, J. (1987) 'Recent Developments in Political Education in the Soviet Union', in G. Avis, *The Making of the Soviet Citizen*.

Morley, J. (1903) *The Life of William Ewart Gladstone*, Vol. II, New York: Macmillan.

Morrissett, I. (1981) 'The Needs of the Future and the Constraints of the Past', in H.D. Mehlinger and O.L. Davis, *The Social Studies*.

Morrissett, I. and Williams, A.M. (eds) (1981) *Social/Political Education in Three Countries: Britain, West Germany and the United States*, Boulder, CO: Social Science Education Consortium/ERIC.

Morrow, G.R. (1960) *Plato's Cretan City: A Historical Interpretation of the Laws*, Princeton, NJ: Princeton University Press.

Muckle, J. (1987) 'The New Soviet Child: Moral Education in Soviet Schools', in G. Avis, *The Making of the Soviet Citizen*.

Muñoz, J.A. (1982) *La Educación Política como Función de Gobierno en el Estado*, Pamplona: Ediciones Universidad de Navarra.

Myrdal, G. (1977) *Asian Drama: An Inquiry into the Poverty of Nations*, Harmondsworth: Penguin.

Naik, J.P. and Nurullah, S. (1974) *A Students' History of Education in India (1800–1973)* (6th edn), Delhi: Macmillan.

NCCI (1967) *Education in Multi-racial Britain*, London: National Committee for Commonwealth Immigrants and Race Relations Committee of the Society of Friends.

Nettl, J.P. (1967) *The Soviet Achievement*, London: Thames & Hudson.

NGLS/Geneva (1986) *Development Education: The State of the Art*, Geneva: United Nations Non Governmental Liaison Service.

Nkrumah, K. (1961) *I Speak of Freedom*, London: Heinemann.

Nussbaum, M.C. (1997) *Cultivating Humanity: A Classical Defense of Reform in Liberal Education*, Cambridge, MA: Harvard University Press.

Nussbaum, M.C. *et al.* (1996) *For Love of Country: Debating the Limits of Patriotism*, Boston, MA: Beacon.

Okeke, P.U. (1964) 'Background to the Problems of Nigerian Education', in O. Ikejiani, *Nigerian Education*.

Oldfield, A. (1990) *Citizenship and Community: Civic Republicanism and the Modern World*, London: Routledge.

Osborne, K. (1988) 'A Canadian Approach to Political Education', *Teaching Politics*, 17.

Osler, A., Rathenau, H.-F. and Starkey, H. (eds) (1995) *Teaching for Citizenship in Europe*, Stoke-on-Trent: Trentham Books.

Oyovbaire, S.E. (1985) *Federalism in Nigeria: A Study in the Development of the Nigerian State*, London: Macmillan.

Ozouf, M. (1963) *L'École, l'Église et la République 1871–1914*, Paris: Armand Colin.

Palmer, R.R. (1959, 1964) *The Age of Democratic Revolution: A Political History of Europe and America, 1760–1800* (2 vols), Princeton, NJ: Princeton University Press.

Palmer, R.R. (1985) *The Improvement of Humanity: Education and the French Revolution*, Princeton: Princeton University Press.

Pangle, L.S. and Pangle, T.L. (1993) *The Learning of Liberty: The Educational Ideas of the American Founders*, Lawrence, KS: University Press of Kansas.

Papastephanou, M. (2002) 'Arrows Not Yet Fired: Cultivating Cosmopolitanism Through Education', *The Journal of the Philosophy of Education of Great Britain*, 36.

Passin, H. (1965) *Society and Education in Japan*, New York: Teachers College, Columbia University.

Payne, S.G. (1980) *Fascism: Comparison and Definition*, Madison, WI: University of Wisconsin Press.

Pennar, J. (1960) 'Party Control over Soviet Schools', in G.Z.F. Bereday and J. Pennar, *The Politics of Soviet Education*.

Peshkin, A. (1967) 'Education and National Integration in Nigeria', *Journal of Modern African Studies*, 5.

Peters, R.S. (ed.) (1967) *The Concept of Education*, London: Routledge & Kegan Paul.

Philp, M. (ed.) (1993) *Political and Philosophical Writings of William Godwin, Vol. 3: An Essay Concerning Political Justice*, London: William Pickering.

Piaget, J. (ed.) (1967) *John Amos Comenius on Education*, New York: Teachers College Press, Columbia University.

Pierce, B.L. (1930) *Civic Attitudes in American School Textbooks*, Chicago, IL: University of Chicago Press.

Pike, G. and Selby, D. (1988) *Global Teacher, Global Learner*, London: Hodder & Stoughton.

Plato (trans. A.E. Taylor) (1934) *The Laws of Plato*, London: Dent.

Plato (trans. F.M. Cornford) (1941) *The Republic of Plato*, Oxford: Clarendon Press.

Plato (trans. W.K.C. Guthrie) (1956) *Protagoras and Meno*, Harmondsworth: Penguin.

Plumb, J.H. (1950) *England in the Eighteenth Century*, Harmondsworth: Penguin.

Plutarch (trans. F.C. Babbitt) (1960) *Plutarch's Moralia* I, London: Heinemann and Cambridge, MA: Harvard University Press.

Plutarch (trans. R. Talbert) (1988) *Plutarch on Sparta*, Harmondsworth: Penguin.

Priestley, J. (1788) *Lectures on History and General Policy to which is prefaced, An Essay on a Course of Liberal Education for Civil and Active Life*, London: J. Johnson.

Prost, A. (1968) *Histoire de l'enseignement en France 1800–1967*, Paris: Armand Colin.

Quintilian (trans. H.E. Butler) (1920, 1921 and 1922) *Institutio Oratoria* I, VII and XII, London: Heinemann, and Cambridge, MA: Harvard University Press.

Rai, L. (1966) *The Problem of National Education in India*, Delhi: Ministry of Information and Broadcasting.

Rathenow, H.-F. (1987) 'Fredenserziehung in Staaten West- und Nordeuropas', in J. Calliess and R. Lob, *Handbuch Praxis*.

Rawson, E. (1969) *The Spartan Tradition in European Thought*, Oxford: Clarendon Press.

Reardon, B.A. (1997) *Tolerance – The Threshold of Peace: Unit 1: Teacher-Training Resource Unit*, Paris: UNESCO.

Reese, D. (1997) 'Emancipation or Social Incorporation: Girls in the *Bund Deutscher Mädel*', in H. Sünker and H.U. Otto, *Education and Fascism*.

Reiss, H. (ed.) (1991) *Kant: Political Writings*, Cambridge: Cambridge University Press.

Riesenberg, P. (1992) *Citizenship in the Western Tradition: Plato to Rousseau*, Chapel Hill, NC: University of North Carolina Press.

Roberts, G.K. (2002) 'Political Education in Germany', *Parliamentary Affairs*, 55.

Robinson, D.W. (ed.) (1976) *Selected Readings in Citizen Education*, Washington, DC: Department of Health, Education and Welfare.

Robiquet, P. (ed.) (1895) *Discours et Opinions de Jules Ferry*, I, Paris: Armand Colin.

Ross, A. (2000) 'Citizenship Education: An International Comparison', in D. Lawton *et al.*, *Education for Citizenship*.

Rousseau, J.-J. (trans. B. Foxley) (1911) *Émile*, London: Dent.

Rousseau, J.-J. (trans. M. Cranston) (1968) *The Social Contract*, Harmondsworth: Penguin.

Rueda, A.R. (1999) 'Education for Democracy in Colombia', in J. Torney-Purta *et al.*, *Civic Education Across Countries*.

Sadler, J.E. (ed.) (1969a) *Comenius*, New York: Collier-Macmillan.

Sadler, J.E. (ed.) (1969b) *Comenius and the Concept of Universal Education*, London: Allen & Unwin.

Samuel, R.H. and Hinton Thomas, R. (1949) *Education and Society in Modern Germany*, London: Routledge & Kegan Paul.

Scanlon, D.G. (ed.) (1960) *International Education: A Documentary History*, New York: Teachers College, Columbia University.

Schapiro, L. (1972) *Totalitarianism*, London: Pall Mall Press.

Schiedeck, J. and Stahlmann, M. (1997) 'Totalizing of Experience: Educational Camps', in H. Sünker and H.U. Otto, *Education and Fascism*.

Schmidt-Sinns, D. (2000) *Political Learning in Historical Context*, Glienecke, Berlin: Galda & Wilch.

Schneider, H.W. (1968) *Making the Fascist State*, New York: Howard Fertig.

Sears, A.M., Clarke, G.M. and Hughes, A.S. (1999) 'Canadian Citizenship Education: The Pluralist Ideal and Citizenship for a Post-Modern State', in J. Torney-Purta *et al.*, *Civic Education Across Countries*.

Seton-Watson, H. (1962) *Eastern Europe between the Wars 1918–1941*, Hamden, CN: Archon Books.

Shelvankar, K.S. (1940) *The Problem of India*, Harmondsworth: Penguin.

Sherwin-White, A.N. (1973) *The Roman Citizenship* (2nd edn), Oxford: Clarendon Press.

Shirer, W.L. (1964) *The Rise and Fall of the Third Reich*, London: Pan.

Shklar, J.N. (1969) *Men and Citizens: A Study of Rousseau's Social Theory*, Cambridge: Cambridge University Press.

Shlapentokh, V. (1998) 'Russian Citizenship: Behaviour, Attitudes and Prospects for a Russian Democracy', in O. Ichilov, *Citizenship and Citizenship Education in a Changing World*.

Shoemaker, E.C. (1966) *Noah Webster: Pioneer of Learning*, New York: AMS Press.

Short, M.J. (1947) *Soviet Education: Its Psychology and Philosophy*, New York: Philosophical Library.

Shu, S. (1982) 'Education in Cameroon', in A.B. Fafunwa and J.U. Aisiku, *Education in Africa*.

Sigel, R.S. and Hoskin, M. (eds) (1991) *Education for Democratic Citizenship: A Challenge for Multi-Ethnic Societies*, Hillsdale, NJ: Lawrence Erlbaum Associates.

Silver, H. (1975) *English Education and the Radicals 1780–1850*, London: Routledge & Kegan Paul.

Simon, B. (ed.) (1972) *The Radical Tradition in Education in Britain*, London: Lawrence & Wishart.

Smith, A.F. (1991) 'The International Perspective: American Citizenship in an Inter-dependent World', in R.E. Gross and T.L. Dynneson, *Social Science Perspectives on Citizenship Education*.

Smith, H. (1976) *The Russians*, London: Sphere Books.

Smith, R.M. (1997) *Civic Ideals: Conflicting Visions of Citizenship in U.S. History*, New Haven, CT: Yale University Press.

Somervell, D.C. and Harvey, H. (1959) *The British Empire and Commonwealth*, London: Christophers.

Spencer, H. (1929) *Education*, London: Watts.

Starke, J.G. (1947) *An Introduction to International Law*, London: Butterworth.

Starkey, H. (ed.) (1991) *The Challenge of Human Rights Education*, London: Cassell.

Starkey, H. (1992) 'Education for Citizenship in France', in E. Baglin Jones and N. Jones, *Education for Citizenship*.

Steele, I. (1976) *Developments in History Teaching*, London: Open Books.

Stewart, R. (ed.) (1986) *The Penguin Dictionary of Political Quotations*, Harmondsworth: Penguin.

Storry, R. (1961) *A History of Modern Japan*, Harmondsworth: Penguin.

Sünker, H. and Otto, H.U. (eds) (1997) *Education and Fascism: Political Identity and Social Education in Nazi Germany*, London: Falmer.

Sutherland, G. (1971) *Elementary Education in the Nineteenth Century*, London: Historical Association.

Sutherland, J. (1999) *Schooling in the New Russia: Innovation and Change, 1984–95*, Basingstoke: Macmillan.

Swanson, J.A. (1992) *The Public and the Private in Aristotle's Political Philosophy*, Ithaca, NY: Cornell University Press.

Sylvester, D.W. (1970) *Educational Documents 800–1816*, London: Methuen.

Szyliowicz, J.S. (1973) *Education and Modernization in the Middle East*, Ithaca, NY: Cornell University Press.

Talbott, J.E. (1969) *The Politics of Educational Reform in France, 1918–1940*, Princeton, NJ: Princeton University Press.

Thomson, D. (1958) *Democracy in France: The Third and Fourth Republics* (3rd edn), London: Oxford University Press.

Thornton, A.P. (1978) *Imperialism in the Twentieth Century*, London: Macmillan.

Tomiak, J.J. (1972) *The Soviet Union*, Newton Abbot: David & Charles.

Tomiak, J.J. (ed.) (1983) *Soviet Education in the 1980s*, London: Croom Helm.

Tomoda, Y. (1988) 'Politics and Moral Education in Japan', in W.K. Cummings *et al.*, *The Revival of Values Education in Asia and the West*.

Torney, J.V. (1979) 'Psychological and Institutional Obstacles to the Global Perspective in Education', in J.M. Becker, *Schooling for a Global Age*.

Torney-Purta, J., Schwille, J. and Amadeo, J.-A. (eds) (1999) *Civic Education Across Countries: Twenty-four National Case Studies from the IEA Civic Education Project*, Amsterdam: IEA.

Toure, A. (1982) 'Education in Mali', in A.B. Fafunwa and J.U. Aisiku, *Education in Africa*.

Toynbee, A. (1969) *Toynbee's Industrial Revolution*, New York: Augustus M. Kelley.

Turner, M.J. (n.d.) *Materials for Civics, Government, and Problems of Democracy*, Boulder, CO: APSA, University of Colorado and Social Science Consortium.

Turner, M.J. (1981) 'Civic Education in the United States', in D. Heater and J.A. Gillespie, *Political Education in Flux*.

Tyack, D. (1966) 'Forming the National Character: Paradox in the Educational Thought of the Revolutionary Generation', *Harvard Education Review*, 36.

Ukeje, O. and Aisiku, J.U. (1982) 'Education in Nigeria', in A.B. Fafunwa and J.U. Aisiku, *Education in Africa*.

UNESCO (1993) *Worldwide Action in Education*, Paris: UNESCO.

Vaughan, M. and Archer, M.S. (1971) *Social Conflict and Educational Change in England and France 1789–1848*, Cambridge: Cambridge University Press.

Warfel, H.R. (1966) *Noah Webster: Schoolmaster to America*, New York: Octagon Books.

Waterkamp, D. (1990) 'Education for Identification with the State in the German Democratic Republic', in B. Claussen and H. Mueller, *Political Socialization of the Young in East and West*.

Wayper, C.L. (1954) *Political Thought*, London: English Universities Press.

Webber, S.L. (2000) *School, Reform and Society in the New Russia*, Basingstoke: Macmillan.

Weber, E. (1976) *Peasants into Frenchmen: The Modernization of Rural France 1870–1914*, Stanford, CA: Stanford University Press.

Webster, C.K. (1926) *The Teaching of World Citizenship*, London: League of Nations Union.

Welter, R. (1962) *Popular Education and Democratic Thought in America*, New York: Columbia University Press.

White, J.P. (1967) 'Indoctrination', in R.S. Peters, *The Concept of Education*.

Whitmarsh, G. (1972) *Society and the School Curriculum: The Association for Education in Citizenship, 1934–57*, M.Ed. thesis, University of Birmingham.

Whitmarsh, G. (1974) 'The Politics of Political Education: An Episode', *Journal of Curriculum Studies*, 6.

Williams, M. (ed.) (1971) *Revolutions 1775–1830*, Harmondsworth: Penguin.

Wilson, M. (1986) 'In-School Development Education: In The Netherlands', in NGLS/ Geneva, *Development Education*.

Winstanley, G. (ed. L. Hamilton) (1944) *Selections from His Works*, London: Cresset.

Wong, J. (1997) *Red China Blues*, London: Bantam.

Xenophon (trans. W. Miller) (1914) *Cyropaedia*, London: Heinemann, and Cambridge, MA: Harvard University Press.

Zajda, J.I. (1980) *Education in the USSR*, Oxford: Pergamon.

Index

nation-states, early 26–7
National Assessment of Educational
  Progress (NAEP) (USA) 122
National Campaign to Promote Civic
  Education (USA) 123
National Council for Social Studies
  (NCSS) (USA) 117, 231
National Curriculum Council (NCC)
  (Britain) 99
National Education Association (NEA)
  (USA) 109–10, 111, 114–15, 117, 226
National Education League (England) 90
National History Project (Canada) 207
national pledges 113, 124–5, 212
National Task Force on Citizenship
  Education (USA) 122
National Teachers' Association (NTA)
  (USA) 109
National Union of the Working Classes
  (NUWC) (Britain) 87
National Youth Service Corps (NYSC)
  (Nigeria) 213
Navarre, J. 36–7
Nazism 21–2, 152, 155, 173, 177–82
Netherlands, The 68–9, 127, 129, 217, 230
New England 53–4
New Secondary Education, The 95
'new social studies' movement 123
Newsom Report 98
Nigeria 145, 209–13
Nkrumah, K. 144
North America *see* Canada, United States
  of America
Norway 230
Norwood, C. 97
Norwood Report 94–5
Nussbaum, M. 233–4

objective totalitarianism 154
objectives of civic education 2
O'Connor, F. 85, 86
Octobrists 169–70, 171, 172
Oertinger, F. 186
oratory 8, 9–10, 19–20
Order Castles (Germany) 178
ostracism 8

paidonomus 5
Pakistan 146
Palestine 203
Palestinians 203, 204–5
Palmer, R.R. 34, 35, 36, 47
Papastephanou, M. 234
Patrick, J. 123

patriotism 224; Britain 92; France 78–80;
  Soviet Union 166; USA 60–1, 118, 121
Paul, St 219
PDG (Parti Democratique de Guinée) 147
peace, education for 226–8
peace studies 229–30
Penn, W. 222
perestroika 171
Persia 4
Phillips, A. 100
Philosopher-kings 13
philosophes 34–5, 36–40
Piaget, J. 221
Pierce, B. 118–19
Pike, G. 230–1
Pioneers, Soviet 169–70, 171, 172
Pius IX 73
Pius XI 154
Plato 7, 8, 9, 11–15, 22, 222
pledges of allegiance 113, 124–5, 212
pluralism 196, 199–200; Canada 205–9;
  Nigeria 209–13
Plutarch 4, 5–7, 19
Poland 38, 197
Politics Association (UK) 98
polytechnic schools, Soviet 163
Portugal 128–9, 217
Pravda 169
Priestley, J. 50–2
primary schools: England 87–8, 91–2;
  France 72, 77, 81; French colonies 131,
  147; Germany 178; India 139–40, 149;
  Nigeria 211; Soviet Union 163–4; USA
  57, 124
private education 3
private schools 46, 54
Progressivism (USA) 108–9, 116
propaganda 162, 168–9
Protagoras 9
Prussia 47, 48, 175
public festivals 15, 38, 44–5, 213
public property 59
Public schools 24, 88–9; ethos 92–3, 210
Public Schools Commission Report 88
Pufendorf, S. von 33–4

Quinet, E. 71
Quintilian 10, 19, 20, 23–4

Rade, K.A. von 47, 49
radicalism 47–53
Rai, L.L. 139
Reconstruction (USA) 107
Red Army 162, 166–7